The Coalition Crumbles, Napoleon Returns

The Coalition Crumbles, Napoleon Returns

The 1799 Campaign in Italy and Switzerland, Volume 2

CARL VON CLAUSEWITZ

Translated and Edited by

NICHOLAS MURRAY
AND
CHRISTOPHER PRINGLE

University Press of Kansas

Published by the University Press of Kansas (Lawrence, Kansas 66045), which was organized by the Kansas Board of Regents and is operated and funded by Emporia State University, Fort Hays State University, Kansas State University, Pittsburg State University, the University of Kansas, and Wichita State University

Library of Congress Cataloging-in-Publication Data

Names: Clausewitz, Carl von, 1780–1831. author. | Murray, Nicholas, 1966– editor, translator. | Pringle, Christopher, editor, translator.
Title: The 1799 campaign in Italy and Switzerland / Carl von Clausewitz ; translated and edited by Nicholas Murray and Christopher Pringle.
Other titles: Feldzug von 1799 in Italien und der Schweiz. English | 1799 campaign in Italy and Switzerland
Description: [Lawrence] : [University Press of Kansas], [2020] | Series: The 1799 Campaign in Italy and Switzerland | Translation of: Die Feldzüge von 1799 in Italien und der Schweiz (Berlin: Ferdinand Dümmler, 1833). | Includes bibliographical references and index. | Contents: Vol. 1. Napoleon absent, coalition ascendant — vol. 2 The Coalition Crumbles, Napoleon Returns.
Identifiers: LCCN 2020016440
ISBN 9780700630240 (vol. 1 ; cloth)
ISBN 9780700630257 (vol. 1 ; paperback)
ISBN 9780700630264 (vol. 1 ; epub)
ISBN 9780700630332 (vol. 2 ; cloth)
ISBN 9780700630349 (vol. 2 ; paperback)
ISBN 9780700630356 (vol. 2 ; epub)
Subjects: LCSH: Second Coalition, War of the, 1798–1801—Campaigns—Italy. | Second Coalition, War of the, 1798–1801—Campaigns—Switzerland. | Napoleon I, Emperor of the French, 1769–1821—Military leadership. | France—History—Revolution, 1789–1799.
Classification: LCC DC223.4 .C5613 2020 | DDC 940.2/7420945—dc23
LC record available at https://lccn.loc.gov/2020016440.

British Library Cataloguing-in-Publication Data is available.

Printed in the United States of America

10 9 8 7 6 5 4 3 2 1

The paper used in this publication is recycled and contains 30 percent postconsumer waste. It is acid free and meets the minimum requirements of the American National Standard for Permanence of Paper for Printed Library Materials z39.48–1992.

This series of translations of Clausewitz's work is dedicated to the late Dennis Showalter. Dennis's support and encouragement played an important role in getting this project off the ground, and he will be much missed.

Contents

Translators' Note

Any translation presents challenges, the most obvious being the tension between adhering to the literal meaning of the author's original words and capturing the spirit of what he is trying to convey. A direct word-for-word translation inevitably sounds cumbersome and clunky, especially if the same sentence structure is retained. Some degree of rephrasing is always necessary, as well as reorganizing sentences and even whole paragraphs to make the work read more fluently. The problem is that the freer the translation, the greater the risk that some important nuance or emphasis may be lost. As we did in Clausewitz's history of the 1796 campaign,[1] we attempted to strike a balance in the translation of the two-volume history of the 1799 campaigns, and we employed a consistent approach and similar style in all three volumes. We hope that in doing so, we have made the entirety of the work more accessible and easier to read while still allowing Clausewitz to make his points as he intended to make them and to speak in his own distinctive voice.

In fact, Clausewitz speaks to us with three different voices. The first is for the bald description of events in chronological order: "A and B did X and Y. C moved to Z. On the nth, W happened." Clausewitz's language here is clear and simple. His sentences are brief. His descriptions are unornamented. That is not to say that this voice is dull. On the contrary, his narration marches briskly and gives us a clear picture of each battle. Furthermore, his selective use of the historic present tense makes certain passages especially vivid. In German as in English, the historic present serves to lend a sense of drama and urgency to descriptions of past events. The effect of this in Clausewitz's history of the 1796 campaign—the battle of Montenotte, when Bonaparte first goes on the offensive—is tremendously powerful. It strikingly conveys the energy and vigor of the youthful Bonaparte bursting onto the scene and emphasizes the contrast between him and his ponderous, elderly Austrian opponent.

Napoleon's dynamism is present here, albeit only in the background, but the plodding Austrians are on hand again, and the language helps convey the dynamic differences between the French and the Austrians in particular.

1. See Carl von Clausewitz, *Napoleon's 1796 Italian Campaign*, trans. and ed. Nicholas Murray and Christopher Pringle (Lawrence: University Press of Kansas, 2018).

Although this change in tense may be disconcerting for the reader, we have chosen to retain it as far as possible and thus remain consistent across all these three volumes of Clausewitz's campaign histories.

Clausewitz's second voice is for expounding on strategic theory and its implications. Here, his prose is as verbose and florid as his first voice is terse and clipped, as he allows himself lengthy and laborious philosophical discursions. The German language is notorious for its long sentences with multiple nested clauses—the so-called *Bandwurmsatz,* or tapeworm sentence. Clausewitz seems especially fond of the humble tapeworm (though we often felt obliged to cut the creature up). This, together with a penchant for not using a simple word or phrase when a more complicated one will do, results in what our good friend Hartmut "Hardy" Steffin exasperatedly dubbed "Clausewitzification." Clausewitz is not averse to a rather English use of the understated double negative that means "very." If at times the translation seems not inconsiderably long-winded, it is not necessarily our fault, nor that of the German language; it is simply Clausewitz in pontificatory mode.

But it is worth putting up with Clausewitz's pontifications for the delight that is his third voice. This is when he wields his quill like a scalpel to dissect the actions of the French, Austrian, and Russian commanders, viewing through the prism of his strategic analysis and flaying them for their manifold failings. He frequently claims to be baffled by their decisions, and his evaluation is littered with phrases such as "it is incomprehensible," "there seems to be no good reason why," or "it makes no sense." His bafflement often provokes him to lapse from philosophical or scientific language into idiom and vernacular: generals are likened to "feeble-minded beetles," their plans are "egomaniacal," they are "clueless." The remorseless logic he deploys to crush the beetles is a pleasure to read, as he shows step by unarguable step exactly why they were wrong and what they should have done instead.

Identifying geographical locations was not always straightforward. For some, he gives German names that are long obsolete, now that these places are in Italy or Slovenia. That would have been less of a problem if his spellings were not so idiosyncratic, and occasionally a misspelled Italian name directs us to a different part of the country entirely. Near-contemporary maps from the Austrian Second Military Survey of 1806–1869 were helpful and can be found online.[2]

2. "Franziszeische Landesaufnahme (1806–1869)," http://mapire.eu/de/map/secondsurvey.

The names of the commanders presented similar challenges. In section 16 of Clausewitz's 1796 history, a chap named "Gugeur" crops up. Later on, we meet a brigadier named "Guyeur." Could these two be one and the same? And if so, could he in turn be related to the French general Jean Joseph Guieu, also known as Guyeux? Then there is the Croat general in Austrian service whom Clausewitz spells as Wukassowitsch but who, in his native Croatian, would be Vukasović, and appears in other histories variously as Vukassovich, Wukassovich, Vukassevich, or Vukaszovich. We found similar inconsistencies in this volume and dealt with them in the same way.

The convention we used for the names of both places and individuals is as follows: When they first appear, we give Clausewitz's spelling, followed by the modern name in brackets. Thereafter, we use the modern name. For places that have different names in different languages, we give both or all—for example, Botzen [Bozen/Bolzano]—and then use one of those names consistently thereafter.

This translation owes a great deal to the linguistic talents of Hardy Steffin. As a native German speaker with an excellent command of English and an interest in translation and wordplay, Hardy was consulted frequently whenever we encountered an obscure or archaic idiom or a particularly tangled passage of Clausewitzification. His generous help was invaluable in eliminating many misunderstandings and the occasional crass error and in tracking down or teasing out the meanings of phrases we could not find in the dictionary. Still, there were some sentences that even Hardy struggled to make sense of. This is perhaps because Clausewitz's writings are often technical and abrupt, as readers of *On War* can attest, and the original work was published posthumously by Clausewitz's widow, Countess Marie von Clausewitz. Some of the denser Clausewitzifications and ambiguities in his text are probably due to the fact that Clausewitz himself never finished editing his work. A number of obvious mistakes he made (such as referring to the wrong bank of a river) would tend to confirm this.

Clausewitz was also fond of emphasizing words or sentences for effect. Where we found instances of this in the original text, we used italic to indicate it. Words or sections emphasized by us, the editors, are identified as such. Foreign words or phrases in Latin or some equivalent are also italicized, following stylistic conventions.

No doubt this work still contains some errors or interpretations some will find problematic. We request the reader's indulgence, as we were not privy to

Clausewitz's thoughts, and the work of translation is as much art as science. If any reader discovers an error, we would welcome being apprised of the correction.

Any such imperfections notwithstanding, we trust that overall we have done Clausewitz justice and prepared a translation that is as faithful and authentic as possible. We hope that you will enjoy reading this work as much as we enjoyed translating it.

Editors' Note

The reader will note that both volumes of the history of the 1799 campaigns contain the same translators' note, note on wargaming, and acknowledgments, which are similar to those in our translation of Clausewitz's history of the 1796 campaign.[1] Not wishing to reinvent the wheel, we also wanted to ensure that readers of either volume had ready access to these thoughts and comments and would not be forced to refer to the other volume. Likewise, each book contains its own index rather than a single index for the two volumes.

The biographic information comes largely from two main sources. For the French, unless otherwise noted, the information comes from Napoléon Bonaparte, *Correspondance Générale*.[2] For the Austrians, unless otherwise noted, the information comes from Dr. Constant von Wurzbach, *Biographisches Lexikon des Kaiserthums Oesterreich*.[3]

Where Clausewitz provides explanatory notes, we include them in the editors' footnotes. For the reader's convenience, we highlighted his name in bold so that his notes stand out.

We hope the reader will find these volumes informative and useful tools for understanding the French Revolutionary Wars and Clausewitz's ideas.

1. Carl von Clausewitz, *Napoleon's 1796 Italian Campaign*, trans. and ed. Nicholas Murray and Christopher Pringle (Lawrence: University Press of Kansas, 2018).

2. Napoléon Bonaparte, *Correspondance Générale*, 15 vols. (Paris: Publiée par la Fondation Napoléon, Librairie Arthéme Fayard, 2004–2018).

3. Dr. Constant von Wurzbach, *Biographisches Lexikon des Kaiserthums Oesterreich*, 60 vols. (Vienna: Universitäts Buchruderei von L. E. Zamarski, 1856–1891), http://www.literature.at/collection.alo?from=1&to=50&orderby=author&sortorder=a&objid=11104&page=.

A Note on Wargaming

Clausewitz's theoretical writings are just one symptom of the broader phenomenon of the increasingly systematic approach to war adopted by the Prussian military in the nineteenth century. Another aspect of this was the development of wargaming as a tool for professional military education.[1]

Since then, wargaming has been widely used by militaries around the world. At the time of this writing, there is renewed professional interest in wargaming in the United States in particular,[2] a movement in which the editors are directly involved. Wargaming gives participants the opportunity to practice rapid decision making in conditions of uncertainty, under time pressure, and in a competitive environment, which can offer profound insights and teach enduring lessons. It is "learning by doing," and it can be tremendously powerful. Both of the editors like wargaming because it places students in the role of decision maker and provides opportunities for hands-on problem solving. For example, when "Major Buttercup" is given the role of Suvorov in 1799, students often find that their job is just as frustrating as their historical counterpart's, experiencing their own version of the testy exchanges they have read about. The process of decision making and planning in an uncertain environment is invaluable, and it allows students to see Clausewitz's ideas and concepts in action, so to speak, leading them to exclaim, "That's what a culminating point is!"

As far as the present work is concerned, the editors encourage readers to explore wargaming as a way to gain a deeper appreciation of how and why the campaigns and battles described and analyzed by Clausewitz took the courses they did. To facilitate an understanding of the campaign as a whole, one of us (Nick Murray) has developed a game for his students that is also used by the US Navy, US Army, and US Marine Corps for training and education. A series of games set in 1796–1797 and 1799–1800 allows students to engage with the key problems and war-fighting scenarios of these campaigns, helping them to

1. Philipp von Hilgers, *Kriegspiele eine Geschichte der Ausnahmezustände und Unberechenberkeiten* (Munich: Wilhelm Fink Verlag, 2008), 58–71.

2. Deputy Secretary of Defense Robert Work, a memorandum for secretaries of the Military Departments, "Wargaming and Innovation," 9 February 2015.

engage with Clausewitz's key ideas as well.[3] For the grand tactical level, many commercial games are available; we favor *Bloody Big Battles!* (*BBB*), which Nick has also used in class. The scenarios and a set of discussion questions related to the operations are available for free via the discussion group at https://groups.io/g/bloodybigbattles.

3. The wargames have been run largely as elective classes over the last ten years (with thanks to Dr. Tim Schultz and his team in the Electives Department of the US Naval War College). Students take on the role of one of the main theater commanders covered in Clausewitz's history. In that role, they confront many of the problems and choices Clausewitz identifies, making these wargames an excellent tool for understanding his thoughts and for practicing decision making.

Acknowledgments

It is an honor for us to recognize the assistance we received during the completion of this book. In this respect, we would like to thank Dr. Tony Echevarria of the US Army War College for taking the time to discuss Clausewitz's writing. This was a great help in thinking about the meaning of Clausewitz's work. Dr. Chris Bassford of National Defense University and his excellent Clausewitz resource (Clausewitz.com) provided some extremely helpful ideas about the timeline of Clausewitz's writings and what that might mean. Vanya Bellinger, author of the excellent *Marie von Clausewitz: The Woman behind the Making of* On War, was kind enough to provide her guidance and proved to be a great help in identifying nuances in the original writing. Though we were less reliant on his help this time around than for the 1796 volume, Hartmut Steffin again contributed his time and knowledge to assist us with some particularly tricky German idioms. Glenda Pringle provided her valuable expertise in indexing both volumes.

We would like to thank everyone at the University Press of Kansas for their professional assistance in the production of this and our previous work, especially Joyce Harrison for her encouragement and support of the project.

These acknowledgments would not be complete without a word of appreciation for Kara McKamey and Glenda Pringle, whose patience was stretched at times when they were neglected in favor of a long-dead Prussian general. We thank them for indulging us.

In spite of all this help, it is likely that we missed something. Thus, any flaws contained herein are our own.

Introduction

The writings of Carl von Clausewitz are among the most important works on war ever written. Much of the focus has understandably been on his great theoretical work *On War*, which has been translated and reprinted across the world. That work, however, formed only the first three of the ten volumes of his published writings. This is significant because, despite the importance of *On War*, it can be difficult to understand and decipher. This is where Clausewitz's historical writing and analysis play an exceptionally important role, as he maintained that his foundational writing helped him think through and more clearly form his theoretical understanding of war, and that the process of so doing was difficult.[1] Therefore, our neglect of his historical analysis, when attempting to understand *On War*, impedes our understanding of his main theoretical writing. This is criminally negligent (as Clausewitz might have put it), since he spent a great deal of time analyzing the conflicts he fought in and creating, in the process, the theoretical underpinnings of *On War*. Thus, by reading and analyzing his histories of the series of wars from 1789 to 1815, the reader can hope to understand *On War* more fully.

What Clausewitz tells us about his historical writing is important, and he addresses this in several of his notes. In *To an Unpublished Manuscript on the Theory of War* (according to Howard and Paret, this was written between 1816 and 1818), Clausewitz criticizes past military writers for their lack of effective analysis of the evidence—that is, the history.[2] He goes further in *On the Genesis of His Early Manuscript on the Theory of War*, where he states:

> The manner in which Montesquieu dealt with his subject is vaguely in my mind.[3] I thought that such concise, aphoristic chapters, which at the outset

1. Jan Willem Honig, "Clausewitz and the Politics of Early Modern Warfare," in *Clausewitz the State and War*, ed. Andreas Herberg-Rothe, Jan Willem Honig, and Daniel Moran (Stuttgart: Franz Steiner Verlag, 2011), 29–48.

2. Carl von Clausewitz, *On War*, ed. and trans. Michael Howard and Peter Paret (Princeton, NJ: Princeton University Press, 1989), 61.

3. If one looks at Montesquieu's *De l'Esprit des Loix*, one can see its resemblance to the structure of *On War*. The work is broken down into multiple smaller books, with each book consisting of multiple smaller chapters, all punctuated with analysis and historical examples.

> I simply wanted to call kernels, would attract the intelligent reader by what they suggested as much as by what they expressed; in other words, I had an intelligent reader in mind, who was already familiar with the subject. . . . From the studies I wrote on various topics in order to gain a clear and complete understanding of them, I managed for a time to lift only the most important conclusions and thus concentrate their essence in smaller compass. But eventually my tendency completely ran away with me; I elaborated as much as I could, and of course now had in mind a reader who was not yet acquainted with the subject.[4]

In other words, his histories and other writings were fundamental to the development of his understanding of war, and it seems reasonable to assume that this would also be the case for a reader unfamiliar with the topic. In his *Note of 10 July 1827* and an unfinished note possibly from 1830,[5] Clausewitz again drives home the point about historical study underpinning his work: "If critics would go to the trouble of thinking about the subject for years on end and testing each conclusion against the actual history of war, as I have done, they would undoubtedly be more careful of what they said."[6] With this criticism ringing in our ears, perhaps it is time to introduce Clausewitz's histories to a broader audience so that they too might benefit from his historical analysis and the testing of his theoretical models against the campaigns themselves. Indeed, that is our primary motivation for translating this work.

It is now important to discuss the text we chose to use: the original version published in 1833.[7] We made this choice because it reduced the chance of encountering the changes and errors sometimes found in subsequent publications. It is also the version of the work sanctioned by Clausewitz's widow, Marie von Clausewitz. Although she did not edit the work herself, she did rely on trusted family friend Major Franz August O'Etzel, who was familiar with Clausewitz's writings, to compile them for publication as the fifth and sixth volumes of the planned ten volumes (the first three volumes being *On War* itself).[8] Major O'Etzel stringently denied making edits to the text, so if

4. Clausewitz, *On War*, 63. Howard and Paret date this note between 1816 and 1818.

5. Howard and Paret believe it to be from 1830. See Clausewitz, *On War*, 70.

6. Clausewitz, *On War*, 70.

7. Carl von Clausewitz, *Die Feldzüge von 1799 in Italien und der Schweiz*, 2 vols. (Berlin: Ferdinand Dümmler, 1833).

8. See Marie von Clausewitz's preface in Clausewitz, *On War*, 65–67.

we take him at his word (and we have no reason not to), the text is largely as Clausewitz left it.[9] Thus, it is ideal for our purpose of using it as a tool to better understand *On War.*

For readers interested in digging deeper into Clausewitz's use of history to support his theoretical understanding of war, and perhaps to aid researchers attempting to date the various parts of his work, we would like to suggest some key concepts for cross-referencing: objects and their value, *Anschauung,* culmination, and *Schwerpunkt.* These are key words in Clausewitz's writing, and they appear here in the context in which he thought about them. As such, their use here is extremely helpful for understanding their actual meaning.

In the translators' note we describe our approach to the translation, and we had much the same ethos when it came to our editors' commentary and analysis. When we use modern terms such as "combat power," the intention is to make the text more accessible rather than to provide an exact replication of Clausewitz's words. We have also cross-referenced the text with *On War* and have attempted to explain what Clausewitz's theoretical ideas mean in relation to the campaign history that is the focus of this work. As such, we hope to make *On War* itself more understandable and usable for students and scholars alike.

For completeness, we have cross-referenced our translation of Clausewitz's campaign history with those of Archduke Charles and Antoine Jomini.[10] These two writers were contemporaries of Clausewitz, and they are considered (both then and now) the other main thinkers about war during the relevant period. Furthermore, Clausewitz used their work to inform his own, and it seemed reasonable to check the veracity of what he claimed they did or said. Thus, comparing their views is illuminating both when they agree and when they do not. We believe that the commentary on and cross-referencing of their work can aid the reader in understanding Clausewitz's history by encouraging

9. Clausewitz, *Die Feldzüge von 1799 in Italien und der Schweiz,* 1:viii. See also Vanya Eftimova Bellinger, *Marie von Clausewitz: The Woman behind the Making of* On War (Oxford: Oxford University Press, 2016), 230; Marie von Clausewitz, "Vorrede zum Dritte Theil," in Carl von Clausewitz, *Vom Kriege,* 3 vols. (Berlin: Ferdinand Dümmler, 1832–1834) 3:v–vi.

10. Karl Erzherzog von Österreich, *Geschichte des Feldzuges von 1799 in Deutschland und in der Schweiz,* 3 vols. (Vienna: Anton Strauss, 1814); Lieutenant-Général [Antoine] Jomini, *Histoire Critique et Militaire des Guerres de la Révolution,* 15 vols. (Paris: Chez Anselin et Pochard, 1819–1824).

critical reflection on Clausewitz's own remarks. In addition, many of the archduke's and Jomini's notes include valuable historical details that either correct Clausewitz's errors or add information to provide a more complete account.

Editorial commentary is not limited to Clausewitz's theory. We have also tried to make the campaign narrative clearer and, where possible, to fill in gaps in our knowledge of the campaign's history. As part of these efforts, we refer to other published histories to make the narrative more accurate. All of the above was done to help the reader better understand what Clausewitz was really trying to say, both here and in *On War*. Our hope is to encourage discussion of this important historical work and to provide a base so that more people will be able to access Clausewitz's writing and understand his ideas.

Original Editor's Note

The kind mention of my assistance with the publication of this work[1] has occasioned the misapprehension here and there that this constituted a kind of editing. This is by no means the case; the legacy of this immortal gentleman who was held in such high regard, and whose premature demise must fill every Prussian heart with the deepest sorrow, was reproduced without a single word added or struck out, and my collaboration consisted entirely in correcting the proofs.

For the printing of the fourth volume (the 1796 campaign)[2] and this present fifth volume, however, I was prevented from doing so by my duties elsewhere, and the business had to be taken care of by a proofreader, who indeed eliminated the actual printing errors with great care, but who, being from another profession, lacked full familiarity with many of the names appearing in these volumes, hence the errors noted here remained.[3]

The publication of the operational maps for these volumes has been delayed by my absence, but they are now close to completion.

O'Etzel[4]

1. See Carl von Clausewitz, *Hinterlassene Werke des Generals Carl von Clausewitz über Krieg und Kriegführung,* 10 vols. (Berlin: Ferdinand Dümmler, 1832), 1:xii.

2. For a recent translation, see Carl von Clausewitz, *Napoleon's 1796 Italian Campaign,* trans. and ed. Nicholas Murray and Christopher Pringle (Lawrence: University Press of Kansas, 2018).

3. The original editor's note included an errata. These errors were mostly typographical and have been corrected in this translation.

4. Major Franz August O'Etzel was a longtime friend of Clausewitz and his wife, Marie, and he assisted her with the publication of her husband's writings after Clausewitz's death in 1831. Major O'Etzel went on to become a key proponent of the use of the telegraph in Prussia and became the first Prussian telegraph director. See Vanya Eftimova Bellinger, *Marie von Clausewitz: The Woman behind the Making of* On War (Oxford: Oxford University Press, 2016), 166.

Clausewitz's Introduction

The two campaigns conducted in Italy and Switzerland in 1799 cannot be separated without depriving them of much of their interest and comprehensibility, because they are so bound together by events and by their effects on each other.[1]

Collectively, they are among the most significant and richest in lessons of any campaigns in the history of warfare. In them, we see four commanders of great repute in action: Suvorov, Archduke Charles, Moreau, and Masséna.[2] Among the generals in the next tier, Lecourbe, Macdonald, Joubert, Soult, Championnet, and Dessolles on the one side and Kray, Melas, Hotze, and Bagration on the other are pretty much the best that both armies had to offer. As for events, we have seven major battles, three opposed river crossings, and a large number of mountain positions in the highest regions of the Alps contested by the most determined attacks and the most steadfast defense. Finally, we have the passage of an army through the St. Gotthard region, held and defended by the enemy, who, after being driven back initially, seals the natural

1. It is interesting and enlightening to compare Clausewitz's introduction with Archduke Charles's in his own history of the campaign. The archduke is more concerned with demonstrating that "the laws of a science only become clear and productive when one takes them back to their source—experience, and provides proof of their application in real-life events. Without theory even the most experienced man remains incapable of comprehending the connections between multifarious manifestations from an area of a practical science, to develop its causes and consequences further, to solve apparent contradictions, to identify the leading principle in its entire purity and to honour the deed in line with its true content: but theoretical knowledge alone does not yet teach us to fill in the chasm between knowledge and action." He goes on to state: "Political influences had to be touched on to the extent that they determined the choice and running of the operations but the appraisal of them lies outside this writer's plan. It restricts itself to assessing the war in line with the laws of science involved and the art, and leaves it to the future to one day lift the veil covering the political motivations. Posterity will then decide whether they deserved to take precedence over the military considerations." Karl Erzherzog von Österreich, *Geschichte des Feldzuges von 1799 in Deutschland und in der Schweiz*, 3 vols. (Vienna: Anton Strauss, 1814), 1:iv–vi.

2. Rather than introduce these individuals here, we do so when they first appear in Clausewitz's main text.

exits like a growing avalanche piling up and obliges the army to seek another way out by winding through the steepest of rocky gorges.

These campaigns, born from the fresh force of a new coalition and furious outrage, are notable in that, through the pettifogging political differences that were clearly present, they soon led to tension, then to misfortune, and thereby to the rapid dissolution of the coalition.[3]

3. We wait until Clausewitz analyzes these campaigns and their political origins in more detail before commenting on his thoughts, except to say that we broadly agree.

6. The Main Armies in Switzerland under the Archduke and Masséna Face Each Other Inactive for Three Months

Lecourbe Defeats the Austrian Left Wing in the Mountains.

57 THE TWO SIDES' POSITIONS

We left the two armies in Switzerland facing each other deployed in long outpost lines to wait for new battles, whether as attacker or defender. Thus a lull of almost three months arose between the main forces from 6 June,[1] the date of the first battle of Zurich, to the end of August, when Archduke Charles departed for the Rhine.

During these three months we have just a few insignificant outpost actions to describe, then Lecourbe's operations against the Austrian left wing in mid-August, which we have already mentioned in the previous volume, plus one abortive attempt by the archduke to cross the Aare and another one against the French right wing likewise abandoned.[2] Thus this period in Switzerland is poor

1. The fighting took place from 4 to 7 June.

2. Karl Erzherzog von Österreich, *Geschichte des Feldzuges von 1799 in Deutschland und in der Schweiz*, 3 vols. (Vienna: Anton Strauss, 1814), 2:7–22, 119–150; hereafter cited as Karl. The archduke spends quite a bit of time discussing these actions and emphasizes his cautious take on campaigning: "The ever so natural wish to use hard-won advantages and to make use of his superiority for further progress has misled many a general into blunders and also prompted the archduke himself as well to think about a fresh offensive. For this there were several paths available to him [the archduke]: on the right wing via a crossing of the Aar, and a move along this river into Masséna's left flank and rear. This operation would have been the most significant as it would have an effect on the enemy's main communications with Alsace, which he could no longer win from the Austrians because the two defiles of the Reuss and the Aar lying behind his position hindered the speed of his movement. There was also the fact that the archduke needed a very superior number of troops to secure the march to the Aar by holding on to Zurich and over the Aar by masking Basel, which then remained in his right flank and where, in addition to a division that manned the Rhine

in terms of actual events but is all the richer in strategic considerations. First, even if the Italian front had become the main theater of operations because of the value the Austrian government attached to it and through Suvorov's energy,[3] still the combat forces massed in Switzerland were not much smaller, and their inaction was not planned but was the outcome of contributing factors in the theater of operations itself; it was therefore inevitable that the use of these combat forces in this theater also raised a series of questions that are essential to the strategic history of the campaign. Second, the few events in Switzerland were not without influence on Italy, as we have already learned, and so the strategic relationship between the two theaters—while far from having the intensity that fantastical theory insists on—was therefore not entirely unimportant. Finally, after the conquest of Piedmont a quite different distribution of forces arose, by which the importance previously attached to Italy was transferred to Switzerland and the Rhine; the archduke left Switzerland and Suvorov went there, and since their change of roles occurs right at the end of this chapter, it retrospectively adds to the significance of the strategic situation.

Thus, while we run through the few events of this three-month period, we will focus our attention mainly on the governments' and commanders' reasons for their actions and inactions so far as we are able to provide them, and try to accommodate them with the requirements of a rational theory.

Before we go on to consider this quiet, uneventful passage, which is like an underground stream that only emerges into the light of day on a couple of occasions here and there, we should like to provide more details of the two sides' deployments, which we outlined in section 38 [volume 1, chapter 3] and which we must think of these armies being in for such a long time.

The French army consisted of ten divisions of various strengths:

---

downstream from the inflow of the Aar, a second one was positioned in the fortified camp." Karl, 2:7–8.

3. We see here the point about the object being sought and its value relative to the effort and means required for success. This is critical to understanding the meaning of purpose and means in war, as well as the value of the conflict's objectives. Each side places a value on the object being sought, and any change to that calculation requires a reassessment of that object and a recalculation of the value of said object and of the means being used to attain it. See Carl von Clausewitz, *On War*, ed. and trans. Michael Howard and Peter Paret (Princeton, NJ: Princeton University Press, 1989), book 1, chaps. 1 and 2 (throughout this volume, references to *On War* are to this version, the most popular translation).

Xaintrailles's division (now under the command of General Tharreau): 8,000 men. This was on the extreme right wing in Wallis and may be considered a separate corps.
Lecourbe's division: 8,500 men. This constituted the right wing proper, in Lucerne. Lecourbe had his right wing in the Hasli valley, where the Aare flows into Lake Brienz; his line then ran along the valley to Lake Sarnen and through Stanz to Bekenried on Lake Lucerne. His left wing was between Gersau on Lake Lucerne and Art on Lake Thun.
Third division (Chabran): 6,500 men. In Zug holding the roads coming down from the high mountains to the eastern shore of Lake Zug, Lake Ägeri, and the Sihl. Its left wing was on the Albis and rested on Lake Zurich.
Fourth division (Soult): 6,000 men. Encamped around Birmensdorf, right behind Zurich, forming the right wing of the actual position on the Albis or Ütli.
Fifth division (Lorges): 8,500 men. Around Urdorf forming the left wing of the main position.
Sixth division (Tharreau): 6,000 men. In and around Bruck, observing the Limmat from Baden to where it flows into the Aare, and the Aare as far as the Rhine.
Seventh division (Klein): 5,100 men. In reserve at Mellingen.
Eighth division (Ney): 5,000 men. Observing the Rhine in the Frick valley.
Ninth division (Souham): 11,000 men. In the entrenched camp in front of Basel.
Tenth division (Montchoisi): 8,000 men. Garrisoning the interior of Switzerland.
Total: 72,600 men.[4]

Facing this position, the Austrians had:

Haddick's corps: 12,000 men. As we have already mentioned, at Aosta facing the two St. Bernard Passes, in the Simplon Pass, and Strauch's brigade in Wallis.

4. Lieutenant-Général [Antoine] Jomini, *Histoire Critique et Militaire des Guerres de la Révolution*, 15 vols. (Paris: Chez Anselin et Pochard, 1819–1824), 12:61 (plan 15); hereafter cited as Jomini.

Bey's brigade of Jellachich's corps: 4,300 men. In the Reuss valley from the Devil's Bridge to Altorf.
Jellachich himself: 9,500 men. From Brunnen on Lake Lucerne, through Schwyz and Sattel, Rotenturm, and Ezel, to Richtenschwyl on Lake Zurich.
The archduke's main army: 47,500 men. Behind the Limmat and the Aare between Zurich and Döttingen.
Observing the Rhine in the Frick valley: 5,600 men.
In Graubündten: 1,500 men.
Total: 80,400 men.[5]

Masséna's headquarters was in Bremgarten, the archduke's in Klotten.

The Swiss have been left out of this reckoning; they came to about 3,000–4,000 on each side.

Furthermore, out of these 80,000 Austrians, General Haddick's 12,000 men belonged to the army in Italy, not to Archduke Charles's. However, we had to include them here, partly because they pinned Tharreau's division, which belonged to Masséna's army, and partly because Strauch's brigade, at least, obviously had a much closer connection with the Swiss theater of operations than with the Italian one.

Since the position south of Lake Zurich was a mountain cordon that was the scene of a series of not insignificant actions during Lecourbe's offensive in August, we should like to describe it in a little more detail.

The purpose of the Austrian left wing and the French right wing alike was to protect the ground behind them and to maintain communications with the Italian theater of operations. Naturally, their extent was far too long to establish a series of small outposts such that they were close enough together to observe the area and to offer one another direct mutual support, which is what constitutes the notion of a connected chain of outposts. But the nature of the high Alps made advancing so difficult, and restricted it to so few places, that it was never very hard for the defender to oppose an advance with proportionate combat forces. The major difficulty for the defender was that which we have already discussed in the first chapter, namely, that the high ridges were too high and inhospitable to establish outposts on them,

5. It is not entirely clear where these figures come from; although they are similar to the numbers Jomini and the archduke give, they are not identical.

and that they would have lacked any lateral communications except via the river valleys, which, because of the huge dimensions of these mountains, were always at least several miles to the rear. For example, on that part of their line from Wasen [Wassen] to Attinghausen, if the Austrians had wanted to have one outpost on the Steinberg[6] at the start of the Meyen [Meien] valley and another on the Surenenberg [Surenen Pass],[7] then these two outposts would have been a little over 8 miles apart with no line of communications between them apart from the one through the Reuss valley, which would have been almost 30 miles long; and a reserve standing behind the two of them could not have been posted any closer than 12 miles away.

This problem caused the Austrians holding the high alpine ridge between the Rhone and the Reuss to go over to the opposite system entirely: that is, to put their defensive line in the valley instead of on the ridge and to site their defensive positions at the exits from the transverse valleys through which the footpaths descend into the main valley.

Thus the Austrian deployment was designed so that Strauch, between Ärnen [Ernen] and Brig, was supposed to use most of his troops in a couple of outposts [near Brig] on both sides of the Rhone to block the valley. Their line cut perpendicularly across it, but without going up onto the topmost height formed by the glaciers. This main position of Strauch's therefore created a left flank arcing back, and his line then ran along the Rhone to the Grimsel. Here it was protected by the trackless glacier, without any other defense or observation. At the Grimsel the road from the Aare valley enters the Rhone valley; Strauch had his right wing there up in the pass itself. His reserve was in the Rhone valley at Münster [Münster-Geschinen]. From the Grimsel the Austrian line carried on along the Reuss. The outpost on the Grimsel likewise protected the first entrance into the Reuss valley, namely, that over the Furka Pass and through the Urseren valley; the next one was via the Meien valley, and the Austrians had an outpost there at Wassen. From the Meien valley to the source of the Aare passing not far from Stanz, the line was again protected by impassable glaciers; but there the pass across the Surenenberg creates the third entrance into the Reuss valley, and the Austrians therefore had more outposts where the road branches to descend at Erstfeld and Attinghausen;

6. This is the Steinberg glacier south of Engelberg-Titlis. For those who like skiing, this is the glacier served by Kleintitlis.

7. The Surenen Pass is almost 5 miles west-northwest from Erstfeld.

then they had one at Seedorf, because a footpath comes out of the Issi [Isen] valley along the lake; and finally, one at Flüelen because of the harbor there.

Between Lake Lucerne and Lake Zurich the terrain loses its high mountainous character, but the approaches between Lake Lucerne and the Sihl are still mostly restricted to the shores of Lakes Lucerne, Lauerz, and Ägeri, so the Austrians put their outposts in Brunnen, Schwyz, and Sattel. Between the Sihl and Lake Zurich the mountains finally end, and the terrain is just undulating hills; there the Austrians had 7,000 men distributed along a 5-mile front in individual outposts close together.

Since we do not have any such detailed accounts of the French position, which was not attacked, we cannot describe it so precisely. But this was not so important anyway, because it was a very refused flank with regard to the front overall, so was not in much danger of being attacked. It was more natural that Masséna should push his right wing forward again than that the archduke should seek to bend his left even further around.

We assert this, even though the archduke says that he did have such a plan and its execution was only interrupted by General Haddick's departure.[8] It is questionable, first, whether his assertion is really serious; second, whether on closer consideration the archduke might not have thought better of it once its difficulties became truly apparent to him, as often happened in the course of his career as a commander; or third, whether he could indeed have embarked on an operation that was against the nature of things and that the critic must therefore regard as unlikely. We shall return to this topic, so leave it at that for now.

The deployment of the two sides' main armies between Lake Zurich and the Rhine was not so much an actual position as an encampment in advantageous terrain. Exceptionally strong positions were available to both armies: to the French on the Ütli, and to the Austrians on the heights Masséna had occupied during the first battle of Zurich and whose front toward the Limmat, as we have already noted, is much stronger than that facing the Glatt. Of the two main armies, it was certainly the French that found itself more on the defensive, since in general it was the archduke who was advancing and who had previously had numerical superiority and could have it again when the Russians under Korsakov arrived. However, the French dispositions were not appropriate for this situation. Instead of the formidable entrenchments they had constructed in their position at Zurich, here there is scarcely a word

8. Karl, 2:8–10.

about any such defensive measures. Of course, two divisions, Soult and Lorges (15,000 strong altogether), stood behind Zurich ready to defend the Ütli; on the other hand, the other 11,000 under Tharreau and Klein were obliged to occupy and defend a 25-mile stretch as far as the Rhine. In the event of an enemy attack, therefore, resistance had to be based on first concentrating the majority of these 26,000 men at the point under attack. Since the Albis and Ütli are 1,200–1,500 feet high, and the Austrian army still had to cross the Limmat, it would not have taken much to make an attack on the Ütli itself as good as impossible, and 15,000 men certainly would have been enough for that; on the other hand, the defense of the Aare was difficult, especially because the troops from the main army that were supposed to help would first have to cross the Reuss and the Aare. Against a decisive commander, in this situation, successful resistance would have been impossible.

We must make the following remark in connection with the distribution of forces. If we leave out Haddick on the archduke's side and Tharreau on Masséna's, both armies are exactly 68,000 strong. Chabran and Lecourbe on the French right wing have 15,000 men; on the archduke's left wing, Jellachich and Simbschen are roughly just as strong. Thus the remaining forces are also equal—except that Masséna has 8,000 of his men in the interior and 11,000 outside Basel who are not operating against the archduke. Now admittedly, the latter still has 7,000 men on the right bank of the Rhine, but neither can Masséna count on Ney's division for the battles that will be fought on the Limmat. Thus the consequence was that between the Rhine and Zurich, where the archduke had 45,000 men, Masséna had only 26,000 available. We may therefore still regard the archduke as being very numerically superior at the main point,[9] and he owed that partly to Masséna's dispersal of his forces.

58 THE TWO ARMIES' INACTION UNTIL MID-AUGUST

In section 38 [volume 1, chapter 3], for internal continuity, we saw ourselves obliged to follow events on the Austrian left wing up to Haddick's departure from the Rhone valley, that is, until 24 June. But now we must set off again from the starting point of this chapter, Masséna's retreat across the Limmat.

9. The archduke hedges on this point, and it is not clear whether he outnumbers the French at all. Karl, 2:7–10.

As we said in section 38, on the day of Masséna's retreat on 6 June, the archduke sent General Jellachich with nine battalions and some cavalry to reinforce his left wing. When the archduke describes this measure,[10] he does not say that it is associated with any offensive aim, and we confess that indeed to us it seems he does it only out of concern that Colonel Gavasini might not be strong enough to cover his left flank. Later on, namely, in his second volume (pp. 7 and following), the archduke returns to this detachment and characterizes it differently, as we are about to see.[11]

Two days later, on 8 June, the archduke reinforced his advance guard under General Rosenberg and had it conduct a reconnaissance of Masséna's position. Not only did it take the villages of Albisrieden, Altstetten, and Schlieren at the foot of the Ütli, but the Austrians even advanced toward Uttikon on the Ütli and captured a redoubt there. Not until the evening did the French gather enough troops together to drive the Austrians away again and to recapture all the villages except Altstetten.

This success from a mere reconnaissance is astonishing. The main strategic factor on which the whole rationale for this episode of the campaign rests, the position on the Ütli, disappears in an instant. What should we think of a position that can be taken and almost held by a mere reconnaissance? The archduke says: "Masséna had dispersed his troops too much to offer resistance soon if the operation had been anything more than a reconnaissance."[12] Jomini says: "This could have been done along the whole line of the Albis if the archduke's main body had been prepared to support this attack."[13]

Thus we see that a serious attack would very easily have produced certain success.

We have nothing to resolve this contradiction except Jomini's expression: "The republicans were surprised,"[14] and we too must certainly see it that way. The French presumably did not believe that the cautious archduke would follow so swiftly, and they had not organized themselves suitably; various misunderstandings of the kind that arise so easily in any new position may have

10. **Clausewitz** notes: "Vol. I, p 384." Karl, 1:384.

11. See Karl, 2:7–12.

12. Karl, 1:381.

13. Jomini, 12:58 ["*C'en était fait de toute la ligne de l'Albis si le corps de bataille de l'Archiduc eut été préparé pour soutenir cette attaque*"].

14. Jomini, 12:57 ["*les républicains furent surpris*"].

played a part, so it is quite understandable that a position that subsequently seemed almost impregnable to the Austrian commander, at least frontally, could be taken almost without bloodshed in the initial surprise attack.[15] But of course, it will be hard for us to forget this episode entirely and not to conclude from it that, given the relatively small number of troops that Masséna used to defend the sector between Lake Zurich and the Aare, it would not have been impossible to overwhelm it frontally with superior force. In any case, this event shows us how often in war a quite unusual success may lie unexpectedly near and can be gained with minimal effort by bold exploitation of a favorable moment. While much in this depends on chance, yet this path along which such favors from fortune are to be sought is not unknown to theory; *it is a bold endeavor, so long as the enemy is still emerging from a crisis.*

The Austrians remained in possession of Altstetten. Masséna found this uncomfortable and retook it on 15 June, using proportionate forces and demonstrations to do so.

Favorable though the outcome of his reconnaissance had been, still the archduke seems to have decided to remain on the defensive until the arrival of the expected 30,000 Russians under Korsakov. In the series of reflections he offers about this, he gives a number of reasons to justify such a decision. We have dug them out as the following nuggets, so far as we are able to do so from the various interpolations and intertwinings of his not very logical manner:

1. He thought he was not particularly stronger than his opponent. According to the overview we gave in the previous paragraph, indeed, he was not stronger overall, but at the key point between Lake Zurich and the Aare, he certainly was. Besides, we must note that our overview presents the strengths as they were at the end of July, and by the archduke's own assertion, Masséna must have received substantial reinforcements by then; we may therefore probably assume that immediately after the first battle of Zurich he would have been 10,000–15,000 men weaker. We make this remark here not to contradict the archduke's reasoning, which we intend to do later, but to establish the facts.[16]

15. **Clausewitz** notes: "Vol. II, p 8." Karl, 2:8.

16. It is worth reminding the reader of the archduke's take regarding the need for caution. See note 2 of this chapter.

2. The archduke says Masséna was driven back but not defeated; in other words, the moral superiority that a real victory provides was lacking.[17]
3. Masséna's position was very strong. The archduke regarded an attack on the front of Zurich itself as almost impossible, crossing the Limmat further down as very difficult and not suitable for producing a major result, and crossing the Aare as no longer an actual attack on the position but rather a maneuver against it, whereby the opponent could be forced to abandon it. But since, in this last case, the aim is not sought by means of an actual test of arms, Zurich itself on the left wing has to be pinned; in turn, to advance with the right wing, Masséna's strong division at Basel also needs to be masked. Altogether, this assumes greater numerical superiority than the archduke thought he had.
4. A disadvantageous situation would also arise in the case of an outflanking maneuver around the French right wing in which the French forces south of Lake Zurich were driven back, because the Austrians could not support their left wing so easily and powerfully as the French could their right.[18]
5. The archduke thinks the French on the Rhine greatly outnumber his corps under Starray and thus are in a position to drive that back and advance against Schafhausen, his natural point of retreat. He calculates that at Basel and Breisach they are about four days' march from Schafhausen, while he would need two days to get there from Baden and Zurich; since he must allow the loss of one day for reporting, he concludes that he can advance at most only one day's march forward, if he is not to run the risk of losing his line of communications through Schafhausen and being restricted to that from Bregenz, which is inadequate for the long term. Since, as we have stated above, he does not consider himself able to compensate for such a disadvantage by a great battle on the Limmat, he does not want to expose himself to it.
6. Finally, the archduke thinks that Switzerland as an objective for his

17. It behooves the reader to remember Clausewitz's emphasis on the need for continuous pressure on the enemy and the role of pursuit in destroying an enemy army. See *On War*, book 1, chap. 1, secs. 12–14, and book 1, chap. 2.

18. This is largely down to the terrain and the difficulties of moving between positions (e.g., the Surenen Pass and Steinberg glacier mentioned earlier).

offensive is not really worth the sacrifice and risk[19] and that, for all the dissatisfaction with the government in France, still an uprising there in support of foreign armies could not be counted on.

All these reasons convince the archduke that his situation dictates that he remain on the defensive until the Russians' arrival gives him sufficient numerical superiority.

We must acknowledge that in our efforts to give these reasons some logical structure, we have totally changed their order. The archduke begins by citing the risk of his base being threatened from the Rhine as the decisive reason why there is no possibility of any operation leading to major success, and then adds the other factors to show that even a more limited operation aimed at a more modest gain would not have been natural in his situation. But if the archduke had been able to strike a decisive blow against Masséna's main army, he need not have worried at all about his rear, since great events and actions drag smaller ones along with them in the same direction, and action against a commander's rear is decisive only when he is no longer able to outbid it with major blows to his front.[20] We believe that the archduke thinks better than he writes and that, at the pace of his judgment—in which all the reasons that would get separated out in a logical exposition have a combined effect as though fused together—each one's individual contribution is quite different

19. **Clausewitz** notes: "Vol. II, p 6." Karl, 2:6.

20. Had the archduke, in the first place, put some effort into his pursuit of Masséna following the battle of Zurich, an attempt at another decisive blow might have been unnecessary. Even if one disagrees with this premise, it is important to consider it. Had the archduke taken the risk of pursuing Masséna, he might have gained enormously in strategic terms. He could have destroyed Masséna's army, leaving a great hole in the French strategic defenses. Had the pursuit not gone well, the archduke's risk was limited, unless he threw his whole army into the effort (which would have been silly); he risked ending up pretty much where he ended up anyway, albeit a bit more disorganized. This last part might have been problematic but for the fact that, had he thrown only part of his force into the pursuit of Masséna, he risked losing only that part of his army, while Masséna's army surely would have suffered greatly, even if it had managed to turn the situation on its head. Thus, the archduke could have risked part of his force, accepting the possibility of losing it, in return for the possibility of destroying the whole French army in front of him. Of course, bad luck might have intervened, and the whole thing could have gone catastrophically wrong. But that can happen at any time.

from what his logical analysis presents. We have therefore preferred to present these reasons in the way we believe they could have motivated the Austrian commander, without running into internal contradictions. We will wait until the conclusion of the chapter to examine whether the point of view from which they are interpreted is a correct one.

After the archduke has shown that he was really constrained to remain entirely on the defensive, he criticizes himself to some degree[21] for an error, in that he nevertheless considered an offensive. That offensive was a joint action by Jellachich and Haddick against the French right wing; indeed, the archduke states that when he detached the former it was entirely with this intention. We find this a little surprising, since when the archduke first tells of this detachment he does not mention this motive at all, and indeed, it seems to us that 6 July, when he knew nothing of Masséna's subsequent actions and had not yet conducted his reconnaissance, could not have been the moment to think about such a joint offensive with Haddick against Lecourbe; also, Haddick did not march out of the Rhone valley until 24 June, and we did not see the archduke press very hard for an operation during that time. If we are to express our honest conviction, it is that we believe the archduke arrived at the idea of an offensive only when Haddick was already gone, frittered away, and that he now places a somewhat stronger emphasis on it to bemoan this general's departure and to justify his own inaction even more.

We therefore cannot attach much weight to this apparently weak notion of the archduke's, which he himself condemns anyway, and we may regard him as being completely passive until mid-August.

Let us turn now to the French commander.

He had retreated behind the Limmat because he saw himself as weaker than his opponent; at the same time, he drew his right wing under Lecourbe closer to him from the St. Gotthard, which also points to his feeling of weakness. Thus, when we see the French commander keeping quiet for the time being, we find that only natural; he was waiting for his reinforcements. We do not actually know what reinforcements he obtained; the archduke says he received significant reinforcements that came from the formations the French government had created since the war began; no one can tell us how strong they were or when they arrived. Since the French situation in Italy was in a very

21. **Clausewitz** notes: "Vol. II, p 7." Karl, 2:7. This was quoted in note 2 of this chapter.

dire state after the battle of the Trebbia on 19 June, we can probably take it as a given that from that point on, whatever combat forces were available were sent exclusively to Italy. It follows from this that Masséna's army could not expect any more reinforcements during the course of July, and that it would have reached the state we gave for it in our overview by the first half of that month.

But Masséna did not think he was strong enough to undertake anything decisive against the main Austrian army in Switzerland. However, in June Masséna does seem to have sent a plan to Paris to give events in Italy a better turn by creating a diversion from Switzerland in that direction. Lecourbe was to invade Italy through the Rhone valley with 25,000–30,000 men, to attract part of the allied army toward him, and to try to make it easier for Macdonald and Moreau to link up. This plan did not come to be executed, because it was too late and the Trebbia had already settled this question. The French government now pressed Masséna to attack his opponent, but he stubbornly refused because he saw the situation in Italy was in ruins and did not think that much could come of an isolated offensive in Switzerland, even a successful one. He therefore stayed quiet.

The Action at Schwyz and Brunnen on 3 July

Meanwhile, Lecourbe decided on a small operation against the outpost and flotilla that the Austrians had at Brunnen. The reason for this limited action was probably just the favorable opportunity to pull a stunt against the Austrians and the wish to keep his troops active, since Brunnen lay within the Austrian outpost line, and the French could not easily hold it.

On 3 July he sent a few battalions out from Gersau to Brunnen and from Steinerberg to Schwyz. The latter appears to have been only a demonstration; indeed, it did not break through, and the Austrians retained Schwyz. However, Brunnen was lost for an instant, and with it a battery of six guns as well as the flotilla the Austrians had here on Lake Lucerne. When the Austrian reserves arrived, the French were driven off again.

Such a result from this small operation was well worth the effort expended on it.

Probably in revenge for this prank, the Austrian General Bey set out from Altorf on 29 July to destroy the French flotilla at Bauen. He moved with two and a half battalions via Attingshausen and Seedorf to Bauen, drove off the French, attained his aim, but let himself be tempted into advancing to Seelisberg to seize that place and thus become master of the whole southern gulf of Lake Lucerne. He probably could have told himself that the French, who had Loison's brigade behind the Aa, would not let him remain in possession of this area; it was an even bigger mistake that, during the advance, he so weakened his force by sending detachments off left and right that he was left with only two companies in Seelisberg. He gained control of this village but was attacked straight away by superior numbers from several directions and was captured together with the larger part of his two companies; two others that had been left in Bauen were also lost, so this operation cost the Austrians 500–600 men and brought upon them the shame of seeing the general in charge of it taken prisoner.

These small operations did not disturb the immovable inaction of the main bodies, and the whole of July and half of August slipped by without anything else happening in Switzerland. However, we do have a few incidents to consider that had transpired on the Rhine meanwhile.

59 THE SUMMER'S EVENTS ON THE RHINE

Until July, both sides' combat forces deployed on the Rhine were under the command of their generals in Switzerland; nonetheless, we would have to regard the Rhine as a distinct theater of operations if the individual incidents there had been important enough to merit their own chapter, because those incidents were not affected in any way by the details of the events happening in Switzerland. But up until the moment when the archduke and his army moved to the Rhine, this theater of operations can be regarded as being in complete quiet and equilibrium, and its influence on Switzerland consists not of events that actually occurred there but rather of imagined possible events. We do have to take a look at this neighboring theater of operations, and we therefore wish to do so now, so that we can better evaluate the two commanders' situations at the point in time when they both feel under pressure to act in Switzerland.[22]

22. In wargames studying the campaign (elective 599B at the US Naval War College, 2019), players found that once one side committed to Switzerland, the other side invariably had no choice but to contest that decision. This is because Switzerland's passes allow the campaign theaters in Germany and Italy to connect, and control over Switzerland presents a threat to the flanks of enemy armies to the north and south.

After the former Army of the Danube had given up its name and a large part of its combat forces had gone to Switzerland, as we said in section 28 [volume 1, chapter 3], about 35,000 men remained behind on the Rhine, comprising Bernadotte's former Army of Observation and the remainder of Jourdan's army. Bernadotte went to Paris, and after he was designated minister of war on 30 *Prairial* (18 June),[23] all these troops came under Masséna's command and were formed into two divisions under Generals Legrand and Collaud—the former at Breisach and Strassburg, the latter at Mannheim. How strong these divisions were, that is, how large the garrisons of Hüningen, Breisach, Strassburg, Kehl, and Mainz were, we do not know. Probably neither of them would have had more than 6,000–8,000 men. Mainz was commanded by General Baraguey d'Hilliers, and because there was no active field corps there, the garrison of that place must be considered as such, since it had a lot to deal with from the popular uprising that had occurred in Mainz. General Dufour, who commanded the interior of the Rhine provinces, probably had only depots and the detachments passing through them.

At the time Jourdan was hurled back across the Rhine, the operation against Holland was not yet an issue, as Russia and England did not even discuss it until June, so the Directory moved significant bodies of troops out of the Netherlands to the Rhine. Reinforcements were also sent there from the interior, so that the French force on the Rhine rose from the roughly 35,000 men it had in April to 45,000 infantry and 7,000 cavalry, not including nine battalions that were considered fortress garrisons.[24] It reached this size in August, after the formation of a new Army of the Rhine under Moreau's command had already been decreed, but we are unable to say when and where the individual reinforcements arrived, nor how strong we should consider the French to have been at any given moment; all that is certain is that the reinforcements did not arrive all at once but bit by bit.

23. Esdaile comments that the repeated defeats undermined the government, leading to a coup on 30 *Prairial*. This promised to lead France back to a more radical revolutionary phase, and it is one of the reasons there was so much pressure on the commanders to gain victories. Charles J. Esdaile, *The Wars of the French Revolution 1792–1801* (New York: Routledge, 2019), 285.

24. For an overview of this campaign, see Esdaile, *Wars of the French Revolution*. See also A. B. Rodger, *The War of the Second Coalition 1798–1801* (Oxford: Clarendon Press, 1964), 176–194.

As we have seen, the archduke had left General Starray facing this mass of troops with eighteen battalions and sixty-four squadrons, but subsequently he must have detailed four of those battalions elsewhere and reinforced this corps with another four squadrons, since he states that it had fourteen battalions and sixty-eight squadrons in June, with a strength of 22,000 men.

Besides these Austrian troops, among the combat forces facing the French on the Rhine we must count the 2,600-man garrison of Philippsburg and the *Landsturm* who had been summoned from the *Waldstädte*[25] to the Main. The idea for this latter measure came from Chur and Mainz Minister of State [*Mainzischer Generalfeldzeugmeister*] Albini,[26] and they were only supposed to protect property against French patrols and pillagers. This mostly happened in Mainz territory and in the Odenwald, where Albini placed himself at their head; the groups of *Landsturm*, supported by two battalions and one squadron of Mainz regular troops, busily fought a running battle along the Nidda with the French garrison of Mainz, without anything much coming of it. Around Philippsburg they were supported by the fortress garrison, and in the Black Forest by Austrian light troops, alongside whom they did outpost duty.

Even if we estimate the value of this whole *Landsturm* mobilization at just 10,000 men, we can well see that so long as the French force did not exceed 40,000 men, and given the number of fortresses they had to keep occupied, the French had no substantial superiority on the Rhine, and thus, for the archduke's part, he had nothing to fear from any new offensive here. Admittedly, the archduke may have greatly overestimated the forces the French had on the Rhine, which could have happened all the more easily as the troops arriving from the Netherlands were mostly only staging there on their way to Switzerland or Italy, but from the other side, he could probably say that the French would also overestimate the south German popular mobilization and would not commit themselves to any serious operation without numerical superiority.

Of the two French divisions, Legrand's had been split up; the smaller part was in front of Alt-Breisach, the larger at Offenburg, whereby they protected

25. These were the "forest towns" of Rheinfelden, Säckingen (now Bad Säckingen), Laufenburg, and Waldshut (now Waldshut-Tiengen), which lay on the main Austrian route west along the upper Rhine River. See volume 1, chapter 1, note 99.

26. This is Franz Josef Martin Freiherr von Albini (1748–1816), who proved to be an able commander. "Deutsche Biographie," https://www.deutsche-biographie.de/sfz313.html?language=de.

the construction work going on in the bridgeheads of Alt-Breisach and Kehl. They had their outposts along the foot of the mountains and in the valleys in which the roads to Breisach and Strassburg run through the Black Forest.

The Austrians had occupied Neustadt, Furtwangen, Triberg, Hornberg, and Freudenstadt, that is to say, the entrances to the Höllen, Kinzig, Rench, and Murch valleys on the eastern slopes of the Black Forest, with eight battalions and twenty-two squadrons; ten squadrons were patrolling between the Murch and the Main, and six battalions and thirty-six squadrons were in an entrenched camp at Villingen, which the forward posts were to fall back on in the event of a serious attack.

These opposing dispositions lasted until July, during which time, apart from minor bickering between outposts, there were just two operations of some significance.

In the second half of June the archduke ordered General Starray to hurl the French outposts back into the Breisach bridgehead. He undoubtedly meant this to divert his opponent's attention to the Rhine so as to prevent Masséna from sending himself any more reinforcements from there to Switzerland.

On 23 June General Gyulai therefore advanced from Freiburg with one brigade, surprised the outposts at Gündlingen and Hochstetten, and drove them into Alt-Breisach.

On the 25th General Meerfeld advanced from Haslach with another brigade in three columns; attacked Ettenheim, Offenburg, and Oberkirch on the 26th; and obliged the French outposts to retreat to Wilstett.

On 4 July, after Legrand had been reinforced by a detachment of troops arriving from the Netherlands that Masséna had sent him for this purpose, he advanced out of Kehl again and retook Appenweier and Renchen, as well as Offenburg on 6 July; but when he heard that the Austrians were bringing up their reserve from Villingen, he left the latter place and limited himself to a crescent of outposts from Marlen through Appenweier to Bischofsheim.

Now everything stayed quiet until September, but the French situation changed. After 30 *Prairial*, in addition to the colossal reinforcements that were to be sent to the existing armies, the French Directory had decided to form two new armies: that of Savoy, led by Championnet, and an independent Army of the Rhine, to be commanded by Moreau. Until Moreau's arrival, General Müller took interim command of this Army of the Rhine. At the end of July he transferred his headquarters to Türkheim, left just six battalions in front of Kehl, and moved the rest of his combat forces to Mannheim, which was newly prepared for defense after actually having two bastions of its fortress demolished according to the previous idea [the French command's view that Mannheim's fortifications were not important for their own defensive scheme but should be denied to the enemy].

Thus in August, at the time when events in Switzerland were coming to a head, a new drive for action on the Rhine emerged, which was made to sound more fearsome than it was by all the grand words being intoned about it in Paris, and therefore seemed a serious threat to Swabia and consequently to the Austrian base.

Throughout this time, Souham's division at Basel remained immobile in the position it had entrenched itself in between Basel and Lörrach.

60 LECOURBE CHASES THE AUSTRIAN LEFT WING OUT OF THE RHONE, REUSS, AND SIHL VALLEYS

Throughout the whole of July, General Masséna had stubbornly resisted the Directory, which was urging him to attack his adversary.[27] Partly, he did not feel strong enough to fight a major battle with any likelihood of success; partly, he felt that an isolated operation in Switzerland could not lead to anything; and lastly, he may well have hoped that the formation of a new Army of the Rhine would cause the archduke to send significant detachments there. But when all reinforcements were diverted to the army in Italy after the defeat on the Trebbia, so Masséna could not expect any more, and when Korsakov had approached so close that he could be expected to arrive in the second half of August, Masséna felt himself compelled by circumstances to act anyway. Now at this time, that is to say, the end of July, the Swiss government began to adopt such a disturbing and threatening tone about the state of the country that the French Directory urged its commander to attack once more because it saw a victory over Archduke Charles as the only means to bring relief to the Swiss.[28]

27. The repeated defeats had led to the 30 *Prairial* (18 June) coup mentioned previously. The new government needed success to cement its hold on power and to prevent a swing toward more domestic revolutionary violence. Esdaile, *Wars of the French Revolution,* 285.

28. The archduke's take on the 30 *Prairial* coup and what it meant for France is worth quoting at length, as it partly matches Clausewitz's ideas about the connection of politics to military action: "Whilst the armies from the Main to the Rhone kept watch on each other and maintained the balance with each other through the advantage of their positions, the revolution of 30 Prairial (18 June) had given the French government a fresh momentum. Every popular revolution is the product of roused passions, amongst which

All these circumstances combined to push the French commander to actually make his decision.[29]

---

imperiousness is the most captivating and the most violent. It generates crimes because only these can satisfy its insatiableness, and immoral people are so bold as to seize the political rudder. If Nature has equipped them with the necessary characteristics and they are strong enough to restrain the extreme competitiveness of their fellow citizens and to rule through fear then they can assert themselves for as long as favorable circumstances keep them terrifying. If they put the iron sceptre down then the suppressed passions destroy their chains. Everyone then deems himself better, everyone wants to avenge himself for the coercion suffered, everyone wants to exert influence on the supreme power. This was the situation the members of the Directory found themselves in. They were scheming, but not strong, men, incapable of leading the common man and proudly reckless over the dangers to the homeland, they indulged only their self-interest, practiced venomous acts and enriched themselves and their followers from the state's means of assistance. In the harshest of conditions the public coffers were without money, the armies without armaments, without pay and without clothing. These most infamous agents of the government plundered defenseless peoples, and mocked the general misfortune through every kind of pressure and through blatant injustices. As the successes of the war went on failing more and more to equate with the sacrifices made, the nation's unwillingness increased and loud complaints resounded from all parts of the empire. Finally, the legislative body rose up and forced the members of the Directory to give up their positions, and they were replaced by others. The sins of the forefathers always appear most vividly in front of the eyes of their direct descendants, this is why they usually also resort to the opposite path as long as self-confidence and inner feelings of strength conceal from them the extent of the difficulties that they have to overcome. The new Directors take up their office with energetic measures for increasing the army and for filling the public coffers. The military manpower of the French Republic, which at that period was only reckoned to be 200,000 men, was to be raised to 500,000, and for this all male inhabitants of France from 20 to 25 years would have to play a part regardless of class, occupation and family circumstances. A forced loan of 100 million francs was imposed on the wealthier middle class." Karl, 2:29–31. All this is significant because the costs imposed on the French people had greatly increased; thus, if we accept Clausewitz's argument, it is likely that the costs associated with the war needed to be matched by gains, and if they were not attainable, then the object needed to be renounced. Given the nature of the trinity, where one has to balance passion, reason, and chance, it is reasonable to argue that great sacrifices might not be easy to renounce and that the gains achieved from the conflict had to increase. If so, then the enemy, logically, would need to make the same calculation. In all likelihood, this would result in an escalation of efforts on both sides. See *On War*, book 1, chaps. 1 and 2. This also demonstrates that the archduke was not as backward thinking as Clausewitz likes to argue.

29. This idea of victory as a means of maintaining or gaining support for the

But this decision was not directed toward fighting a major decisive battle right away. Any attack between Lake Zurich and the Rhine must necessarily lead to such a battle, and Masséna saw this as a very dangerous undertaking, not without reason. For the time being, an offensive from the Rhine or against the Austrian left wing in the Rhone, Reuss, and Sihl valleys could only have the effect of a maneuver, that is, causing the archduke to adopt a different deployment, which would then have to create some advantage for the French commander and lead to further operations by him; on the other hand, these flanking operations unarguably entailed fewer difficulties or dangers. The Rhine option ruled itself out for the French commander, since command of these troops had been taken away from him again. He was therefore left with the option of an attack on the Austrian left wing, which he executed in mid-August.

We have seen that if we include General Haddick and his entire corps, the Austrian left wing was deployed as four distinct detachments, namely:

Jellachich between Lake Zurich and Lake Lucerne.
Simbschen, who had replaced Bey, in the Reuss valley from Lake Lucerne to the Devil's Bridge.
Strauch in the Rhone valley.
Haddick with the rest in the Simplon Pass and at Aosta.

This line of deployment was 110 miles long, and about 26,000 men were used to occupy it.

The French decided to attack that part of the line between the Simplon and Lake Zurich, which was about 70 miles long and was occupied by about 20,000 men, at all points on the same day. At that period of the revolutionary wars, they always expected a special effect from attacking a very long strategic front at all points at the same time, even though it is clear that such a system is contrary to the concentration of one's own forces and

---

government closely ties in with Clausewitz's conception of the value of the object one is seeking (*On War*, book 1, chaps. 1 and 2). The object does not necessarily have to be something physical. In this case, it is clear that the Directory sees a direct link between military success and domestic political power. It is reasonable to say that Napoleon firmly grasped this connection during his entire career.

cannot be favorable for cutting off and enveloping individual elements of the enemy deployment.[30]

Masséna detailed Tharreau's, Lecourbe's, and Chabran's divisions for this operation, which were reinforced with a few thousand men from the center and formed a force of about 25,000 men. Overall command was given to General Lecourbe, and 14 August was set for its execution.

Lecourbe divided his attack into three major groupings: Tharreau in the Rhone valley, his own division in the Reuss valley, and Chabran in the Sihl valley. The detailed plan was, however, quite complex.

Tharreau was to drive Prince Rohan out of the Simplon Pass with his right wing and attack Strauch in the Rhone valley with his left. Lecourbe's division's right wing under Gudin was to take the Grimsel, in Strauch's rear; his center was to advance into the Reuss valley; and his left was to attack Schwyz and Brunnen. Chabran was to take Jellachich's outposts. But besides that, there was a kind of interweaving of the columns. After overwhelming Strauch's outpost on the Grimsel, Gudin, with the right wing of Lecourbe's division, was to turn left through the Furka Pass and via Realp into the Reuss valley and attack General Simbschen's left flank. Lecourbe himself, with a reserve of five grenadier companies, was to embark on his flotilla, first landing at Brunnen to support his left wing, then embarking again and landing a second time at Flüelen to help the center against Simbschen. This double use of two detachments in different directions and against different parts of the enemy deployment is certainly one of those truly contrived creations, but from this distance in time and space, we cannot allow ourselves to pass too harsh a sentence upon its value or otherwise.

To prevent the archduke from reinforcing his left wing, Generals Soult and Lorges were to engage him with a feint attack against the front of his main body.

The overall intention of this attack was to gain possession of the Rhone and Reuss valleys and consequently of the St. Gotthard Pass, to drive the Austrians back into the Rhine valley and behind Lake Zurich and Lake Walensee, and in this way to threaten Graubündten. Masséna could imagine that such a success would cause the archduke to detach forces to his left wing, which would then make an operation against his main body easier. What trophies this might yield would depend on the activity and talent of individual leaders, as well as on the enemy's mistakes.

30. This plan is the one detailed in volume 1, chapter 1.

Complete success was then achieved within a couple of days and, astonishingly, with all the tasks of this very complex plan being accomplished.[31] We wish to divide the story of how this was done according to the three Austrian corps under Strauch, Simbschen, and Jellachich, and we begin with the first.

Colonel Strauch had eight battalions and one squadron totaling 6,000 men. Apart from these, Prince Rohan had some 2,000 in the Simplon Pass. In order to have direct communications with the prince, and probably also to protect the upper part of the Rhone valley, Strauch had pushed his deployment forward to the area around Ernen. His outposts, or indeed his actual positions, if you will, straddled the Rhone between Roswald [Rosswald] and Ried [Ried-Mörel] facing Naters and Brig, and each consisted of one battalion. He had one and two-thirds battalions in the Binna valley to support the outpost on his left wing, and a battalion on the Theisberg [presumably the heights above Fiesch or Deisch, opposite the Binna] to support the right. Thus, this was Colonel Strauch's actual front. To protect his rear against the French in the Aare valley, there were two battalions on the Grimsel. This left one battalion in reserve in Münster [Münster-Geschinen]. Two companies were detached to the Italian slopes of the Alps to obtain supplies. The squadron was attached to the infantry in small groups.

The French in Wallis had been on the move since 8 August, and besides, Strauch received word from Switzerland of an impending offensive. However, this did not make him change his position.

On 13 August Tharreau attacked the battalion on the Rothwald with greatly superior numbers, dispersed most of it, and drove the rest into the Binna valley. His right wing likewise drove Prince Rohan out of the Simplon. But in the evening the French retreated out of the Binna valley again. On hearing news of this attack, early on the 14th Colonel Strauch sent—one might well say carelessly—four companies, or two-thirds of his reserve, into the Binna valley under Major Richter in order to drive the French completely out again from possession of the outpost the Austrians had had there.[32]

On the 14th Gudin and his five battalions arrived from the Aare valley and attacked the two battalions on the Grimsel. Strauch now rushed up with both

31. Despite the risk, bold action on the part of the French again showed what was possible. See Clausewitz's thoughts on boldness in *On War*, book 3, chap. 6, 190–193.

32. The archduke covers the episode; see Karl, 2:11, 105–112.

of his remaining companies, but this weak support and the natural strength of the position could not prevent the Austrians from being overwhelmed by the superior force and losing their line of retreat across the Furka Pass to the St. Gotthard. Strauch now concentrated his troops near Ober-Gestelen [Obergesteln], occupied Zum Loch at the exit from the Egge valley that led to the Nufenen Pass—the last way out of Wallis to Italy that he had left—and sent an order to the troops at the front facing Tharreau to come and join him. But it was too late.

For on the 14th the French had also returned to the attack here, first overwhelming the outpost on the right bank of the Rhone and forcing it to retreat into the Binna valley, to where Major Richter then also began his retreat. When Strauch's order reached these troops, it was too late to march back up the Rhone valley, as the French were already between them and Strauch.

On the 15th, having lost the larger part of his troops and having just 500 men with him, Colonel Strauch was left with no option but to retreat over the Nufenenberg to Airolo. Since a French battalion had advanced through the St. Gotthard on the 15th, on the 16th Strauch moved to Bellinzona.

Colonel Carneville and the actual main body of Strauch's corps moved through the Val Maggia to Locarno on Lake Maggiore, where he arrived on the 19th, and from where he joined Strauch in Bellinzona on the 21st. The corps was now about 3,000 strong, so it had lost half its men and its artillery. It received a reinforcement of two battalions from the Milan area.

If we reckon General Tharreau, reinforced with some Swiss troops, at 10,000 men, Gudin at 3,000, and deduct a few battalions that stayed facing the Great St. Bernard, then about 12,000 men fought against Strauch and Rohan, who were 8,000 strong altogether. If we consider the strength of the local terrain, the Austrians' orders and actions certainly do not gain much honor from the result of this fight.

The archduke seems quite justified in accusing Colonel Strauch of having pushed his front so far forward that not only was his position much more extended but it also reached into the area where the French were able to use the road leading to Brig to bring a superior amount of artillery to bear against him.[33] But leaving aside this mistake in the layout of the defense overall, the Austrians do not seem to have put up suitable resistance even in their individual positions. When the attacker has to work his way forward in single

33. Karl, 2:106–107.

file along footpaths over glaciers, as on the Grimsel, one might expect that 2,000 men could hold out against an attack by 3,000 for longer than half a day.

General Simbschen had six battalions and a squadron. Of these, two occupied Wassen as the main entrance into the Reuss valley, namely, from the Hasli valley over the Steinerberg through the Meien valley; one battalion was at the mouth of the Reuss and occupied Seedorf, Attinghausen, and Flüelen; one battalion was in Erstfeld, where the track over the Surenenberg arrives in the Reuss valley; and the other two were in Urseren [near Realp] and Amsteg, to protect the rearward entrances into the Reuss valley. This general's 4,300 men were thus extended across 20 miles in the Reuss valley and were actually protected by nothing other than that river and the difficulty of the approaches over the mountains. But since the highest points of these approaches were only observed, not defended, all they gained was that they learned about the enemy advance in time. Only at Wassen did the position itself have a kind of strength, because there was an old walled redoubt there [the Meienschanze],[34] which the Austrians occupied with one battalion and two guns.

In accordance with the French plan, Loison advanced into the Reuss valley in three columns on the 14th. The strongest, which he led himself, had three battalions and moved through the Meien valley upon Wassen; the second, consisting of two battalions under Daumas, moved across the Surenenberg upon Erstfeld and Attinghausen; the third, likewise consisting of two battalions, moved out of the Issi valley at Lake Lucerne to Seedorf.

Of these three columns, on the 14th Loison advanced to Wassen but could not make himself master of the redoubt that day. Likewise, the other two columns were only able to advance to the bank of the Reuss but could not effect a crossing, since the Austrians had demolished the bridges and were defending the right bank with their fire.

Toward evening Lecourbe himself landed at Flüelen and Seedorf, not without difficulty, although the Austrians had only one gun there. He had landed a detachment at Sissingen [Sisikon] earlier, which came across the Axenberg and descended at Bürglen into the rear of the outposts at Attinghausen and Seedorf. Now the defense of the mouth of the Reuss came

34. The redoubt is no longer there, but there is a more modern building and a memorial on or near the site on the *Alter Sustenweg* about 500 meters west of the center of Wassen. Given the difficult terrain, this would have been quite an obstacle to any attack.

to an end. Part of the Austrian battalion moved into the Schächen valley and part up the Reuss valley, whereby the defense at Attinghausen and Erstfeld was taken in its right flank and abandoned on the 14th. Lecourbe now advanced to Amsteg.

On the 15th a new attack ensued at Amsteg and Wassen. Lecourbe, who may have had four or five battalions with him, broke through at Amsteg, and the two or three Austrian battalions that had been shoved together there were driven into the Maderaner valley, from where they retreated across the mountains to Tavetsch [Tujetsch] in the Anterior Rhine valley.

At the same time, Loison had taken the redoubt at Wassen, after repeated assaults, by delivering heavy fire against the garrison from the neighboring heights that overlooked it. The Austrians now retreated from there with one and a half battalions to the Devil's Bridge, behind which they made another stand against Loison.

But on the morning of the 15th Gudin had begun his march into the Reuss valley, easily overcame the resistance the Austrians put up against him in the Urseren valley, and now entered Urseren itself toward evening. This made further resistance at the Devil's Bridge impossible, and during the night of 15–16 August General Simbschen retreated with the three battalions he had there to the Crispalt, after demolishing the curve of road leading to the Devil's Bridge.

Lecourbe started work on repairing the bridge immediately on the 16th and joined up with Gudin at 7:00 a.m. He then sent one battalion through the St. Gotthard to seize Airolo and to threaten the Anterior Rhine through the valley of the Middle Rhine. He himself advanced with a few battalions to attack General Simbschen. The latter held out for a while on the difficult approaches to his position, but toward evening he had to retreat, with the loss of three guns and 1,000 prisoners. We may imagine this did not leave him with much. He descended into the Rhine valley at Chiamut [Tschamut-Selva] and San Giacomo [San Giacomo Pass][35] and moved to Somvix [Sumvitg] on the 17th, Ilanz on the 19th, and Chur on the 20th, after having his right wing join him at Tavetsch [Tujetsch]. In total, his losses probably came to more than

35. The pass at San Giacomo is the most likely place. It is just south of All'Acqua on the Ticino River. The archduke places French and Austrian troops in the valley at roughly the same time, and the valley connects to the Usereren via the St. Gotthard Pass. Karl, 2:80–101.

2,000 men, or half his corps, the same as Strauch. This success was obtained by the cooperation between Gudin's brigade and the reserve that Lecourbe himself led across the lake, thus by about 8,000 men against 4,300.

The outpost at Schwyz and Brunnen belonged to Jellachich's main body; it covered the entrance to the Muota valley and thereby his strategic left flank. It comprised two battalions in Schwyz and one and a half with three guns in Brunnen to command the lake. As a link between this outpost and the position proper, there was one battalion at Sattel; one battalion had occupied the lake trail at Rapperschwyl, which still left the Austrian general with seven and a half battalions and five squadrons in his position between Richtenschwyl and the Sihl, which was about 5 miles in extent.

The French attack on the outpost at Schwyz was carried out by Boivin's brigade (the left wing of Lecourbe's division) and by the reserve led by Lecourbe in person. The French actually attacked this outpost in three columns. The main column under Boivin, which Masséna was with as well, moved through Seewen upon Schwyz, three companies moved from Gersau against Brunnen, and the third column was Lecourbe with his flotilla. The outpost at Brunnen was soon taken, so Lecourbe had to put in only a brief appearance before embarking again for his landing at Flüelen.

The outpost at Schwyz held out longer, and the French even began to have doubts about the outcome. Masséna's chief of general staff, Oudinot, led the troops into the enemy fire once more and was wounded during the action, which was decided in favor of the French. The Austrians withdrew into the Muota valley, leaving a couple of guns behind; they were attacked again at Muota on the 15th and driven as far as the Klöntal lake, from where they continued their march to Netstal, near Glarus.

General Jellachich's main position was attacked by Chabran's division in three columns. We cannot state Chabran's strength precisely, but he probably had twelve battalions and six squadrons. We are equally unable to give details of the Austrian general's deployment or the French plan of attack. On the 14th the column on the left wing attacked the Austrians in their position proper at Richterswil, Wollerau, Schindellegi, and Hütten. Jellachich held out on this day, albeit not without bringing all his troops into action. Meanwhile, a couple of small columns had advanced through Ägeri and Morgarten against the Austrian communications outpost at Sattel, driven this off without any trouble, and forced it to retreat to Einsiedeln and then from there toward the Etzelberg. The French column following it sent a detachment into the Wägi valley to the [Wägitaler] Aa, which threatened the Austrian main body's line of retreat to Uznach. At nightfall General Jellachich retreated from his first position to a second one further back on the Etzelberg. Here he was attacked once again on the 15th and again forced to retreat. The outflanking move into the Wägi valley seems to have made its effect felt in this retreat, since, as the archduke himself says, at Grynau (close to Uznach) Jellachich was driven back in disorder across the Linth, behind which he deployed again. General Jellachich's losses are not stated but can probably be assumed to be no fewer than 3,000 men, since two entire battalions were lost during the retreat across the Linth alone.

The combat forces the French employed between Lake Zurich and Lake Lucerne may have come to about 11,000–12,000 men, so they were little stronger than Jellachich, who had between 9,000 and 10,000, and here too the result does not especially enhance Austrian honor.

The demonstrations by Lorges's and Soult's divisions consisted of them attacking the Austrian outposts at Witikon, Wollishofen, and Leimbach on the 14th and seizing these places, which were then retaken by the Austrian reserves when they arrived.

Thus, the result of these two days was that the Austrians had been driven out of the Rhone valley to Lake Maggiore, out of the Reuss valley into the Rhine valley, and from the Sihl to behind the Linth; the French had not followed any further and had their outposts toward the Linth at Reichenburg, Bilten, and the Klöntal lake and at Somvix in the Rhine valley.[36]

Thus, in the blink of an eye, the Austrians lost possession of the St. Gotthard just when it was quite seriously important for the first time, namely, when

36. **Clausewitz** notes: "It would of course have been better if instead of telling us about the French outposts, the historians had provided the positions of their main bodies. But since they do not offer a single syllable about that and even say nothing about the archduke's attempted reaction on this wing a few days later, we can only make do with assumptions, which we mainly draw from the state the French were in four weeks later when Suvorov moved against the St. Gotthard. According to this it is likely that Tharreau stayed in Wallis, while Lecourbe occupied the St. Gotthard and the Reuss valley and had pushed forward advance posts into the Rhine valley at Disentis, as well as in the Schächen and Muota valleys." He is sarcastically referring to Jomini and the archduke, neither of whom offers details about the positions of the main bodies of troops. The best we get from the archduke is that there were forty-four battalions of infantry and sixty-eight squadrons of cavalry between the outflow of the Aar and Lake Zurich. Karl, 2:96. See also Jomini, 12:55–94.

Suvorov was about to begin his march to move through it into Switzerland. The St. Gotthard also had a certain strategic value as a shorter line of communications with the Italian army, since communications now had to run through the St. Bernard and Splügen Passes; even so, the Austrians' biggest problem was not this loss of territory but their losses of men and guns and the effect on morale these produced. These losses came to at least 7,000–8,000 men and fifteen to twenty guns, while the French most probably lost fewer than 2,000 men.[37]

61 REFLECTIONS ON THIS ACTION

This attack of Lecourbe's and the Austrians' defense against it give us cause for some reflections, which we wish to present from two points of view, one concerning the strategic dimension and the other the tactical. The first viewpoint is the strategic value of the success of this action; the second, how effective the cordon adopted by the Austrian corps proved to be.

The loss of the St. Gotthard and of the outpost line leading up to it could have no influence on the archduke's strategic situation beyond somewhat lengthening his line of communications with the army in Italy; instead of running through the St. Gotthard to Bellinzona, it now ran through the Splügen Pass to Chiavenna. But since there were no troop movements along this line and no mutual support between the two armies, and since it was used only by couriers, we cannot attach any great value to such a change.

The line of communications through the St. Gotthard acquired greater value from the moment Suvorov wanted to climb through it with the Russians in order to betake himself from Italy to Switzerland; however, it is still hard

37. **Clausewitz** notes: "We estimate the losses as being so high from what emerges about them from the archduke's historical account, although Jomini himself gives them as only 6,000 men and eleven cannon. As far as the guns are concerned, the archduke gives those eleven as Simbschen's and Jellachich's losses, and out of gallantry toward him, Jomini lets that stand; but the archduke attaches so little value to trophies that he neglects to list his own, so we cannot be surprised if he does not count the enemy's accurately. Most likely the two cannon that were in the Wassen redoubt were also lost, and it is just as likely that Strauch's corps would not have been entirely without artillery but could not have brought any of it out along the route he took for his retreat. The losses of men are made up of 2,000–3,000 from Strauch and 2,400 from Simbschen, leaving another 2,000–3,000 for Jellachich, which is certainly not too many, since two entire battalions were cut off."

to see why he could not just march into Switzerland along the same road on which Bellegarde had marched out, through Chiavenna and the Splügen. But anyway, Masséna was not even aware of this factor at the time he decided to drive the Austrians out of this area, since that was before the battle of Novi.

It is natural that the archduke could not have been happy to lose the upper part of Graubündten and the small cantons, mainly for the sake of the inhabitants, but this consideration was not one that affected his own situation.

We believe the archduke would have been in a much better position both for defense and for attack if he had rested his left wing on the St. Luciensteig rather than on the St. Gotthard.

Thus, if General Masséna and his historian, General Jomini,[38] are supposed to have thought that the loss of the line through the St. Gotthard before Korsakov's arrival could have prompted the archduke to abandon Switzerland, we would not want to declare this impossible, because with a commander such as the archduke, we cannot vouch for that, but we can argue that there was absolutely no objective reason for it.

However, if Masséna simply thought that this operation, which Jomini calls a preamble [*un préambule*], would cause the archduke to reinforce his left wing and that this might give him a chance to do something against the archduke's main army, there are certainly *objective* reasons for that.

A commander who has once been in possession of a stretch of territory will not gladly give it up unless force of circumstance obliges him to, especially if its inhabitants have been heavily involved in fighting alongside him, and will see it as a matter of military honor to protect them.[39] If, in addition, the loss of this territory comes, as it does here, with a series of reverses in which the enemy has gained considerable trophies and moral superiority, then reaction is much more likely, and indeed, this equation proved true here.

38. Jomini worked with the Swiss army, seeing to the administration of the arsenals, and thus witnessed little of the campaign. That should not undermine his immense knowledge of events, as he was an excellent historian. For his role at the time of the fighting, see Ami Jacques Rapin, "Jomini at the Time of the Helvetian Republic (1798–1801)," Université de Lausanne, https://applicationspub.unil.ch/interpub/noauth/php/Un/UnPers.php?PerNum=851054&LanCode=37&menu=pub.

39. This sentiment ties in closely with Clausewitz's idea of the interaction of passion, reason, and chance in his trinity (*On War*, book 1, chap. 1). Even if it were logical and strategically sound to give up ground, it is hard to return something so expensively gained, and it is also hard to abandon people alongside whom one has been fighting.

Thus we cannot fail to applaud Masséna's operation as preparation for a larger one, especially as it had already conferred a very good result in itself.

It could also have further strategic value in connection with the Army of Italy. Despite their significant distance away, Suvorov had shown that he was never entirely indifferent to the events occurring on the southern slopes of the Swiss Alps.[40] If Lecourbe had been able to advance through the Simplon Pass with part of his force, the loss of the Rhone valley certainly would have resulted in Suvorov sending significant detachments to these areas, just as we have already seen Kray on the march (section 55) [volume 1, chapter 5]. Perhaps only the presence of General Lecourbe in person with Xaintrailles's division reinforced by 2,000–3,000 men would have been needed to produce an extraordinarily large effect. But we really cannot criticize General Masséna if he did not dare to strike a blow into Italy with his right arm when he felt he needed to grasp his sword in both hands against the archduke.

But as far as timing is concerned, we can certainly say that, as a demonstration rather than being decisive in itself, Masséna's operation came fourteen days too late, since it coincided with the two events against which it could have been directed: the battle of Novi and the arrival of Korsakov, who entered Schafhausen at this time. If Masséna's attack had happened fourteen days earlier, then in Switzerland, the archduke would not have been able to regard Korsakov's arrival as offsetting his losses, and in Italy, the loss of the Rhone valley could have had an effect on the battle of Novi.

We now come to the second topic of our reflections, which is obviously one of the most difficult in the whole theory of war, because it is so difficult not to lose sight of *the essence of the matter*. Because of that, a host of major errors has nestled here as well.

We feel we must take this opportunity to present a theoretical consideration mainly because, for the first time, we see a considerable corps deployed cordon fashion on an extensive front and organized for defense, attacked by an enemy who is not particularly superior in numbers and whose success therefore cannot be ascribed mainly to great superiority nor to surprise, as was the case with events of this kind that occurred earlier in this campaign.[41]

40. Again, this has been a routine observation among players taking Suvorov's role during historical wargaming conducted at the US Naval War College.

41. It would behoove the reader to look at what Clausewitz has to say regarding the defense in *On War*, book 6. Pay particular attention to chaps. 1–5 on the relationship

A long defensive line is easy to break through. This is a very natural finding, so inevitably, whenever such a line is broken through and the defender suffers all kinds of damage, the critic is at hand to claim that it was a mistake to deploy in the cordon or to fight in it. Can we be satisfied with such a judgment? If we think honestly about it from what we know, instead of being content with half-truths, obviously we cannot; for not only do we see such lines occurring constantly in the conduct of war—from which we can conclude that there is some intrinsic need for them whenever certain situations arise—but also it is not hard to deduce the need for their occurrence from the nature of how things work.

When two armies face each other without seeking a major battle, nor expecting the enemy to do so, they both need to secure the territory to their left and right that is roughly level with them; no one likes to be wrapped around by his opponent, and there is no need to explore the reasons for that in detail here.[42] Such a deployment is therefore the normal one, as modified by the local terrain and individual circumstances, so each of the two adversaries strives toward it.

In a flat region, this aim is achieved by corps posted left and right of the army in concentrated positions; whatever is not covered by the position itself, the corps covers by maneuver. In the mountains, it is quite different. Because one cannot freely march to the left and right in the mountains, any deployment in them entails *a certain extension,* since in the mountains even more so than on the plain, one cannot expose oneself to the danger of getting into a fight while surrounded on all sides and perhaps cut off from all lines of retreat. This intrinsic need for extension increases in proportion to the size of the mountains, since the higher they are, the further apart the approaches are from one another.

Thus, in the case of a commander who wants to retain possession of a

---

between attack and defense and the character and means of defense, chaps. 15–17 regarding the defense in mountain warfare, and chaps. 27–30 on defense of a theater of operations. Then look at book 7, chaps. 1–6 regarding the attack, chap. 11 on the attack in mountains, and chaps. 15–17 regarding the attack in a theater of war. It seems clear that the historical analysis contained herein closely parallels the topics in *On War* and that the histories were written to enable an understanding of the phenomenon of war and thus to support the reading of *On War* itself.

42. Suffice it to say that the risk posed by a flank attack or a double envelopment is too great to ignore, even if they are difficult to pull off in practice.

mountain region and therefore deploys a corps in it, this corps cannot avoid extending itself to some degree: first, because otherwise it would not be holding the ground, and second, because of its own tactical needs. This extension is therefore a quite necessary requirement. How the corps organizes itself on this extended line, whether it lets local defense or maneuver predominate, depends, of course, partly on the talent and tastes of the general commanding it, as well as on the characteristics of his troops; but mainly, yet again, it depends on the character of the area, since the more this impedes maneuver, the more the general will be steered toward local defense. Since this tendency is in the nature of the business, it is fatuous to declare oneself against it in general. Instead, there is no option but to examine in each case what else the defender could have done that would have been better.

Thus, cordon deployments often arise from necessity and not, as people usually think, from some misguided effort to defend every village every time.[43]

When people compare the difficulty and danger of such a deployment with how easy it is to attack and therefore give precedence to the latter, they are comparing things of very different kinds. The attack aims to gain possession, the defense to retain it; one is an action, the other a state. It strikes us as like someone saying that jumping is easier than standing because the soles of his shoes do not press his feet when he is in the air.

Let us accept, then, that cordon deployments necessarily must occur, even though attacking them may be *much easier* and defending them *much more risky*; in that case, one might ask, why not merely occupy them but abandon them immediately if attacked, so as to retake them from the enemy later through an attack of our own? Any expert will probably shake his head at this question. It is understandable that one might concede an individual place to the enemy, especially a village, so as to then drive him out again quickly before he has reorganized; but a long line with many individual outposts in an extremely inaccessible region? However much one might advocate that in theory, its execution would never seem practical; but anything that is impractical is also wrong theoretically. The fact is that people exaggerate

43. Again, although the evidence is anecdotal, there is a clear trend among players wargaming these campaigns to try to balance the need for some form of cordon and the requirement to concentrate in the face of the enemy. Players might well make sensible decisions regarding one or the other course of action, but sometimes bad luck, mistiming, and the like can make even well-thought-out plans look rather silly.

these notions of the ease of the attack and the danger of the defense. This exaggeration becomes palpable when one has to decide whether to abandon an individual strong position with the intention of retaking it later. No one will gladly abandon a decent earthwork to have to storm it later, or fall back across a long bridge so as to cross it again under enemy fire, or clamber down from a high Alp so as to clamber back up it under fire. All these elements occur during the defense and are an advantage that should not be underestimated; if in most cases they are nevertheless overcome eventually, that is in the nature of the business, but given suitable arrangements, it should not happen without costing the attacker more casualties than the defender; or in other words, resistance in the mountains is a disadvantage for the overall outcome, but an advantage temporarily.

But what constitutes the real fear for a cordon defense is the losses that are often incurred as soon as the line is broken through, because then individual outposts are surrounded, and others are cut off or forced back. We have seen these losses suffered by Auffenberg in March, Ménard in May, and now Strauch, Simbschen, and Jellachich. But we maintain that these losses are simply the result of bad dispositions or poor-quality troops or very great numerical superiority, and not in any way a necessary result every time a mountain defense is overcome.

If General Ménard with his 6,000–8,000 men had been forced to withstand an attack by 18,000 men on the plain, would his losses have been any fewer than the 3,000 prisoners his defense of the St. Luciensteig cost him on 14 May?

Do we not see Lecourbe resist a very superior force on 30 April and then abandon this resistance on 1 May without any significant loss? And likewise in the last days of May, when he had to vacate the St. Gotthard in the face of Haddick and St. Julien?

Was Dessolles's huge success against Laudon on 25 March not achieved against a *concentrated position* and without any numerical superiority on the part of the attacker, and thus simply the result of the poor performance of the Austrians? And against Dessolles in exactly the same place on 4 April, did Bellegarde not have to be content with very few trophies, despite his superior numbers?

Thus, the heavy losses that arise in some cases when mountain positions are breached are always ascribed to the nature of the business, when they are really due to the commanders and the troops involved.

We therefore stand by our claim that any mountain position can be broken through and thereby overcome; that it is therefore a dangerous measure for absolute resistance; but that where it would not have been possible for the defender to defeat his opponent anyway, the duration of resistance and the losses it costs the enemy are greater than would be the case on the plain. Whenever this result is not demonstrated, that arises from poor defense.[44]

If we bring these points of view to bear on the actions of 14 and 15 August, this shows that if we look at them carefully, the brief duration of the Austrians' resistance and their significant losses are not a result of the long cordon they adopted.

In particular, despite the long extent of the Austrian line, we do not see the French overcoming the points they attack due to any great numerical superiority. We do not know how many troops Xaintrailles used against Strauch's left wing; on the Grimsel, where their superiority was greatest, two and a third Austrian battalions fought against five French, which is about 1,900 men against 3,500. Certainly, on the first day, Simbschen with 4,500 men had to deal with no more than 5,500; and at Wassen, one and a half Austrian battalions fought three French, or 1,200 against 2,100; while against Jellachich, the French also seem to have had only a few thousand men more. From this, we can see that at none of the main points was the French superiority so great that it must necessarily defeat even *a strong locality*; if the resistance on the Grimsel lasted only a few hours, and if the garrison of the Wassen redoubt let itself be driven out by mere musketry from the mountains,[45] we are probably justified in assuming that the Austrian troops did not do enough here to be able to claim that they were on a par with their adversaries, and therefore the moral superiority of the latter played a part in their success.

As for the significant losses the Austrians suffered here compared with the French, again, we can blame this on the poor leadership and weaker structure of the Austrian units. None of the individual outposts was cut off, each of them found a way out through the villages to their rear, the pursuit was extremely slow because of the inaccessibility of the area and because cavalry was out of the question, yet the Austrians lost 4,000 men taken prisoner. This can only be ascribed to the inept leadership of the individual detachments and to the

44. This ties in again with Clausewitz's idea about the value of the object being sought and the degree of effort (or cost, if you will) required to attain that goal.

45. The location of that redoubt should have allowed its garrison to resist quite well, given the difficulty of circumventing the position.

great disorder into which poor-quality troops fall after losing a fight. We have already said that the Austrians never managed to obtain any similar successes against Lecourbe.

Yet it still seems to us that the Austrians could have expected better results if they had organized their line differently.

The archduke himself criticizes Strauch[46] for pushing his left wing too far into the Rhone valley in the area where the road begins, so that the French could begin their attack with artillery while he seems to have had none there of his own. But if he really wanted to advance his outpost so far, it would have been more sensible to keep that area only lightly held, since it was not distinguished by any strong position, and to keep a reserve of four battalions at the foot of the Grimsel; then the latter could not have been taken and, if necessary, Strauch could have turned against Xaintrailles with his force united if the latter came up the Rhone valley. Lecourbe did this successfully in the Engadin twice.

Simbschen probably would have put up better resistance if he had established and held outposts at the end of the Meien valley and on the Surenenberg itself, just as Lecourbe in the Engadin had his outposts in the Schärljoch and Tschirfser Joch. If Simbschen had posted one battalion in each of these two passes and one at Seedorf, and if he had stayed in the valley with three battalions and a squadron to set upon whoever first came down it, a good result might very well have been expected. Lecourbe admirably repelled General Laudon in this way at Schuls on 11 March, after he had already advanced into the valley.

It is quite natural that the outposts at Schwyz and Brunnen should have been driven off after resisting for half a day, since the locality is probably not that strong and the 1,500–1,600 Austrians were attacked by about 3,000 French. But the effect of these outposts must have been intended to enable a stubborn resistance in the Muota valley. The fact that the Austrians let themselves be driven back beyond the Klöntal lake, that is, 25 miles within twenty-four hours, again demonstrates no great steadfastness. In what follows, we shall see how much more the Russians under Rosenberg achieved in these same passes, as did the French under Molitor.

The success Chabran obtained against Jellachich may be ascribed either to the latter's dispositions or to the French superiority, but it was still not a

46. Karl, 2:106–107.

consequence of a cordon deployment, since the nature of the area was such that Jellachich could maneuver to the right and left and thus act with his force united. If Jellachich had beaten the enemy to his front, he could have remained quite unconcerned about the few who came through the Wägi valley into his rear. But to his front, he would have to do more than just hold out; he would actually have to be *victorious.* The fact that two battalions were cut off during his retreat should also be regarded as simply a failure of leadership.

Thus we believe that in the present cases, the brief duration of the resistance and the heavy losses were not due to the nature of the mission but to how it was carried out; not to the tool, but to how it was used.

As for the French attack, despite its fine success, we believe it was too structured and contrived. Nowhere did it have truly decisive superiority, and therefore, if the defense had been better or if by chance something had disrupted its complex organization, it might have gone completely awry.

Besides, one would misunderstand us if one were to draw the conclusion from our two assertions—that cordon positions in the mountains are not always to be avoided, and that they are not as risky as people usually claim—that we consider those used so often by the Austrians and French during the 1799 campaign to have been unavoidable. We are much more of a quite different opinion, but we shall not express it until the conclusion of the campaign.

62 THE ARCHDUKE TRIES IN VAIN TO CROSS THE AARE

While Masséna was winning the day over the Austrian left wing, personally leading the action against Jellachich and moving some of his troops from his left wing to his right, thus weakening the former, the archduke was planning his revenge. It is likely that he had already been informed of the troops moving from the French left wing before 14 August, since Masséna did not commit to his decision so quickly, and the preparations for it could hardly have been completed in two days.[47]

47. See section 60, where Clausewitz mentions that pressure from the Directory and the Swiss government at the end of July finally pushed Masséna to action; then, later in the same section, he says that "the French in Wallis [facing Strauch] had been on the move since 8 August."

The archduke knew there were no more than 2,000 enemy troops behind the Aare from its confluence with the Limmat to the Rhine, a stretch of 7 miles, and according to his reports, there were only the same number in the Frick valley. He therefore decided that before forces could flow back again from the enemy right wing to the left, he would cross the Aare at Döttingen[48] with the larger part of his main army and with Korsakov's corps, which had just arrived at Schafhausen, and seek out the enemy force on the far side of the river for a decisive battle, in the event it did not simply abandon the area when he crossed.[49]

Since none of the reports tell how much Masséna had reinforced his right wing, we cannot judge how much he had weakened his left. If the bulk of his reinforcements were not used against Jellachich, we can hardly imagine where they would have been left, but what we are told about Lecourbe's dispositions for his attack leaves us to conclude that he was reinforced by at most four or five battalions. Jomini explicitly states that the reserve under Klein at Mellingen was taken from there;[50] this comprised 5,000 men, and it is very likely that this constituted the only reinforcement for the right wing. But then that would leave Soult's, Lorges's, and Tharreau's divisions with 20,000 men between Zurich and the Rhine, and Ney's in the Frick valley with 5,000. Thus, either the archduke had received false reports or he did not express himself precisely and is not including the troops cantoned further back in his figure of 2,000 in each of those places. Jomini also states positively that General Ney, who had taken over command at this point the previous day (in place of Tharreau), managed to concentrate a mass of 10,000 men on the 17th.[51] From this, we would have to think that the French force between Zurich and the Rhine came to some 20,000 men. We present this deliberation because we feel the need to dispel the quite erroneous picture that could be inferred from the vague utterances of the two main historians (namely, the archduke[52] and

48. For readers examining Jomini's account, he spells this Dettingen, which might be confusing, as there are several towns with this name. Jomini, 12:55–94.

49. Karl, 2:119.

50. We could not find this reference in Jomini, but it was in the archduke's account; see Karl, 2:119.

51. Jomini, 12:88–89.

52. The archduke blames the poor quality of the troops and their training for the failure. According to the archduke's account, he thinks he got most things right: "The

Jomini), these being calculated merely for effect, but we certainly do not think we have established our own result with any real certainty.

But it was not only the weakness of the enemy left wing that demanded action from the archduke. He had already been ordered to march to the Rhine and admits that he gladly would have used the Russians' arrival to strike one more glorious blow before his departure, which would have completely justified his inaction until then, restored his reputation, perhaps even averted the march to the Rhine, and, in any case, made the job easier for the Russians when they took it over from him. A motive that the archduke probably just forgot to mention was to make up for the damage he could very reasonably expect to receive on the 14th and 15th. The archduke thought that, in the event of a successful outcome, the Austrian government would soon forgive the fact that such an operation basically ran contrary to the instructions he had been given.[53]

To the critic's eye, this decision and this disobedience certainly need no apology. When we consider that the archduke could cross with 60,000 men and could reasonably expect to strike with 50,000 of them against 15,000–20,000, and that this blow would probably fall while Masséna was still elsewhere, and that the direct consequence of a successfully executed crossing would have been either a precipitate French retreat or their complete defeat and, in any event, their evacuation of Switzerland, then such an operation simply seems absolutely imperative, and its omission a huge mistake.

The major problem, indeed, the only one, seemed to be the task of getting across the Aare successfully, that is to say, in superior force. But since this river is only 200–300 paces wide, the route to the crossing point was fairly well concealed by the terrain, the French only held it weakly from the confluence of the Limmat down, and the archduke was equipped with a substantial pontoon train, this problem could not be regarded as a very serious one; in any case, even if the operation should fail at this point, there was no fear of it causing him heavy losses.

Archduke quickly took the decision to cross the Aar and now he proceeded to select the most favorable point, to decide on the date, to gather a fully effective volume of forces, and to prepare the necessary arrangements." Karl, 2:122. For an account of the crossing as a whole, see Karl, 2:119–135; Jomini, 12:60–90.

53. Karl, 2:122. He is hoping that success would allow a change of policy to match the changed circumstances or at least show him in a good light.

The Action at Dettingen [Döttingen] on 17 August

The archduke had chosen the point between Gross- and Klein-Döttingen because the Aare curves out toward the Austrian side there, the right bank significantly overlooks the area inside the bend, the village of Klein-Döttingen is well suited as a bridgehead, and it was occupied by only two enemy companies of Swiss.[54]

The archduke's dispositions during the night of 16–17 August were that Korsakov with 20,000 infantry and 1,600 Cossacks should enter Ober-Endingen, 3 miles from Döttingen, and join up there with 23,000 infantry and 6,000 horse from the archduke's army. Hotze was to stay in Zurich with 7,500 men and defend the city to the utmost but follow the enemy should they retreat; 5,000 men stayed distributed along the Limmat. Where the Limmat flows into the Aare, batteries were to be brought up to command the road running along the opposite bank of the Aare. There were to be two bridges thrown across the Aare, one above Gross-Döttingen and one below it, so as to cross in two columns. The first of these columns, 25,000 strong, was to seize the heights along the Aare and then take the crossings at Bruck [Brugg] and Aarau; the second, with 12,000 men, was to move into the Frick valley; a third column of 10,000 men was to guard the crossing and then follow in reserve behind the first column, so that in this way, a force of 35,000 men[55] would be massed.

On the same day, 17 August, Starray was to demonstrate against Alt-Breisach and Basel, and a cannonade was to be fired at Waldshut and Koblenz to the same end.

54. The archduke describes it thus: "At the lower Aar, and downstream from the inflow of the Reuss and Limmat, where every move of the enemy out of the upper area to the place of the crossing is made difficult, the point between the village of Gross Dettingen on the right bank and Klein Dettingen on the left bank of the river offered the most advantages. There the Aar formed a bend to the East and this was crowned with favorable high ground dominating the flat Klein Dettingen on the other side all around. In the center of the bend lay the small insignificant village, a completely suitable location for the erecting of a bridgehead and only occupied by two companies of French [Swiss]. The winding of the Aar did moderate the torrential flow here, but its bed is rocky and without a bottom suitable for anchoring, of which circumstance the Austrians took too little account." Karl, 2:122–123.

55. The original had this as 38,000, but it appears to be a typographical error, as the numbers add up to 35,000.

The troops concentrated on the evening of the 16th, and numerous batteries were driven to the near edge of the valley; construction of the bridges began during the night at 2:00 a.m., without the enemy suspecting anything. But now the whole operation foundered on the bridge construction itself. Incomprehensibly, the construction was begun without ferrying troops across by boat first; the archduke had thought that the couple of enemy companies could just be driven off by artillery fire, and he also makes the excuse that there were no boats available and that it would have delayed the bridge construction if they had used some of the bridging pontoons. The consequence was that as soon as they heard noise down by the river, the two rifle companies began aiming shots there. An Austrian battalion that had occupied Gross-Döttingen replied to the sharpshooters with battalion volleys, and the artillery opened up a fearsome fire. Klein-Döttingen was soon ablaze, but amid all this din, the Swiss riflemen[56] would not let themselves be driven away but continued to shoot. Despite the dark night, this seems to have seriously disrupted the work of building the bridges.[57] In addition, it now turned out that the river had a rock bed in which the anchors would not catch, that the current was too rapid, that the bank down which the boats had to be brought was very steep, and that the preparations had not been the best. So it came to be that after they had worked all night and then with the benefit of a thick fog until 9:00 a.m., only thirteen boats had been constructed for the first bridge, and still fewer for the second; and now that the fog had lifted and the enemy troops had increased to a considerable corps behind Klein-Döttingen, it was deemed no longer possible to complete the bridges and force a crossing. The archduke abandoned the crossing and offered General Ney a truce, according to which he would cease fire and suspend his bridge building if the French allowed him to retrieve his pontoons again undisturbed, to which Ney swiftly agreed.

The archduke then had his troops return to their previous positions, while the Russians went into quarters behind the Austrians at Seedorf.

56. Jomini describes them as chasseurs from Zurich armed with excellent rifles. Jomini, 12:88–89. It is not entirely clear which Swiss unit this was or whether the men were simply hunters from Zurich. General Ney's memoirs describe them as Helvetian carabiniers, noting their great accuracy and the "immense range" of their pieces. A. Bulos, *Memoirs of Marshal Ney*, 2 vols., 2nd ed. (London: Bull & Churton, 1834), 1:299, https://archive.org/details/memoirsmarshalno2bulogoog/page/n9.

57. See note 52 above. The archduke had neglected to do a proper reconnaissance of the crossing site.

The main cause of this failed bridge building is really not to be found, as the archduke says, in poor reconnaissance of the river or its rocky bed or poor preparations by the general staff of the pontoon corps but in neglecting to ferry across an advance guard.[58] The lack of transport craft cannot serve as an excuse for this, since all that mattered for the moment was to have one bridge, so the boats from the second one could have been used to ferry over a couple of battalions, which not only would have quickly driven off the two enemy companies but also would have got a foothold themselves and, steadily reinforced by ferry, held off the enemy that hurried there; indeed, so as not to disrupt this ferrying, the second bridge should not have been begun until the first had been completed. During his crossing of the Po in 1796, Bonaparte got as many troops across just by ferry as were necessary to hold off the first Austrian division.[59] We have seen this method used everywhere since time immemorial, and the means for it were so close at hand that we cannot see how the archduke did not resort to it, so we virtually have to believe that he just shied away from gambling the first couple of battalions.[60]

Whether the archduke abandoned the operation too soon, as his army seems to have believed, since the first disagreement with Korsakov stemmed from this, we do not wish to presume to judge; the position of Klein-Döttingen and other features of the locality are very important for that determination. No one will ever persuade us that a bridge can be built while a couple of hundred men are firing on it from close range; but on the other hand, of course, the alacrity with which Ney accepted the truce demonstrates that at that moment, which would have been during the course of the morning, he still had very few troops at hand and was very worried himself.

General Jomini criticizes the archduke for not using the failed operation as a demonstration under cover of which to carry out another—namely, to march his 50,000 men quickly back to Zurich and have them cross there to take the Ütli while the French had already pushed a large part of their forces to Döttingen, thus denuding their center.[61] This proposition does not stand up to any criti-

58. For Clausewitz's ideas about defending and attacking river crossings, see *On War*, book 6, chaps. 18–19, and book 7, chap. 8, respectively.

59. See Carl von Clausewitz, *Napoleon's 1796 Italian Campaign*, trans. and ed. Nicholas Murray and Christopher Pringle (Lawrence: University Press of Kansas, 2018), 64–71.

60. He certainly had plenty of troops to warrant the risk.

61. Jomini, 12:93–94.

cism. Döttingen is 25 miles from Zurich; the troops had moved there on the 16th and had probably spent that night and the next morning under arms; if they were to march off at 10:00 a.m., they probably would not arrive in Zurich before 7:00 or 8:00 in the evening, by which time they would have marched another 25 miles and thus would hardly have been able to undertake yet another attack on the Ütli, even if there had still been time to do so. Besides, by our estimate, the area between Zurich and the Aare was held by 20,000 men, and even if 6,000–8,000 of them really were on the march to Döttingen, that still would have left about 12,000 who could be concentrated to defend the Ütli before the Austrians emerged from Zurich, while the French troops sent to Döttingen would have soon turned back, since a failed and abandoned attempt at bridge building is not especially suitable as a demonstration.[62] Indeed, a breakout from Zurich would have been much more likely to succeed on any other day but that one, as the bridging pontoons could have been used for alternative crossings over the Limmat and all the preparations could have been made in silence, whereas on the 17th the French were already alerted and naturally did not take their eyes off their opponent for a moment.

63 THE ARCHDUKE TRIES TO RETAKE HIS LEFT WING'S FORMER POSITIONS BUT GIVES UP

The archduke had failed to obtain the magnificent revenge with which he wanted to make up for the losses in combat forces, territory, and honor that he had suffered on the 14th and 15th, and he felt uncomfortable about leaving Switzerland without at least using his present numerical superiority

62. The archduke's comments regarding his pontoniers indicate that such a demonstration would have been a waste of resources: "In the Austrian army the pontonier corps was not brilliantly trained. In peacetime there was hardly any practice taking place or else only where the terrain and the known course of the rivers particularly favored bridge building and where all requirements lay conveniently to hand so that the work could proceed at leisure and with ease and where the corps' exercises looked more like useless parades than combat operations. Inexperienced in that knowledge whereby the lack of proper means is replaced by other aids and, in extraordinary ways, gets there where ordinary means cannot, if only the pontonier officers had also equipped themselves with even the necessary requisites for the most basic method of bridge building." Karl, 2:134.

to regain the line of the St. Gotthard and thereby facilitate Suvorov's march into Switzerland, so he now decided to attack the French right wing itself and to drive it back again to its previous position. On the evening of 17 August he therefore sent General Hotze with 8,000 men through Rümlang and Grüningen to Rapperswil with the mission of taking over command of the whole left wing and attacking the enemy right wing.

On 14 August General Jellachich had been 13,800 strong, not including Strauch. If we reckon his losses as being around 5,000 men, that left him with 9,000. These may have been distributed so that Jellachich had something like 5,000 men between Lake Walensee and Lake Zurich, a couple of thousand in the upper Linth valley, and a couple of thousand in the Rhine valley.

Hotze arrived in Rapperswil on the 19th and ordered a general attack in three columns on the 21st.

The first column was to advance across the Grynau bridge against the enemy position between Lake Zurich and the Sihl, the second from Glarus through the Muota valley upon Schwyz, and a third from Graubündten through the Anterior Rhine valley upon the Crispalt.

The archduke does not provide strengths for the individual columns,[63] but since a significant alteration in their deployment could hardly have been accomplished within the short space of about thirty-six hours, the troops in the Rhine valley at least certainly could not have been reinforced. We may therefore estimate that the second and third columns would have come to no more than a couple of thousand men each. Thus, out of the total force of 17,000 men that was formed by Hotze joining with Jellachich, about 12,000 men would have been left for the first column.

None of the historians describes the course of the action. Rather, the archduke is content to say:

> The outcome of this operation was that Hotze advanced with his first column to the Aa and his forward elements to Altendorf on the lake, from where the French withdrew into their advantageous position between Pfäffikon and the Etzelberg. The second column had to remain at Schwanden [now in Glarus Süd] in the Linth valley to cover the flank of the first, which the

63. He does provide strengths for his main divisions at the beginning of August, albeit by location rather than by the name of their respective commanders. See Karl, 2:96.

enemy threatened to outflank from the Schächen valley. The third arrived at Ilanz on the 23rd and pushed its outposts to Disentis.[64]

It is clear that this operation failed entirely or was again abandoned during its execution. If we assume that Masséna reinforced General Chabran again when he learned about the detachment sent off by the archduke, then, since Chabran was originally (section 57) only 6,000–7,000 strong, we cannot imagine that he could have had more than about 10,000 men with which to oppose Hotze's 12,000. But of course, against these 10,000 in a good position, Hotze's chances of success could be seen as very doubtful. Still less could anything be expected of the two small columns advancing against Lecourbe's division in the Rhine and Linth valleys, so the whole thing seems like a half-measure, and we can back up this verdict on the affair with the archduke's own confession, in that he says about himself at this point in time: "The archduke's desire conflicted with how the court had ordered him to act, which he felt it was his duty to comply with, and this generated an extraordinary fluctuation in his decisions."[65]

He goes on to say: "Hotze dithered and requested reinforcements, since when the commander in chief is not entirely resolute, each of his subordinates also falters to the same degree."[66]

Obviously, the reinforcement of the left wing was too meager if anything decisive was supposed to be achieved against the French right, and this was due to the archduke's indecisiveness; Hotze sensed that it was a half-measure and therefore did not allow it to come to anything decisive.

The archduke's indecisiveness lay in his character and not in the conflicting circumstances, as he would give us to understand, since a general should never be indecisive.[67] But by this the archduke means that, on the one hand, he was

64. Karl, 2:136.

65. Karl, 2:136.

66. Karl, 2:137.

67. This could also be due to a lack of imagination. The archduke makes it clear that he believes history can tell commanders what to do in the present: "In the bed of the Trebbia the fate of Upper Italy was now decided for the third time. On the very same battlefield in 218 B.C. Hannibal had defeated the Romans, in 1746 Lichtenstein defeated Maria Theresa's enemies, and in 1799 Suvorov was victorious over the French. It is so very true that the course of operations depends on the nature of the terrain because the position of the mountains and the course of the rivers immutably determine those lines

reluctant to leave Switzerland without having made amends and thereby leave the Russians, who were not in a particularly great situation before Suvorov's arrival, in an even worse position; but on the other hand, with each passing hour, his responsibility for not marching away increased. The French army on the Rhine was beginning to stir, and anything it might do against Swabia and the Austrian base would be charged to the archduke's account, since he had delayed his departure. In these circumstances, he thought any further operation that he allowed himself in Switzerland could *only* be justified by *a successful outcome*, so he therefore had to refrain from any that was at all doubtful. But these conflicting motives would have made a decisive general even more careful to avoid doing things by halves.

Hotze requested reinforcements only because he wanted to make a proper job of it, and that should not be held against him. To crown his indecision, the archduke had the quaint idea of asking General Korsakov to send Hotze a few thousand Russians. Korsakov had taken no great pleasure from the events of 17 August; he had argued (probably unwisely) that they should force the business through, and now he had gone rather unhappily into quarters at Seebach, where he wanted to wait for his cavalry. He refused the archduke's request outright because he did not want to split up his corps. The archduke could reasonably have anticipated this, and his discretion should have told him that it was not entirely appropriate to make such a proposal as soon as Korsakov

---

and points at which the armies have to clash with each other. This is why, under quite different conditions and with other weapons, several decisive battles have occurred on the same battlefields, of which some deserve to be listed as examples: Four battles at Cassano: 1509—1658—1705—1799. Four at Verona: 249—312—489—1799. Three at Caldiero: 1796—1805—1813. Three at Turin: 312—1640—1706, as well as six sieges. Two at Novi: 1745—1799. Three at Rheinfelden: two in 1638—1678. Three at Höchstädt: 1703—1704—1800. Four at, and in the area of, Nördlingen: 1634—1645—1796—1800. . . . Three next to, and on, the Marchfeld at Vienna: 1278—two in 1809. Thus history guides us to the knowledge of battlegrounds designated by nature and teaches us to determine the main features of future events according to the models of the past." Karl, 2:64. If he did indeed believe this, and it seems reasonable to suppose that he did, given that he wrote it, then it is also reasonable to assume that he might struggle to make a decision when there is no clear historical event to act as a guide. How different this is from Clausewitz, who argues that all events need to be critically analyzed back to their root causes and that superficial analysis and dogma whereby historical events demonstrate specific fixed outcomes to be rigidly followed are to be scorned. See *On War*, book 2, chap. 5, especially 167–169.

arrived. Anyway, it is thoroughly incomprehensible why the archduke did not send further Austrian reinforcements to Hotze, since he had decided not to take all his men away with him.

General Korsakov probably took this opportunity to explain that he would prefer to join the left wing with his whole corps, and after a few days' discussion between the two commanders, this was the reason for him setting off for Uznach, where he arrived on 25 August.

Because he felt there were now too many troops massed on the left wing after this maneuver, the archduke took six battalions from General Hotze back to Zurich. He united his troops near the city in order to support the left wing's attack by an advance, as he puts it, thus really by a demonstration against the Ütli.

This again made General Korsakov mistrustful and unhappy. He asked that the six battalions stay with Hotze and promised to participate only if the archduke committed himself to take part in the proposed operation with the whole Austrian army; for simply pushing the left wing forward could not achieve anything, since after the archduke's departure, the Russians would be obliged to relinquish the places they had taken again. Indeed, Korsakov would then have no option but to take position behind Schafhausen, since Suvorov had ordered him to send 10,000 men to Italy.

While these objections on the part of General Korsakov can partly be ascribed to his own sullenness, in the main, they cannot be said to be without foundation. Suvorov's order dated from 11 August, before Suvorov was instructed to march to Switzerland, so Korsakov could well say to himself that he no longer needed to comply,[68] but apart from that, we can very well understand the Russian commander's unhappiness with his situation. What he had seen of the Austrian army so far did not inspire any great confidence; he knew that the archduke had been ordered to march away to the Rhine more than eight days ago and that he was poised to do so; Suvorov, for his part, had not yet begun his march at that time (25 August), and it would take him at least another two to three weeks to arrive; even if the archduke actually left some of his troops behind, the allies' situation in Switzerland would still be awkward; facing a superior enemy who was about to go on the offensive, with allied troops

68. That is, the way the situation had changed in the intervening two weeks meant that Suvorov's order to Korsakov to reinforce him in Italy was void, since Suvorov was no longer staying in Italy but was marching to Switzerland.

some of whom were unfamiliar with the theater of operations or the conditions and without an adequate commander in chief—that was a situation that might well alarm General Korsakov. A decisive victory over Masséna would have thoroughly remedied the matter, but it is certainly debatable whether a partial operation in extending and pushing forward the left wing might not have made it even worse, so we cannot entirely disapprove of Korsakov's protests.

Because of this new appeal from the Russian general, more time was lost; Hotze, who was waiting for reinforcements on the far side of the Linth and thought he might become the victim of this dispute, left his position behind the Aa[69] on 26 August and retreated behind the Linth again.

This delayed things even more; the archduke was unhappy with this too, became sick of the whole affair, and decided to comply with the order he had received to march away and let matters in Switzerland go as God may please.

The immediate result of this decision was that on 27 August Korsakov marched back from Uznach to the Limmat to relieve the archduke's army in its positions on the Limmat and the Aare, while Hotze remained on the Linth.

64 MASSÉNA MAKES A FAILED ATTEMPT TO CROSS THE LIMMAT AND DRIVES HOTZE BEYOND LAKE WALENSEE

The Directory had been constantly urging Masséna to go on the offensive, which finally resulted in the operation of 14 and 15 August, as we have seen. On that very day, 14 August, the minister of war, General Bernadotte, submitted a report to the Directory about the military situation, which, as is so often the case, did not offer any penetrating clarity but left everything vague. But this report is remarkable for the perversity of the proposals it leads to. General Bernadotte sees Italy as central, but that does not lead him to want to do something in Italy; instead, he says:

> "The enemy can always be superior to us in Italy, because he holds the lines of communication between there and Switzerland and can reinforce

69. **Clausewitz** notes: "This little river that creates the Wägi valley and runs into Lake Zurich at Nülen should not be confused with the one that runs past Stanz into Lake Lucerne."

himself continuously; consequently we must drive him out of Switzerland. We can best do this if we reinforce our Army of the Rhine, which has only 20,000 men available, up to 40,000 and advance with it toward the Danube into the archduke's right flank. To provide that reinforcement, Masséna would have to move 20,000 men to the Rhine. But," he goes on to say, "the Rhine is a sensitive spot for France; if this army were to fail, we would be drawing the enemy toward a weak point, and anyway if the archduke were to attack Masséna after those 20,000 men had left, Switzerland could be lost." The minister therefore presents *a different* proposal: "To conquer Graubündten, to occupy the St. Gotthard Pass, and to get into the rear of the enemy occupying Piedmont and the Cisalpine. By sending a corps of 20,000 men to Glurns [Glorenza, South Tyrol, now in Italy], we would interrupt the enemy lines of communication and support the Army of Italy and the Army of the Alps in a powerful way." "Nothing," he says ruefully, "stands in the way of this excellent plan except supply difficulties."[70]

This plan bears the imprint of all the strategic views of the time. Indirect action by diversions is preferred to direct action for no specific reason; its success is presupposed without any further argument for it, and the effects attributed to this success are lost in vague lines and phrases that largely lack any reality. We do not wish to get involved in any further presentation of the errors and contradictions it contains, nor to try to shed any more light on the arcane significance of Glurns, which plays such a magical role in the French plans here for the second time. Indeed, we would have skipped the whole thing if it were not important from time to time to give a glimpse of the kind of strategy that came up in cabinet meetings, and if this plan—albeit one that did not come to be carried out—were not to some degree intertwined with the strategic fabric of the campaign.[71]

As a result of this, Bernadotte wrote to Masséna on 17 August,[72] imparting

70. This exchange of letters is found in Jomini, 12:432–447.

71. This argument ties in with Clausewitz's view on the object of the conflict and the corresponding need for campaign objectives to clearly line up and match the political objective. As such, the plans proposed by Bernadotte and the Directory would not make the cut.

72. Jomini, 12:437–442.

the government's decision as a *captatio benevolentiae*[73] [i.e., ingratiatingly], according to which the earlier intention of giving Moreau supreme command over the armies in Switzerland and on the Rhine was rescinded as far as the former was concerned, and Masséna retained his previous full authority. Bernadotte then offered Masséna the choice of either fighting a major battle

73. This is a rhetorical technique used by Roman orators to gain the goodwill of the audience at the start of a speech. Bernadotte's letter is wonderfully over the top: "Citizen General, I hereby send you a new decree from the Executive Directory by which you remain commander in chief of the Army of the Danube, and which confers on General Moreau command of the Army of the Rhine. In transmitting to you this decree, which furthermore confirms the Directory's confidence in your talents and zeal, I inform you of its absolute intentions concerning the military operations which the present circumstances require. Though the Army of the Danube's defensive posture has served it well so far since the enemy has not dared to undertake anything against it, it is time for it to sally forth with the *élan* of the victory that is assured for it by its numerical superiority over the enemy, and especially by the eager zeal which the soldiers of the Republic have to regain that ascendancy which has been the wonder of Europe for so long and which has destroyed so many coalition armies. Numerous Russian reinforcements will join the army of Archduke Charles any day now; let us not wait for these new forces to combine. The Army of the Danube will show itself worthy of its previous campaigns by attacking, beating, and routing the enemy army; it must do so in a major battle. We must strike unexpectedly; the safety of the Republic demands it; the Directory desires it; let us obey. This great and imposing victory is expected by all republicans; and they see it guaranteed by the heroic valor of the French under your skillful leadership." ["*Je vous adresse, citoyen général, un nouvel arrêté du directoire exécutif, qui vous conserve le commandement en chef de l'armée du Danube, et confère au général Moreau celui de l'armée du Rhin. En vous transmettant cet arrêté, qui est pourtant la confirmation de la confiance du directoire dans vos talens et votre zèle, je vais vous faire connaître ses intentions absolues sur les opérations militaires qu'exigent les circonstances présentes. Telle bonne qu'ait été jusqu'ici l'attitude défensive de l'armée du Danube, puisque l'ennemi n'a osé rien entreprendre contre elle, il est temps qu'elle en sorte avec l'élan de la victoire que lui assure sa supériorité numérique sur l'ennemi, et surtout l'ardeur impatiente qu'ont les soldats de la république, de reprendre cet ascendant qui a si long-temps étonné l'Europe, et qui a détruit tant d'armées coalisées. Des renforts nombreux de Russes arrivent chaque jour à l'armée du prince Charles; n'attendons pas que ces nouvelles forces y soient réunies. L'armée du Danube va se montrer digne de ses dernières campagnes: attaquer, battre et disperser celle de l'ennemi; c'est une bataille générale qu'elle doit livrer à celle-ci. Il faut frapper inopinément; le salut de la république l'exige; le directoire le veut; obéissons. Cette grande et imposante victoire est attendue par tous les républicains; et ils en prennent pour gage la valeur héroïque des Francais dirigée par vos talens.*"] Jomini, 12:347–442.

against Archduke Charles or, if he was not entirely sure of winning such a battle, sending 20,000 men to the Rhine, in which case the lovely plan to take Glurns would be shelved.

When he wrote this, Bernadotte believed the Russians would not arrive for another three or four weeks but, as we know, *by this time they were already on the Limmat.*

Masséna, who did not think the very moment Korsakov joined the archduke was a suitable one for a major battle, and who was therefore supposed to send 20,000 men away to the Rhine just when his opponent had been reinforced with 30,000, was so indignant at such an unreasonable demand that he asked to be relieved of his command.

Meanwhile, the reports of Masséna's success against the Austrian left wing and of the battle of Novi had arrived in Paris at the same time; this gave the Directory a respectable excuse to let its outraged general have his way, and on 26 August it canceled its order to send away 20,000 men. Instead, it urged General Masséna to undertake a decisive offensive against the archduke to prevent him from uniting completely with the Russians, even though these had already joined his army twelve days earlier. Masséna was promised a diversion by the Army of the Rhine against Philippsburg.

Masséna hereupon decided not only to remain in his post but also, since he had meanwhile been reinforced with another few thousand men, to give in to the constant urgings and go on the attack once more. He probably had not had any reliable reports about the archduke's definite intention to depart for the Rhine; otherwise, he probably would have delayed his attack for a couple of days.

We find ourselves greatly at a loss concerning the French commander's operation. Since it was largely a failure, the historians only touch on it briefly, so we remain uncertain about its aim and character, and there is no mention of an actual plan.

It is said that Masséna, still ignorant of Korsakov's return to the Limmat that occurred on 29 August, decided to cross the Limmat on the night of 30–31 August while at the same time diverting the allies' attention to the Linth by an attack on their position there. He chose the point where the Limmat flows into the Aare, but not one historian tells us whether the crossing was supposed to be across the Limmat or the Aare.[74]

74. **Clausewitz** notes: "Dedon, who directed the engineering for the river crossing

There is not a single word about how many troops Masséna concentrated for this, or what he hoped to do after crossing.

The French had chosen the point of confluence for their crossing because they could easily have the necessary transport brought there from the Aare and the Reuss. But greater problems than had been anticipated were encountered during its execution, which Jomini ascribes to the swollen river, Dedon to damaged boats. Since it was now thought (apparently mistakenly) that the Austrians had already been alerted to the operation and had taken the necessary measures to defend against it, Masséna abandoned it for now.

The Actions at Näfels and Glarus on 29, 30, and 31 August

But Soult, who had taken over command of Chabran's division, had set his 10,000 men in motion toward the Linth in the direction of Uznach on the 29th, while Lecourbe's left wing under Molitor, 3,000 strong, moved through the Klön valley upon Glarus and Näfels. The latter seized both these places but was driven off again by an Austrian reserve.

Soult had halted on the Linth on the 29th. On the 30th he attacked Näfels, and Molitor attacked Glarus again; the first of these two places was taken once again, but the Austrians held on behind the Linth bridge. The French did not take Glarus.

On the 31st Hotze, who had hastened up from the lower Linth, wanted to advance through Glarus for a reconnaissance, but he ran into Soult, who was on his approach march right then and who intended to press across the Linth in this area. Hotze was surprised, fiercely attacked, beaten, and thrown back across the Linth in disorder.

This unfavorable action, and probably more so the worry that the French superiority would increase after the archduke's departure and that a position in the Linth valley could not be held, prompted General Hotze to retreat with his left wing behind the Seez between Lake Walensee and Sargans. Small detachments continued to hold the Rhine valley as far as Ilanz.

---

as brigade artillery commander and commander of the pontoon corps, only mentions this crossing in passing in his *Relation detaillée du passage de la Limmath* and, with all due respect for his otherwise excellent book, we may say with much vagueness and confusion." He is referring to François L. Dedon, *Relation du Passage de la Limmat* (Paris: Didot Jaune, 1801), https://books.google.com/.

65 ARCHDUKE CHARLES MOVES TO THE RHINE

The archduke decided to leave General Hotze behind in Switzerland with thirty battalions and thirty-four squadrons of Austrians, as he puts it, "so that the Russian corps would not be exposed to any certain mishap, and Hotze could await its arrival in a creditable defensive position."[75] Since the units he designated for this came from the left wing, which had suffered the most and had the weakest battalions, this Austrian corps did not come to more than 22,000 men; in addition, there were 3,000 Swiss, and since Korsakov's corps may be assumed to have had about 30,000, together these formed a force of 56,000–57,000 men.

The archduke also had three battalions reinforce the brigade that, until now, had stood on the right bank of the Rhine between Waldshut and Basel; gave General Nauendorf command of this corps; and marched off to the Rhine on 31 August with his remaining 30,000 men.

As we said in section 57, in July the archduke had 68,000 men, excluding Haddick. Now 22,000 were with Hotze, about 6,000 stayed behind on the Rhine, and he left with 30,000; the missing 10,000 can be estimated to be his losses by the end of August.

Before his departure, he and Korsakov established that the Austrians under Hotze should take over the left wing and occupy the area from the Italian border to Meilen, a place on the northern shore of Lake Zurich about halfway between Rapperswil and Zurich. The Russians were to hold the area between Lake Zurich and the Rhine.

Since Masséna had to observe Colonel Strauch (who had taken position in the valleys leading to Lake Maggiore since being driven out of Wallis) and also had to leave troops facing Nauendorf, the archduke calculated that Masséna would have a superiority of at most 10,000 men over Korsakov and Hotze. If we go by Jomini's account, the archduke's estimate of this superiority still seems too high, and it must have been at most 5,000 men.[76] But because of it, General Korsakov still found himself in a much worse situation than the archduke had been in, for first, the allied forces were distributed quite differently: at the main point between Lake Zurich and the Rhine, where

75. Karl, 2:139–140.

76. It is hard to be certain, as the numbers given are only sometimes tied to a particular place or date. See Jomini, 12:244–247.

before there had been 47,000–48,000 allied troops, now there were about 30,000; and second, the 63,000 men[77] were divided into three corps, probably none of whose commanders regarded themselves as strictly subordinate to the others. The archduke does not say that Hotze and Nauendorf were placed under the command of General Korsakov, and indeed, it emerges from several places in his work that this was not the case; but even if it had been so, we can well imagine that neither of them could be regarded *purely* as instruments, as completely *flexible* and *obedient members* of the whole, while they served a *different* master and were dedicated to their own *particular* mission. The actual commander of this whole force was Suvorov, but it would be another three weeks before he arrived in the theater of operations, and by then, anything could have happened! The decisive blow that was struck in the second battle of Zurich actually befell under the aegis of his supreme command that had already come into effect; but it was supreme command from a distance that led to the pernicious idea of deciding in Asti on 5 September what should happen in Zurich on the 25th.

All these factors were bound to cause concern for Switzerland, so long as Suvorov had not yet arrived there. The archduke recognizes this very well, talks a lot about shortening the line of deployment, criticizes himself[78] more or less for not having waited with his army (or at least not having stayed behind *in person*) until Suvorov arrived or until the last moment—that is, until there was danger on the Danube. All these things may be as true as they like, but they do not hit the nail on the head: *before he departed, the archduke should have used his obvious superiority to vanquish Masséna.* The fact that he did not do this is more than caution; *it is timidity.*[79]

77. It is not clear which "63,000" these are supposed to be. Clausewitz presumably meant to say "56,000–57,000," the figure he gives at the start of this section for the total allied forces left in Switzerland after the archduke's departure. Perhaps 63,000 is his figure for the French facing them if they had the 5,000-man advantage Clausewitz concludes from Jomini.

78. Karl, 2:148–150.

79. This is reasonable in the circumstances. The archduke had a number of opportunities to deal a decisive blow to Masséna and failed to take any of them. Thus, another missed opportunity, even if it might have proved more difficult than Clausewitz argues, warrants criticism of the archduke.

66 REFLECTIONS ON THE AUSTRIAN COMMANDER

After what the archduke showed us of his spirit of enterprise in April and May, we certainly could not expect much from his crossing of the Rhine either. However, from that moment until the first battle of Zurich, he had made steady progress, and as our gaze follows him from the Rhine to the Limmat, we cannot resist hoping that he might try to continue in this vein. But from the battle of Zurich onward, his positive intent leaked away like the river Rhine in Holland; just as it divides into many shallow branches, he dissipates his effort in small operations.[80]

In fact, this is no surprise if we examine all the circumstances closely. It is true that he had not beaten Masséna, so he could not flatter himself that he had any morale advantage, and it was not a case of exploiting the momentum of an existing maneuver; his numerical superiority had also entirely disappeared, if the total forces were compared; the defender had very strong terrain on his side, so the archduke's passivity was certainly quite natural, *given the resources* he had available. If we consider *the aim*, this could not provide any great motivation either. Italy was the Austrians' main concern, they sent their

80. Clausewitz comments on the suspension of action in war (*On War*, book 3, chap. 16), which relates closely to his discussion in this section. As such, he is worth quoting at length: "Suspension of action in war is a contradiction in terms. Like two incompatible elements, armies must continually destroy one another." He then notes that the suspension of action is common for three main reasons: The first is "fear and indecision native to the human mind. It is a sort of moral force of gravity, which, however, works by repulsion rather than attraction: namely, aversion to danger and responsibility. . . . The second cause is the imperfection of human perception and judgment, which is more pronounced in war than anywhere else. We hardly know accurately our own situation at any particular moment, while the enemy's, which is concealed from us, must be deduced from very little evidence. . . . The third determinant, which acts like a ratchet wheel, occasionally stopping the works completely, is the greater strength of the defensive. A may not feel strong enough to attack B, which does not mean that B is strong enough to attack A. . . . In this type of war, where military action is reduced to insignificant, time-killing flourishes, to skirmishes that are half in earnest and half in jest . . . many theorists see the real, authentic art of war." *On War*, 217–218. He is really driving home the point that war is not simply algebraic or scientific; that passion, reason, and chance dominate all aspects of war; and that theorists and generals such as the archduke completely misunderstand the nature of war. One can almost hear him saying, flabbergastedly, "They just don't get it!"

main forces there, and they had the satisfaction of seeing everything there progressing toward the completion of its conquest. Beyond that, they did not really care about Switzerland. The French invasion of Switzerland in 1798 was certainly one of the main arguments in the Austrian manifesto for the war, but that had more to do with the violation of neutrality, not because the Austrian government felt any great pity for the Swiss. The democratic party that pervaded the country had brought this misfortune on itself, and at those moments when victory would not come straight away, the Austrian government, happy to have got the loyal-minded Graubündten under its wing, probably *thought it would not do any harm for the Swiss to be chastised a bit.*

So it came about that the Austrian government was happy so long as nothing was actually lost in Switzerland, and it did not wish to take any risks as the price for conquering the country. Thus the archduke would hardly have been encouraged by the government, and whatever he might have had left in terms of ambition and desire for the glorious success of his campaign was soon dispirited by the departure of Bellegarde and Haddick.[81]

Taking all these things into account, we certainly cannot be surprised that nothing happened in Switzerland and that the pendulum stopped of its own accord.

But does this really justify his inaction? To answer this question, we need to know more details of the tactical factors of the French position between Zurich and the Rhine. The archduke could have deployed almost twice as many combat forces as his opponent on this stretch, namely, 45,000 men against 26,000, and the possession of Zurich assured him a crossing that his adversary had to keep covered by a substantial force. The terrain advantages therefore must have been very considerable and the French tactical dispositions quite excellent if a crossing of the Limmat or the Aare that would have led to favorable combinations for battle was not feasible in such conditions. An enterprising commander would quite certainly have attempted it and would probably have produced a major result by doing so.

81. This also tells us that Austria's motives for war were fairly limited in scope. As such, it is reasonable to suppose that the Austrians did not feel the need to put in much effort. After all, why assume more cost and risk to destroy the French if one's goals were already broadly attained? See Clausewitz's thoughts on what is war (*On War*, book 1, chap. 1), purpose and means in war (book 1, chap. 2), strategy (book 3, chap. 1), and war plans, the military objective, and political aim (book 8, chaps. 4–9).

The fact that the French dispositions were not so excellent as we would have to imagine them to be in order to excuse the archduke's passivity is proved by the action of 8 June, so when we see the archduke making no such attempt, we may well say that at least for this section of the campaign, his military leadership lacks *the daring to take advantage of a favorable opportunity.* Since war is not purely the product of rigid functions between ends and means, but rather always retains something of the nature of gambling, so the art of command cannot entirely dispense with that element either; and *a commander* who is too reluctant to gamble will fall short in his winnings, and in the great ledger of military success he will get deeper into debt than he thinks.

We have already said during the narrative that the archduke attached a false worth to the security of his strategic base, but we have to agree with his verdict when he rebukes himself for not having endowed his Rhine bridges at Schafhausen with bridgeheads on both banks.[82]

Furthermore, we are in complete agreement with him that both commanders attached too high a value to possession of the St. Gotthard Pass and that, simply for strategic reasons, a much shorter line with his left wing resting on the St. Luciensteig would have been preferable. This had just two accessible sectors, namely, between Lake Zurich and Lake Walensee and then between the latter and the Rhine, each about 10–15 miles across. But even these sectors only needed to be observed, not defended, since if the French were unwise enough to have a corps advance across the Linth, they could easily be punished for it. Here, this really was absolutely a case where the area could be defended offensively. To suggest that such a shortened deployment would leave the approaches to the Tyrol open is fatuous, since the French truly were not in any state to send anything to the Tyrol.

If the archduke had chosen this deployment, then, instead of using 14,000 men on his left wing, 4,000 could reasonably have sufficed, which would have left him with 10,000 more against Masséna's main army. This would have made his relative strength even more favorable, since Masséna could not have concentrated to the same degree, because occupying the St. Gotthard virtually obliged him to disperse his troops more widely.

We single out the archduke for these reflections because similar considerations occur so often in mountain warfare, but we must acknowledge that the archduke certainly had a political reason that we must not overlook and that

82. Karl, 2:15.

really motivated his occupation of the mountains. The war had begun with the Austrians occupying Graubündten; they had reconquered it after Generals Auffenberg and Laudon were wiped out; the government attached value to protecting this country with which it was suddenly involved politically, and it could certainly ask the archduke to do this so long as he did not try to undertake anything major.[83] We are of the opinion that, despite the archduke's own half-criticism of himself, the extension of the position to the St. Gotthard cannot be blamed on the archduke, and that he could have abandoned it only if he was undertaking something major that would bring Switzerland and therefore Graubündten swiftly into his hands again. But of course, these reasons have nothing in common with the imaginary importance people want to attribute to mountains per se, whatever the situation.

Such is our view of the archduke's conduct prior to Korsakov's arrival; but once they joined up, from that moment on, a major blow against Masséna was *absolutely imperative.* Indeed, on 17 August the archduke seems to have intended one; the fact that this operation failed did not prove that a similar one was impossible; the archduke therefore should not have left it at that but should have considered a second one. What the archduke did with his left wing did not count, since a decisive blow could be struck only by the main body, and not by leaving 40,000 men on the Limmat. If the archduke felt a crossing of the Limmat was impossible, he should have decided to leave a strong garrison in Zurich and to cross the Linth and Sihl with more than 60,000 men in order to bring about a major battle south of Lake Zurich. Masséna probably would have been able to bring his forces into action only gradually, and so, as the saying goes, he would have been rolled up from his right wing to his left. The fact that this would expose his line of communications through Schafhausen to French raids until the decisive battle does not merit any consideration; the remote possibility of being beaten and then no longer being able to retreat through Schafhausen should have deterred him equally little, since he retained the road through Bregenz, and even a makeshift way out seems sufficient insurance—if we really had to take every such *remote* possibility into account in warfare, our calculations would never end.[84]

83. See *On War*, book 1, chaps. 1 and 2. The political purpose of the conflict should match the strategic goals of the military campaigns.

84. This is a crucial point because it is unlikely that commanders can ever know or take into account everything, yet they still need to make decisions. Clausewitz states:

But we cannot concede that an attack on the Limmat was impossible either. If one has almost 70,000 men with which to operate against 20,000–30,000, if the river is only 100–200 paces wide, and if one has two bridging trains and already holds one crossing, then the enemy certainly cannot hold a river line 25 miles long.

The archduke's demeanor in the period from 17 August to 11 September really is as though he wanted to act *the part of a ditherer*; he even rebukes himself for it in a roundabout way, though he thinks he can find an excuse in the difficulty of his task. But this difficulty escapes us, and even if it really had been that great, then, as we have already said, indecision can never be excused when it is in the dock in the critics' court, any more than cowardice could. It must be understood that we are not referring to indecision while deliberating what to do, which can and must increase with the difficulty of the case; here it may take as long as it likes, so long as it does not spill over into the operations and generate half-measures and vacillation there.

67 REFLECTIONS ON THE FRENCH COMMANDER

We have three observations to offer in regard to the French commander. The first concerns the question of whether he could have attacked the archduke in a major battle at any point; the second, the possibility of a diversion toward Italy; the third, Masséna's deployment in defense.

The French Directory constantly urges its general to attack the archduke, and General Jomini also considers it a major error that he did not do so at the end of July because, at that time, Masséna himself could not expect any more reinforcements, while the archduke was waiting for Korsakov. Jomini says of this opportunity, "for it is an immutable principle of war to forestall an enemy who is on the verge of being joined by a considerable corps, when one

---

"Circumstances vary so enormously in war, and are so indefinable, that a vast array of factors has to be appreciated—mostly in the light of probabilities alone. The man responsible for evaluating the whole must bring to his task the quality of intuition that perceives the truth at every point. Otherwise a chaos of opinions and considerations would arise, and fatally entangle judgement. Bonaparte rightly said that many of the decisions faced by the commander-in-chief resemble mathematical problems worthy of the gifts of a *Newton* or an *Euler*." *On War*, 112.

cannot hope for any reinforcement oneself."[85] We wish to examine whether the government's urgings should be condoned, whether Jomini's judgment is right, and whether his principle is as incontrovertible as he says.

If we go by the strength reports given by Jomini for the French and by the archduke for the Austrians, at no time did Masséna have numerical *superiority* over the archduke, not even at the end of July, when he was at his strongest. If Masséna wanted to attack the archduke with the aim of a major battle, this could happen only on the Limmat or the Aare, for if he had led his main body across the Linth, his base for that operation would have been in the high mountains, and he would have run the risk of entirely losing his natural line of retreat through Bern; he could put himself in such a situation only if he was very sure of victory over the archduke or, conversely, if desperation forced him to take this perilous course. Neither was the case. An attack on the archduke on the Limmat and the Aare can be regarded as very difficult, since the archduke's position was just as advantageous as that of the French, and he had twice as many troops as they did. It seems to us to follow from this that if General Masséna regarded attacking his opponent in a major battle as very difficult and success as very unlikely, the critic of later times can hardly object to that.

General Masséna furthermore objected that even if it succeeded, such an operation would not be of any particular consequence, and this again seems entirely correct to us.

If Masséna attacked the archduke and did not inflict an absolutely total defeat on him, the latter would retreat behind the Rhine, and it is unlikely that the French commander could have got involved in an operation on the far side of that river. Since Masséna was weaker than his opponent from the outset, and the latter was expecting Korsakov, there could be no question of an operation forcing his way any further into Germany. Thus, if we want to stick to reality rather than being happy with mere fantasies, we must recognize that the risks associated with an attack by Masséna were not accompanied by equivalent advantages, and that even if it were successful, the effect of the

85. In the original French: "*Car il est un principe immuable à la guerre, c'est de prévenir un ennemi qui est à la veille d'être joint par un corps considerable, lorsqu'on n'espère soi-même aucun renfort.*" Jomini, 12:65. Jomini admonishes in a footnote on the same page: "Wellington defeated Marmont at Salamanca, by the application of this maxim which his opponent forgot completely."

enemy superiority that could be foreseen for August would scarcely have been weakened in any significant way. It is hardly conceivable that such a success would have had any influence on matters in Italy.

Thus, if the French commander deemed an attack to be very risky and its results insufficient, he was left with no option but to remain on the defensive.[86] The fact that the archduke would be 30,000 men stronger in August was an evil he would just have to endure, if he had no effective means to avert it.

While the French commander thus remained on the defensive so as not to tempt fate under adverse conditions, he still held the defense's greatest advantage in his hands—*to wait and see.* It was very questionable whether the archduke's reinforcement would have all the consequences that were feared from it. With an *indecisive commander* like the archduke and a pair of *allied generals*, no unity or energy could be expected from that.

If Frederick the Great had followed General Jomini's principle in 1761, he would have had to attack Laudon at any cost before he linked up with Soltikov, but he did not do so; instead, he went into the camp at Bunzelwitz, where he discovered that with 60,000 men, one can withstand 150,000 allies for three weeks without matters reaching a decisive result.[87] In fact, Masséna made a similar discovery. The archduke and Korsakov had been united for fourteen days without putting any serious decision into effect, apart from the attempted crossing at Döttingen, and they probably could have been together for another four weeks without anything better coming of it.

The French government's urgings mainly emanated from Minister of War Bernadotte, whose way was always just to press on without regard for the situation, and whose logic consisted merely of grand turns of phrase.[88] His assertion that Masséna was numerically superior to his opponent seems to have been not so much a forgivable error as a casual assumption, just like his assertion that the Russians would join the Austrians four weeks later than they actually did.

As far as Jomini's principle is concerned, simple though it appears, it is by

86. See note 81 above regarding the objective, purpose, and means in war.

87. For an analysis of the role and effectiveness of fortification, see Nicholas Murray, *The Rocky Road to the Great War: The Evolution of Trench Warfare to 1914* (Washington, DC: Potomac Books, 2013), 1–44. For a more detailed look at the camp and the context, see Dennis E. Showalter, *The Wars of Frederick the Great* (New York: Longman, 1996), 304–305.

88. For an example, see note 73 in this chapter.

no means as absolute as he thinks. The inventors of theories and the historian-critics are always ready to label this or that a universal principle, whereby they merely demonstrate that they do not understand the nature of a theory. The universal applicability of this principle is opposed by this single observation, and we shall leave it at that: *that mere ratio of forces alone never constitutes a reason for action.*[89]

Thus, it seems to us that a fair critic could not blame the French commander for not attacking the archduke in a major battle.

In section 61 we have already declared our view of the value of Masséna's attack on the Austrian left wing on 14 and 15 August. This operation was of a quite different kind: since it was of a secondary nature, it was not accompanied by any great risk; its success was fairly likely and also not insignificant, since its moral importance continued to have a visible impact once Korsakov had arrived, when the enemy commanders could not come to a decision.

As far as the possibility of an effective demonstration toward Italy is concerned, that depends solely and simply on how the allied commanders in Italy viewed the danger that could accrue from it; for if we look at the matter purely objectively, in fact, we cannot see how a corps of 25,000–30,000 men could do anything important enough in upper Italy to offset the danger that its absence from Switzerland would create. But *among the allies, the opinion certainly did exist* that some major danger could arise from that, and there is no doubt that a thrust from Switzerland toward Italy shortly before the battle of the Trebbia or the battle of Novi could easily have had such an influence on either of these events as to produce a quite different outcome. The only question, therefore, is to what extent Masséna was in a position to create such a diversion. At the time of the battle of the Trebbia in June, it was as good as impossible, since at that time, Masséna was not yet as strong as the archduke and was expecting to be attacked by him any day; but at the end of July, when Masséna's reinforcements had reached their culminating point[90]

89. Furthermore, it seems unreasonable to attack just because one assumes the enemy will be reinforced. Of course, as noted earlier, Jomini believed the attack was the stronger form of war, so his logic makes sense if one believes him. If one believes that the defense is stronger, per Clausewitz, then Jomini's conclusion is illogical as an absolute guide to action.

90. This is a key idea of Clausewitz's. The success of an attack comes about because of a superiority of force, but as the attack continues, that force degrades physically or morally or both. This does not necessarily mean the attacker grows weaker in

and the Russians had not yet arrived, such an operation was not impossible. If, instead of the attack that Tharreau's, Lecourbe's, and Chabran's divisions carried out against the Austrian left wing in mid-August, Lecourbe and Tharreau—reinforced with 4,000 men from the main army to bring them up to 20,000—had limited themselves in late July to attacking the Rhone valley and the St. Gotthard, had barred the way to the latter from the Reuss valley at the Devil's Bridge, and had marched one column to Vercelli and the other toward Milan, then they would have attracted a corps of at least 20,000–30,000 men toward them from the allied army. Whether that would have sufficed to enable General Joubert to win a victory remains uncertain, of course, but it surely would have helped him considerably. In Switzerland, the situation on the Limmat would have remained much the same, while Chabran was still facing Generals Simbschen and Jellachich on the Sihl, and we cannot see how the Austrians could have retaliated effectively there. Extended in a long chain of outposts, probably eight days would have passed before the archduke could have made all his preparations for an attack on the Sihl, and even if he had then pushed General Chabran back to the Albis, he would not have gained much thereby, because Lecourbe's return would have obliged him to abandon this enveloping position.

But the French government rightly rejected the proposal Masséna and Lecourbe put forward for a similar operation in June; if 25,000–30,000 men had marched off to Italy then, Switzerland would have been lost. If it had been undertaken later and with a smaller force, that would have been *a quite different measure.*

---

relation to the defender, but in most cases, the strength of the attack diminishes with time and distance. Of course, if key ground is captured or key political objectives are met, the cost is worth the effort, assuming these gains can be traded after the fighting concludes and the costs do not exceed the object's value. Eventually, the attack will exhaust the necessary levels of will and physical might necessary to continue, at which point the attack will cease or be driven back. If the attacker has secured the gains it sought, it is possible that negotiations and peace will ensue. If not, then a stalemate is likely, or the defender may be in a position to counterattack to regain the lost objects. Either way, if the attack has culminated without securing the necessary objectives, it is unlikely that the conflict will end. The reader should compare *On War*, book 7, chaps. 1–7 (particularly pp. 527–528 and the note on p. 528) with book 7, chap. 22, on the culminating point of victory. Then it is worth reading book 8 and book 1, chaps. 1 and 2, to see how the various parts fit together.

We now come to the topic of our third observation, namely, Masséna's deployment for defense.

As we have seen, the archduke had a political reason for extending his left wing as far as the St. Gotthard. That was not the case for the French commander. As the result demonstrated, so long as he kept his right wing north of the high Alps, he was not obliged to abandon his occupation of the Rhone valley if he attached some value to maintaining it because of the uprising there. If the armed insurrection by the inhabitants of Graubündten and the minor cantons had not been so thoroughly suppressed by the measures taken against them in early May, concern about that uprising could have justified occupying the mountains. But during the six weeks the Austrians were in occupation, we see nothing of the kind stirring. Thus, on closer examination, we think that the value the French placed on occupying the high mountains per se, and on holding the St. Gotthard as the key to them and to Lombardy, had no basis in reality that could make up for the costs of doing so.[91]

But the French commander should be criticized still more for deploying a division of 11,000 men to Basel, which was a scarcely comprehensible waste of his forces. This division occupied the *right bank of the Rhine* there and was constructing an entrenched camp at Lörrach. It therefore appears as though General Masséna wanted to *threaten* there and to treat this point as a classic demonstration, whereby the archduke's bridge at Schafhausen and Starray's left flank would be under constant threat. But the archduke would have kept the 5,000–6,000 men he had on the right bank of the Rhine between Schafhausen and Basel there anyway, without this, and there was really nothing to worry about from Starray. It seems to us that if the bridge at Basel had been destroyed, it would not have needed to be occupied at all or, at most, by one battalion. How valuable 11,000 more men behind the Limmat would have been to General Masséna!

We cannot evaluate his actual dispositions for the position behind the Limmat because we lack precise details of them. But it would be extremely interesting to have his detailed maps of the area behind the Aare and the Limmat, since it is indisputably one of the strongest of strategic positions and must play a role in any campaign conducted in Switzerland.

91. Again, this relates to the value one places on the object to be attained and to the degree of effort judged to match the object's value.

7. Suvorov Moves to Switzerland

Korsakov Is Beaten by Masséna at Zurich. The Allies Retreat behind the Rhine.

68 THE TWO SIDES' NEW PLANS

We now come to the most important section of the whole war, when a major change in the cast of armies and commanders occurs, new commanders are summoned, and new theaters of operations open up; when the allies' very complex strategic plan is the cause of a major disaster, when we have a battle to describe that, after Rivoli,[1] is the largest of the war so far in terms of its consequences, and a passage through the mountains that has no equal in the whole history of warfare and that demands exertions and endurance bordering on prodigious; the section when finally the impact of all these events brings about an utter reversal of the situation and makes the new coalition disintegrate even faster than the previous one, so that the ensuing campaign only has to overcome its remnants and the French colors once again visit the Austrian capital to dictate peace terms to emperor and empire. This all happens because, in the Austrian cabinet, petty politicking played its insolent games for so long with the colossus of war until it was shattered by it.

Italy had been virtually conquered by August, and the fall of the fortresses could be foreseen with reasonable certainty, so it seemed nothing more needed to be done after the great test of arms there; and the agreement between England and Russia for a joint landing in Holland had been concluded in July, and its implementation was approaching.[2] At this point, the particular interests of the Austrian and English cabinets led them to wish to introduce a different

1. For a detailed analysis, see Clausewitz, *Napoleon's 1796 Italian Campaign*, 213–257.

2. For a brief overview of this campaign, see Esdaile, *Wars of the French Revolution*, 287–288. Rodger describes the entire episode in scathing terms: "The operation in North Holland was, from the allied standpoint, an ill-conceived, ill-planned, muddle-headed fiasco. . . . In its inception, planning, and conduct the British and Russian Cabinets and War Offices made almost every blunder possible, and it is an object lesson in how not to carry on combined operations." Rodger, *War of the Second Coalition*, 176.

division of forces and of roles for the remainder of the campaign. According to this, the Russians would have their whole force move into Switzerland under Suvorov, while the Austrians would continue the war in Italy on their own until the country was completely conquered; at the same time, the Austrians should return to the Rhine with a major army.

Neither England nor Austria wanted the Russians to acquire political toeholds in Italy. England feared the Russians gaining possession of Genoa because, in connection with his relationship with the Knights of Malta, Tsar Paul had expressed his determination to take possession of Malta; because other harbors on the Italian coast could easily fall into the hands of his troops in the Adriatic; and because they would thereby gain a firmer foothold in these waters than English interests could tolerate.[3]

The Austrians saw those Italian provinces that had not belonged to them as being in a provisional state after their conquest. They knew very well that the king of Sardinia had made peace with the French in 1796 and had subordinated himself to them at the start of the war this year (1799) only because he could not do otherwise, but he was not really a member of the coalition; he himself had contributed nothing to the reconquest of his country and, strictly speaking, could not regard himself as de facto having any vested rights in what the Austrians and Russians had taken from the French by force of arms. Tsar Paul had undertaken the war in an entirely chivalrous spirit against the usurpations of the French government and the danger of its revolutionary principles; he thought that anywhere these great European thieves could be hounded out of again should be returned to the rightful owners without further ado. But the Austrian government saw these conquests as quid pro quo that they could use to negotiate with afterward, partly to make it easier to even out the difficulties of a general peace treaty, and partly to better establish themselves in Italian politics one way or another. Naturally, the Russians must have been an embarrassment to them in this regard because they knew Tsar Paul took a different view of this matter, and also they could probably tell themselves that the Russian cabinet would exploit the situation in Italy to establish lasting bonds of gratitude, on the one hand, and protection, on the other, as a result. Furthermore, Suvorov entirely shared his tsar's view and

3. For an overview, see Piers Mackesey, *Statesmen at War: The Strategy of Overthrow 1798–1799* (London: Longman Group, 1974), 72–92.

was a very temperamental and irritable fellow into the bargain, who easily lost his poise, let himself get carried away and act hastily, and was therefore very difficult to cope with in that respect.

Apart from these Italian sensitivities, the three powers had another reason for changing the distribution of forces, especially England. The landing that the English and Russians wanted to undertake in Holland in August or September with 40,000 men seemed to need a diversion on the Rhine for the sake of ensuring its success. Starray's corps on the Rhine seemed inadequate for this, all the more so because, since 30 *Prairial*, the French had been busy creating a new army on the Rhine to attack south Germany. Thus, partly out of consideration for England, partly to keep south Germany safe, and finally to make it easier to get the Russians out of Italy, the Austrians appeared willing to have Archduke Charles move back to the Rhine with the Austrian main army as far downstream as it might be feasible for him to operate.

Tsar Paul had no objection to these wishes on the part of the two allied governments. The reason for creating a diversion for the benefit of the landing seemed so obvious and was of such a normal kind that probably not many cabinets would have rejected it. But for the tsar of Russia, they also needed the argument that it must definitely redound to the benefit of the whole if each power kept its own combat forces together as far as possible and each acted independently in its own theater of operations, because thereby the pernicious disunity and friction that had revealed itself several times in Italy would be precluded. Since Switzerland was the colder country, it would be appropriate to unite the Russian forces there under Suvorov.

Thus, in August the agreement among the three cabinets for this change of roles came into effect, according to which Suvorov and Archduke Charles received their orders in mid-August, the former to move to Switzerland with the Russians, the latter to move to the Rhine with his main army.

Although a change of roles of this kind usually brings danger with it because forces engaged in marching may be considered neutralized, this did not really happen in the present case because they did not miss much either in Italy or on the Rhine. But there is a debatable point here that we cannot get straight because we do not know either the date or the content of the aforementioned agreement among the three powers. On his arrival in Swabia, Suvorov bemoans the archduke's departure from Switzerland and says, among other things: "The position at Zurich, which was supposed to have been defended by 60,000 Austrians, had now been left to 20,000 Russians."[4] Furthermore, in his published report we find the following excerpt:

> Lord Mulgrave had once again promised me that the English minister was not thinking of having Your Majesty's troops move to Switzerland until the Archduke had driven the enemy out of that country. He had added that Mr. Thugot had formally assured the English minister in Vienna that the Archduke would not leave Switzerland; and that he had written to the Archduke accordingly. Yet his promise was wrong, and he gave the Archduke enough time to evacuate Switzerland.[5]

This situation Suvorov describes probably means simply that the archduke was to wait for his arrival in Switzerland, which may very well be imagined to have been in the agreement among the three powers. If we now find the following excerpt from the archduke himself— "the court of Vienna made it mandatory upon the archduke to keep secret the order given to him (to march away) and to comply with it soonest without any further objection"[6]—that certainly must have induced mistrust toward the Viennese cabinet as, to say the least, it had not acted in entirely open accord with Suvorov. Of course, the archduke could not keep his actual departure secret, but since perhaps another eight to fourteen days passed in making preparations for it, it seems to have been important to the court of Vienna that the Russians should not be aware of it because old Suvorov might have abandoned his move to Switzerland if he had heard about it.

If the Austrian cabinet's behavior in this matter indeed caused mistrust, it is also apparent from the instruction that Suvorov issued to Generals Korsakov,

4. "*La position de Zürich, qui devait être défendue par 60,000 Autrichiens, avait été abandonée à 20,000 Russes.*" **Clausewitz** notes: "*Campagne des Autrichiens et Russes en Italie.* Paris 1802. P. 188."

5. "*Lord Mulgrave m'avait de nouveau promis que le Ministre anglais ne pensait pas à faire venir les troupes de Votre Majesté en Suisse, avant que l'Archiduc eut chassé l'ennemi de ce pays. Il avait ajouté que Mr. Thugot avait formellement assuré le Ministre anglais à Vienne que l'Archiduc ne quitterait pas la Suisse; qu'il avait écrit à l'Archiduc. Pourtant il se trompa avec cette promesse et procura assez de temps à l'Archiduc pour évacuer la Suisse.*" This report from Suvorov to Tsar Paul, 20 September (Gregorian), Lucerne, Switzerland, can be found in German in D. A. Milyutin, *Geschichte des Krieges Russlands mit Frankreich unter der Regierung Kaiser Pauls I. im Jahre 1799*, 5 vols. (Munich: Commission der Jos. Lindauer'schen Buchhandlung, 1856–1858), 3:456.

6. **Clausewitz** notes: "Vol. II, p 94." Karl, 2:94.

Hotze, and Linken on 5 September that by then he no longer envisaged the archduke being present at the time of their joint operation. Thus, we may well assume that the complaint he lodges against the archduke's departure is one of those excuses that people gladly put forward alongside other reasons for an unsuccessful operation when they do not even regard it as one of the direct causes. Suvorov may indeed have believed earlier that the archduke would wait for him, and in any case, he would not have been able to bring this up afterward if the Austrian side had been completely open with him.

We have had to bring up these circumstances here because they delivered the final blow to Suvorov's goodwill, but the crack that split the alliance started from Suvorov first.

As we have already remarked, the divergence of particular political aims had already made its presence felt during the course of the campaign. Suvorov had wanted to proclaim to all of Italy that the allies' aims were to give back to everyone what was theirs and simply to restore the old order of things everywhere. The Austrian generals disagreed with such a declaration; they took possession of Piedmont's fortresses in the name of the emperor of Austria; although the king of Sardinia had been recalled by Suvorov and arrived in Livorno, they denied him entry into his own state; in Piedmont they exercised authority in the name of the emperor of Austria, etc.

Thus the rift began in Italy, and it was inevitable that this created a negative attitude toward the coalition in Tsar Paul's mind; add to this the military disasters, the heavy losses of combat forces incurred, the plaintive reports from Suvorov, Grand Duke Constantine, Korsakov, and Prince Gorchakov expressing nothing but unhappiness with the Austrians, whose conduct seemed to them to border on betrayal, and it was almost inevitable that this would prompt a man like Tsar Paul to leave the coalition and abandon the fight against France. Thus it is Suvorov's move to Switzerland together with the impure motives of the Austrians and the poor results in the execution that became the cause for the dissolution of the new alliance.[7]

We are considering the later consequences of these political strategic dispositions now because it sheds light on the state of affairs, on people and relationships, which makes their actions more understandable.

Since Suvorov's army marched out of Italy about 20,000 strong and

7. For an overview of the Russian position, see Christopher Duffy, *Eagles over the Alps: Suvorov in Italy and Switzerland, 1799* (Chicago: Emperor's Press, 1999), 152–154.

Korsakov had 30,000, this formed a force of 50,000 in Switzerland. To these should be added the Swiss formations, which they hoped to expand further; Condé's 3,000-strong émigré corps; and a division of a few thousand Bavarians as a result of a special treaty Tsar Paul had concluded with the elector of Bavaria. Altogether these would have brought the total allied force to 60,000 men, which thus would have remained at least 10,000 stronger than the French. Apparently, it was not the Austrian cabinet's intention for the Austrian troops the archduke had left in Switzerland under Hotze to remain there after Suvorov's arrival, and it seems to emerge from the archduke's account that he had left this corps there not on the court's orders but out of his own consideration for the situation.

The Austrian army's mission in Germany is not specified, beyond saying that it should leave a corps of 20,000 men to protect southern Germany and undertake an operation on the lower Rhine with the rest (which would have been close to 70,000 men, including Hotze). No one seems to have known exactly what this *operation* was supposed to be, which is nothing unusual, given the vagueness of thought in these matters. To undertake an operation seems to people to be as sufficient a mission as when the ballet master prescribes a *pas de deux*. In considering this new task, the archduke says: "At whatever point below Philippsburg the Austrians wanted to direct their operations, they would have been so weakened after deducting all the troops they would have had to leave behind to protect their extended line of operations that the most they could have engaged in would have been raids between the fortresses of Landau, Mainz, and Düsseldorf."[8] We present this simply to show that the commander who was supposed to operate in this new theater did not know exactly what he was supposed to do there himself.

The landing of 40,000 men in Holland was seen as an effective diversion for all the other theaters of operations and as a means of awakening a new foe for the French among the inhabitants of these areas. It is easy to see that England had a special interest in seizing the Dutch fleet and obtaining a foothold on the coast, and this special interest must be regarded as the silent motivation for the operation. If the Austrians wanted to pursue their own interests in Italy, they had to allow the English to seek theirs in the Low Countries, and only the ostensible reasons were presented to Tsar Paul's chivalrous view.

Thus, at this point of the war, 30,000 men under Korsakov, 6,000 Bavarians

8. Karl, 2:91.

and émigrés, and 40,000 men in the Low Countries arrived on the battlefield, that is, new allied combat forces worth 76,000 men in total.

After the Second Congress of Rastatt dispersed, the German Empire [Holy Roman Empire] was also asked to muster its contingents for the emperor; but the northern princes were protected by the Demarcation,[9] and the southern were not in a hurry to arm themselves anew either, so apart from the Bavarian division we have already mentioned, only a few reinforcements for the garrisons of Philippsburg, Ulm, and Ingolstadt were forthcoming.

This is what we had to say about the new arrangements for the war on the part of the allies. The French will detain us less.

After their disasters in Italy and the events of 18 *Prairial* that they led to, the French too had decided on a regeneration of the war, if we might express ourselves thus. We have already told how 200,000 more men were supposed to be conscripted,[10] the armies in Italy and Switzerland were to be reinforced, and the new Army of the Alps and Army of the Rhine were to be created. But as is usual with republican forms of government, these decisions, which sounded so portentous and awesome, were very difficult to put into effect. None of the new conscripts could be put into the field immediately, and the 150,000 men remaining from the conscription levied at the start of the war in 1798 had already been rushed to the frontiers piecemeal.

We have also told how in Italy the project died in its infancy, partly because the Army of the Alps could never be raised up to a tolerable size, and partly because in mid-August the battle of Novi already brought its operations there to a standstill again. Since then, the Italian combat forces had been formed into one army again under Championnet's command.

Establishing the Army of the Rhine was doubly difficult because, since then, a new army in Holland had become necessary. By September, this came

9. The 1795 Treaty of Basel had seen France and Prussia agree to a line of demarcation in Germany whereby the princely states to the north of the Main River would remain neutral. See Steven T. Ross, *Quest for Victory: French Military Strategy 1792–1799* (London: Thomas Yoseloff, 1978), 89–91; Georges Lefebvre, *The French Revolution from 1793 to 1799*, trans. John Hall Stewart and James Friguglietti (New York: Columbia University Press, 1964), 149–153.

10. In many ways, the step to further mobilize the French population shows that the conflict was far more important to the French than to the allies. In turn, this meant that the French were more likely to increase their efforts, and the allies would have to do likewise or renounce their goals.

to 34,000 men, including those troops tasked as garrisons in Belgium, so the force on the Rhine could only be increased to 54,000, of which the larger half had to be deducted for garrisons.

Initially, General Moreau was to take over command of both the army on the Rhine and that in Switzerland; but when Masséna took this badly and wanted to quit, the Directory retracted this order so that Moreau only took over the Army of the Rhine. But even this was soon changed again; Moreau withdrew, and Lecourbe was named commander of the Army of the Rhine in September. Until then, while this army was forming, it was commanded by General Müller.

Thus the French government's overblown projects melted away under the pressure of reality like soap bubbles under atmospheric pressure.[11]

The actual state of French military power in the latter half of September was 247,000 men on the frontiers and 134,000 in the interior, not including the army in Egypt. Thus, this was some 30,000 more men than at the start of the war. Since, at the time, some 150,000 of these men were still in the process of formation, this actually reveals a reduction of 110,000–120,000 men, which must be thought of as not just from the armies on the borders but from the entire combat force. Indeed, it is also likely that of the 382,000 combat forces available in September, 40,000–50,000 men had been levied from the latest conscription, formed into *bataillons auxiliaires* (auxiliary battalions) according to Bernadotte's system, and rushed to the frontiers, so the reduction can be assumed to be about 160,000 men. This steep reduction is the consequence of a constantly changing, weak, and disorganized administration. Probably a third of the young men ran away before being placed under arms or rotted in the neglected hospitals. The French army of the time was as excellent in action—like a molten mass tempered in the flame—as it was lousy and corrupt in everything that lay behind the fighting, right up to the highest levels of its administration.

Of the 247,000 men posted on the frontiers, as we have said, 34,000 were in the Netherlands and 54,000 on the Rhine; there were 82,000 in Switzerland, 64,000 with the Army of Italy, and 12,000 in the Italian fortresses.

11. Again, Clausewitz is using a contemporary scientific concept as a metaphor for his ideas. For example, he mentions a Bologna flask shattering upon being scratched (*On War*, book 7, chap. 22, 572) and refers to the interaction of magnets in terms of his trinity (*On War*, book 1, chap. 1, pt. 28).

The Directory did not believe its Army of Italy was strong enough either in numbers or in quality for a powerful offensive, and on the Rhine, it could only put enough troops in the field to invest Philippsburg. The French government therefore put its main trust in the army in Switzerland because it was the strongest, because Masséna inspired the most confidence, and because the events of mid-August were regarded as good preparation for further success. In addition, the French government had no idea of the new decisions the allies had made, and at the start of September, it still thought Archduke Charles had been instructed to send 20,000 men to Italy to reinforce Suvorov. Since the Rhine army's diversionary attack was bound to oblige Archduke Charles to send troops to the Rhine as well, the French had no doubt that Masséna would be very numerically superior in Switzerland. On 5 September Minister of War Bernadotte therefore pressed Masséna most keenly to undertake something major.[12] He gave him the choice between invading Graubündten, combined with a diversion in the direction of Lake Maggiore to divide Suvorov's force in Italy, and fighting a major battle with the Russians wherever possible. This latter directive is not without merit, and the allies' mistakes meant that Masséna was able to comply with it. The defeat at Zurich essentially divided the alliance, and in such cases, a blow suffered by one ally alone always has a pernicious effect on his goodwill.

69 STRENGTHS AND POSITIONS OF THE TWO SIDES IN SWITZERLAND

The positions of the two sides in Switzerland changed fundamentally in a few places over the course of September. We must therefore present them as they were at the time of the decisive events as precisely as the available reports allow.

On the allied side, the main change was that General Korsakov did not think, as Archduke Charles had, that the Limmat and the Aare were best defended by deploying behind those rivers.[13] Instead, right at the start of

12. See Bernadotte's 5 September letter to Masséna in Jomini, 12:444–447.

13. The archduke's thoughts on the Russians are enlightening and tie in with some of the problems identified in the previous section: "All the army's requirements were hauled along by the Russians in a gigantic train, complicating every move. Organized for war in the inhospitable plains of the Turkish border, they barely envisaged the

September, he moved his main body through Zurich into a camp beneath the guns of that fortress. It is stated that eight battalions and ten squadrons under General Durassov were left behind the rivers in one main camp at Wettingen and a smaller one at Würenlos, as were another three battalions under General Markov at Kloster Fahr.[14]

The historians' reports are extremely sketchy, though, and we must therefore determine the distribution of the Russian corps according to probability.

According to one precise report, when it marched through Augsburg, the bayonet strength of Korsakov's corps was approximately:

21,000 infantry
6,000 cavalry
3,000 Cossacks
30,000 men

The Cossacks should generally be counted as being of little combat value. Except when they are present in very large numbers, the Russian armies

possibility, in line with the more modern system of war, of doing without a lot, of finding that which is the most necessary everywhere, and making do with only a little baggage. Since 1763 they had only waged significant wars against the Turks, in which decisiveness, personal courage, and the holding together of the troops in dense masses without any particular assistance from the art of maneuver usually decide victory. Therefore most of their generals and officers were trained exclusively according to this principle and remained strangers to every other area of warfare. Proud of their recent victories over the Turks, impassioned by the French émigrés with contempt for the New French and, consequently, also for the Austrians, who were unable to bring the so easily misunderstood war to an end, convinced that only Suvorov's arrival had decided the good fortune in Italy—they and their general were blinded by a sense of superiority. It was not that noble self-assurance, which elevates the soul and puts it in the mood for great deeds, but the sign of moral weakness, and a worrying weariness in misfortune. Korsakov believed himself certain of such superiority that the enemy would necessarily be swayed by him and that no more care need be taken in Switzerland than in the steppes of the Dniester. As if, generally, the immovable could determine the decisions of the more mobile and as if not every enemy and every country required a different application of the principles of warfare. In this mind-set and mood, the Russians took over the defense of the Limmat. It was therefore not surprising that they despised all the precautionary measures of their predecessors as the product of fear, thus preparing their own undoing!" Karl, 2:189–192.

14. Karl, 2:192.

mostly use them for guarding the baggage train and for personal and orderly duties for the officers. Any left over from these duties were probably used to observe the Limmat and the Aare.

If we take the eight battalions to be 4,500 men, and if we say a couple of thousand men were left behind to guard the Rhine bridges around Schafhausen, that leaves 14,500 infantry for the main body; if we reckon 4,500 cavalry in addition, it was 19,000 strong. But it seems that these 19,000 were not all in or in front of Zurich, since Dedon and other authors as well speak of a reserve camp at Seebach. At the time of the decisive battle, this no longer existed, or at least not with any significant number of troops, and since the 5,000 men sent to Hotze on the 25th per Suvorov's order were mostly taken from this camp, it seems to have held 4,000–5,000 men.

However, at the time that primarily matters to us, the moment of the decisive battle at the end of September, we must take the number of combat troops to be a couple of thousand fewer than when they marched through Augsburg. This then yields the following as the likely result: from 30,000 men, take away a reduction of 2,000, another 2,000 detached to the bridges, and 3,000 Cossacks, and that leaves 23,000 men; of these, about 6,000 were behind the Limmat and the Aare, and 5,000 had been sent off to Hotze, leaving 12,000 for the corps in and in front of Zurich.

It is also remarkable that Korsakov moved not only his headquarters into Zurich but also *his artillery park and the entire baggage train.*

The archduke gives the reason for the deployment of the Russian main body as being that Korsakov was informed of Suvorov's intention to go on the offensive at all points simultaneously, and therefore wanted to ensure his breakout from Zurich thereby.[15] But first, the breakout from Zurich could never have presented any great difficulty, since the fortress itself constituted a bridgehead, the archduke had always maintained an advance guard on the Sihlfeld,[16] and the difficulty of an attack at this point lay not in crossing the Limmat or the Sihl but in scaling the Ütli; second, Suvorov's circular to the generals in Switzerland in which he most likely first expressed his intention was dated 5 September at Asti, and General Korsakov had already adopted this position at the start of September.

We consider it very likely that General Korsakov thought to impress the

15. See note 13 above.

16. The Sihlfeld is now a suburb of Zurich, but it was an open floodplain at the time.

French by his deployment and that perhaps he had once heard tell of the principle that the near bank of a river is best defended from the far side; besides, heaven knows what muddle-headedness from the general staff had befogged his common sense. A child could understand that it was impossible to apply that principle in the present case.[17]

Of the deployment of the Austrians under Hotze, we know only the general outline, and even that general outline is not at all precise.

The archduke says that Hotze and the Swiss had 25,000 men;[18] 5,000 Russians were supposed to be added to these, of whom a couple of thousand joined him before the battle of Zurich, but 3,000 of them only on that day. The total would therefore be 30,000 men. But from the 25th onward, we find fewer than 20,000 men engaged against the French. This contradiction, which none of the historians has worried about, needs to be resolved so far as it can be.

The Russians who had moved to join Hotze on the 25th turned back again, and from this army, only those 2,000 men who had arrived earlier came into action with him.

Bachmann's Swiss Legion was likewise sent off to General Korsakov by Hotze on the 25th.

According to the archduke's account, Hotze was left with thirty battalions and thirty-four squadrons of Austrian troops, or 22,000 men in total.[19] From his account and that of other historians, those that came into action were:

Hotze himself: 10 battalions and 14 squadrons = 8,000 men.
Jellachich: 6 battalions and 3 squadrons = 4,000 men.
Linken: 5 battalions and 1 squadron = 3,000 men.
Auffenberg: 4 battalions = 2,400 men.
Total: 25 battalions and 18 squadrons = 17,400 men.

Thus, there are five battalions and sixteen squadrons missing, or about 5,000 men. The five battalions can probably be assumed to be garrisoning Rapperswil, the St. Luciensteig, and elsewhere in the Rhine valley, but the sixteen squadrons must have received some other mission. Most likely they had just set off to follow the archduke to the Neckar, since, in what follows, we shall

17. More sarcasm. See volume 1, chapter 4, note 64.
18. Karl, 2:139.
19. Now that the Swiss contingent of 3,000 had been sent off. Karl, 2:139.

see General Nauendorf being joined after the battle of Zurich by a couple of thousand Austrian cavalry who had this mission and who could only have come from Hotze's corps.

According to these assumptions, at the time the decisive battle occurred, we may give the strength of Hotze's corps as: 13,000 men between Rapperswil and Lake Walensee under Hotze's personal command, 4,000 between Lake Walensee and the St. Luciensteig under General Jellachich, 3,000 between the St. Luciensteig and Reichenau under Linken, 2,400 in the upper Rhine valley as far as Disentis under General Auffenberg, and 2,000 men garrisoning Graubündten, making 25,000 men altogether, including 3,000 Swiss and 2,000 Russians.

The strengths and deployments of the allies before the moment of the decisive battle were thus:

Russians behind the Limmat: 6,000 men
Russians outside Zurich: 12,000
Russians in the camp at Seebach: 3,000
Russians in the bridgeheads: 2,000
Cossacks: 3,000
Austrians, Russians, and Swiss under Hotze: 13,000
Austrians under Jellachich: 4,000
Austrians under Linken: 3,000
Austrians under Auffenberg: 2,400
Austrian garrisons in Graubündten: 2,000
On the march from Hotze to Nauendorf: 2,600
Total: 53,000 men

We gave this force as 55,000 men when the archduke left Switzerland. The difference lies in the 2,000-man reduction we have estimated for the Russians.

Furthermore, of these 53,000 men, the 6,000–7,000 appearing under items 4, 10, and 11 should not be considered as engaged with the enemy, which leaves just 46,000–47,000 actually in the line.

Strauch's and Haddick's corps belonged to the army in Italy and were still at the Italian exits of the roads from the St. Gotthard and Wallis. Nauendorf, who basically should not be counted among the combat forces in Switzerland either, had 5,000–6,000 men on the right bank of the Rhine between Schaffhausen and Basel.

The French deployment had also changed somewhat. General Chabran had taken over Souham's division outside Basel, while General Soult got Chabran's old division on the Linth. Their strengths and deployments were now as follows:

Tharreau's division in Wallis facing Strauch and Haddick: 9,000 men
Lecourbe's division:
Gudin's brigade from St. Gotthard to the Urseren valley: 3,500
Loison's brigade in the Reuss valley as far as Altorf: 6,000
Molitor's brigade around Glarus: 3,000
Soult's division on the Linth and up to Rapperswil: 10,000
Mortier's division on the Albis and the Ütli: 8,000
Lorges's division toward Baden: 10,000
Ménard's division above and below the junction of the Aare and the Limmat: 9,000
Klein's division in reserve, partly behind Ménard's division, partly on the Rhine: 10,000
Chabran's division in front of Basel: 8,000
Total: 76,500 men

Finally, Montchoisi's division of 2,500 men in the Swiss interior also belonged to Masséna's army, which was therefore about 80,000 strong.

Thus, leaving out Haddick, Strauch, and Nauendorf from the allied side and Chabran, Montchoisi, and Tharreau from the French, we find that the French had 60,000 men and the allies 53,000; but as soon as Suvorov and his 20,000 Russians arrived, as well as the Bavarians and the émigrés, the allied force would rise to 80,000, so the French would be very outnumbered.

70 SUVOROV'S PLAN FOR LINKING UP

Such superiority of numbers on Suvorov's part undoubtedly would have cost the French their possession of Switzerland, and on the side of the allies, particularly Suvorov, this outcome was seen as almost beyond question. To make it properly glorious and magnificent, the Austrian general staff talked old Suvorov into a plan for linking up that would at the same time be an enveloping strategic attack on the enemy's combat forces in Switzerland and would lead to the complete defeat of the enemy commander.

The way Suvorov's headquarters staff saw it, he had three routes by which he could invade Switzerland. The one via Bellinzona and the St. Gotthard through the Reuss valley was the shortest. The one via Como, Chiavenna, the Splügen, Chur, and Wallenstädt, which Bellegarde had taken in the opposite direction, entailed a detour of about three days' march. Finally, he could move left via Ivrea, Aosta, the Great St. Bernard, and Martigny to the canton of Freiburg. We cannot say that this third route was either closer or further away, since it led to a quite different point and not to any junction with Hotze and Korsakov.

Thus, if Suvorov had wanted to invade by this last route, a junction with those generals for a combined attack could not have been his intention. Instead, it would be a strategic outflanking maneuver and, consequently, an operation of a quite different kind. It would certainly have been a good one if the 55,000 Austrians and Russians had been led by an enterprising commander who exploited the effects of this outflanking for a major battle, which, however, under the prevailing circumstances, would have been a very daring gamble. Since the question about this point is such an interesting one, we want to pick up on it in our reflections at the end of this chapter, but here it would divert us too far from the events. At Suvorov's headquarters in Asti, the question seems to have been discussed in the way one might consider a salesman's route according to its length and practicability, apparently in total innocence of how completely different such an operation is from a simple route march.

Out of the other two routes, the one through the St. Gotthard was in the hands of the French and would therefore have to be captured first; also, only small 2-pounder mountain guns could be brought across it, while all the other artillery, parks, and baggage would have to be taken through either the Splügen Pass or the Adige valley.

Against these disadvantages, the Austrian general staff thought they saw the following advantages. First, this route was closer. Second, from the moment Suvorov arrived at the St. Gotthard and attacked the position there, he was basically having an effect already and drawing part of the enemy force toward him, whereas if he went through the Splügen he could not be considered as being present until after he joined up with Hotze; since Suvorov could be expected to reach the foot of the St. Gotthard by the 19th but could not meet up with Hotze before the 25th, the time difference was certainly appreciable. Third, heading for the St. Gotthard would aim into Masséna's right flank; the Austrian general staff therefore thought that if the march was undertaken in this direction, and if the first thrust was made at the St. Gotthard and could be continued toward the Albis while the corps on the enemy's front attacked at the appropriate time, this would be nothing less than an attack in the form of an envelopment or, as it is usually expressed, with an outflanking. Since such an attack is usually considered the more effective form, an advantage seemed to arise here entirely of its own accord, one that in most cases has to be obtained specifically by sending a column to detour around.

Now, since the St. Gotthard Pass could not be regarded as an impregnable position but only as one of those strong alpine positions that one can be sure of overwhelming with significant numerical superiority, the first of the disadvantages mentioned above basically disappeared completely, and the second was outweighed by the supposed advantages. Thus it was decided to take the route over the St. Gotthard.

As we described in section 56, Suvorov had already received the order for his departure from Italy on 25 August but stayed until the fall of Tortona on 11 September. During this time, he decided on his plan and on 5 September issued a circular from Asti to the generals commanding in Switzerland, which we must regard as the general dispositions and which we present here in detail, because it constitutes the basic foundation of the ensuing decisive events:

> Circular from Marshal Suvorov to Generals Hotze, Korsakov, and Linken
> Asti, 5 September 1799
>
> The Russian imperial troops who have been with the army in Italy until now shall leave Piedmont on 8 September to move to Switzerland. I expect to arrive with them at Airolo on the 17th, at the foot of this side of the St. Gotthard, which I propose to attack on the 19th.
>
> As Colonel Strauch's troops, Prince Victor Rohan's, and Count Haddick's must all cooperate in this attack, it will be very important that the two imperial courts' united armies in Switzerland should resolutely and steadily carry out a general simultaneous and combined attack on all the enemy's positions; but above all, the left wing, under the orders of my lord Baron Linken, shall concentrate all its forces and make every effort, perhaps even reinforced beforehand, to assist and support the Russian corps in traversing the St. Gotthard mountain, the upper valley of the Reuss, and that of the Linth. As well as possibly attacking the enemy in the rear, then by rapidly linking up with the left wing of the imperial army and advancing in concert the enemy may also be prevented from overwhelming the Russian corps coming from Italy and destroying it in detail.

As I do not know the exact positions of the two united imperial armies in Switzerland, only from occasional reports, I must presume that the corps of Russian troops under command of General Korsakov is deployed between Zurich and the Aare along the right bank of the Limmat, and that of the royal and imperial [i.e., Austrian] troops under command of my lord Baron Hotze between Lake Zurich and Lake Walensee, through Maienfeld in the Rhine valley as far as Disentis. Above all I must expect to link up with the latter's forces. I wish to learn from him himself where and how this should be done since he knows the area best. Likewise for my part, once the linking up has been achieved, I think that the Russian troops from Italy can no longer be stopped and will penetrate along the two shores of Lake Lucerne, those of my lords Linken and Hotze between Lakes Zurich and Zug, and finally all will meet up with the Russian troops of General Korsakov near the right bank of the lower Reuss and the Aare; this will be the only maneuver that could promise a decisive result for subsequent operations.

As I shall hasten to let you know from Bellinzona when the Russian column arrives there from Italy, likewise you should let me know by courier at Bellinzona at the latest (if you should not be able to do it sooner by the route via Novara and Varese) the positions and strength of all our troops concentrated in Switzerland, Russian and Austrian alike, as well as the enemy positions, strength, and distribution. I likewise desire that my lords Generals Barons Hotze and Linken should advise me of their opinions and their local knowledge of the terrain and of how to conduct war in this country, while indicating how the rapid cooperation of all the troops already in Switzerland and those marching there from here may be achieved most efficaciously and most usefully; I shall thereby be enabled to prepare my attack and to decide the most favorable day and time for it.

P.S. For the general attack, I must recommend the precaution which is always necessary of keeping the forces concentrated as far as possible, so as not to render the attack inadequate by unnecessary fragmenting and gratuitous weakening; in addition, the commander of each sector should have accurate knowledge of the strengths and positions of the enemy corps facing him; these should also be reported swiftly beforehand, since we should communicate daily by courier with detailed reports of our first steps.

I also desire that on the free days in the interlude before the general attack, the concentrated units should practice assaulting in three columns with bayonet and saber.

By attacking exclusively according to this method, we shall multiply our successes and make them much less costly. And for this exercise I advise that my lord Lieutenant-General Korsakov should lend Russian officers who are familiar with this method to the Austrian corps in Switzerland.

The above-mentioned General Korsakov is authorized by the orders attached.

Signed: Suvorov.[20]

20. **Clausewitz** notes: "We give this letter in French as it is found in *Campagne des Austro-Russes en Italie sous les orders du Maréchal de Suwarof.* The original was probably in French, and indeed probably exactly as it is here. The translations which are found in other authors' works diverge from it somewhat, because such gibberish really cannot be translated."

"*Circulaire du maréchal Suwarof aux généraux Hotze, Korsakof et Linken*

Asti, le 5 septembre 1799

Les troupes impériales de Russie qui, jusqu'à present, étaient à l'armée d'Italie, partiront le 8 septembre du Piémont pour se rendre en Suisse, et je compte arriver avec elles le 17 à Airolo, au pied de ce côté du Saint-Gothard, que je me propose d'attaquer le 19.

Comme les troupes du colonel Strauch, celles du prince Victor Rohan et du comte de Haddick doivent coopérer à l'attaque, il sera très necessaire que les armées des deux cours impériales, réunies en Suisse, fassent avec fermeté et constance une attaque générale simultanée et combinée sur toutes les positions de l'ennemi; mais surtout l'aile gauche, sous les orders de M. le baron de Linken, réunira tous ses moyens, fera tous ses efforts, peut-être même avec des renforts préalables, pour faciliter et soutenir le passage du corps d'armée russe par le mont Saint-Gothard, la haute vallée de la Reuss et celle de la Linth. De même qu'il sera possible d'attaquer l'ennemi à revers, on pourra aussi, par la junction rapide de l'aile gauche de l'armée impériale, et en avançant de concert, empêcher l'ennemi de culbuter le corps russe d'Italie et de le détruire en detail.

Comme je n'ai pas eu connaissance exacte des positions des deux armées impériales, réunies en Suisse, et que seulement par des rapports prise en passant, je dois présumer que le corps de troupes russes, sous les orders du general Korsakov, est posté entre Zurich et l'Aar, le long de la rive droite de la Limmat, celui des troupes impériales et royales, sous les orders de M. le baron de Hotze, entre le lac de Zurich et celui de Wallenstadt, par Maienfeld dans le Rheinthal jusqu'à Disentis, je dois avant tout, attendre la junction des troupes de ce dernier. Je desire d'apprendre de lui-même, comme connaissant mieux les localités, où, et comment l'opérer. De même, de mon côté, dès que la junction aura réussi, je pense que les troupes russes d'Italie, ne pouvant plus être arrêtées, pénétreront sur les deux rives du lac de Lucerne, celles de MM. de Linken et Hotze entre les lacs de Zurich et Zug, et enfin la reunion totale des troupes russes du general Korsakov près la rive droite

According to the archduke's testimony, this general plan of Suvorov's, for which the Austrian general staff provided the idea but which seems to have been drafted either by Suvorov himself or by someone from his inner circle, was followed on 10 September by a later and somewhat more precisely defined arrangement that was established in agreement with Hotze and Korsakov:

> Namely that on 21 September Suvorov would set off from Bellinzona to attack the St. Gotthard. Colonel Strauch, who was observing General Tharreau on the routes to Italy, was to cover this movement and an Austrian brigade was to push across the Crispalt from Disentis to Am Steg in the Reuss valley. Suvorov hoped to be in possession of the mountain by the 24th, to continue his march to Altorf on the 25th, to Schwyz on the

---

de la basse Reuss et de l'Aar; ce sera la seule manoeuvre qui puisse promettre un résultat décisif pour les operations ultérieures.

Comme je me hâterai de vous faire connaître, de Bellinzona, l'arrivée de la colonne des troupes russes d'Italie, c'est aussi à Bellinzona, au plus tard, à moins que vous ne le puissiez plus tôt, par la route de Novara et Varèse, que vous me ferez connaître, par courriers, la position et la force de toutes les troupes, tan trusses que royales-impériales, qui se trouvent réunies en Suisse, ainsi que les positions de l'ennemi, ses forces et leur distribution. Je desire aussi que MM. les généraux baron de Hotze et de Linken me communiquent leurs avis et leurs connaissances locales sur le terrain et la manière de faire la guerre dans ce pays, en indiquant comment la cooperation précipitée de toutes les troupes qui sont déjà en Suisse, et de celles qui y marchent d'ici peut être le plus efficacement et le plus utilement exécutée; je serai par là en état de préparer mon attaque et d'en déterminer le jour et l'heure positifs.

Post-scriptum. Je dois, pour l'attaque générale, recommander d'avoir la précaution, qui devient chaque fois necessaire, de tenir les forces tant que possible réunies pour ne pas rendre l'attaque insuffisante par des parcellements non nécessaires et des affaiblements gratuits; en outre, chaque commandant de section doit connaître au vrai la position et la force des corps ennemis qui son ten face; il doit aussi chaque fois s'empresser de l'annoncer préalablement, puisque nous devons journellement nous addresser réciproquement, par courriers, des rapports très détaillés de nos premiers pas.

Je souhaite aussi que les troupes réunies s'exercent, dns l'intervalle des jours libres jusqu'à celui de l'attaque générale, à executer sur trois colonnes cette attaque avec la baïonnette et le sabre.

C'est à cette manière d'attaquer que nous devons, ici exclusivement, nos succès multipliés et très peu sanglants. Et d'après mon avis, M. le lieutenant général Korsakov pourra répartir, pour cet exercice, les officiers russes qui s'y connaissent, au corps royal-impérial qui es ten Suisse.

Le susdit général Korsakov est autorisé par les ordres ci-joints.

Signé: Souvarov."

26th, and to Lucerne on the 27th, to where he would send a detachment from the Reuss valley via Engelberg on the western shore of the lake.[21]

Hotze, reinforced with 5,000 men from Korsakov's corps, was given the mission of advancing simultaneously from Uznach toward Einsiedeln, and of having this maneuver supported by flank columns which were supposed to head from Flums through Schwanden and from Sargans through Glarus up the Klön valley to Einsiedeln.[22] Hotze's subsequent mission was to attack the French position on the Albis in the flank; meanwhile, Korsakov would storm it frontally from Zurich and link up with Hotze.[23]

The archduke continues:

> The successful result of these preliminary actions would have given the allies possession of the whole course of the Reuss and put them in a position to reach the Aare with their forces united. Suvorov had no doubt that as the attacker he was bound to carve his way through the mountains everywhere, and anticipated danger all the less as reaching the crest of the mountains would leave him free to invade either along the road through the Linth valley or, in the worst case, into Graubündten, according to the situation.[24]

To these not very exactly arranged dispositions as imparted by the archduke in his history of the campaign, we must add the following more precise instructions from the Russian account. The flank columns the archduke mentions were those of Generals Jellachich and Linken. The first of these was to advance from the area of Sargans and Walensee to Netstal and Näfels in the Linth valley, seize the crossings over the Linth, and then push on toward Einsiedeln. General Linken, meanwhile, was to advance from the area of Chur and Ilanz into the upper Linth valley as far as Glarus and march from there

21. Karl, 2:181.

22. This plan has been cross-checked with the archduke's account, and what is here makes no sense. The two columns would be forced to cross each other's paths. It is worth examining on the online map at https://mapire.eu/de/map/europe-19century-secondsurvey/?layers=here-aerial%2C158%2C164&bbox=922216.9166959223%2C5923756.634562108%2C1116596.2796251255%2C5984906.257190249.

23. Karl, 2:182.

24. Karl, 2:182.

through the Klön valley across the Bragel Pass to Muota, where he was to link up with Suvorov.

On 26 September, the day Suvorov expected to arrive at Schwyz, Korsakov and Hotze were supposed to attack the French—the former on the Limmat, the latter on the Linth—while Generals Jellachich and Linken were to reach the areas of Einsiedeln and Muota. At the last minute, on the 24th, Hotze and Korsakov met in Zurich and agreed that the main attack should be carried out by Hotze, while that by Korsakov should be no more than a demonstration. This agreement was indisputably the consequence of Suovorov's order that Korsakov should send 5,000 men to reinforce Hotze. We can well imagine how reluctantly Korsakov agreed to this; he seems to have hesitated to do it until the last moment, and then only gave in to Hotze's personal representations when Hotze finally betook himself to Zurich on the 24th, but presumably, only with the express warning that now he could not undertake anything more than a demonstration. We cannot say the Russian general was wrong in this.

We are loath to interrupt the apparent coherence of this plan and its associated rationale with an observation that would disrupt it completely and that, to our amazement, seems not to have occurred to anyone in Suvorov's headquarters and that none of the historians has made either: namely, that under the conditions at the time, there was no road for Suvorov and his 24,000 men leading from the St. Gotthard to Schwyz, since the Gotthard road ends at Altorf and the route to Schwyz can only be completed by water across Lake Lucerne or else on a couple of shepherds' and hunters' tracks through the Schächen and Muota valleys. Now, they could not possibly have imagined that the enemy would leave a small fleet at Flüelen in readiness to carry the Russian army; indeed, it was far more likely that not a single vessel would be found there, and the gentlemen in Asti could have had equally little expectation of the Russian army being able to use the track that it actually took later in desperation.[25] It seems to us that this observation should have cut short any discussion of the possibility and usefulness of marching over the St. Gotthard as absolutely as Lake Lucerne cuts the road. The fact that this did not happen,

25. This is an interesting observation, as Clausewitz previously criticized the French outside of Verona for hesitating to cross difficult terrain, even though Napoleon had crossed the same terrain in 1796 and shown that it could be done. See volume 1, chapter 2, section 20.

that Suvorov's general staff first had to stick its nose into Lake Zurich[26] before such an observation occurred to it, and that none of the historians mentions this factor either until the moment the story has led to Lake Zurich, thereby making the same mistake to some degree, has caused us more astonishment than any other point in the history of warfare. If anyone swears it was just a moment of absentmindedness, then we are put in mind of Voltaire, who, when a member of parliament offered the excuse for condemning Damiens, who was known to be insane, that "*the best of horses may stumble once*," replied, "*yes, but not a whole stableful of horses at the same time.*"[27]

Since very few points of this plan were actually carried out, we wish to postpone the commentary it requires and the observations it gives rise to until the end of this chapter.

Having presented Suvorov's intentions and the missions given to the generals in Switzerland through these general dispositions, as well as the conditions under which they were operating, we now wish to turn to the events themselves. We start with those on the allied right wing because, although Suvorov's breakthrough begins a day earlier, it takes much longer and can only be properly understood if these other events are already known.

71 MASSÉNA'S PLAN OF ATTACK

As we saw in section 64 [volume 2, chapter 6], General Masséna was to some extent prepared for an offensive, since he had already tried to launch one before the archduke marched away. Because of chance circumstances, he had not managed to do so. One might therefore suppose that the French commander would just wait until the archduke and his army were far enough away and then carry out the intended attack, but that did not happen. It is said that Masséna busied himself with the preparations for it and set 26 September as the day for its execution, since he could not be ready any sooner. But when he learned later that Suvorov was already on the march to the St. Gotthard and

26. Clausewitz has this as Lake Zurich, but we believe it should be Lake Lucerne, as it is on the route from the St. Gotthard Pass.

27. Robert-François Damiens was a French peasant brutally tortured and executed for attempting to murder Louis XV. "Chateau de Versailles," http://en.chateauversailles.fr/discover/history/key-dates/assassination-attempt-king-louis-xv-damiens-1757.

that the Bavarians and émigrés might also arrive toward the end of the month, he worried that his attack might be too late, but he could only bring it forward one day and fix it for 25 September. This date seems to have been set on 20 September, as was the plan for the attack.

When we consider that Suvorov feasibly could have set off from Asti a few days earlier, that Masséna cannot have had very precise information about this, and that, without the halt Suvorov made at the foot of the Alps, he reasonably could have beaten Lecourbe on 25 September and linked up with Hotze, then we can well see that by delaying his operation so long, Masséna was sticking his hand in a lucky dip and that important obstacles must have been present if we are not to regard his delay as a mistake. Nonetheless, it seems that these obstacles consisted only of unfinished preparations for building the bridges. Despite the laborious reports of the bridge construction that we have in Dedon's work,[28] we find it difficult to explain the pause this caused, since Dedon explicitly says that as soon as the attempt at crossing on 31 August failed, they began busily preparing for another. Indeed, with the main army, everything was actually ready by the 20th, but Soult's division was not; perhaps it was there that the time was wasted.

Masséna's plan was to attack General Korsakov with his main body, while Soult's division and Molitor's brigade of Lecourbe's division attacked the Austrians in the Linth valley. The former was to be the main attack and lead to the major decisive battle, while the latter was more to pin the Austrian forces and prevent them from rushing to Korsakov's aid. Both attacks were to happen on the same day.

The troops Masséna wanted to use against Korsakov were the four divisions under Mortier, Lorges, Ménard, and Klein, which were 37,000 strong altogether. Masséna had to assume that Korsakov had about 30,000 since, at the time, the French knew nothing of him recently detaching 5,000 men to Hotze.

Soult and Molitor combined had 13,000 men, and Masséna must have expected that the Austrian troops on the Linth would be 15,000–20,000 strong, or at least that they could bring that many into action there gradually, even if Masséna had heard or assumed that they had moved a significant detachment to the Anterior Rhine valley to facilitate Suvorov's breakthrough. Masséna therefore absolutely could not count on any numerical superiority for his right wing, though for its intended purpose, that did not seem necessary anyway.

28. Dedon, *Relation du Passage de la Limmat.*

If General Korsakov and his 30,000 men had actually been behind the Limmat, then the French 7,000-man advantage would not have been so great that they could have been considered very likely to succeed. The position on the right bank of the Limmat is perhaps no weaker than that on the left, and the archduke did not dare crossing against Masséna with much greater superiority. Thus, if we may regard the two sides' armies as being quite equal in terms of their military virtues, that is, their skill and maneuverability, the outcome of a crossing must seem very doubtful. But of course, we must concede that the Russians and their commander may not have been entirely suited to such a role and that, against them, Masséna could have attempted a crossing with some likelihood of success, even if they had stayed behind the river, as the archduke did. But the Russian commander had come halfway toward solving the French commander's problem for him, in that he deployed his main body in front of Zurich and left only about 8,000 men behind the river line. Thereby the success of the operation became not just much more likely but almost inevitable, for it is clear that 8,000 men were not capable of holding the river line. As for the suggestion that Korsakov could have gone on the offensive with his main body, beaten the French corps left facing him, and thus compelled the other corps that had crossed the river to either retreat soon or be cut off by him: to that we may reply that despite their crossing, the French could have left a significant corps facing General Korsakov that was no weaker than he and in very strong terrain; thus there was no reason why this corps should be beaten by him.

General Korsakov indisputably had in mind the general idea that the French would have to divide their force while crossing and that it would then be feasible to beat them while they were separated by the river and his force was united. But he forgot that he would also have to divide his force, that the French were stronger, and that the terrain on the left bank of the Limmat made attacking very difficult.

But there is yet another very important point to consider.

Any time an attack is supposed to be responded to with an attack at the opposite point—and thus with the idea that if both succeed, a change of front will arise—*the relationship of the lines of retreat* comes into question, and only he who has the advantage in that respect can outdo his opponent, unless victory is largely ensured by other factors. If Korsakov really had beaten the French left wing and advanced to the bridge, he would have succeeded only in cutting off the corps that had crossed from retreating back the same way it had come; indeed, the latter would have been able to find a crossing at another place further downriver, since the right bank would have been vacated by the Russians and the French could easily arrange a second bridge for themselves. However, on the other hand, if the French left wing had advanced to Zurich after its own victory, it would have entirely cut off the Russian main body's retreat, that is, the Russians could not have regained it by falling back but would have had to fight their way out. But how difficult it would have been to break out from Zurich along the road to Schafhausen if the enemy held the heights surrounding Zurich on that side! A glance at the map shows it, and the history of 25 September proves it.

We are therefore convinced that the situation was entirely unsuitable for responding by attacking and that, consequently, it seems that deploying the main body in front of Zurich was an immense error.

This is so even if we do not consider the 5,000 men who were detached and if we imagine that Korsakov could advance to the attack with 16,000–18,000 men; but if we then have to deduct these 5,000 as well and leave him with just 11,000–13,000, it emerges that we are not overstating it if we regard the success of the French attack as inevitable simply because of General Korsakov's deployment.

Having examined in detail the circumstances in which the second battle of Zurich developed, let us now describe the battle itself.

72 THE SECOND BATTLE OF ZURICH[29]

Masséna ordered Lorges's division and half of Ménard's, 15,000 men altogether, to cross the Limmat near Dietikon, 7 miles from Zurich, to beat any Russian troops opposing them on the right bank of the Limmat and advance to outside Zurich. The other half of Ménard's division was to demonstrate in the area of Bruck and build a flying bridge there.[30] Klein's and Mortier's divisions, 18,000

29. See also Jomini's and the archduke's accounts of the battle. Jomini, 12:244–263; Karl, 2:181–212.

30. "A FLYING BRIDGE is formed by suspending a floating body in a river, so as to receive the action of the stream obliquely; from which a force is derived to move the vessel across the river. . . . These are particularly useful in all enterprizes of a bold, desultory character; and are essential in attempting to pass a river in face of an enemy,

strong, were to be used against Korsakov's main body in front of Zurich either to repel it if it went over to the attack or to attack it themselves.

Masséna chose Dietikon for the following reasons:

1. The Limmat forms a convex bend there, which is always favorable for a crossing for well-known tactical reasons.
2. Because of the convex bend, the foot of the mountain range is close to the river there, which makes a covered approach easier for the force that is crossing, something that is very important at a river that is just 150 paces wide.
3. The carriage road from Ober- and Nieder-Urdorf comes out of the mountains right at that point.
4. The river was less rapid there and its bed good for anchoring the pontoons.
5. At the point where the bridge itself was to be built, the left bank was very high, so it strongly dominated the right, which was quite flat.

But precisely because of these distinct advantages at Dietikon, the Russians had posted General Markov there with three battalions, or about 1,600–1,800 men, who were only a couple of thousand paces from the crossing point and had their outposts at the river itself. This very major disadvantage was further increased by the fact that in the bend formed by the Limmat, about 800 paces from the crossing point, there was a height detached from the high mountain ridge, covered with forest and (if we may trust Archduke Charles's map)[31] with a short but steep slope facing the river. Thus, 800 paces from the bridge there was a very strong position that would have to be overcome. Finally, the right bank at the actual crossing point is forested, which would have been an

either by stratagem, or by a combination of force with it." This type of bridge is a little unusual, but it is extremely useful for crossing a river where there is no bridge and the crossing might be opposed. An anchor is placed in the river, to which a narrow barge is tied. The flow of the river provides the energy to move the barge across the river in a manner similar to a pendulum. See Major-General Sir Howard Douglas, *An Essay on the Principles and Construction of Military Bridges, and the Passage of Rivers in Military Operations* (London: T. Egerton, 1816), 94–102, https://books.google.com.

31. Karl, 3:chart VIII. See also https://maps.hungaricana.hu/en/HTITerkeptar/25641/view/?pg=8&bbox=441%2C-6980%2C10724%2C-1216.

advantage for those crossing if the enemy was not already in occupation but in these circumstances must be counted a disadvantage, since the skirmishers posted in it could not so easily be driven off by artillery fire.

If General Masséna chose this place despite its disadvantages very much canceling out its advantages, this is sure evidence that there were very few usable crossing points within a few miles of Zurich, and Masséna could not cross the Limmat more than about 10 miles downstream without his operation turning into something quite different. We can see this just by looking at the archduke's map, even if such things virtually cannot be judged from the usual maps.

The French had fairly plentiful and well-prepared crossing equipment, since they had been working on it for three weeks. They had collected a depot of barges of various kinds at Bruck [Brugg]; the largest of these were capable of carrying 2,000 men each, but since they were too big to be carried on wagons, they were allocated to the feint attack on the Aare and to the flying bridge to be built there later. As for smaller vessels that could be transported by wagon, they had twelve there from Lake Zurich and ten small wooden pontoons that had belonged to Zurich's pontoniers; to these they added another fifteen boats from the other Swiss lakes, so they had thirty-seven such boats dedicated to carrying the troops across, which could take 900 men at a time. The bridge itself was to be built on sixteen pontoons that, until then, had served as a bridge across the Reuss at Rottenschwil behind the Albis.

These transport and bridging craft had to be taken to Dietikon by land, which was certainly a major problem. The pontoon bridge from Rottenschwil could be taken downriver at least as far as Bremgarten by water, but on the other hand, it seems not to have been possible to bring the thirty-seven boats from Brugg up the Reuss to Bremgarten; instead, they were carried there overland, albeit on a fairly good road. Transporting these fifty-three pontoons and boats from Bremgarten to Dietikon, 5 miles across a high mountain ridge on a poor path through a ravine, was an even more difficult task because the French lacked suitable wagons. In the circumstances, naturally there was no question of getting this done in a single night so as to reach the river unnoticed, as always happens at river crossings normally. It was therefore a matter of transporting them over the mountains a few at a time and in a way that was not too obvious to the enemy. This was done by first taking the wagons along the road as far as they could without being observed by the enemy, and then by night from there to Dietikon, where the boats were unloaded and hidden behind hedges. Here most of them had to be repaired, since they had usually been damaged on the way. After the thirty-seven craft allocated for ferrying across had been made ready at Dietikon like this, in the evening of 23 September—twenty-four hours before the designated time for the crossing—the bridge at Rottenschwil, which had been left standing for as long as possible so as not to arouse any suspicion, was dismantled. In those twenty-four hours it was brought on its own wagon train through Bremgarten to Dietikon, where it arrived in the evening and halted. In the last few days of these preparations, which lasted several weeks, they made some ostensible preparations at Brugg to attract the enemy's attention thither.

Now the crossing equipment was about 1,500 paces from the point where the ferrying across and the bridge construction were supposed to happen. Since the Limmat is only 110–120 paces across and the far bank was held by enemy infantry, even bringing up the equipment to the bank could not be done in the usual way using horses, because against so many helpless vehicles having to ride up, unload, and turn around in a tight space, effective enemy fire would soon have thrown them into the greatest disorder. Brigadier Dedon therefore proposed that the boats and equipment for ferrying troops across should be carried to their designated points by 1,000 bearers from among the infantry, while the pontoons should wait on their trailers at Dietikon until the advance guard had established a foothold on the other side. This measure was so completely successful that all the craft were arranged on the bank with the pontoniers behind them without the Russians becoming aware of it.

With this the arrangements were finished and the bridge construction prepared so completely as very rarely happens; indeed, this was virtually essential if the crossing was to be forced against three enemy battalions.

General Markov had set up his camp behind the forest on the slope of the foot of the mountain running toward the river. It was therefore a few thousand paces from the river's furthest point. The copse along the riverbank itself was occupied by infantry who must, however, be regarded as mere outposts and therefore be thought of as very weak. Since according to Dedon's account the whole river was thick with sentries, we can well imagine that General Markov must have had to provide other detachments as well, and that his three battalions would have been left with not many more than 1,500 men. He had seven guns with him.

From these dispositions it follows that the French had to expect to be attacked by 1,500 men about half an hour after the moment they embarked their advance guard, or, in the event Markov remained on the defensive, that they would have to fight his force in a fairly strong position, though apparently it had not been strengthened with any man-made defenses.

During the night General Masséna had concentrated the designated crossing force (Lorges's division and Quétard's brigade of Ménard's division, 15,000 men altogether) behind the crossing point, where he was in person. Lorges's divisional artillery was deployed on the banks in such a way that it surrounded the area enclosed by the river bend, whose chord was about 4,000 paces across, and commanded it with its crossfire.

At 4:15 a.m., with the first glimmer of dawn, the signal was given to launch the boats into the water, which was done quickly but immediately attracted the fire of the enemy sentries. The advance guard commanded by General Gazan embarked. While it was being ferried across, the French artillery opened up the most lively fire on the enemy bank, whereby the enemy infantry there seemed to be driven off. One-third of the first wave went to the Russian-held island below the bridging point, while the other two-thirds, 600 strong, ferried straight across to the opposite bank, which they reached three minutes later. At the first noise, the Russian battery had directed its fire against the area of the crossing but had so little effect that not one of the craft was damaged and not a single man drowned.

The first wave of French met no resistance on the bank itself and advanced with drums beating, whereupon the French fire from the left bank ceased and the ferrying across of the next wave was expedited. When the first couple of waves were across, they felt sufficiently sure of success to begin building the bridge. The pontoon train that had been held at Dietikon quickly trotted up, and bridge construction began at 5:00 a.m.

The Russians had withdrawn from the bank into the pine forest, and Markov had taken position there with his three battalions. The French advance guard advanced against him, and a fierce musketry and artillery duel arose.

During this initially indecisive action, the French shipped ever more troops across. Since they needed about ten minutes for each round-trip, including embarking and landing, after an hour they had got 6,000 men across. These were enough to outflank General Markov; to defeat him despite his stubborn resistance, by the end of which he had formed square; and to capture his artillery as well as, apparently, the majority of his infantry. He himself was wounded and taken prisoner.

After an hour and a half, at 6:30 a.m., the bridge was complete, by which time 8,000 men had already got to the right bank by ferry alone. Now the other 7,000 men followed, and toward 9:00 a.m. the entire corps was in battle order at Kloster Fahr on the right bank. General Masséna, who had been present during the crossing, handed over command of this corps to his chief of general staff, General Oudinot, while he himself hastened to Altstetten and the Sihlfeld. While 15,000 men crossed at Dietikon between 5:00 and 9:00 a.m. and wiped out General Markov's corps in this way, General Ménard with the other brigade of his division had demonstrated as though to cross above and below the confluence of the Limmat and the Aare, thereby deceiving General Durassov into marching his main body to Freudenau [Burgruine Freudenau, opposite Stilli], in the area of these demonstrations. General Ménard himself managed to get a small group across the Limmat above the confluence, secure the right bank, and bring up from the Aare a flying bridge that had already been prepared there and have it set up at Vogelsang, by means of which his troops could cross the river the following day. Thus General Durassov and his 6,000 men were not only prevented from coming to the aid of General Markov, who was in any case two or three hours' march away, but also neutralized for the whole of the 25th, as we shall see from the subsequent course of his maneuvers.

Around 7:00 a.m., a few hours after the crossing at Dietikon and the demonstration near Brugg began, Mortier attacked the Russian main body in front of the Sihl.

With his main body, which we estimated above at 13,000 men, Korsakov had taken position in front of the Sihl so that the suburb of St. Jacob that lies along it was just behind him; but at the same time, he had sent a corps of about 5,000 men under Prince Gorchakov from there to occupy the area of Wollishofen between the Sihl and Lake Zurich. The reasons for pushing his left flank 3,000 paces beyond his main position must have lain either in the nature of the terrain or in his effort to secure a suitably broad area for his intended offensive.

Mortier had his right-wing brigade under General Drouet cross the Sihl to attack the Russians at Wollishofen, while the left-wing brigade advanced to attack Wiedikon.

General Drouet threw the Russian outposts out of Wollishofen but was then himself attacked by Prince Gorchakov with his whole force, driven back across the Sihl, and pursued as far as the Ütli.

The brigade advancing against Wiedikon was likewise met by superior forces, so that Mortier had trouble hanging on enough not to be completely driven from the field.

Just after the action at Kloster Fahr began, Korsakov had betaken himself to the area of Höngg, but he thought this crossing was merely a demonstration. In this, he was probably led astray by two things: first, the action starting just then at Wollishofen, which probably sounded lively at that time; and then the guns falling silent at Kloster Fahr at 6:00 a.m. after General Markov was defeated and captured. With a hastiness most unworthy of an experienced general, he deployed an insignificant detachment at Höngg and left it at that, hurrying back to the Sihlfeld, where he believed the main attack to be.

Thus, if we picture the situation at 10:00 on the morning of the 25th, we find Mortier's division in the process of giving way; Gorchakov scaling the Ütli in supposed victory; Klein's division behind Altstetten, where Masséna has just joined it; Oudinot at Kloster Fahr about to advance; and Durassov arrived at Freudenau. Let us pick up the thread again at Kloster Fahr.

The French advance diverged along four radii of a semicircle: Oudinot with the main body comprising Gazan's brigade and part of Bontemps's, about 8,000 strong, moved up the Limmat to Höngg to attack and defeat whatever troops Korsakov might send against him from Zurich; General Bontemps with the rest of his brigade and part of Quétard's, about 4,000 strong, moved in two columns to Regensdorf and Dällikon with the mission of preventing Generals Durassov and Korsakov from linking up; two battalions of Quétard's brigade, about 1,500 men, moved down the Limmat to Oetwil, likewise to bar against Durassov pushing through; and finally, yet another part of Quétard's brigade stayed in reserve by the bridge.

Since these detachments did not encounter any substantial bodies of enemy troops, they reached their designated places without further incident; those few troops that Oudinot found on the mountain near Höngg were soon driven off, and he gained the Wipkingerberg without any serious fighting.

While the left wing was engaged in these maneuvers, Masséna had committed part of Klein's division to support Mortier's left wing and part to advance against the right wing of the Russian main body. The latter, weakened still more by its ill-timed offensive against the Ütli and not in any state for stubborn resistance, found itself obliged to retreat behind the Sihl, and Korsakov had to recall Prince Gorchakov back to him. With this, the actual fighting on the left bank of the Limmat seems to have ended; both sides were content to bombard each other here while they moved some of their troops to the opposite wing. Let us then also betake ourselves to that wing.

Oudinot had hastily had some earthworks thrown up on the Wipkingerberg,[32] occupied them with some of his troops, and toward 3:00 p.m. advanced with the rest against the Zürichberg, at the same time dividing his force again by sending General Gazan to Schwamendingen on the road to Winterthur, probably to hold off any reinforcements that might come from the reserve the Russians had in that area earlier.

After the Russians retreated across the Sihl, Masséna had sent part of the reserve division through Kloster Fahr to reinforce Oudinot.

Korsakov had finally begun to sense his huge mistake and sent some troops from the main body through Zurich to the Zürichberg; but moving through the city along narrow streets packed with artillery, wounded, wagons, and baggage trains of every kind was so difficult that the units emerged on the other side like drops of water through a filter, so not enough men could get through to hold the Zürichberg against Oudinot. Thus the French gained possession of the Zürichberg as well, and with it the heights tightly encircling the city on its northeastern side,[33] from which they pushed down to the Schlössli and the village of Fluntern.

At this time, getting on to 6:00 in the evening, Korsakov seems to have withdrawn all his troops from the position on the Sihl to Zurich and been busy making enough space for himself on the right bank again, with the idea of either beating the French corps or at least opening a line of retreat. This was made much easier for him during the evening, in that four battalions of the Russian troops sent off to Hotze returned, and Bachmann's Swiss Legion, which Hotze had sent to support him, likewise arrived. This body of troops, which we may assume to be around 4,000–5,000 men, was immediately committed to retake the Zürichberg. The French seem not to have seriously defended this point; Masséna himself says in his report that he did not risk occupying it in force. It seems that no heavy blow was struck there, but even if the French retreat was voluntary, it was certainly the arrival of these 4,000–5,000 men that caused it. If we consider that after Oudinot sent Gazan off to

32. This was typically done to secure a location to provide a safe base of operations for other ventures. For an explanation of the reasons for using field fortifications, see Murray, *Rocky Road to the Great War*, 1–44.

33. Clausewitz has this as the northwestern, but it should be northeastern.

Schwamendingen, he himself was just 5,000–6,000 strong, that the couple of thousand men Masséna sent from the reserve to reinforce him had perhaps not yet arrived, and that he was offering his naked left flank to the arriving Russians, we find the withdrawal of his left wing very understandable.

Basically, no serious fighting had happened anywhere on the right bank of the Limmat since the action at Kloster Fahr because the French had not run into any sufficiently strong enemy and because, by the time the troops coming from the Linth arrived, the French had already weakened themselves so much by continually splitting up that they spontaneously withdrew. Even so, the skirmish fire went on until late in the night, as always happens in the mountains, so long as neither side marches away entirely. Consequently, this skirmishing on one side of the Limmat and the cannonade on the other until late into the night made this day's battle seem like one of the bloodiest and most incessant in history, which, however, it was not.

None of the reports gives details of either side's positions during the night; we learn only that General Gazan maintained his position in Schwamendingen on the road from Winterthur, presumably because no Russians came down it. We must therefore think of the French being on a line from Schwamendingen to Wipkingen, and it remains uncertain whether they held the Geissberg.

Late in the evening, probably thinking the Russians were in retreat and wanting to either speed that up or discover more details about it, Masséna sent an envoy to Zurich to demand the fortress's surrender. Naturally, the Russians sent no reply and detained the negotiator.

During the night, General Durassov arrived at Zurich. After realizing his error, he had left one battalion and a few cavalry around Freudenau to observe General Ménard's movements and had marched over the range of hills that accompanies the right bank of the Limmat toward Zurich. When he reached the area of Adlikon, he ran into General Bontemps, who had apparently united his two columns. Durassov, who probably would have been roughly as strong as the French general, did not think it advisable to open the road to Korsakov here by force but preferred to make a detour, probably via Seebach and Dübendorf, to join Korsakov, which, as we have said, he managed to do that night.

Another two of the Russian battalions that had been detached to Hotze also rejoined Korsakov during the night.

On the other side, General Bontemps, who probably guessed where General Durassov was marching, moved to General Oudinot and stationed himself on Lorges's left wing.

Thus, on the morning of the 26th we find the French on both sides of the Limmat, separated by Zurich, and divided so that there were roughly the same numbers on each side. Oudinot had crossed with 15,000 men; he had received a reinforcement from the reserve—let us take that to be 3,000 men—and, on the other hand, we must deduct 4,000 men for detachments at the bridge and on the various roads that had to be observed, as well as his losses on the 25th, which leaves 14,000 who found themselves in the position between Schwamendingen and Wipkingen. On the left bank of the Limmat, Mortier and Klein had started with 18,000 men; deduct the 3,000 who joined Oudinot and 1,000 for those lost in action, and that likewise leaves 14,000 men outside the fortifications of Zurich. We cannot say with total certainty which part of his army Masséna himself was with, since it is not explicitly stated in his report nor in any account. Most probably he was on the left bank of the Limmat for the whole of the 25th but on the right bank on the 26th.

It is more difficult for us to say anything definite about the strength and distribution of the Russians with quite as much likelihood. Basically, Korsakov had concentrated pretty much his whole corps, for which, at this point in time, we have assumed a bayonet strength of 28,000. We know of no detachments other than that which General Durassov left on the Aare and three battalions under General Titov that were still with Hotze; if we take those two combined to be 3,000 men, allow for 2,000 at the Rhine bridges, add 3,000 Cossacks, which would be of no account on such a day, and 3,000 men for the losses of the 25th, that comes to 11,000 men. After subtracting these from 28,000, that leaves the Russian force at 17,000 men, along with a couple of thousand Swiss, so that we can probably consider the combat force available to Korsakov to be 20,000 men.

As for how they were distributed, we can only infer this to some degree based on what the archduke says: on the morning of the 26th Korsakov had sixteen battalions at hand. By that, the archduke undoubtedly means those troops facing General Oudinot outside Zurich.[34] If we take these sixteen battalions to be 8,000 men, plus the cavalry, almost all of which must have been here, at just 5,000 men, then for the corps on the north side of Zurich

34. **Clausewitz** notes: "We regard General Oudinot as the commander on the right bank of the Limmat, as per Jomini, and because we do not know exactly where Masséna was." Jomini, 12:253–255.

we get 13,000 men, so there still would have been about 6,000–7,000 men in Zurich itself.

Korsakov had reservations about decisively beginning his retreat on the morning of the 26th, justifiably so, in our view. Suvorov had hoped to enter Schwyz on the 26th. Hotze, instead of being in Einsiedeln on this day, had been beaten on the 25th; he himself had fallen, and his corps was in full retreat, which must have been known to Korsakov by early on the 26th. His commander in chief, Suvorov, was therefore put in an awkward situation, which would have been made much worse if Korsakov either began his retreat to the Rhine without further delay or just sat idle on the 26th, because then Masséna could turn against Suvorov with most of his force; the latter, abandoned by everyone else and put in the most dangerous situation against a superior force, would have held General Korsakov highly responsible for doing nothing at all on the 26th. Korsakov therefore thought he should attack the enemy on the right bank of the Limmat, hoping to push them back and thereby hold his position in and around Zurich, at least until Suvorov could get through.

It was with this in mind that General Korsakov attacked the French on the right bank of the Limmat at daybreak on the 26th. We know nothing of the dispositions for this action, beyond the fact that the Russians were in two lines and that the attack had both its main effort and its main success on their right wing. It seems that they actually drove the French back somewhat further there and thereby opened the road to Winterthur and Eglisau. This success was assisted by the fact that Oudinot, probably as instructed by Masséna, attached particular value to advancing toward Zurich with his right wing to be able to attack the fortress and thereby facilitate its storming from the Sihlfeld side, since Masséna felt his divided deployment growing more dangerous with every passing moment and wanted to gain possession of Zurich as soon as possible.

But the Russians could not achieve a decisive success, one that could promise victory over Oudinot's corps. On the contrary, toward midday the balance shifted against them; probably during the course of the action Korsakov had taken some troops out of Zurich to reinforce himself and was now worried about keeping possession of the fortress. Since his line of retreat was an extension of his front, his experienced eye recognized the full danger of his situation, and he decided to begin his retreat before any major breach of his position made that impossible. He therefore apparently gave the order to retreat around midday. According to Jomini, who, however, does not absolutely vouch for it, he placed the infantry at the head of the columns, then the cavalry, followed finally by the baggage. Meanwhile, he had the artillery move out to the side in order to protect the flank march that this retreat entailed.[35]

To gain time for Zurich, an offer was made to General Masséna that the city would be vacated that evening, provided it was not attacked before then, which the French commander naturally rejected.

Without attaching too much importance to the arrangements made for the retreat, because ultimately we do not know them for certain and also because even the best arrangements would not have proved very successful, we wish only to describe the result and try to explain it.

As soon as the French saw that Korsakov had begun his retreat, they renewed their attack with all their forces. The consequence was that while they could not entirely cut the line of retreat along the road to Eglisau, they did break through the column in several places, spreading much disorder and making it impossible for any wheeled transport to get away, so that all the artillery and baggage were lost and 100 guns fell into French hands.

It is not hard to explain this outcome. A flank march that has to be carried out under the eyes of the enemy, indeed, under enemy fire, and that has to wriggle its bloody way out of the crisis of a battle is certainly one of the most difficult of tactical problems, and it cannot conceivably have a happy result if the battle is already half lost. If we add to this unsuitable dispositions and ponderous troops, it is inevitable that even in the best case the army marching away will come out of it quite ravaged. After Korsakov neglected to send away his baggage train early on the 25th, it was impossible for it to get away, and the fact that it was taking up the road was probably part of the reason the artillery could not escape. The loss of all the artillery also proves that the march was very poorly conducted. All the artillery seems to have been used to cover the march against the enemy for as long as possible. Even if this did facilitate the escape of the infantry and cavalry, it is questionable whether this should be condoned. In our modern battles, the loss of guns is equivalent to the loss of standards in earlier times; it is the true measure of the scale of a victory and the index of its impact on morale. An army that loses all its artillery has let the banner of its honor fall soiled and trampled on the path of its rout.[36]

Korsakov retreated partly on the road through Bülach to Eglisau and partly

35. Jomini, 12:255–257.

36. It also meant loss of the arm that had become one of the key combat enablers.

along the road from Winterthur to Schaffhausen. We do not know whether this was due to orders or to disorder, as perhaps many who could no longer get through along the former road threw themselves onto the latter one.

While this was going on with the army, in Zurich there were only weak posts at the gates and disorderly groups of train personnel, baggage escorts, etc., 500–600 men in all. When the French on the left bank noticed that the Russians were withdrawing from Zurich, at 1:00 p.m. they pressed into the city from its shortest side,[37] opening the gates with cannon fire, although the city mob must have helped them with this; now a fight of sorts began in the city, which ended with the Russians being taken prisoner or massacred.

Apart from his entire artillery of 100 guns and his entire baggage train, including a considerable war chest, Korsakov's losses came to 8,000 men killed, wounded, or taken prisoner, so that he got away with just 10,000 Russians.

Since Masséna could achieve nothing further against Korsakov, he left just Lorges's and Ménard's divisions and the cavalry reserve facing him, or about 20,000 men under Oudinot's overall command. He himself turned against Suvorov with Mortier and Klein.

73 REFLECTIONS

Although we are deferring our reflections on the commanders' strategic actions in this chapter to the end, we still need to give an evaluation of the battle of Zurich before the vividness of its impression is lost. We will start from the standpoint of the morning of the 25th and not cast our gaze over how the situation at that time had arisen until our concluding remarks.

Let us first consider the river crossing.

The unanimous view of the French preparations for the crossing is that they were excellent and, likewise, that their measures for its execution were suitable. Its success is indeed sufficient proof of this.[38] We wish to remark on just a few factors in particular:

37. It is not entirely clear what Clausewitz means here, but given the location, he is presumably referring to the short stretch of fortifications facing southwest, between the Sihl and Lake Zurich. This is more accessible than the stretch protected by the Sihl.

38. See *On War*, book 6, chaps. 18–19, for the defense of rivers and book 7, chap. 8, for crossing them.

1. The essential difference between this exemplary crossing and the archduke's total failure obviously lies in the fact that here 8,000 men were transported to the enemy bank *by ferry alone* before and during the bridge construction, while the archduke took no such action at all.
2. Although the Limmat was only about 120 paces wide and probably did not need all sixteen pontoons that had bridged the Reuss, it still took one and a half hours to build it. From this, we can see that one must beware of assuming that the time it takes in a peacetime exercise, which in such cases could be counted in minutes, would be the time required in war. We still regard one and a half hours as a very short time for its completion.
3. Manhandling the barges to the river, over which Dedon took so much trouble, is almost inevitable at such small rivers when the enemy actually occupies the bank.
4. It was certainly decisive good fortune that the preparations with which the French busied themselves for three weeks did not betray their intention to the Russians, who easily could have rendered it impossible to carry out.[39]

Concerning the manner in which General Markov should have acted with his three battalions to prevent the crossing, this could only have consisted of

39. This relates to Clausewitz's views on boldness, surprise, and cunning (*On War*, book 3, chaps. 6, 9, and 10, respectively). Clausewitz values boldness, as he believes that "timidity will do a thousand times more damage in war than audacity." The point he is making is that the mental state of the commander is often negatively affected by the weight of command the further up the ranks one goes. Thus, "boldness grows *less common in the higher ranks.*" He goes on to argue that "boldness governed by superior intellect is the mark of a hero. This kind of boldness does not consist in defying the natural order of things and in crudely offending the laws of probability; it is rather a matter of energetically supporting that higher form of analysis by which genius arrives at a decision: rapid, only partly conscious weighing of the possibilities" (*On War*, 191–192). One can see why he was so consistently critical of the archduke's caution. In addition, regarding surprise and cunning he makes the point that achieving surprise at the tactical level is much simpler than achieving it at the strategic level. At the higher levels, preparations for a cunning surprise may take months and require great resources; as such, they are more vulnerable to exposure and friction, thus making surprise less likely, despite the immense effort (*On War*, 198–201). Hence his comment regarding "decisive good fortune." This is the role of chance, and it closely ties in with his concept of the trinity.

either rapidly attacking the first troops to cross, blasting them into the water or capturing them to prevent the next wave from landing, or else taking a defensive position so close that the enemy could not get out of the semicircle formed by the river, thus gaining time to bring up more troops.

General Markov was 1,500–2,000 paces from the bank; if he had wanted to position himself right on the bank, he would have had to divide his troops, and since the area he would have had to occupy was 6,000 paces across, each battalion would have been about 2,000 paces away from the next, so not much would have been gained for the speed of their initial arrival, and much would have been lost by their dispersion. It would have taken fifteen to twenty minutes to cover those 1,500–2,000 paces, and if we also allow ten minutes for communication, standing to, etc., then half an hour was bound to pass. In that time, as we have seen, the French could have ferried a couple of thousand men across; since these would have been fighting for their lives, it would not have been easy to overwhelm them and prevent the later arrivals from landing. In a word, as things stood, an attack by General Markov probably would have been repelled, and it would not have impeded the bridge construction.

The terrain certainly seemed to offer favorable conditions for organizing and defending a position within the river bend. But when we consider that the chord from Kloster Fahr to the opposite curve of the river is 4,000 paces long, it is clear that a position for three battalions could consist only of occupying a couple of stout redoubts connected by an abatis. Naturally, these redoubts could not prevent the crossing or the bridge construction, but they would have to be taken before the French could advance out of the bend. It was not too much to expect that, in this way, the Russians could have held on for a few hours, but of course, the general arrangements would have required that, within these few hours, a substantial Russian corps could arrive; otherwise, the redoubts would have been lost, along with the troops in them.[40] From this, we see that whichever type of resistance the Russians chose, it was never going to give rise to any very favorable result, and that is due to their misguided mission. Only major rivers can be defended on their banks, and only under certain favorable conditions, never ones that are just 120 paces wide. If these are to be defended, it can happen only if the general arrangements are set up

40. The use of redoubts to defend a key location and to enhance the fighting power of the troops defending them is a key idea in relation to the use of field fortifications. Murray, *Rocky Road to the Great War*, 25–44.

not, as here, to prevent the crossing itself but *to attack the corps that has crossed soon after its crossing and in an advantageous situation.* Since the Russians had far too few troops behind the Limmat and the Aare, such a combination could hardly be expected. Nonetheless, the overall result would have turned out better if Generals Markov and Durassov had stationed themselves on the slope of the heights instead of at the river and had they not been tasked with resisting at the river; then they would not have been separated from each other, Markov would not have been entirely wiped out, and even assuming they would have combined and moved against Oudinot only after four or five hours, they still would have significantly delayed and impeded his advance against Zurich, gaining time for Korsakov to make a suitable decision.

Since no entrenched position had been prepared for General Markov and he probably did not feel justified in quitting the area without a fight, and since he could not have anticipated how quickly the French would be ferried across, it seems to us that *his most natural decision* would have been to pounce on the arriving enemy with his three battalions and then retreat if he could not defeat them. To opt to fight immediately with no entrenchments in an area that was three times too large for the size of his force, letting himself be outflanked and having every line of retreat cut off, was indisputably the worst thing he could have done.

Let us turn now from this individual episode to the broad outlines of the actual battle, starting with the attacker's intentions and plan.

Masséna intended to defeat the allies in Switzerland before Suvorov could arrive; the main blow was to fall on Korsakov. The simplest way to attain this aim unarguably would have been to attack Korsakov's main body in front of Zurich. Basically, its position there was anything but advantageous, as its center and right wing sat on a flat plain. Since Masséna could employ more than 30,000 men against these 12,000, it is beyond question that he would have driven them back into Zurich and that the more stubbornly they fought to avert this, the heavier their losses would have been. But a battle in which there can really be no pursuit[41] hardly allows a victory, and Masséna wanted a victory. This compelled him to break through the enemy position behind the Limmat by crossing with half his army, while the other half stayed to observe the enemy's main body on the Sihlfeld. This is entirely understandable. The

41. As discussed previously, pursuit is one of the main means of destroying an army and inflicting a decisive result. See *On War*, book 4, chaps. 11–12, in particular.

corps that crossed could hope to win a victory over part of the enemy force, since the French certainly thought the Russians behind the Limmat were stronger than they actually were; this initial advantage could then serve as good preparation for the battle, as directing the crossing force against Korsakov's line of retreat would surely force him to abandon his position on the Sihlfeld to confront his opponent on the right bank of the Limmat. This was what the French commander needed: then he would find his adversary no longer protected by a fortress but out in the open field, and if he just applied the whole of his force there, he could exploit his numerical superiority to obtain his victory.

But this series of suppositions we make here due to our need to understand their logical progression was apparently not how the French commander thought at all. In particular, we watch with astonishment as he stays on the left bank with the other half of his force on the evening of the 25th, when Korsakov has already withdrawn his own into Zurich and is about to break out on the other side; and we watch him persist in this divided deployment all night and the next day until the end of the battle, even though he is only about 5 miles from his bridge and another 5 miles from there to Oudinot. This is not only a major error that is recognized as such by all the historians; it also casts the whole attack before that in quite a different light, so that we no longer know what General Masséna was actually cooking up for himself. Perhaps he thought that while Oudinot was fighting on the right bank, he could carry the part of Zurich on his side[42] by storm. But we do not see him making any preparations for that during the morning of the 26th. Or was General Masséna thinking of blockading General Korsakov in Zurich and forcing him to surrender? But he lacked the forces to aim so high. For 20,000 men to be captured by 33,000 in this way presupposes other preceding favorable events. In any case, a breakout by Korsakov could only be expected on the right bank of the Limmat, and consequently, Masséna should have had a much larger part of his force there. Most probably Masséna's concern about Suvorov prevented him from moving a stronger force to the right bank of the Limmat. But on the 24th Suvorov had still not taken the Devil's Bridge, as Masséna must have

42. Clausewitz actually says "*die kleine Seite*," which could be a printer's error for "*die linke Seite*," or "the left side," or it could be referring to the smaller part of Zurich on the western side of the waterway, or the shortest face of its fortifications, as per note 37 in this chapter.

known on the morning of the 26th; from the Devil's Bridge to Zurich is four days' march by the shortest route, and Lecourbe was still in between them, so what did Masséna have to fear from Suvorov on the 26th that would not have been amply compensated by a great victory over Korsakov?

However General Masséna saw things and whatever his plan actually was, no one can dispute that on the evening of the 25th and early on the 26th, the situation he had created was far from advantageous: he was divided and the Russians were united, and once things turned out like that, his experienced judgment[43] should have made him rush to join Oudinot with at least the whole reserve, and the fact that he did not do so is recognized by everyone as a definite mistake on his part.

Thus, if it drives us crazy when we see the French commander implementing a wise plan but failing to execute it in the way the developing situation seems to us to dictate, then of course we must say that he does not seem to deserve this quite brilliant victory.[44]

Let us turn now to General Korsakov.

In connection with his intended actual or feint attack, this general attached great value to his position on the Sihlfeld. It was therefore natural that he should not want to abandon it too early. The fact that he initially took Oudinot's crossing at Dietikon for a demonstration is excusable, but it is inexcusable that he did not *investigate* it, for which he only needed to send an officer to Kloster Fahr, who could have been back in an hour. But in any case, from midday onward, General Korsakov could have been in no further doubt about the nature of the attack, since by that time, every inhabitant of Zurich, dreaming of victories, could watch in amazement as the French appeared on the heights north of the city. Since General Korsakov had a considerable force facing him on the left bank, he now had a very clear overview of the situation, and he must have recognized immediately the one advantage he had in his generally difficult position: namely, that the enemy was divided by the Limmat, while he himself was in a position to operate with his whole force against one of the two parts of the enemy, and naturally, this part could only be the one that had crossed the Limmat and was in the process of seizing his line of retreat. The

43. Clausewitz uses the word *Anschauung.* See note 73 of this chapter.

44. But then there is the role of friction, chance, and probability. Even if the French did not deserve their victory, they got it, and it is worth pointing out that this is partly Clausewitz's point.

most natural thing therefore would have been to leave a couple of thousand men to man the walls of the western part of Zurich, move quickly through the city with all the rest, and attack General Oudinot with his concentrated force of about 10,000 men so as to at least regain the area of Höngg. Since the French had dispersed themselves along every radius of a semicircle during their advance, he most probably would have succeeded in this; in any case, he would have achieved his two main objectives, namely, to put up a tough fight and to enable an orderly retreat in the event the enemy's numerical superiority and the test of arms made it necessary.

General Korsakov was prevented from following this simple course of action because he had not considered it beforehand; nor had he prepared systematically for it with his previous actions. Such a plan would have demanded, first, to feed as few troops as possible into the fight on the Sihl[45] and keep the rest in reserve ready to march away; second, to send back all impedimenta well in advance; and third, to identify a position on the right bank of the Limmat, keep the routes to it clear, especially those through the streets of Zurich, and issue preliminary orders for the march to be carried out in several columns.

Not a single one of these preparations for marching away seems to have been made, and instead of committing troops to the fight on the Sihl with the great circumspection that was required, quite the opposite seems to have occurred: Prince Gorchakov seized the initiative from General Drouet and piled into him so well, charging at the double as decreed by Suvorov, that he hurled him back on to the Ütli. Naturally, this aimless offensive, which was quite inappropriate in Korsakov's situation, had the effect that the latter was completely pinned on the Sihl, feeling as though he had been banished to *the wrong battlefield* while he was losing the right one. A considerable amount of time must have been lost before Prince Gorchakov could extricate himself and return from his inconvenient victory, and now it had also become necessary to defend the Wiedikon area doggedly against Mortier's left wing; indeed, it is likely that preparations were made here to go over on to the offensive to support Prince Gorchakov, which could not have happened without getting more heavily engaged than was desirable for an intended march away.

Since General Korsakov did not make any preparations for marching

45. The use of entrenchments (as Clausewitz suggested) would have gained him time, allowed him to defend the Sihlfeld with fewer troops, or possibly both.

away, and since he certainly did not disapprove of Prince Gorchakov's attack, it follows that he had not clearly thought through his mission at all, so he had not sorted things out so he could avoid dangerous developments in good time; as generals who have no clue about the higher art of war are so wont to do, he wanted to make every decision according to the circumstances of the moment—*on the spot*, as they say—and so these circumstances dragged him down into ever deeper embroilment.[46]

Assuming the way we have presented the actions of the two commanders here is not entirely inaccurate for lack of information, for ourselves, we may declare: never has it so pleased willful fate to reward the equivocation of one commander with such a rich bounty of victory because of the shortsightedness of another!

74 HOTZE IS BEATEN ON THE LINTH BY SOULT

We turn now to Generals Soult and Hotze. The latter had hoped to advance to the area of Einsiedeln on the 26th. To that end, his left wing under Jellachich and Linken had already been on the move for several days, arriving in the upper Linth valley on the 25th, while on that day, Hotze with the right wing still stood quietly behind the Linth. Two quite distinct episodes ensued from this, namely, Hotze's defense of the Linth against Soult's attack, and the actions Jellachich and Linken fought against Molitor's brigade of Lecourbe's division during their advance into the upper Linth valley on the 25th and 26th. We will describe General Soult's attack on Hotze's right wing first.

According to the archduke's account, between Lake Zurich and Lake Walensee, Hotze had ten battalions and fourteen squadrons that the archduke estimates at 8,000 men altogether.[47] He says Hotze had distributed these troops along the Linth in such a way that he had a reserve of only two battalions with him in Kaltbrunn, which is one hour's march from Grynau and two from Schänis. This stretch of the Linth is only sixty paces wide but is mostly bordered by marshy meadows, which makes crossing it very difficult. This undoubtedly

46. Clausewitz is pointing out the problems many generals have when dealing with purpose and means in war. The political goals need to match the strategy, which needs to connect to the tactics so as to provide the best chance of achieving one's goals.

47. Karl, 2:214.

persuaded General Hotze to spread most of his troops out along the river and close to it, so they could hurry to defend its bank as soon as the enemy prepared to cross. The stretch from Lake Zurich to Lake Walensee is about 15 miles long, which of course was a considerable extent for such a narrow river. We do not have precise details of how the troops were distributed or of any other arrangements that were made, nor can we draw any conclusions about this from the course of the action.[48]

The French had their bridging equipment at Lachen on Lake Zurich. This comprised eight portable boats that were to be used for the main crossing between Bilten and Schänis, twelve larger boats that were to ferry troops across the lake, and three gun sloops to protect the landing.

General Soult's dispositions were as follows:

His division comprised Boyer's and Laval's brigades, 10,000 men altogether. Of these, Boyer's brigade was to cross between Bilten and Schänis and carry out the main attack. For this crossing, the eight boats were to be brought overland from Lachen to Bilten, with some used for ferrying and the rest for a flying bridge. A thousand men from General Laval's brigade were to embark at Lachen; 300 of these were to land at Schmerikon, have every vessel there taken to the south shore of the lake, and then march on Uznach, while 700 men under *chef de brigade* [Colonel] Lochet were to sail up the Linth to land near the Grynau bridge, drive off the Austrians, and repair the bridge. General Laval himself was initially to appear with his brigade opposite Benken, between Bilten and Lake Zurich, to pin the enemy in that area and then move quickly to Grynau to cross there.

The troops were concentrated in such a way that the crossing could begin at 3:00 on the morning of the 25th.

Since the marshy meadows at the point chosen for the crossing had to be either bridged or made passable with a causeway of logs and fascines for a breadth of 600 paces,[49] this necessary labor meant that they could not hope

48. The archduke describes the defensive line as a "chain of posts" and questions their defensive viability. Karl, 2:214–215.

49. **Clausewitz** notes: "Dedon says: The convoy which had left Lachen at five in the evening debouched from the village of Bilten to move to the riverbank, which is 1,200 meters away of which more than half is marsh, to cross which it had been necessary to build a plank road. The noise of the wagons on this surface attracted the attention of the enemy outposts who opened fire on the convoy. [*Le convoi qui, la veille, étoit parti*

to surprise the enemy completely, so a volunteer company of 150 skillful swimmers was formed, armed with pikes, sabers, and pistols, and specially rehearsed in Lake Zurich. These carried out the first crossing.[50] They drove off the Austrian outposts on the bank, which seem to have been only sentries and offered no serious resistance. Now the ferrying across began, and once six companies of grenadiers were on the right bank, they carried out the first attack on the village of Schänis, a mile from the bank, which they seized. Until then, the Austrians must have had only a few troops at this point. But before the French could be reinforced, the Austrians returned and drove them out of the village again; now the village was contested, retaken, and lost several times. Gradually, the French ferried over another six grenadier companies and a battalion of infantry, while on the other side, Hotze arrived with the two battalions from Kaltbrunn. Fighting was still going on around Schänis when Hotze and his chief of general staff, Colonel Plunket, were shot and killed. This seems to have been between 7:00 and 8:00 a.m. It immediately settled the question of possession of Schänis, and the Austrians retreated through Dorf to Kaltbrunn.

On the left wing, the 300 men destined for Schmerikon had been landed there and had taken the place, but Colonel Lochet found it impossible to sail up the Linth under the direct fire of the Austrian outposts, as probably could have been expected, so he likewise made his way to Schmerikon and went ashore there. From here, Lochet made his way to Grynau, while the 300 moved against Uznach. The former drove the Austrians out of Grynau and hastily began repairing the bridge, but at the bridge between Uznach and Schmerikon,

---

de Lachen, à cinq heures du soir, déboucha du village de Bilten, pour se rendre au bord de la rivière, qui en est éloignée de 1200 mêtres dont plus de moitié en marais, à travers lesquels on avoit été obligé de pratiquer un chemin avec des madriers. Le bruit des voitures sur cet espèce de plancher attire l'attention des postes ennemis qui firent feu sur le convoi.] From this we are supposed to conclude that they actually *bridged* the marsh. But if we consider the quantity of materials and labor that would have been needed for this and that, in that case, an engineered construction would have been so much easier and more natural than using fascines, we must doubt this, all the more so as Dedon was not on the spot here, and also there are many internal contradictions and confusions in his book which weaken his authority somewhat. We prefer to imagine that an existing path was improved with fascines, logs, beams, planks, in short, with anything they could get." See Dedon, *Relation du Passage de la Limmat,* 102–103.

50. The archduke says there were 300 of them. Karl, 2:215.

the 300 encountered an Austrian outpost that they could not drive off; in fact, the Austrians were soon reinforced enough to go over on the attack and chase this detachment back to Schmerikon and onto the boats. Meanwhile, the bridge at Grynau had been repaired, and General Laval had arrived with the rest of his troops, but as the first ranks were crossing, it collapsed again. Just at that moment, two battalions of Russians under General Titov appeared. The French had nowhere to retreat to, so they had to defend themselves; thanks to the narrowness of the river, they were powerfully supported in this by four cannon and two battalions deployed on the left bank, so after softening up the Russians somewhat with fire, they managed to drive them off with a bayonet charge.

With this, the line of the Linth was taken, but it seems the French did not cross the river at all at Grynau and only very slowly at Bilten; just getting the infantry across is supposed to have taken until 9:00 in the evening,[51] while the flying bridge for the cavalry and artillery to cross was not in operation until 4:00 the next morning. This cannot be explained unless we assume that General Laval's troops were unable to cross at Grynau and only reached Bilten toward evening.

The fact that the French crossed so very slowly provides the strongest criticism of the Austrian defense. How unsuitable their dispositions must have been, or how feeble their efforts, if, in the course of the whole day, they could not concentrate 5,000–6,000 men at a single point; but they cannot have done so, since no serious resistance occurred, and in the evening Soult ejected them from Kaltbrunn, even though it is easy to see that he could have led no more than 5,000–6,000 men against the place.

General Petrasch had taken over command after Hotze's death. He still had the good intention of making an attempt during the night to turn the next day's destiny in his favor, probably by a surprise attack. One of his columns not only seized the village of Kaltbrunn again but even pushed forward as far as Benken. But either this was not coordinated with the operation as a whole or else it was intrinsically rash; the result was that the column that had pressed ahead, comprising 1,800 infantry, a squadron of hussars, and five guns, was surrounded on all sides by Soult and forced to lay down its arms.

On the 26th, before doing anything else, Soult sent *chef de bataillon* [Ma-

51. **Clausewitz** notes: "Dedon." Dedon, *Relation du Passage de la Limmat*, 96–115.

jor] Godinot with a few battalions against Wesen, where there were another two Austrian battalions with eight guns. The French outflanked them, and the result of the action was that they captured the eight guns and took 700 men prisoner, which is hard to understand, since the Austrians could have gone across the bridge and joined General Jellachich, who was fighting at Näfels at the time. We may well allow that this was the result of major confusion.

On this day, Petrasch continued his retreat to St. Gallen, then crossed the Rhine at Rheineck on the 27th, demolished the bridge, and summoned the Vorarlberg militia to defend the border.

The Russian General Titov had retreated to Grüningen on the 25th; he was driven out of there on the 26th by French light troops, moved to Wil, and reached Konstanz on the 28th.

The trophies from these two days were 3,000 prisoners, twenty guns, and the Austrians' flotilla on Lake Zurich.

General Soult pursued the two enemy generals only with his light troops, since Masséna had turned with part of his force against Suvorov in the area of Schwyz, and as matters there were not yet resolved, Soult could not advance to the Rhine on his own. In early October Masséna sent him to Näfels with part of his force, probably one brigade. However, we are unable to give a precise account of his positions in late September and early October.

75 JELLACHICH AND LINKEN ATTACK MOLITOR IN VAIN IN THE LINTH VALLEY

From Suvorov's plan that we imparted in section 70, we saw that Generals Jellachich and Linken, of whom the former was between Lake Walenstadt and the Luciensteig and the latter between the Luciensteig and Reichenau, were supposed to advance into the upper Linth valley so as to drive the French out of it; and by 26 September, when Suvorov intended to be in Schwyz, Jellachich was to be in Einsiedeln and Linken in Muota. To this end, it was necessary for Jellachich to launch his attack against the upper Linth valley a day ahead of Hotze's attack on Soult, thus on the 25th; but Linken had to begin to move even earlier because he had further to go and had to organize himself to reach the area of Glarus on the 25th, so that he and Jellachich could attack the French in the upper Linth valley together. If this succeeded on the 25th, then Linken would be able to enter Muota on the 26th.

The Actions at Mollis, Näfels, and Netstal on 25 September

The only French in the Linth valley were Molitor's brigade. This belonged to Lecourbe's division and took no part in Soult's offensive on the 25th but stayed in the Linth valley with its main body between Netstal and Näfels. General Molitor had 3,000 men. From the course of events during the attack, we see that he had one battalion at the Wichler-Bad [on the Wichlenbach] in the upper end of the Sernf valley to watch the path that arrives there from Graubündten.[52] Most likely he also had something along the upper tributaries of the Linth valley itself, so what he had between Netstal and Näfels cannot have been much more than 2,000 men. If we assume General Jellachich had 4,000 men and General Linken 3,000, then there could not have been any doubt that they would succeed against Molitor if their actions were properly coordinated. If the French did not attack General Hotze on the 25th, a decisive successful result against Molitor would have greatly facilitated Hotze's crossing of the Linth on the 26th, and it would have been a powerful corrective for the events that took place on the lower Linth on the 25th, since Soult hardly could have taken possession of Weesen and instead probably would have turned back on the 25th to take on these two generals.

In any case, this is the effect the attack by Generals Jellachich and Linken would have had if it had been successful; what connection it had with Suvorov's march, we shall be able to make clear when we describe that. But while the allies were beaten at Zurich and on the lower Linth, where the French had greater numbers, they did not manage to break through at a single point where they themselves had decisive superiority. The reason for this lies partly in their defective dispositions and partly in the faintheartedness of their commanders.

On the 25th General Jellachich set off for the Linth valley from the area of Sargans and Walenstadt with six and a half battalions and three squadrons in three columns. The right column of three battalions and three squadrons, which he himself was with, moved through Mühlehorn upon Mollis; the second column of three battalions moved across the Kerenzerberg and the Fron Alp to Netstal. Two companies were sent through the Weisstannen valley to maintain communications with Linken.

The first column encountered the French in the area of Mollis and drove them back across the Linth to Näfels. These were probably only Molitor's

52. This path travels via the Panixer Pass.

outposts, as he seems to have taken position at Näfels with three battalions and four guns. The bridge at Netstal had been demolished. On the 26th Jellachich attacked the bridge at Näfels but could not make it his. Since he was twice as strong as his opponent, some exceptional helplessness or timidity seems to have prevailed for him not to manage to get across the Linth somewhere else. But Mollis is only 5 miles from Bilten, so Jellachich was bound to have learned about General Hotze's fate on the 25th, and this news may have still weighed heavy on him and his corps. Now on the 26th, when the fight was renewed, the French who had dispersed the troops at Weesen and taken most of them prisoner pushed forward from there against Jellachich and pounded him with the eight guns taken in Weesen; he then felt he had already endured enough and that he was therefore justified in commencing his retreat. The two columns went back the way they had come; only weakly pursued by the enemy, they reached the Kerenzerberg and Murch [the Mürtschenstock][53] on the 26th, moved to Walenstadt on the 27th, and because Petrasch continued his retreat across the Rhine on the 27th, Jellachich felt he had to do the same and crossed the river at Bad Ragaz the same day.

The Action at Wichler-Bad on 25 September

General Linken and his corps of five battalions and one squadron had begun his march from Chur and Ems to Flims on the 23rd. From here he sent one battalion over the Flimsberg through the Martinsloch [the Segnas Pass] to Elm in the Sernf valley. With the main body he moved to Panix [Pigniu] on the 24th, to advance from there into the Linth valley in two columns on the 25th. The right column, comprising two and a half battalions and one squadron, moved over the Ringgenkopf and through the Jätzischlund [the gully below the Jätz Alp] to Wichler-Bad, which is a path usable by horses; the second column of one and a half battalions went across the Panten Bridge over the Linth and then down the Linth valley.

All these major moves were designed to trap the one battalion Molitor

53. The Mürtschenstock is the mountain to the south of Lake Walensee, but Clausewitz might have been referring to the small town of Murg, which is on the southern shore of the lake itself. Either location makes sense in the circumstances, although Murg seems more likely, as it is on the direct route to Walenstadt.

had at Wichler-Bad, which is indeed what happened. This battalion was defending itself staunchly at the bridge[54] when the Austrian battalion coming through the Segnas Pass arrived, cutting its route into the Sernf valley, and the detachment sent over the Panten Bridge cut its path over the high Alps into the Linth valley. Thus it was captured, along with another that arrived from the Schächen valley to support it.

But all this cost precious time, since it was not until the 26th that General Linken's columns reunited at Schwanden, by which time Jellachich had already begun to retreat. On that day he had only an insignificant fight with the French outposts at Mitlödi.

On the 27th Molitor moved against Linken with four battalions of his brigade. Linken drove Molitor back to Glarus and took position outside the town, but he seems to have found it too difficult to move through there and attack him on the other side. Indeed, perhaps he did not think it mattered much whether he did so; since his orders were to join Suvorov via the Klön valley, he may have thought he was already fully prepared to do that from his position behind Glarus, so he could wait there until he got word of Suvorov's arrival. He therefore stayed near Glarus on the 28th and 29th. As we shall see below, Suvorov had arrived in Altdorf on the 26th and then spent the 27th, 28th, and 29th moving out of the Schächen valley over the Chinzig Chulm into the Muota valley. If General Linken heard nothing of this, that must be ascribed mainly to his position, which left the French controlling the entrance from the Klön valley. If he had driven Molitor away from Glarus, the latter would not have been able to hold the Bragelberg [Pragel Pass] as he did on the 28th and thereby bar the way to the Cossack detachment that Suvorov had actually sent that day from Muota to Glarus. But apart from that, it seems almost incomprehensible that General Linken learned absolutely nothing of the Russian army's movements, for when 25,000 men arrive in a valley like the Schächen or Muota, we have to think that every last chamois must have known about it, let alone the people. However it came about, suffice it to say that General Linken heard nothing and amused himself on the 28th with minor skirmishing. But during the night of 28–29 September his opponent received a letter from General Lecourbe with the news that Suvorov had taken the St.

54. This was probably the Wallenbrugg, as the archduke comments on a French battalion defending itself bravely there. Karl, 2:223.

Gotthard, advanced to Altdorf, and was about to attack his rear in the Linth valley. Molitor now felt he had to get General Linken off his back quickly, so at the crack of dawn on the 29th he attacked him vigorously, at the same time threatening to outflank his right along several alpine paths. We shall leave it open to question whether the attack was so lively that Linken could not withstand it, as Molitor believes, or whether, having learned meanwhile that Hotze and Jellachich had retreated, Linken did not think it advisable to fight it out against a serious attack. Suffice it to say that on the 29th Linken commenced his retreat, continuing it unpursued on the 30th through Panix to the Rhine valley, where he deployed at Chur and occupied the passes with a few troops.

In this way, General Molitor and his brigade, of which he probably had no more than three or four battalions with him, were able to repel eleven Austrian battalions and to knock out the base that Suvorov had been counting on for his difficult descent from the St. Gotthard.

Thus misfortune had spread infectiously through the Austrian corps from right to left like the plague. Because Hotze was beaten, Jellachich felt he could not win, and because Jellachich balked, Linken did not dare to carry out his mission. Because Korsakov had been forced to retreat behind the Rhine, Petrasch did not want to linger behind either the Thur or the Sitter, nor Jellachich on Lake Walenstadt, while in the Linth valley, Linken became anxious. We see now that none of these generals' retreats was really dictated by the actual circumstances at the time; they were only the result of excessive caution. Of course, this wildfire of terror is not unusual in such cases in the history of war, but it is always a sign that the second-rank commanders are men whose personal interest in acts of war for their own account, their own fame and glory, is outweighed by their interest in most obediently but perfunctorily discharging their duty as mere instruments. The desire for glory, the enthusiasm, the warrior spirit of the French division generals at this time provide a stark contrast, and the success of French arms in the campaign of 1799 owes far more to this than to the high command.[55]

55. Again, Clausewitz is pointing out that military genius and boldness are key factors dictating success in war and that commanders must possess these characteristics.

76 SUVOROV'S SITUATION: THE MARCH OVER THE ST. GOTTHARD

From section 70, we recall what Suvorov's actual immediate purpose was in advancing through the St. Gotthard and along the Reuss valley, namely, to link up with Hotze between Lake Lucerne and Lake Zurich in the vicinity of Schwyz and Einsiedeln. Hotze should have been 30,000 strong, including his Russian reinforcements, and Suvorov was bringing 20,000 with him. Thus, if the execution of this plan had gone without incident, then, after deducting a few thousand men lost in crossing that last gap of only about 15 miles, they would have had close to 50,000 men combined, while Korsakov still would have been on the Limmat with some 20,000. If the French forces had been divided in the same proportions, then it would have become very difficult for General Masséna to appear between the two lakes in similar strength, as he had only about 60,000 men between the St. Gotthard and the Rhine. But in such a case, one always counts on one's measures being somewhat concealed from the enemy and that he therefore will not be able to distribute his forces entirely suitably; the attack along the Limmat ordered for the 26th was supposed to operate with exactly this in mind. This is how matters were seen in Suvorov's headquarters, so it was expected that once they got beyond Schwyz, any difficulties would have been overcome because of:

1. Their probable numerical superiority,
2. The principle of the offensive,
3. Suvorov's energy,
4. The moral impact of the march as a whole and of the successes won against Lecourbe along the way,
5. And the principle of strategic outflanking that lay in the direction of this march.

These factors would leave scarcely any doubt that they could overcome any resistance Masséna might offer in this area and thus oblige him to abandon his position on the Limmat and to carry out a major retrograde maneuver. The fact that Masséna's resistance between the lakes was only expected to be feeble and insufficient, and that the principle of strategic outflanking was expected to have a dominant effect, emerges from the intention contained in Suvorov's plan—placed somewhat in the background, but nevertheless clearly expressed—that Suvorov and his corps were to move to Lucerne along both shores of Lake Lucerne.[56]

We wish to disregard this intention, which was conceivable only in the most fortunate case, and to assume that during its *execution*, Suvorov was deterred from doing this by Masséna's strength and was obliged to advance through Schwyz with his whole corps.

If we just look at the material factors that developed here, at numbers and time and space, we cannot possibly say that the strategic position Suvorov would have attained after his breakthrough at Schwyz would have been an advantageous one. The allies were not superior to the French overall after Suvorov's arrival in Switzerland, so the division of their force caused by Lake Zurich must be regarded as a very major disadvantage. This put the French commander in a position to attack their main body with a superior force, or at least with a stronger one than would have been possible in any other situation; this becomes especially marked when we consider that out of all the allied corps combining between the two lakes, only Hotze's on the lower Linth could be adequately endowed with artillery, while the rest, that is, three-quarters of the total, only had 2- and 3-pounder mountain guns.

Nonetheless, we consider it not unlikely that, if Suvorov had reached that goal, then mainly because of the moral impression of this bold move and Suvorov's name and the overestimation of the Russian strength,[57] and finally because of misguided concern for his strategic flank, in the position that these circumstances would have created, Masséna would not have dared to undertake any major operation, so his retreat would have been unavoidable.

In saying that Suvorov hoped to see a force of 50,000 men united under his command beyond Schwyz, we mean only to establish the point of view that might have been held in his headquarters; but of course, in fact, the matter was less favorable, since instead of Hotze combining with the Swiss and the Russians to form 30,000 men altogether, he would move only about 20,000 to

56. Duffy points out that subsequent historians have claimed that Suvorov could not march west around Lake Lucerne, but Duffy shows that this is not correct. Duffy, *Eagles over the Alps*, 155–161.

57. Duffy notes the poor Russian logistics for the march. For instance, the mules Austria supplied were unlikely to sustain the Russian army across the alpine passes. Duffy, *Eagles over the Alps*, 161.

the line between the two lakes. This was the first difference between plan and execution to reveal itself.

Suvorov's immediate purpose was to get to the area of Schwyz. To oblige his general staff and to proceed according to their chain of thought, let us assume the possibility that he would have taken the boats at Flüelen and Seedorf by surprise before the French could get them away, thereby obtaining the necessary means to get to Brunnen, and that his disembarkation there was unopposed. This extremely arbitrary and unlikely notion was the first way by which he could get to Schwyz. If this did not succeed, then the second way of reaching Schwyz was a march through the Schächen and Muota valleys along the most arduous footpaths,[58] and then it would depend not on a landing, as in the previous case, but on debouching from the Muota valley. An enemy who was present in force could prevent this just as well as he could the landing. Then the area of Schwyz could not be reached, and instead of this enveloping direction, Suvorov would have to head in another less enveloping one that would lead primarily to a rapid junction with the Austrians; this was the direction of the Linth valley.

If Suvorov could not advance out of the mountains at Schwyz, he would have to move through the Klön valley into the Linth valley and from that out into the open country at Urnen. If the Austrian corps were there, the French could not defend against this breakthrough, but if the Austrians had been beaten, which had to be foreseen as being possible, then breaking out from the Linth valley could also become unfeasible; Suvorov would then have to turn right yet again to attain the Rhine valley, which, if the French were already in force at the exit from the Linth valley, could hardly happen via Mollis and Kerenzen but only along the tributaries of the upper Linth.

But the Rhine valley, too, could have already been barred to him at Sargans and the St. Luciensteig, so then he would have had to march through the valley of the Lanquart or the Plesser to the Ill and finally, in the event the position at Feldkirch had been lost, to the Inn valley.

58. This is where the issue of Russian logistical failings is important. The Russians overestimated their ability to live off the land in Switzerland and received only about a fifth of the mules promised to them by the Austrians. This led to Suvorov's decision to use Cossack horses as pack mules, even though the Cossacks owned their own horses. One wonders what effect this had on Cossack morale, as well as on their ability to scout for the army. Duffy, *Eagles over the Alps*, 161–165.

Of these various detours, those from the Schächen valley to the Muota and from the Linth valley to the Rhine were on such rugged tracks that they alone could wreck an army.

All these various degrees of failure lurked in wait for Suvorov's move through the St. Gotthard,[59] and if we must regard the last of them as a very unlikely case, the success of the first case is equally so; and in planning this whole episode, the reasoning for it should never have been biased toward either of these extremes.

Having thus made the situation clear, let us describe how the march was carried out, along with the battles that arose from it.

77 SUVOROV ATTACKS THE ST. GOTTHARD AND DRIVES LECOURBE BACK TO SEEDORF

Suvorov had set off from the area of Asti and Alessandria on 11 September, via Valenza and Varese, and reached Taverne on the 15th. In Varese, the whole of the artillery together with an escort of Cossacks departed for Lake Como, to embark there and travel through Chiavenna and the Splügen Pass to Graubündten. The heavy baggage had already been moved to the Adige to take the road through the Tyrol. All that stayed with the army was 2-pounder guns that could be transported on mules.

By now, Suvorov's army had dwindled to 16,000 infantry and 3,000 Cossacks, but including noncombatants, it numbered close to 23,000 men.

In Taverne, it had to be equipped with mules to transport guns, ammunition, and provisions, of which they needed at least eight to ten days' worth for the march through the high Alps. It would be very interesting to have detailed reports about these transport arrangements, but these are entirely lacking. Because of the poor arrangements by the Austrian administration, the mules

59. Duffy comments that "the nationalistic Russian historiography represents Suvorov as arriving at Altdorf and finding, contrary to the assurances of his Austrian staff, that no path led around the eastern lake shore." Duffy, *Eagles over the Alps*, 159. He shows that this is almost certainly untrue, and a detailed look at the near contemporary maps indicates that he is likely correct. See https://mapire.eu/de/map/europe-19century-secondsurvey/?layers=osm%2C158%2C164&bbox=906580.8098823754%2C5917319.972018652%2C1003770.491346977%2C5947894.783332722.

that Suvorov expected in Taverne arrived too late and in insufficient numbers, namely, only 400 of them, and Suvorov was obliged to dismount most of his Cossacks[60] and use their horses to carry provisions. The dismounted Cossacks were used as light infantry.

All the historians ascribe a loss of five days to the vainly awaited mules because Suvorov and his corps did not set off for Bellinzona until the 21st, and some go so far as to blame this negligence for the loss of the battle of Zurich and for all the consequences that followed.

Suvorov himself complains about this delay in his official report. But we have seen that it was decided at Asti on 10 September that Suvorov would set off from Bellinzona on the 21st and that, at that time, he hoped to be in possession of the St. Gotthard on the 24th;[61] now this tallies with Suvorov's actual movements, so a five-day pause at the foot of the mountains must have already been allowed for at that time, which could quite understandably be necessary to obtain provisions and to make arrangements for their transport.[62] Thus, if the Austrians' failure did indeed result in significant handicaps, these were not such that they could have had a critical influence on the course and outcome of the operation, and we must not be misled by the Russian commander's expression of his unhappiness, since he was already upset with the Austrian authorities and certainly ready to attach the maximum importance to any mistake they made.

60. Duffy states that 1,500 of 2,500 Cossacks were forced to give up their horses as pack mules. In addition, he notes that the muleteers often deserted with their mules. Duffy, *Eagles over the Alps*, 165.

61. **Clausewitz** notes: "On p 181 of Vol. II of his history of the 1799 campaign, the archduke says: 'When Suvorov began to make serious preparations to move to his new destination in Switzerland, he came to an agreement with Hotze and Korsakov about their joint operations. After several discussions, on 10 September it was finally decided that he would set off from Bellinzona on the 21st to attack the St. Gotthard.' Suvorov's circular to Generals Korsakov, Hotze, and Linken is dated 5 September. It would certainly have been possible to receive an answer from Korsakov and Hotze between the 5th and the 10th and to have reached a new decision accordingly. Since we must attach great value to the account of the extremely truth-loving and on this point certainly well-informed archduke, we have regarded the change of timing agreed in Asti as a fact, although the archduke himself also complains about the delay that the lack of mules caused General Suvorov at Taverne."

62. Duffy has mules still arriving on 18 September. Duffy, *Eagles over the Alps*, 165.

The Action at Airolo on 24 September

When Suvorov arrived at the foot of the St. Gotthard, the position of the French right wing, namely, Lecourbe's 12,000-strong division, was the following:

Since the actions at the end of August that had left him in possession of the Linth valley, Molitor had held his position there with 3,000 men. The right-wing brigade under Gudin, 3,500 strong, was in the St. Gotthard. Lecourbe with Loison's 6,000-strong brigade was in the Reuss valley with his headquarters in Altdorf, as well as occupying the Maderaner and Schächen valleys, thereby serving partly as communications between Gudin and Molitor and partly as reserve for them both. Gudin's brigade connected with Tharreau's division, which was in Wallis holding the passes against Haddick.

All we know of Gudin's position is that he was defending the St. Gotthard with three battalions, had one battalion in the Furka, and, as Jomini puts it, had a detachment on the Crispalt.[63] By that, we do not know whether General Jomini means the outpost the French had by the Oberalpsee or whether this detachment also had outposts toward Disentis and covering the Maderaner valley. In any case, we must assume it to be a couple of battalions, since the French report refers to the 67th Demi-brigade that had fought at Oberalpsee. Gudin's brigade then would have had six battalions, which would give it a strength of roughly 3,500 men.

If we take a closer look at the approaches through the Gotthard mountains, there seems to be scant reason for this position of Gudin's, by which we do not mean to say that it could not have been fully justified, only that we lack reports about it. Apart from the Gotthard road itself, which runs from Airolo through the Tremola valley past the Hospitium [Ospizio] to Hospental, there are another three footpaths that lead over the mountains so as to join the road at Urseren (Andermatt) at the entrance to the narrow Reuss valley, so should be seen as outflanking the St. Gotthard. The first runs left through the Levantin valley[64] to the Furka and from there down the Urseren valley through Realp to Hospental; the second runs right from Airolo through the Val Canaria and over a very high rocky pass, the Pontenera [Passo Bornengo], to the Unteralpsee and down its valley to Urseren; the third runs through Santa

63. Jomini, 12:82.

64. This is the name given to the part of the Ticino River valley running from roughly Faido to Biasca, where the Ticino meets the Brenno River.

Maria[65] at the entrance to the Medel valley, starting either from Brugnasco past Lake Ritom and the Lukmanier [Passo del Lucomagno] or else earlier through the Brenno valley and then from Santa Maria through the Medel valley (the Middle Rhine) and the Anterior Rhine valley to the Oberalpsee.

This quite naturally yielded these dispositions: that the main position defended the Gotthard road, that the three side roads were either defended or observed at suitable points, and that a reserve was in the Urseren ready to repel any enemy who might advance on a side road as soon as he got close enough.

If we examine the French dispositions, admittedly, there was no reserve in the Urseren, but General Lecourbe with Loison's brigade in the Reuss valley could be regarded as such, since Altdorf is only about 20 miles from the Urseren and he could arrive in good time if the St. Gotthard was threatened. There was one battalion in the Furka Pass and apparently two at the Oberalpsee, but on the other hand, there is nothing to be found about anything guarding the path leading over the Passo Bornengo. But this is understandable to some degree, because Gudin took position just behind Airolo with his main body, so that path was right beneath his eyes; perhaps also, at this time of year, that pass was no longer usable.

The Gotthard Pass itself, that is, the saddle in the mountains where the road crosses the watershed, does not offer any strong position for a force of a few thousand men, since it is a fairly wide, low plateau. The most difficult places on the road ascending from Italy are in the steep and narrow valley of the Tremola, which begins behind Airolo and leads up toward the Hospitium, and in the multiple steep, sharp bends with which the road works its way up from this valley to the small terrace that lies between it and the Hospitium.

The French usually had their main position at Airolo, and on this occasion too, rather than anywhere in the Tremola valley, because this place also covers the roads leading off through the Val Bedretto (the upper Ticino valley) and through the Val Canaria and keeps the most difficult part of the Gotthard road behind it, making it feasible to defend this part step by step.

Since any mountain pass can be outflanked in the end by small bodies of infantry on or above the mountain slopes that form it, then in cases such as this, where resistance is to be offered in the face of great numerical superiority, this resistance will probably last longest and be the toughest when it relies on not just one but several successive positions. Since these positions cannot be

65. This is now under a reservoir, the Lai da Sontga Maria.

overcome frontally, the time it takes to outflank them provides the duration of their resistance. We can easily imagine how in this way an attacker can be obliged to spend much more time to get through the pass than if everything is just geared toward the defense of the narrowest gap or the most advantageous position.

Suvorov's strategic dispositions for the attack were to send one column of 6,000 men under the command of General Rosenberg through the Brenno valley and the Middle Rhine valley to the Anterior Rhine valley; there it was to establish communications with Austrian General Auffenberg's 2,400 men concentrating at Disentis; both were then to advance into the Reuss valley on the same day, the latter through the Maderaner valley, the former past the Oberalpsee, while Suvorov himself attacked the St. Gotthard. Thus Lecourbe's division would be attacked in three places on this day. The attack through the Maderaner valley was partly to act as a demonstration against the St. Gotthard itself and weaken its defense; partly to bar the way to the St. Gotthard to the troops coming from Altdorf, and to pin others above it and prevent them from supporting the St. Gotthard; and finally to actually cut off the line of retreat of those withdrawing from the St. Gotthard. It could not be foreseen in which of these four ways General Auffenberg would be most effective, but he was bound to be very effective for Suvorov's breakthrough in one way or another. The attack along the Oberalpsee path was an attack on the rear of the Gotthard position itself. Of course, the enemy had the advantage of finding himself between the attacker's separate columns, as he always does against attacks on the rear; but in a high mountainous region, the attacker has to expose himself to that because the narrow roads and paths do not allow him to bring his superior numbers into effect to any degree in any other way. The main thing was just that this column's attack should coincide exactly with that by the main body, and then superior numbers would mean that the only possible result was that the enemy would be overwhelmed.

Suvorov placed the Brenno valley column under the command of General Rosenberg as we said, made it eight battalions and two Cossack regiments strong, and had it move to Bellinzona two days earlier, namely, on 19 September.

He himself set off at the head of about 14,000 combat troops on the 21st.

The columns advanced thus:

On the 21st: Suvorov to Bellinzona; Rosenberg to Dongio.
On the 22nd: Suvorov to Giornico; Rosenberg to Santa Maria.
On the 23rd: Suvorov to Dazio; Rosenberg to Tujetsch.

On this day [the 23rd], Suvorov was joined by Colonel Strauch with his 4,000-strong brigade arriving from the Maggia valley, and Rosenberg established communications with Auffenberg, who was at Disentis with his 2,400 men. General Haddick and his corps participated in the Gotthard crossing only by making demonstrations against the Wallis passes to keep Tharreau occupied, in which he was indeed completely successful.

On the 24th, now 18,000 strong, Suvorov advanced to attack the St. Gotthard, that is to say, Gudin's position at Airolo. He again formed three columns, of which the main column was to attack frontally along the main road while Colonel Strauch was to go around the right flank with three battalions and General Schweikowsky around the left with eight.

Gudin had apparently taken position on the height known as Alcino del Bosco [Cima del Bosco][66] behind Airolo with only about 1,000 men, so we must assume that he had made other detachments from his three battalions. This position seems to have been outflanked on its right side by Colonel Strauch advancing along the right slope of the Ticino valley, whose bottom is cultivated to a fairly wide extent and therefore passable.

The outflanking that Schweikowsky carried out on the [Russian] right side encompassed not only the position at Airolo but also all of the Val Tremola and therefore the whole of the defense of the Gotthard. This general and his eight battalions scaled the main ridge of the Alps by its steep slope, that is, without being able to use a reentrant valley, moved around the source of the Val Sorescia (a small tributary of the Val Tremola), passed the Lago della Sella (another tributary of the Tremola), and headed to the right for Hospental, with the Gotthard road roughly a couple of thousand paces to his left.

General Schweikowsky's route, which a few of the local people can still point out, is absolutely astonishing, and in that respect, this is the most extraordinary episode in all of Suvorov's march. According to the locals, the Russians are supposed to have used crampons for it, which the Austrians had had made in large numbers.[67]

Thus, here we see the route through the Val Canaria left unused, while Schweikowsky moves through an area that all experience would have led one to regard as completely impassable. Whether the Val Canaria path was

66. The series of hairpins on the road north traveling to the St. Gotthard Pass.

67. Duffy notes the Russians' use of Austrian-supplied crampons for this part of the march. Duffy, *Eagles over the Alps*, 156.

unusable at that time of year, or whether Suvorov did not want to use it because it entailed a detour to Andermatt and thus a strategic outflanking, we cannot say.

Schweikowsky's outflanking maneuver must have been a complete surprise to the French; however, since it took a long time, it could not entirely cut short the duration of the defense. Consequently, between Airolo and the Hospitium, Suvorov encountered very stubborn resistance that lasted until 4:00 in the afternoon and cost the Russians 1,200 dead and wounded. These very heavy losses stemmed mainly from the fact that Suvorov was too impatient to wait for the outflankings to take effect and constantly drove the fight forward frontally, whereupon the French skirmishers hiding in gorges and behind boulders were able to fire on the dense columns of advancing Russians to great effect.

In this first encounter with alpine warfare, the Russians seem to have felt a kind of shiver. They came from the rich, fair plains of Italy and now entered the serried ranks of snow-covered Alps. The tiny path, the narrow valley, the jagged rockfaces, the endless scaling of the rubble of bygone epochs of upheaval of heaven and earth made a fearsome impression on their imaginations from first to last.[68] The enemy himself, in possession of these towering masses and as at home in these ravines as if he were on his native soil, must have become a giant in their eyes. They balked and did not want to advance any further. Only the voice of their commander, who himself seemed to them like a kind of giant, overcame these qualms, and the fight dragged itself slowly and bloodily up through the narrow ravine of the Tremola valley to the St. Gotthard. At 4:00 in the afternoon Suvorov arrived at the Hospitium and was able to descend to Hospental without further difficulty. Thus the first knot of this tangled mission was untied.

The Action at the Oberalpsee on 24 September

On the 24th General Rosenberg had advanced out of the Rhine valley toward the Oberalpsee. At 3:00 he first ran into the enemy outpost, whose strength is not given by the Russian reports but appears from Masséna's report to have consisted

68. This also inspired some rather fanciful paintings, including *The March of Suvorov through the Alps* by Vaily Surikov and *Suvorov Crossing the Panix Pass* by Alexander Kotzebue.

of the 67th Demi-brigade. But since this constituted half of Gudin's brigade, we can probably assume that no more than two battalions of it were here.

It resisted obstinately, and the fighting lasted several hours, but finally superior numbers led to the outpost being overcome,[69] and the French were driven back to the Urseren. General Rosenberg did not arrive at the heights of the Urseren until toward evening.

Meanwhile, Lecourbe had hurried up with the larger part of Loison's brigade. He had probably begun to march to the Urseren the previous day on hearing reports of Suvorov's approach. No report says what time he arrived, but it must have happened before Rosenberg had taken the outpost at Oberalp and after Gudin had abandoned that at the St. Gotthard, since Lecourbe contented himself with leaving a reserve in the Urseren and taking position with the rest of his troops outside Hospental. Thus, he had the town and the western tributary of the Reuss behind him and was determined to go on the attack against Suvorov the next morning, from which it follows that he did not suspect that such a substantial column had advanced across the Crispalt, which at that time was already covered with snow and ice, and that it must have been too late in the day to do anything to retake the St. Gotthard.

General Gudin had apparently retreated to the Furka Pass with the majority of his troops; we do not know exactly why. Suvorov, meanwhile, had halted to rally his troops at the Hospitium and therefore likewise did not arrive in front of Lecourbe's position at Hospental until the evening, where he halted.

69. **Clausewitz** notes: "Several authors, among them the archduke, have recited one after the other that the Russians killed or captured 1,500 French from the 67th Demi-brigade. Jomini, to whom the matter probably seemed very unlikely but who has great respect for the archduke's statements, finds a way out by saying of the detachment posted on the Crispalt that *il fut en majeure partie pris ou tué* [the bulk of it was captured or killed]. But the Russian report itself says nothing about this large a number killed and captured, but only mentions a few hundred. This lets us guess that an error must have got into those large numbers, and it turns out that this probably arose from a somewhat garbled version of the translation of the French report. According to this translation (*Allgemeine Zeitung Jahrgang 1799, No. 320*), Masséna says: '*Die einzige 67. Halbbrigade hatte sie bei der Passage von Urseren 1500 Mann einbüßen machen.*' ['The 67th Demi-brigade alone caused them the loss of 1,500 men during the passage of the Urseren.'] It is undoubtedly a hasty misreading of this that was the reason for people believing that it was the 67th Demi-brigade that had lost 1,500 men." What Clausewitz says is not strictly true. Neither the archduke nor Jomini mentions the 67th Demi-brigade. See Karl, 2:239; Jomini, 12:267.

When General Rosenberg observed more enemy troops in the Urseren without having heard anything yet from Suvorov's main force, at first he was worried about advancing any further, and it was not until 9:00 in the evening that he decided to attack the Urseren. Rosenberg has been criticized for this, as people have maintained that a bold advance would have cut off Lecourbe's retreat. The report of a very reliable Russian witness[70] says that this and similar delays and pauses were caused more by the troops' fatigue and unfamiliarity with this type of warfare than by any bad intent. We must add that if Rosenberg's delay really was deliberate, it can still only be regarded as an act of normal caution from which few generals would have refrained. Nor do we see how a bold advance by Rosenberg would have resulted in Loison's brigade being captured, since in the worst case, the road through the Furka remained open to General Lecourbe, and indeed, even the way we shall shortly see him resort to would not have been lost to him. Such a success would have been much more likely to occur if Rosenberg had marched against the Urseren and Hospental even later than he actually did—that is, not until the next day while Lecourbe was engaged in attacking Suvorov, if indeed he still took that step. Naturally, General Rosenberg could not have worked out such a combination, since he could not have known all this; anyway, we only want to excuse his lingering, not to praise it, since the danger to which he would have been exposed by advancing without delay was not great, and in that case, boldness is always better than caution; it is the most golden of military virtues.[71]

Be that as it may, and whether it was an order from Suvorov or the news of his arrival at Hospental or something else that set General Rosenberg in motion again, it was enough for him to hurl himself impetuously upon the French in the Urseren at 9:00 in the evening and force them to retreat as fast as possible to the Devil's Bridge. It was completely dark, and thick fog covered the mountains, so it was impossible for the Russians to tread on the heels of the fleeing French so as to press through the Urnerloch and over the Devil's Bridge at the same time as them; instead, they halted in the Urseren and refreshed themselves from the provisions left behind by the French.

When Lecourbe learned that his reserve had been defeated and that the enemy had arrived in the Urseren in force, he realized there could be no more

70. **Clausewitz** notes: "Jomini in an annex." This is "*Relation raisonnée de la marche de l'armée de Suwarof d'Italie en Suisse.*" Jomini, 12:455–467.

71. Duffy recounts the series of fights set out here. Duffy, *Eagles over the Alps*, 171–198.

question of him making a stand at Hospental and that fighting his way through toward the Devil's Bridge could put him in a hopeless position if Suvorov set upon him from the other side. He therefore quickly made the decision to have his reserve demolish the Devil's Bridge, for heaven's sake, and to lead his troops from Zumdorf, climbing across the high ridge and down to the Göschenen valley, so that he could get into the Reuss valley again there. Since he could not get his artillery out along this path, he had it all thrown into the Reuss gorge so that the Russians could not use it against him and to deprive them of these trophies, after first using it all to discharge a mass salvo against their camp so they would be too stunned and deafened to notice him leaving.

So ended the 24th of September. Apart from their artillery, the French had suffered only negligible losses, while those of the Russians may be estimated at a couple of thousand men. The latter had gained control of the St. Gotthard and, to that extent, had achieved the aim of their plan; but the French were still in possession of the Urnerloch and the Devil's Bridge, two defiles of a kind found hardly anywhere else. Suvorov could certainly expect so much resistance there that he could calculate it would be impossible to reach Altorf, another 20 miles away, on the following day as his plan envisaged; rather, there was a very high risk that he would not be able to get through the Urnerloch or across the Devil's Bridge and would then be forced to go over the Crispalt and down into the Rhine valley, because it was unthinkable that Suvorov and his army could or would follow the same path Lecourbe had taken. Indeed, the only guarantee of crossing the Devil's Bridge was General Auffenberg's advance upon Amsteg, whereby the French resistance at the Devil's Bridge could certainly be hindered. However, it was very uncertain whether General Auffenberg would succeed completely. It could therefore be foreseen that Suvorov would either get to the area of Schwyz on the 27th at the earliest, or else indeed, not at all; consequently, the Austrian corps that were supposed to attack on the 26th were in danger of being beaten before Suvorov arrived.

78 SUVOROV TAKES THE DEVIL'S BRIDGE

Suvorov left Colonel Strauch and his brigade at the St. Gotthard to cover the pass against Wallis, joined up with Rosenberg early on the 25th, and then moved against the Urnerloch. This 80-paces-long tunnel blasted through the rock 1,000 paces from the Devil's Bridge, through which the St. Gotthard road runs, had not been blocked or made impassable in any way by the French; nor was it defended directly, but only by fire from skirmishers on the opposite bank of the Reuss.

If arrangements had been made here sooner, we can imagine that a breastwork of timbers with a cannon posted behind it would have been able to hold out indefinitely, or at least for a very long time, perhaps achieving more than was achieved at the Devil's Bridge. If the enemy did finally capture the entrance, the cannon could be abandoned and the few troops there could escape across the demolished arch using single planks. But the exit from the Urnerloch was not defensible, since the road from it falls steeply down toward the bridge and provides no suitable place for a position.

The French had not demolished the Devil's Bridge itself, but only the arch supporting the road beyond it. This one physical obstacle was entirely sufficient against the Russians advancing directly along the road itself, but as far as repairing the broken road after they had captured it was concerned, of course complete demolition of the bridge arch would have been a much more effective measure. Perhaps the French spared this bridge because they told themselves it could be very useful to them later.

But the main thing in defending this point was to be suitably strong on the left bank of the Reuss; since the Reuss was wadable and the foot of the mountain ridge the Urnerloch goes through is not totally sheer on that side but forms a ledge about 50 feet above the Reuss from which one could get down to the riverbed if need be, the defense was not limited just to the broken arch.

Thus, if Lecourbe had posted himself with Loison's brigade behind the Devil's Bridge instead of going to Hospental, we do not see how the Russians could have taken a single step forward; they would have been obliged to turn across the Crispalt into the Rhine valley. But Lecourbe had gone to Hospental imagining that he could fling the enemy back down from the St. Gotthard, and we cannot really blame him for this intention. After he was cut off from the Devil's Bridge by Rosenberg and had to save himself by a detour to Göschenen, from there he still would have been able to appear behind the Devil's Bridge in time to defend it; but the news of one Austrian column advancing through the Maderaner valley and another in the upper Linth valley may have dissuaded him from the idea of resisting in the upper Reuss valley. He naturally would have been forced either to defend the Reuss as far as Altdorf or else to be happy to be cut off from Altdorf and have his line of retreat restricted to the single mountain path through the Meyen valley. We can understand that he did not want to get involved in either of these options and therefore continued on his way as far as Amsteg at the mouth of the Maderaner valley. So it came to be that the two strongest defiles in Switzerland, the Urnerloch and the Devil's Bridge, were defended lightly or not at all. Even the troops that had fallen back through them from the Urseren seem not to have awaited the attack but to have continued on their way, leaving one company as a rear guard.

This is how matters stood on the morning of the 25th when the head of Suvorov's column advanced against the Urnerloch. The first battalion plunged boldly into the black maw from which some nameless doom chilled the foreboding soul; the next ones pressed on behind, and now, when they arrived at the open gorge of the Devil's Bridge, it was impossible for those at the front to shy away; they were shoved together in dense masses on the narrow road between the cliffs and the chasm, riddled with bullets by the enemy's musketry to murderous effect, and their chaotic milling around toppled many of them into the abyss. In this desperate situation, the Russians again wonderfully demonstrated their boldness and resolution. In constant danger of plummeting, and under close-range musket fire from the enemy, they climbed down the very steep, 50-foot-high ledge between them and the surface of the Reuss; waded the river, whose rushing waters came up to their armpits; scrambled up the equally high bank on the far side; and drove off the French from beyond the bridge. That they could do this in such difficult circumstances was of course because of their numbers; that is to say, they crossed along a considerable stretch of the river while the few French were partly engaged at the end of the bridge, but nobody would deny that this was among the finest episodes of martial resolve. Thus the Russians gained control of the bridge and of the demolished arch and could devote themselves to repairing the crossing by filling the gap with logs and planks.

This labor took them until 5:00 p.m., so it was not until late in the evening that the column reached Wassen, where it halted.

General Auffenberg and his four battalions had set off from Disentis on the 24th to go through the Val Strem, over the Chrüzli Pass, down the Etzli valley to Amsteg at the mouth of the Maderaner valley, and into the Rhine valley. From a contemporary personal document it appears that General Auffenberg had summoned 4,000 of the Graubündten militia for his operation, but since it does not say whether these turned up, it is very doubtful whether this measure produced any noticeable result, and no historian mentions it, so we cannot assume that there was any significant reinforcement of this kind.

The route from Disentis to Amsteg is only 25 miles long, yet General Auffenberg did not reach Amsteg on the 24th but remained in the Maderaner valley, where, as Archduke Charles puts it, nightfall took him by surprise.[72] This pause before the objective was probably partly due to caution; General Auffenberg knew that Suvorov would attack the St. Gotthard on the 24th, he probably learned from the locals that Lecourbe was on the march to there, and he wanted to allow Lecourbe time to move further away from him so as not to have to deal with too superior a force.

On the morning of the 25th Auffenberg set off for Amsteg, drove off the weak French outposts, and moved through the village. Now reinforcements appeared from Altdorf, allegedly 2,000 strong, but it is inconceivable that the French still had so many troops in that area, and Auffenberg was certainly facing no more than a couple of battalions here. He had just repelled their attack when Lecourbe appeared from Wassen with Loison's brigade. Now Auffenberg had to deal with a very superior enemy against whom he would have had to form front to both north and south at the same time, so naturally he avoided such a fight, all the more readily as he could probably tell himself that Suvorov would not be in a position to follow on the heels of General Lecourbe, and the Maderaner valley gave him the opportunity to avoid a fight without actually retreating.

Lecourbe had now opened his road, so he halted beyond Amsteg, having covered the stretch from Hospental to Amsteg in a single march and having put 15 miles of the most arduous mountain passes behind him.

He could have waited for Suvorov and tried to make a stand again here, since he was now just 10 miles away from Lake Lucerne. General Linken had initially been threatening his rear but, by heading for Glarus, had moved further away from the Reuss rather than approaching it; for the next three days, there was no prospect of Masséna approaching to where Lecourbe could fall back on him, since he had just set off across the Limmat on the 25th to attack the Russians. We therefore do not really see what deterred General Lecourbe from attempting to put up the same resistance at Amsteg on the 26th as he had intended to offer at the St. Gotthard on the 24th. If that had been his idea, then naturally, he would have fallen on Auffenberg on the 25th with his whole force, and we can probably assume that the latter would not have been able to withstand this. Now the action between Auffenberg and

72. Karl, 2:237.

Lecourbe is always portrayed as though Lecourbe was not in a position to push him away from the entrance to the Maderaner valley, but if Lecourbe had seriously wanted to do so, it is hard to believe that he could not have managed it. Since none of the reports and none of the historians tell of any such serious and sustained fighting, we can see that it did not happen, from which we can conclude that when he entered Amsteg, Lecourbe was already intent on continuing his retreat, so he certainly had no interest in tangling with Auffenberg any further.

Lecourbe therefore had the bridge across the Chärstelen stream burned and let his troops rest until evening, when he continued his retreat, crossing the Reuss at Erstfeld and contenting himself with taking a flanking position on the left bank of the river, destroying the bridge, and keeping only the one at Seedorf intact, with his advance guard posted in front of it. Since he had had every boat on Lake Lucerne taken to its western shore, he was sure that Suvorov could not continue on his way to Schwyz by any other route than through the Schächen and Muota valleys. That being the case, it seemed to General Lecourbe that a flanking position like that behind the Reuss would be especially effective because from there, he could block any subsequent return through the Reuss valley and could win a glorious victory over the rear guard.

Suvorov had set off again from Wassen during the night of the 26th and had reached Amsteg before daybreak. When he saw a large number of campfires near the town, he halted, but soon learned that it was General Auffenberg. He joined up with Auffenberg and moved to Altdorf, arriving at midday.

When Suvorov arrived in Altdorf, he realized with his trained eye[73] what

73. Here again, Clausewitz uses the word *Anschauung* (see note 43 of this chapter and volume 1, chapter 2, note 33). We have chosen to translate this word in a manner that fits the context in which it is used. However, *Anschauung* is often translated as "intuition." See Immanuel Kant, *Critique of Pure Reason*, trans. and ed. Paul Guyer and Allen W. Wood (Cambridge: Cambridge University Press, 2000), 757. In simple terms (and any budding philosophy majors will need to cover their ears), Kant is using *Anschauung* to mean a combination of intuition and inference. Clausewitz uses the word a number of times in *On War* too; see *On War*, 106, 115, 140, 192, 274, 352, 365, 396. For those checking the original German, see book 1, chaps. 3 and 5; book 2, chap. 2; book 3, chap. 6; book 4, chap. 14; book 5, chap. 18; book 6, chaps. 3 and 10. See also his use of the concept of coup d'oeil and military genius, in particular, in book 1, chap. 3. Essentially, a great commander can see through the fog and friction of war and visualize (intuit) what is unseen.

a huge blunder the perverse stupidity of the Austrian general staff had led to. The Gotthard road ended at the waves of Lake Lucerne, without a single vessel available. An impassable mountain massif confronts him, stretching its bare rocky arm up the gloomy Schächen valley like a gigantic signpost of destiny. He can only move through this valley; he has to cross these massive, jagged rocks by clambering up and down precarious shepherd and hunting tracks to Muota, where he will then be greeted by Schwyz's less hostile terrain. But he must hurry, because he is already a day late arriving in Altdorf, and the thunder of battle has been rolling along the Linth and the Limmat for two days already. It is too late to influence and decide that battle, but if he loses a moment in freeing himself from this rocky net that a pernicious plan has caught him in, the enemy may appear, and the enemy's sword may prevent him from getting out of it.

And Suvorov's army has already been assailed by the destructive forces of marching, fighting, and privation, eating away its solid structure like nitric acid on metal.[74] For six days it has hauled itself up and down across the rocky rubble of the mountains; for three days it has fought along tracks and footbridges, waded the Reuss, scaled its steep banks, slid along narrow bridges and timbers; torrential rain pours down from the thick clouds hanging on the mountain slopes, swelling the streams and rivers and making every step more difficult. The provisions brought with them on pack animals have not been able to keep up, and the exhausted troops are reduced to what little they can find from the locals or have taken from the French. Thus exertion and privation gnaw[75] at their strength with double effect, and the army's march from Airolo to Altdorf creates an endless, intermingled queue of pack animals and stragglers.

This was the state in which Suvorov arrived in Altdorf on 26 September. The most immediate, most urgent necessity would have been to concentrate his army, to give it a couple of days to recover and wait for the provisions. Nothing would have directly prevented Suvorov from doing so, since the only enemy nearby was Lecourbe's 5,000–6,000 men, and the rocky masses surrounding him everywhere were also protection against the more distant enemy. If the entry to or exit from the Muota valley were to be barred to him

74. Here is another example of Clausewitz using a contemporary scientific concept as a metaphor for his ideas; see note 11 in this chapter. See also volume 1, chapter 2, note 108, for a related discussion of the term *Schwerpunkt* and its scientific origin.

75. See *On War*, book 1, chap. 5, "On Physical Effort in War."

while he granted his army a couple of days' rest, he could still use the route over the Klausen Pass into the Linth valley or even through the Maderaner valley into the Rhine valley. While these paths were difficult enough, they could not compare with the one into the Muota valley. Here he had to continue along a footpath the likes of which he had not yet encountered, and indeed, such as perhaps no army has trodden for as long as war has been waged. To demand this of his army in the exhausted state in which it arrived at Altdorf required uncommon strength of will, and to obtain it from his troops took remarkable command of their emotions. A cautious commander—if we can even imagine one like that getting into such a situation in the first place—would have halted and then retreated. But Suvorov felt he was too strong to shrink back from such difficulty and too proud to stomach the idea that he should be the one to miss the rendezvous for battle that he had instructed his subordinates to make; it drove him to get there without losing a moment, nor did he lose one. Next morning he set off for Muota.

79 SUVOROV MOVES OUT OF THE SCHÄCHEN VALLEY INTO THE MUOTA VALLEY AND FALLS BACK FROM THERE INTO THE LINTH VALLEY

A road leads out of the Schächen valley above the Balm cliff face and through the Klausen Pass into the Linth valley; but there are just two footpaths leading to the Muota valley that are trodden only by shepherds and hunters. The easier of the two goes through the Bisis valley, while a shorter but much steeper one goes over the Chinzig Chulm and through the transverse valley that starts at Muota itself. Suvorov chose the latter alone, without making any use of the other, which naturally must have been due to some local circumstances.

The Russian army had probably camped far enough up the Schächen valley that it could not be overlooked by the French. But Generals Rosenberg and Auffenberg stayed at Altdorf as an advance guard against Lecourbe, whose advance guard Suvorov had made the mistake of tolerating on this side of Seedorf instead of driving it off and destroying the bridge.

Early on the 27th the advance guard began its march to Muota. The route from the one valley to the other is scarcely 8 miles long but is so arduous that an individual hiker would need seven or eight hours to cover it. Indeed, the first couple of hundred Cossacks forming the head of the advance guard only entered Muota at 5:00 p.m., after taking twelve hours to cover these 8 miles. In Muota, they surprised a couple of companies of French who had been sent there from Schwyz and captured some of them. These were probably troops Lecourbe had left behind, or else perhaps they belonged to Soult's division.

Suvorov himself arrived in Muota with the first division shortly before daybreak on the 28th. Thus he had spent the night on the ridge and taken perhaps twenty hours to cover this small stretch of the route. This slow progress was naturally due to the column constantly breaking up at places where the men could only clamber and stumble individually and with difficulty and danger along the cliffs, or where they had to help one another carefully along narrow bridges over chasms. The battalions then had to reassemble from time to time, each waiting for the next, so this very naturally explains how twenty hours could pass before one division of 8,000–10,000 men had completed this difficult crossing.

But the march of the whole army in uninterrupted succession took from the morning of the 27th until the evening of the 29th, sixty hours in all. During this whole time, we must therefore think of the Russian army, now numbering 25,000 after joining up with Auffenberg, as crawling slowly over the huge mountain ridge in a caterpillar motion. In the Muota valley, the first to arrive have to wait longingly for the rest, so as to be able to hurry out into more open country; in the Schächen valley, the battalions crammed together at the foot of the mountain have to wait impatiently to begin their march and to put the mountainside behind them, because the sustained rattle of musketry is already echoing from Altdorf, where the rear guard is covering their departure against Lecourbe's attack; on the slopes of the mountain itself, the poor heavily laden soldier, starving and barefoot, wheezes up the steep rockfaces slippery from rain and waterfalls and only presses on with a last-gasp effort because he feels it is the only way he will escape the arms of Death reaching out after him. In every cleft, detachments lie scattered around catching their breath, sick and exhausted men, tired and lame pack animals. How many fell victim to Death here because the last spark of their willpower gave out before they reached the goal or because a false step plunged them to be shattered in the abyss, no report tells us. But still to this day, the inhabitants of these valleys remember this unprecedented march with pity and admiration.[76]

76. Again, it is worth reading *On War*, book 1, chaps. 4 and 5, on danger in war and on physical effort in war, respectively.

Lecourbe attacked Suvorov's rear guard under General Rosenberg on the 27th, but this action had no decisive result; they fought with fluctuating fortunes. While this is understandable for the 27th, so long as the Russians were still superior, it is hard to see why Lecourbe could not obtain a glorious success on the 28th against the last troops to withdraw, which he obviously did not, since Masséna's report makes no mention of it. According to Suvorov's report, Rosenberg had already followed on by the 27th and had left only two infantry regiments facing Lecourbe; according to the archduke's account, which is probably based on General Auffenberg's report, Rosenberg's division did not arrive in Muota until the night of the 29th–30th,[77] from which it follows that it probably did not set off until the 28th. Since the archduke is always scrupulously careful in his accounts, whereas Suvorov's report has the character of much less clear and more confused recollections—as they must have been for the Russian officers concerning an event in a theater with which they were still unfamiliar—on this point we have followed the archduke's account.

As we said, we cannot quite understand how the bold and energetic Lecourbe did not achieve more against the rear guard, nor how he failed to capture a large number of pack animals. If it was the result of very good arrangements for the Russian withdrawal, we must very much regret not learning about these, since in that case, detailed reports of their dispositions and of the course of this march would be extremely instructive.

While Suvorov spent the 27th, 28th, or 29th covering the 8 miles from Altdorf to Muota and suffering effects from the march that were almost equivalent to those of a defeat, on the first two of those days, Masséna had been able to cover the 25 miles from Zurich to Schwyz without exerting himself in the least, so on 28 September he was already prepared to meet his opponent at Schwyz. That amply demonstrates the major strategic advantages that can be gained from possession of the more accessible terrain.[78]

77. Karl, 2:249.

78. What Clausewitz is getting at here is the role of terrain and the fact that accessible terrain facilitates maneuver. Thus, it provides an advantage to the side able to use it. See the discussion of terrain in *On War*, book 5, chap. 17. Although some of his ideas relate to the tactical, they also have broader implications for strategy, as difficult terrain precludes the effective use of cavalry, which in turn means that it is more difficult to inflict a decisive blow and employ pursuit.

On the 26th, on the Zurich battlefield, the French commander had learned of the events at the St. Gotthard. At the end of the battle he therefore gave General Ménard command of Ménard's and Lorges's divisions and the cavalry reserve, forming a corps of 18,000 men altogether, with which he was to pursue Korsakov to the Rhine and then observe him. Masséna set off to march to Schwyz with Mortier's 7,000-strong division; he ordered the infantry of Klein's division, about 6,000 men, to move to the area of Richterswil to support Soult, who was to march with the majority of his division to Weesen and Schänis.

To make some sense of these orders of General Masséna's, we must remember that when he issued them on the 26th, he perhaps did not yet know of the victory Soult had won on that day but had been told of Generals Jellachich's and Linken's advance into the Linth valley, without knowing of the former's subsequent retreat on the 26th. He therefore thought he had to send half of his available combat forces to the Linth (about 15,000 men) and appear on the Reuss with the rest (about 12,000). The fact that Klein's division was sent only to Richterswil and not directly to Soult's division is an utter half-measure, unless that was just careless drafting of the report and Richterswil was meant to indicate only the direction, not the destination.

At this time, there was a change of division commanders: Lecourbe had been appointed to take command of the Army of the Rhine; Masséna ordered Soult to take his place and transferred command of Soult's division to General Gazan.

Having made these dispositions, Masséna betook himself in person through Lucerne to General Lecourbe at Altdorf and was with him in the Schächen valley on 29 September. However, they found nothing there but dead or dying men and horses, the tragic traces of Suvorov's march away. General Masséna hereupon took Loison's brigade, which was the only unit Lecourbe had with him, across to Schwyz.

Masséna's presence in the Schächen valley proves that on the 29th the French still did not really know what had become of Suvorov.

Because of that, the 29th elapsed as well without the French doing anything significant in either the Schächen or Muota valley, and Suvorov and his army had time to haul themselves up and away over the mountain ridge.

On the 27th, when Suvorov himself was still on his way to Muota, he received news of a victory that General Linken had supposedly won in the Linth valley, a rumor that undoubtedly stemmed from that general's successful action at Wichler-Bad on the 25th. He believed this rumor unreservedly and saw it as a result of his overall plan being fulfilled, and as soon as he arrived in the Muota valley, he sent a detachment of Cossacks to Glarus to let General Molitor know that he was surrounded on all sides and to summon him to surrender. Here, the antics that so often pervaded Suvorov's personal actions seemed to spill over into actual warfare for once. When the Cossacks arrived, a French battalion was just in the process of occupying the Pragel mountain that forms the pass between the Muota and Klön valleys; the Cossacks were driven back and brought the first news of Korsakov's and Hotze's defeat. Since this news was supplied by the French, Suvorov thought it was a trick and would hear nothing of his officers' proposal that he should march across the Pragel to join Linken and break out of the Linth valley together; he much preferred to advance to Schwyz without delay. But it was not until the 28th that part of his army reached Muota in a state of considerable fatigue and disarray; exactly what enemy forces might be encountered at Schwyz could not be foreseen, so finally Suvorov had to accept that it was wiser to concentrate his forces first and to cancel the order he had already given. The march on Schwyz was now postponed until the 29th. But soon the rumor of Korsakov's and Hotze's defeat arrived from other quarters, and it became more certain and was further confirmed with every hour; impacted by this new obstacle to the execution of his plan, Suvorov called a council of war. In this, the quite natural view must have been asserted that anything Suvorov's army—now probably numbering no more than 15,000 infantry, including Auffenberg's, and with hardly any artillery and very little ammunition—might achieve on its own between Lake Zurich and Lake Lucerne would not be able to compensate for Korsakov's and Hotze's disaster; therefore, even if a further advance through Schwyz were initially successful, this could never lead to reversing the outcome overall; rather, it was much more likely that as soon as he left the protection of the mountains, Suvorov would be in the greatest danger of being attacked on all sides by superior forces, trapped by defiles in every direction, and in a completely hopeless situation. This conviction naturally must have pushed him toward the only option that was left, namely, to secure the Pragel as quickly as possible so as to join up via the Klön valley with Linken, who was still thought to be winning there. Besides, even though this road from Schwyz to Glarus is not suitable for wheeled traffic, it is one of the better ones, so it was not a question of another march like the one out of the Schächen valley. Nonetheless, it took a long time before the fearless Suvorov's proud spirit could accept the idea of retreating. In his simple strategy, retreat and defeat are the same thing,[79] so this retreat would have destroyed both the enemy's belief in Suvorov's invincibility and his own. We see here that, among commanders whose main principle in leading their army is simply one of courage and energy, this principle must often be caught like a wild animal and led in the right direction if it is not to destroy rather than to create. The collective vote finally won out over Suvorov's feelings, and he grudgingly gave the order for Auffenberg to set off for the Pragel bright and early on the 29th. But since the army itself had still not reassembled by that day, its departure had to be postponed until the 30th.

On the 29th, then, while Suvorov's rear guard is still moving over the Chinzig Chulm, Masséna and Lecourbe are inspecting his old campsite, and Molitor is hard on General Linken's heels, Auffenberg easily ejects the battalion Molitor had posted on the Pragel and advances to the Klöntal lake. But that did not actually open the pass. Upon hearing news of the attack on the Pragel, Molitor had let General Linken go, pursued by just two battalions, while with the third he quickly turned back to the Klöntal lake and reached its eastern end before Auffenberg could get past the narrow defile formed by it. Molitor's arrival in this advantageous position brought Auffenberg to a standstill.

On 30 September Suvorov began his march to the Klöntal lake. He left General Rosenberg with Rosenberg's and Förster's divisions, about 8,000 men, as a rear guard at Muota. Molitor had meanwhile moved up a third battalion, and that same day, early on the 30th, he vigorously attacked General Auffenberg but could not drive him off. Both of them now stayed quiet until the afternoon, when, after Suvorov's first division had joined Auffenberg, Molitor made a reconnaissance in force against the allies. Auffenberg let his troops on the road give way, while he kept the rest concealed on the heights; when the French imprudently pursued, he pounced on them and pushed after them through the defile along the lake, reaching the eastern end at the same time as them. The allies got no further than that on this day; night fell, and Suvorov still could not reach Glarus that day.

79. This argument ties in with Clausewitz's thoughts on purpose and means in war as well as his thinking on military genius. Suvorov was a good commander, but he struggled, according to Clausewitz, to see that retreat was the best option to keep alive any hope of overall success in the campaign. A short-term loss might lead to a longer-term gain.

On 1 October the allies attacked General Molitor anew and forced him to retreat first behind the bridge at Netstal and then down both banks of the Linth to Näfels and Mollis. But this retreat was conducted as an obstinate fighting withdrawal, and although the Russians repeatedly charged the French with the bayonet and, as Molitor himself says in his report, often got in among his men, he did not lose a single gun. He was able to hold on at Näfels and Mollis against his pursuer, Bagration, until toward evening; then, when Bagration had finally taken the villages of Näfels and Mollis, Gazan hurried up in support with a couple of battalions and forced him to relinquish them again.

Thus Molitor and his four or five battalions had fought against Jellachich on the 25th and 26th, against Linken on the 28th and 29th, against Auffenberg on the 30th, and against Bagration on 1 October, with admirable success against them all. We must regard this force multiplication of a single brigade, this unwavering resistance against foe after foe, as one of the finest episodes of the campaign.[80]

Suvorov and the troops he had with him moved to Glarus on 1 October, where he found a store of provisions with which he could remedy the lack, which had become extreme.

While Suvorov was carrying out this two-day march with his advance guard fighting all the way, Rosenberg's outstanding bravery on the one hand and Masséna's overly cautious measures on the other were saving him from the risk of being caught between two fires.

General Masséna had returned to Schwyz on 29 September and had contented himself on the 30th with a reconnaissance in force into the Muota valley. This drove back the Russian outposts, but when it came up against their main body's position at Muota, it was attacked and thrown back to Schwyz.

Having convinced himself by this reconnaissance that Suvorov and his main force had moved to the Linth valley, on the same day, General Masséna sent a few battalions of Mortier's division there via Einsiedeln.

On 1 October Masséna apparently advanced for a serious attack on Muota with all his troops, apart from one demi-brigade of Lecourbe's division, thus 8,000–10,000 strong. But although he had superior numbers and his opponent had almost no artillery, he was so completely beaten that he was driven back to Schwyz, losing five guns and 1,000 prisoners. The reasons for this extraordi-

80. His resistance also shows us what was possible, leading us to ask why the Austrians in particular could not seem to fight as hard or as well as the French.

nary result were partly the Russians' exceptional courage and partly an all-too-simple overhasty advance by Masséna along the valley bottom without having secured its slopes.

Masséna now gave up completely on advancing into the Muota valley and, *because Korsakov was once more threatening the corps he had left behind on the Thur, and (as Masséna put it) he would not be so fortunate as to lure Suvorov through the exit left open at Einsiedeln and into Switzerland's open country, he decided to turn against Korsakov again; but first he wanted (in his words) to completely finish off Suvorov and therefore to attack him in the Linth valley.* We must make do with these confused and unsatisfactory motives for the French commander, which we have taken from his official report, because none of the historians can offer anything better. We will defer closer examination of these to the end of the chapter.

Masséna therefore left General Mortier with six battalions in the Muota valley, under orders to follow the Russians' movements, and took the rest of the troops with him, perhaps 4,000–5,000 men under General Soult, to join Molitor's brigade and Gazan's division in the Linth valley.

80 SUVOROV MOVES THROUGH THE SERNF VALLEY INTO THE RHINE VALLEY

As for the Russian commander, whom we left as he arrived at Glarus, his next steps and particularly his sojourn at Glarus need careful examination; all the more so as the two main historians, the archduke and Jomini, have presented views of this part of Suvorov's march that are not clearly expressed nor perhaps even clearly thought through.

Suvorov came to Glarus on 1 October. On the 2nd, as Jomini relates[81] (though not the archduke), he sent General Auffenberg to the Sernf valley to secure the pass there leading to Graubündten. He now had one division at Muota, a second facing Näfels, and a third in the Sernf valley, with his center in Glarus. He stays here on 2, 3, and 4 October; the archduke says it is *because he cannot decide what to do.*[82] We indeed concede that men like Suvorov, who are absolutely dynamic so long as they can follow one simple desire, can

81. Jomini, 12:276–279.

82. Karl, 2:253–255.

become very indecisive when the situation is more complicated, in that they let these situations they do not themselves understand be explained to them by conflicting advisers and thus come to no clear view. Still, it would be foolish to imagine that this indecision would be such that Suvorov would have been continuously wrestling over it for three days, since even a weak man would not behave so at a moment when the situation demands action; rather, such indecisive vacillation arises from incidents that cast the matter in a different light yet again and upset the previous decision, but which a strong-minded and forceful character will not allow to induce him to make an error.[83]

When Suvorov arrived in Glarus on 1 October, he was as astounded as he was indignant to find not one of the Austrian corps in the Linth valley. It follows from this that he did not know their true situation and indeed must not have had any discussions with them before then; communications between them could not have begun before 1 October.

If we enumerate the various routes that Suvorov could take, they were the following:

1. To advance along the left bank of the Linth;
2. To advance through Weesen, on the right bank of the river;
3. To march to Walenstadt via Mollis and along Lake Walen, since there is no direct overland route across the mountain ridge that runs to Lake Walen between Weesen and Mühlehorn;
4. To move through the upper Linth valley to Panix [Pigniu] in the Rhine valley.

The first and second of these routes were to be regarded as continuing the offensive and were conceivable only on the one precondition that the Austrian corps would cooperate. Even if we wish to concede the possibility that, with the 10,000 men that he could use if he occupied the passes behind him, Suvorov was in a position to drive the French before him into the plain, the same consideration arises here that had deterred him from advancing out of the Muota valley through Schwyz; that is, he could not even things up on his

83. This section ties in with the chapter in *On War* (book 1, chap. 3) on military genius and a commander's ability to be bold and make decisions despite the fact that the further up the command chain one goes, the more difficult the decisions become. A commander needs the right intellect and temperament to do this.

own, and he could not let himself be trapped between Masséna's army and the French-held Linth. It was equally impossible for him to stay on the right bank of the Linth between the river and the high ridge that runs along the northern shore of Lake Walen to the Linth unless the Austrians had recaptured that ridge from the French.

When we consider that the Austrian corps, which were now perhaps 15,000 strong and whose precise positions at this time are unfortunately not given by the archduke in his history, had been spread out from Reichenau to Bregenz, it is very understandable that even if only 10,000 of these men were supposed to be concentrated on the banks of the lower Linth for a joint operation with the Russians, that would have required at least four or five days, and the allies would have been about 20,000 strong with very little artillery. But by that time, it was reasonable to expect that Masséna could have been ready with just as many or more of his own combat forces; the allies would have had to operate in separate corps again, which, at various points in their vicinity as they headed out, would have had lakes, mountains, marshes, and the enemy between them, while Masséna had his force united and totally in hand. It is quite obvious that a successful outcome could not be expected in this situation. But if the outcome were not successful, Suvorov could easily lose his line of retreat, since the line from the Linth valley led over nothing but narrow mountain roads that the enemy could have seized behind him. When we consider all these difficulties, we cannot believe that Suvorov could adopt such a plan.

The third route was the closest to the Austrian corps and the shortest for getting into the Rhine valley, which must be regarded as Suvorov's actual and natural aim. The road to Walenstadt goes through Mollis and over the mountains to Mühlehorn on Lake Walen and then along the lake; it is about 10 miles long. Suvorov could expect to find the Austrians in Walenstadt about 4,000–5,000 strong, for since he could establish communications with them, and since they were bound to be able to concentrate such a force near Sargans within one day, then if Suvorov allowed them just a couple of days, there was nothing to prevent them moving to Walenstadt; even if the French had already advanced to that place, it could only be with a weak detachment that could not prevent them linking up. The only difficulty on this route lay in gaining control of Näfels and Mollis. However, we do not wish to close our eyes to the fact that here too, there was a great risk of losing any line of retreat. Suvorov must have heard the fighting at Muota on the 30th; he could not in any way rely on Rosenberg winning the victory he did the following day, so when he heard the action there begin again on 1 October, he had to expect that on the 1st or 2nd Rosenberg would arrive in Glarus pursued by the French. In these circumstances, to move away from Glarus in the opposite direction from his one secure line of retreat, uncertain whether he would be able to open another one, was always an extremely risky venture.

On the fourth route, the only difficulties to be overcome were natural ones. However, these were not trivial. The ways out of the upper Linth valley through the Martinsloch to Flims and across the Panten Bridge are very difficult footpaths; the route through Wichler-Bad is a small road whose passes are much higher than the Chinzig Chulm and, at that time of year, was already covered in snow. Admittedly, Linken had just moved through these passes, but with a much smaller body of troops.

Of the four routes mentioned above, Suvorov chose the last, because after the resistance Bagration had encountered at Näfels and Mollis on the 1st, he judged that it was too risky to carve his way through Mollis to Lake Walen and then fight through to the Austrians via the continuous defile alongside the lake, when he did not know for certain whether they actually held the area of Sargans and Walenstadt.

The archduke criticizes the Russian commander's decision, whereas General Jomini[84] defends it, but neither says exactly what they think of Suvorov's breakout from the Linth valley, and they obviously confuse the first three routes we listed, so we are left feeling as dissatisfied by the one verdict as by the other. Along with that, the archduke makes the scarcely understandable assertion that even if Suvorov did have to fear a collision with Masséna's main force, he should not have let that deter him, for as the archduke says, "what else can a man do when every exit is barred?"[85] But two lines later he opines, "the rigors of the one way out that remained open to Suvorov (namely, through the Sernf valley) would have cost him more than fighting his way through Masséna's whole army."[86] First, this is an exaggeration; second, the archduke forgets that even if the losses from retreating were just as great as they might have been from fighting his way through, at least the outcome of the former was not subject to any doubt, unlike the latter; and third, he overlooks the

84. Jomini, 12:278–279. Jomini flatters the archduke by referring to him as "an illustrious historian," even as Jomini disagrees with him.

85. Karl, 2:255.

86. Karl, 2:255–256.

fact that the main difficulty Suvorov encountered in crossing the ridge was a recent snowfall, a chance circumstance that could have been unknown or unnoticed at the moment Suvorov made his decision.

From what we know of the matter now, we may be sure that if Suvorov had marched against the French on 1 October with everything he had in the Linth valley, he certainly would have chucked out Molitor and whatever had arrived of Gazan's division, gained possession of Mollis and Näfels, and opened the way to Lake Walen and to joining up with the Austrians; for when Jellachich learned of Suvorov's arrival at Glarus, on 2 October he returned to Sargans, left a garrison in Walenstadt, and pushed his advance guard along the lake, where he ran into the first French at Kerenzen, who fell back before him. Petrasch too, ordered by the archduke to support the Russians,[87] concentrated part of his force between Fläsch and Maienfeld on 4 October. But on 1 October Suvorov could not have known about this advance by General Jellachich; he could and indeed must have learned of it the next day, and perhaps then there was still time to take Näfels and Mollis and clear the road as far as necessary. But by the 2nd it was already dangerous to move away from Glarus, since Suvorov could not be sure whether Rosenberg had not already been pushed into the Linth valley that day.

Thus we see that marching to Lake Walen must have seemed an extremely awkward business, and since it certainly could not have been imagined that the move across the mountains to Panix would be as terrible as that march turned out to be, we can very well understand why Suvorov, or rather his general staff, could have preferred the latter route.

As far as Suvorov's lingering at Glarus from the 1st to the 5th is concerned, at first glance, this is certainly something very remarkable, since he found himself in a position in which he absolutely could not stay and that could get significantly worse with every hour; but upon closer examination, this remarkableness disappears. Jomini tries to conceal the gap in his understanding, as historians so often do, by having Suvorov march away on the 4th, the day Rosenberg joined him, and by saying that Suvorov had wanted to wait for Rosenberg.[88] But General Rosenberg was only 15 miles from him and, consequently, could have joined him on any day. Also, Suvorov did not march away on the 4th but only sent his pack animals ahead then; he himself

87. Karl, 2:256–257.
88. Jomini, 12:278–279.

did not set off until 3:00 on the morning of the 5th.[89] But if we tell ourselves that Suvorov sensibly did not want to have General Rosenberg leave Muota before he himself had made the decision to move through the Sernf valley, and that he in turn could not start the march until Rosenberg had arrived, then we can explain Suvorov's halt at Glarus simply by the delay in reports coming from the Rhine valley. If, for example, he had not learned until the evening of the 3rd what the Austrians had decided and where they were, and whether Auffenberg had successfully reached the Panixer Pass 20 miles from Glarus and what news he brought from the Rhine valley, it follows that he would not have had Rosenberg join him until the 4th and could not have marched away himself until the 5th. These are, of course, only conjectures, but it is still better to stand by a not unlikely conjecture than by some literal bankruptcy of intellect on the part of the Russian commander in having his mental machinery stand still for seventy-two hours. This waiting for reports that were perhaps not absolutely necessary, this hearkening to rumors that probably changed from hour to hour, might still deserve to be called indecisiveness, since, as we have already said, this is exactly the way it can sneak unnoticed into a commander's headquarters and into his soul; but to express such a verdict, we would have to have reports from Suvorov's headquarters directly before our eyes. The archduke probably did not lack such reports, and in this respect, we certainly believe that he is not without justification in accusing the Russian commander of indecisiveness.

We do not need to demonstrate in any detail the danger from General Suvorov's lingering at Glarus. Those poor lines of retreat that were still open behind him could be taken from him at any moment through the Schächen and Rhine valleys, and the utter lack of provisions must very soon drive him out of the Linth valley, like the fox from its den.

Rosenberg joined Suvorov on 4 October; therefore, he must not have marched away before the 3rd, and Mortier must not have attacked him again on the 2nd and 3rd; nor was there any rearguard action to indicate a serious pursuit.

After the convoy of all the pack animals had begun to move on the afternoon of the 4th, Suvorov set off on the morning of the 5th and moved to Elm. On the 6th he began the march across the Panixer mountains that Auffenberg had already completed three days earlier on the 3rd.

The route leading out of the Linth valley through the Sernf valley via Matt,

89. Duffy has this as 3:00 p.m. on 6 October. Duffy, *Eagles over the Alps*, 248–249.

Elm, and Wichler-Bad, through the Jätzischlund [Jetzbach], over the Rinkenkopf, close by the Haus massif to Panix is one of those little mountain roads that is still usable by animals; it is the usual connection between Glarus and Chur. However, this is not the only way to get to the Rhine valley from the Linth, as there are several other footpaths over the Alps, though these are partly just hunters' and shepherds' tracks and are very dangerous; coming through these with a large body of men and animals would have involved the same difficulties encountered between the Schächen and Muota valleys, and because this northwestern major ridge of the Alps is significantly higher and larger, it probably would have been quite impossible. Therefore, there could have been no question of Suvorov retreating by any other way than this road, and this was, in itself, certainly not to be compared with the footpath over the Chinzig Chulm; but because fresh snow had fallen a few days earlier that was loosely packed and several feet deep,[90] it had become almost unusable.

Thus the poor Russians who had not yet recovered from their march over the Chinzig Chulm, carrying a host of sick and wounded with them, mostly barefoot and contending with serious privation, were once again ordered to make unspeakable exertions in scaling one of those high alpine ridges that had confronted them everywhere for the last fourteen days and that must have made them feel as though they were under the spell of some demonic power that had decided on their downfall among these crags.

In his description of this march, the archduke says:

> From Elm the march crossed the steep frontier of Graubündten on the 6th. A fresh snowfall two feet deep that gave way underfoot covered the narrow footpaths by which the rocky masses of the mountain range had to be clambered over laboriously in single file. Looking down from the summit, as far as the eye could see, Graubündten and the Tyrol were revealed as a huge snowy wasteland: no sign of habitation, no path to be seen; not one bush provided the possibility of making a fire; no rocky pinnacle stood out to serve as a landmark or pillar for the traveler. On the slope on the other side the cold wind had frozen the snow so slippery that only the plummet of the men and horses in front could warn those following them

90. Several feet of snow in early October is certainly unlucky. If the archduke's description is accurate and two feet of snow had fallen (see the quotation at note 91), it is reasonable to surmise that it had blown around and formed deep drifts. This is a classic example of the fog and friction of war.

> to swap one dangerous track for another just as dangerous. The whole day passed like this. The advance guard and headquarters got to Panix with difficulty. The bulk of the column spent the night on the highest peak and on the slopes either side of the mountain under frosty open skies. More than 200 men and most of the pack animals lost their lives; one by one the mountain guns that had been brought with them plunged into chasms, and by the 8th the tail of the column had still not reached Panix.[91]

Thus, this march had taken three whole days. Suvorov had had to leave the sick and wounded, several thousand in number, in the Linth valley and entrust them to the enemy's sense of humanity.

Suvorov transferred his headquarters to Ilanz on the 8th, and on the 10th all those who had not fallen victim to fearsome nature were united there.

The French had followed the Russians withdrawing from around Näfels only as far as Matt on the 5th and had not disturbed their retreat thereafter.

With this, Suvorov's alpine march and his army's suffering ended. In the Rhine valley he found provisions and a good road to Lake Constance held by the Austrian corps.

This march over the high Alps had lasted three weeks from 21 September to 10 October with constant fighting, exertion, and privation and had cost the army a third of the men, a majority of the horses, and all the artillery it had set off with from Varese. These losses are comparable with those from losing a battle, but the moral effect was different. If Suvorov and his army could perform this march in a flash through a country that was so awesome to them, and of which they had only confused images and fantastic impressions afterward, it must have seemed to them as though they were a rushing torrent that had breached every dam put in front of them by the enemy at the St. Gotthard, the Crispalt, Amsteg, Altdorf, and in the Klön valley, and surmounting each of these must have seemed like a victory over the enemy army. They had scaled these incredible mountains on paths no army had ever trodden and probably none would tread again, and when they sank down exhausted like a hunted animal in the Muota valley after their most strenuous effort and the enemy commander himself hastened up to overwhelm them risk and trouble free, then like a bear in its cave they turned on him, tore him to pieces, and chased him out again in fear and confusion. Thus, when we see Suvorov report this march out of

91. Karl, 2:262–263.

his critical situation like a great flood of victories, we should not mistake this for the usual boasting employed to offset the impression of utter defeat. While Suvorov's march was more a defeat than a victory in all its material effects, in its moral impact, it was more a victory than a defeat.[92] And so it would have proved, had it not been that alongside the feeling of achieving something most extraordinary and being capable of extraordinary things, its twin brother of hatred for the Austrians was also awakened and the last embers of the Russian commander's goodwill extinguished, so that like a headstrong khan with his horde of Tartars, he suddenly turned aside and rode home.[93]

81 MASSÉNA COMPLETES THE CONQUEST OF SWITZERLAND

In section 79 we said that, after leaving Mortier with six battalions in the Muota valley, on 2 October the French commander marched off to the Linth valley with 4,000–5,000 men. The road from Schwyz to Näfels via Einsiedeln is only about 20 miles, so Masséna reasonably could have arrived there on the 3rd. Likewise, the elements of Gazan's division that Masséna had ordered there on 26 or 27 September must have arrived on 3 October. Since Gazan's division had presumably advanced after the Austrians as far as the Rhine, we can imagine that it was very spread out, so General Gazan probably had only a few thousand men with him in the Linth valley; if we assume he had 4,000 men, General Molitor 1,500, and the troops Masséna brought with him (of which he left one battalion in Einsiedeln) at 4,000, then the whole force concentrated in the Linth valley would have come to 9,000–10,000 men. The French commander, of whom the history makes no mention for eight whole days, seems to have waited for the Russians with this force in a position at Näfels and Mollis for a couple of days, that is to say, on the 4th and 5th. This was indeed quite natural, since in advancing against Suvorov, he would have

92. A veritable triumph over adversity, despite the cost.

93. This last point is important, for after this episode, one can see why the Russians felt they were paying both too high a price and far more of a price than Austria for a war from which Austria hoped to achieve more than Russia did. The problems during this part of the campaign certainly must have enhanced the already considerable ill will between the army commanders.

had to leave the Austrians on Lake Walenstadt almost in his rear. There is not a single word about the reserve under Klein, which had moved to Richterswil; it probably remained there.

After Suvorov had begun his march through the Sernf valley on the 6th, Masséna too left the Linth valley and presumably betook himself in person to his left wing in order to drive those allied troops still on this side of the Rhine at the bridges at Büsingen, Diessenhofen, and Konstanz back across the river. He ordered General Loison to drive the allies out of the St. Gotthard and from the outposts they still had on the left bank of the upper Rhine.

This gave rise to the following new distribution of the French army:

Tharreau's division remained in the Rhone valley facing Haddick.

Loison concentrated his division in the Reuss valley again to take the St. Gotthard Pass.

Mortier, with most of his division, moved to Walenstadt, Mels, and Sargans.

Soult, with a small part of Mortier's division and a brigade of Gazan's, moved to Rheineck to observe the Austrians on the Rhine; Gazan himself, with his other brigade, moved to Konstanz; and Klein's infantry moved to Andelfingen as reserve for Oudinot's left wing along the Thur, which comprised Lorges's and Ménard's divisions with the cavalry reserve.

On the allied side, Colonel Strauch had not stayed for long in the position indicated to him by Suvorov in the St. Gotthard; he left only outposts in the St. Gotthard and the Bedretto valley (the western source of the Ticino), with two battalions in support in Dazio Grande, and had moved to Bellinzona with the rest. The archduke sees this as a quite natural measure for reasons of supply,[94] but the Russians seem to have taken this retreat from the St. Gotthard badly as well.

When we consider how Suvorov's march through the area at the foot of the St. Gotthard must have devoured its resources, we can well understand how, right at this time, Colonel Strauch would have had great difficulty keeping his main body in Airolo.

Generals Linken and Auffenberg had joined up in the Rhine valley and moved up it so that they were between Ilanz and Disentis.

94. Karl, 2:268.

Jellachich was in the vicinity of Maienfeld, while still occupying the Kunkels Pass and the Tamina valley on the left bank of the Rhine.

Petrasch had occupied the position at Feldkirch and was observing the Rhine as far as Lake Constance.

On the right wing, Korsakov had joined up with the 4,000-strong Bavarian division and Condé's corps of 2,700 men and taken position between Schafhausen and Lake Constance.

General Titov and his three battalions that had fought at Walenstadt on the 26th had retreated to Konstanz, but when a weak enemy reconnaissance approached the town on the 30th, he had abandoned it, destroyed the bridge, and then moved to join Korsakov. The French then moved into Konstanz and were busy repairing the bridge to Petershausen, where there was still a magazine, when a couple of squadrons of Austrian dragoons rushed up just in time, dismounted, drove the French off again, and then occupied Konstanz itself.

Korsakov himself had a bridgehead at Büsingen that he had occupied with 1,800 men. To cover the second bridge at Diesenhofen, he had six battalions and twelve squadrons establish a camp in front of the town. He was with the rest of his troops behind these two points.

General Nauendorf's troops had hitherto been spread out between Schafhausen and Basel. He now concentrated them more at a single point and reinforced himself with a couple of thousand Austrian cavalry that were on their way to follow the archduke to the Neckar. These cavalry were probably some from Hotze's corps that had moved away before the French attack. This made Nauendorf 8,000–10,000 strong and in a better state to rush to General Korsakov's aid. But the French had followed only as far as the Thur, so Condé's corps was ordered to occupy Konstanz.

Let us now recount the few events that transpired in these opposing positions and completed the French conquest of Switzerland.

Since Strauch was in Bellinzona, Loison was able to regain possession of the St. Gotthard easily by driving off the Austrian outposts. He pushed across the Crispalt on 10 October and presumably through the Maderaner valley as well, into the Anterior Rhine valley. He probably moved through the Linth valley itself over the Klausen Pass and through the Schächen valley straight to Altdorf, since, if he had had to take the detour via Einsiedeln and then by water from Brunnen to Flüelen, it would have been impossible for him to appear at Disentis and be able to attack on the 10th, the day the last of

Suvorov's troops reached Ilanz. Perhaps his foremost troops were just those from Gudin's brigade who had retreated to the Furka Pass on 24 September.

General Linken, who, as we already said, had pushed left toward Disentis when Suvorov descended into the Rhine valley so as to cover the Russians' debouchment, was therefore attacked on the very day this was completed. It is not clear from the accounts whether he was driven off forcibly by Loison or whether he voluntarily withdrew again, having fulfilled his mission. He took position at Reichenau and occupied the Domleschg valley as far as Thusis. For the time being, the Austrians also retained possession of the Kunkels Pass and the Tamina valley, since Loison did not move beyond Ilanz. This enabled Suvorov to continue his march undisturbed.

Three serious actions were fought on the French army's left wing on 7 October.

Upon Suvorov's arrival in the Muota valley, he learned of Korsakov's defeat and wrote to the generals in Korsakov's force on the 28th: "You will answer with your head for any backward step you take: I am coming to fix your mistakes."[95] It was probably this letter received by Korsakov in early October that made him feel the full weight of the responsibility that would fall upon him if he did not do something for his commander in chief. After he had rallied his forces again behind the Rhine, then including the Bavarians and émigrés, they could have come to 18,000–20,000 men, but with very little artillery; Lorges's and Ménard's divisions were roughly just as strong. Admittedly, General Nauendorf was nearby with 8,000–10,000 men, but these were actually facing Chabran's division at Lörrach, and besides, Korsakov was not in charge of Nauendorf. Now, even if Korsakov had actually been able to complete his preparations for a new offensive right at the start of October, thus before Masséna arrived with his reserve, the situation did not promise any particular success. But his attack was postponed until the 7th, on which day Masséna was already at Andelfingen with the reserve under Klein; the prospect of success was therefore even smaller. But Korsakov's situation was such that he had to do something, even against the odds. In this case, it was certainly better for him personally to be beaten once again than to stand by undefeated and watch whatever misfortunes might be befalling General Suvorov at that moment. But in such a case, criticism cannot disallow that personal interest, assuming

95. In French: "*Vous répondrez sur votre tête de chaque pas de plus que vous ferez en arrière: je viens réparer vos fautes.*"

that we are talking not about useless sacrifice but about great daring; for in his practical actions, no man can ever be a mere dutiful automaton, especially not a general. It is in exactly such personal interest that the missions he is tasked with and the duties imposed on him must find the surge of energy in his own noble efforts by which they are supposed to be carried out. Thus, we find Korsakov's decision entirely natural; all that the critic can find fault with is that instead of acting with the prudence and caution the situation required, he let half-measures creep in.

Before Korsakov could be ready for his offensive, Masséna had ordered his left wing to move against the Russians' bridges. This happened on the 6th, when Ménard's division advanced on Büsingen and Lorges's on Diesenhofen and toward Stein. On this day Oudinot moved to Kloster Paradies with a couple of thousand men and drove the Russian outposts back into the bridgehead redoubts. When the garrison sortied and attacked him determinedly, he withdrew again some way.

On the 7th the French themselves were trying to advance with both their columns, probably to drive the Russians entirely back across the river, when the latter moved against them.

In his account, the archduke characterizes this advance by Korsakov very well:

> On the 27th [*sic*][96] General Korsakov advanced from Büsingen out of the bridgehead and through the Scharen woods with 10 battalions and 22 squadrons—uncertain about what to do—since in his soul, his wish to avoid getting involved in anything serious vied with his fear of being rebuked for being inactive for a long time and of being blamed for having done nothing to alleviate Suvorov's situation. The whole affair was therefore designated as a reconnaissance in force. Like someone who has reluctantly resolved to do something and is trying to get it over with quickly, without waiting for his cavalry to cross Korsakov dashed up with only his infantry to the heights at Schlatt and Trüllikon against Ménard's division. This and Lorges's division were just in the process of advancing to the attack against Diesenhofen. The Russian infantry thrust in among the enemy's ranks with such impetuosity that he was beaten back to Andelfingen with heavy losses. Here Masséna restored the situation at the head of the grenadiers from his

96. This should read 7th and is clearly an error.

reserve, wrested the Russians' victory away from them, and forced them to fall back through the Scharen woods into the bridgehead. The French sat quietly occupying these woods until 7:00 in the evening; but then they suddenly burst out to storm the bridgehead, but were nonetheless twice beaten back steadfastly and successfully, whereupon Masséna withdrew to Trüllikon again and the Russians finally occupied the Scharen woods.[97]

In combination with Korsakov's attack, General Voinov also approached from Diesenhofen with two battalions and one squadron. Fortune favored his advance initially: he captured an enemy cannon and several prisoners. But when the main column had to concede its gains, Voinov could not withstand the pressure from Lorges's division. He returned to Diesenhofen, where he held out with great courage until nightfall, but then abandoned the left bank of the Rhine and destroyed the bridge behind him.[98]

The allies did no better at Konstanz. Condé's 2,700-strong corps was here, composed mainly of cavalry, which had just arrived from Volhynia, where it had been enjoying the Russians' hospitality until then. When it reached Stockach, the archduke was there again, back from the Neckar; this was the moment the Russians abandoned Konstanz, to his great displeasure, and it became the reason why the archduke deployed this corps there, because he attached great value to this crossing point in connection with a new invasion of Switzerland. For God knows what other random reasons, and as if this corps did not have too many cavalry already, a Russian hussar regiment was attached to it, so that it took position in the very broken country of the vineyard-covered hills in front of Konstanz with 3,000 French, Russian, and Austrian cavalry and very few infantry. On the 7th Prince Condé was attacked by Gazan, the left wing of his position was overwhelmed toward evening, and the Kreuzlingen gate into Konstanz was taken before his right wing had begun its retreat. The French now pressed into Konstanz, but instead of seizing the Rhine bridge immediately, they dispersed into the city, fell into disorder, and began looting. This and the arrival of night made it possible for the right wing to fight its way through the French in Konstanz itself and to succeed in getting across the bridge, which was then demolished.

The archduke, who, as we said, was back from the Neckar at this time, was

97. Karl, 2:274–275.
98. Karl, 2:275.

unhappy about what had happened in these three places and was concerned for the pontoons used to build the bridges at Büsingen, since he realized the Russians were not serious about defending the bridgehead any longer. He therefore authorized General Korsakov and his troops to retreat and gave the order to dismantle the bridge.[99]

Now, with the exception of the Kunkels Pass, which they did not take until early November, the French held the whole of the left bank of the Rhine, thus all of Switzerland except Graubündten, just as they had at the start of the campaign. But Suvorov's army in Graubündten was moving toward Lake Constance from one side, as was Archduke Charles's army in Swabia from the other, and these two commanders in chief, linking up with Korsakov and Petrasch, would again give the allies a marked preponderance that could put the outcome of the whole campaign in question once more. The following section, in which we have to recount the events on the Rhine, will lead us back to that situation and to the end of the campaign in Germany.

82 REFLECTIONS: THE ROUTE ACROSS THE ST. BERNARD

As we have already said, in the section of the campaign we have just finished, there lies the turning point of the campaign and of the whole war, and actually, this is all the more remarkable because, until then, the war had followed a constantly successful course. The whole of Italy up to the walls of the fortresses of Genoa and Cuneo had been wrested away from the French, and even the bastion of Switzerland seemed about to fall, when two intrinsically unremarkable measures brought about events that, three weeks later, breached the alliance between Austria and Russia and thereby caused a general turnaround in the fortunes of war.

Those two measures were the departure of Archduke Charles for the Rhine and of Suvorov to Switzerland. However, because their higher-level significance belongs more to the campaign as a whole than to this section, we wish to defer our reflections on that until the conclusion of the campaign and for now just engage ourselves with Suvorov's march to Switzerland, so far as its intended immediate outcome and the events associated with it

99. Karl, 2:277.

are concerned. Although we have already presented our observations about the most important of these events, the battle of Zurich, we must crave our readers' attention and perhaps their patience for longer than usual. It would, of course, be briefer and indeed might look better to say in a couple of words what the end result of our reflections will be—that the only sensible way Suvorov could have gone was through the Splügen Pass—but then a host of circumstances and questions of general interest would be left undiscussed. The march through the St. Gotthard is such an extraordinary event, one might say such a gigantic mistake, that any active spirit of inquiry must find it absolutely essential to take a really close look at it to understand it clearly.

The march through the St. Gotthard cannot be considered in a comprehensive way without considering a march through the St. Bernard, as was actually discussed in Asti.[100] We therefore regard it as being necessary in the interest of theory to also take into consideration this alternative that was so close at hand, and we wish to do this before we examine the march through the St. Gotthard in more detail as to its *aim, plan, and execution.* The theoretical consideration of that question will make our critical investigation of this event easier, in that it will allow some preliminary light to be cast upon it.

The march through the St. Bernard leads through Martigny into the Rhone valley, then along the Rhone to Vevey on Lake Geneva, from which several roads lead into Switzerland's open country. Of these roads, none was so natural for Suvorov's purpose as that through Fribourg to Bern.

The route through the St. Bernard was a *strategic outflanking*, that is, one that either would not lead to a decisive battle at all but would *interrupt the French lines of communication*, or else would lead to a decisive battle that would *not* be fought *in combination* with the combat forces facing the enemy's front. As far as the latter was concerned, we must ask how General Suvorov could have thought of striking in combination with Korsakov and Hotze, since it would take him at least four or five days to reach Vevey from the mo-

100. Clausewitz argues in his chapter on critical analysis (*On War*, book 2, chap. 5) that for analytical purposes, all available courses of action should be examined critically, not just the one ultimately chosen. Only then can one know and understand whether the correct decision was made, as it is not enough to look at a decision in isolation and pronounce judgment on it without examining the alternatives. During wargaming of this campaign, students often find that, after analyzing multiple potential courses of action, they still cannot identify one that guarantees a good result. They often point out that they are forced to choose "the least worst option."

ment it became apparent that he was heading for the St. Bernard, but Vevey is 110 miles from Zurich, so it would simply be up to the French commander to decide exactly where along the last 50–70 miles of that route he wanted to fight Suvorov.

If we ask ourselves which of these two kinds of strategic outflanking Suvorov's march could have resulted in, it is undoubtedly only the second, namely, decision by battle.

If we take the French army's line of deployment to be along the Limmat and the Linth, of course it had Lake Geneva directly to its rear, but still the canton of Vaud was not its base, much less its line of retreat. Its true base lay behind the Jura, and the most important section of it was obviously that from Besançon to Basel. An enemy army that advanced through Vevey but could not advance too boldly because it did not want to force a test of arms obviously would not threaten this base in any effective way, since if one of the southern roads was taken away from the French commander, he could transfer his communications to the next one to the north of it. There was certainly no place in Switzerland of any decisive importance to the French; the most important might be Bern, and that was a good halfway toward the French army. What might have happened if Suvorov had taken position somewhere between Lake Geneva and Lake Thun and raided across Switzerland? It could only have been regarded as a demonstration, which *might* have scared the French commander and induced him to retreat to the Bern area. But Suvorov had not marched out of Italy with the intention of making a demonstration; a demonstration is indeed the method of someone weak who does not feel strong enough for a real operation, but the allies had numerical superiority and wanted to exploit that superiority for the conquest of Switzerland.

Demonstration or not, any operation against the French strategic flank that did not lead to a rapid decision by battle but was supposed to take effect gradually entailed the utmost danger for the allies. While they were using a third of their forces at this remote place for an operation of slow and uncertain effect, the French commander could make his superior numbers count against the isolated commanders near him—as indeed, he actually did—and whatever form Suvorov might devise for his attack on Switzerland, one of the first considerations must always be to end as soon as possible the dangerous situation that existed in Switzerland.

Compared with a *normal* attack, a strategic outflanking with the intention of fighting a decisive battle (which is what we have led Suvorov's march back to) has the more decisive character, since the scale of its success is increased, even though its likelihood is reduced.[101] Such an operation is therefore suitable for the stronger party who is already sure of success to some degree by virtue of his numerical superiority and who is anxious to obtain a major success. But of course, in war we can never hope to know how much weight a commander gives to his own powers, that is, his own talent and luck; this must always be left absolutely up to him, and likewise the degree of boldness with which he pursues his chosen course of action. All that theory can ask is that he recognize all the objective conditions and evaluate them correctly, thus taking only calculated risks.[102]

101. Here, it is worth noting the geometrical factor (*On War*, book 3, chap. 15), which Clausewitz decries. By taking aim at geometry, he is criticizing those writers (the archduke and Jomini, among others) who make a case for more scientific and mathematical methods of warfare. Clausewitz argues that siege warfare might find geometry useful, but as soon as things are mobile, its utility evaporates (*On War*, 214–215). See also book 7, chap. 7, on the offensive battle, where Clausewitz argues that the typical lack of clarity about the opponent's location means that an outflanking movement is more likely to be successful than an envelopment (*On War*, 530–531). If one wants to destroy one's enemy, outflanking or enveloping is a good way to maximize combat power against part of an enemy's force. But of course, it is the pursuit that truly does the damage (see *On War*, book 4, chap. 12, on the strategic means of exploiting victory).

102. Here, Clausewitz is implicitly recognizing that war is a gamble and that calculated risk taking is governed by chance. In *On War*, book 1, chap. 1, he notes the similarity to a game of cards. He mentions this again in book 8, chap. 3B, where he notes that cards are "dealt by time and accident" (see pp. 86 and 590, respectively). Elsewhere (book 6, chap. 28, and book 7, chap. 16), he mentions the phrase *Vorteil der Hinterhand*, translated here as "the advantage of playing last," which is an expression found in a German card game called *Skat* (which Howard and Paret translate as "riposte"; see pp. 489 and 550, respectively). Given Skat's relationship to gambling and its popularity in Prussia, it is reasonable to assume that Clausewitz had this or similar games in mind when making his card-game analogy. As such, it is worth pointing out how complex the game is, how large a role luck plays, and that very few hands are guaranteed to be successful. "The game of Skat allows of so many different combinations that it keeps all the players in continual suspense and excitement. Herein lies the great charm of the game, and hence arises the success it has obtained. Very few hands, and those of very rare occurrence, are absolutely certain to win a given game; while, on the other hand, a concurrence of lucky accidents may enable you to bring a very poor, indeed a downright hopeless-looking hand, to a successful issue, and overthrow one which seems to be all but certain of winning." A. Hertefeld, *The Game*

The critic's business is therefore to present the conditions under which this march would have taken place.

If Suvorov had linked up with General Haddick, who had at most 14,000 men, including Colonel Strauch's force, he would have become 34,000 strong. If, after leaving a few thousand men behind, he had advanced with this corps 25,000–30,000 strong, overrun whatever French confronted him to start with, taken the route through Fribourg to Bern, and been able to give battle to whatever Masséna led against him from Zurich, which could hardly have been much stronger than him; and if he had won that battle, which a commander like Suvorov probably could have felt confident of doing in such circumstances, then Switzerland would have been conquered with this one blow, and this march through the St. Bernard would have stood as one of the most glorious of military operations, not unworthy of being ranked alongside the march that Bonaparte carried out through this pass in the opposite direction nine months later. It is quite understandable that such a result could tempt a bold commander to take a big risk. But only a superficial conception of the affair

---

of Skat, trans. and ed. Professor Hoffman (London: George Routledge & Sons, 1893), 15. Blackjack is often cited as a card game to explain Clausewitz's point; however, it is unlikely that he was familiar with blackjack, which had only recently been invented in France, and its relatively calculable predictability does not match Clausewitz's argument. Essentially, with effective strategy, blackjack players can increase the odds in their favor in a precisely calculable fashion. This is not possible in Skat, as its stochastic and probabilistic nature does not allow it to be managed in the same way one can manipulate blackjack by counting cards. (Dr. Michael Dennis deserves credit for help with this idea during an email exchange on 2 October 2019.) Thus, it seems absurd to argue that this might be the case in war, given the role of human decisions, chance, and friction. As such, the use of a blackjack analogy in relation to strategy is at best unhelpful and at worst completely misleading. For an excellent history of card games, see David Parlett, *A History of Card Games* (Oxford: Oxford University Press, 1991). See also Clausewitz, *Napoleon's 1796 Italian Campaign,* 279–280n11. An email exchange (6 November 2018) with Vanya Bellinger, author of the excellent *Marie von Clausewitz: The Woman behind the Making of* On War (Oxford: Oxford University Press, 2016), proved most useful. She pointed us toward an essay Clausewitz wrote on strategy in which he uses the example of the card game Pharaoh. See Carl von Clausewitz, *Ausgewählte militärische Schriften* (Berlin: Militärverlag DDR, 1981), 384. That game does not have a clear equivalent of *Vorteil der Hinterhand,* so it seems less likely that the examples cited in *On War* refer to Pharaoh, but it supports the contention that Clausewitz was thinking of contemporary gambling games involving complexity and incalculable chance when writing about war.

could envision it thus; a detailed examination was bound to show that it could hardly have developed that way.

General Tharreau was in the Rhone valley with 10,000–12,000 men. If this general had retreated from Suvorov toward Vevey, and if Lecourbe had completely abandoned the St. Gotthard and the Rhone valley at that moment, it might come to pass that Suvorov would proceed through a 70-mile series of the narrowest of alpine defiles and that his sole line of communications and retreat to Italy would run through these *narrow pipes*, as we might say. But the French would never, ever have abandoned Wallis; if there was ever an opportunity anywhere in the world for a genuine flank position, this was it. If Tharreau remained in Wallis with the larger part of his division, there was no way Suvorov could drive him out of there if he did not want to get involved in a side operation that took away all his time and forces from the main operation; thus he could do nothing but drive him back up the valley somewhat and then have him observed by a suitable corps. Since he would now have to occupy the St. Bernard itself as well as the Aosta valley, in which Haddick had had part of his force until now, it follows that he could hardly take any of Haddick's corps with him to Vevey, so he would be left only 20,000 strong, of which only 16,000 were infantry.

Thus Suvorov would have had to seek a decisive battle with this force while his line of retreat over the St. Bernard was so threatened that it could be lost to him from one day to the next; for as long as the French held the St. Gotthard, Suvorov could never be sure that the majority of Lecourbe's division would not march down the Rhone valley, join up with Tharreau, and then inevitably seize the St. Bernard and the Rhone valley as far as Lake Geneva.

To think that General Hotze should have come toward General Suvorov to meet him halfway is to presuppose that the former would have beaten his opponent, General Soult, before Suvorov had exerted any influence at all; but if we take that assumption as given, then the reconquest of Switzerland did not require any operation as risky as Suvorov marching through the St. Bernard. But even if Hotze really was still numerically superior to General Soult and to whatever Lecourbe could oppose him with, the course of events on the Linth from 25 to 29 September demonstrated all too well the uncertainty of such an assumption.

Therefore, for Suvorov to march through the St. Bernard would not have been much better than a landing in which he burned his boats behind him. Even the boldest of men would resolve on such a daring deed in only two cases: if he is almost certain of the success ahead of him, so that the danger threatening him from behind may be disregarded because of its small probability (like Bonaparte at Jena),[103] or if a desperate situation forces him to. For as soon as the probability of success can no longer be increased with prudence to such a degree as to give an acceptable result, then quite different principles of operation apply, and a slight chance of success can only be obtained by the greatest audacity, because great audacity always brings with it the advantage of the unexpected; then the greatest audacity becomes the greatest wisdom. Suvorov was in neither of these two situations, so we believe that, although at first glance a march through the St. Bernard has an attractive ingenuity, when considered in detail, it would have been inexcusably rash.

Thus, when the author of the account that Jomini includes as an annex regards this route as the best one for Suvorov's march because Suvorov would have debouched into Switzerland 140 miles behind Masséna, this is one of those common empty phrases whereby the author does not actually mean anything specific, that is, any ultimate effect.[104] There is nothing more common in strategic reasoning than to stop at such a midpoint and fail to follow the reasoning through to its conclusion, where one would otherwise realize that the significance of this intermediate element is quite different from what it seemed to be initially.

83 THE MARCH THROUGH THE ST. GOTTHARD PASS

The actual decisive event in Switzerland that mainly led to the unhappy outcome of the campaign for the allies consists in the fact that Generals

103. The battles of Jena and Auerstadt were where Napoleon destroyed the Prussian and Saxon armies on 14 October 1806. Clausewitz was captured at the battle, and the humiliation of Prussia seems to be one of the main factors driving his thinking and writing, as he uses the example of Jena repeatedly in *On War*.

104. Jomini, 12:455–467. **Clausewitz** notes: "It is comical that in this account that is otherwise sensibly and carefully written, the author says Suvorov would then have been able to link up with Haddick's corps, with 5,000 men who were in the Aosta valley, and with Strauch and Victor and Rohan. Yet Strauch and Rohan belonged to Haddick's corps; those 5,000 men were actually Haddick's main body; 'Victor' is merely Rohan's first name; this correspondent probably thought these five corps had well over 12,000–14,000 men."

Korsakov and Hotze were beaten by Masséna, the former losing his entire artillery and the Austrians losing a large number of prisoners, as usual. But these events are quite simply the consequence of the interregnum that affected the allies in Switzerland due to the archduke's early departure and Suvorov's late arrival. Any sensible person would have arranged things so that these two events coincided, but all experience shows that to demand that a cabinet or Aulic Council in charge of military affairs act like a sensible person at all times is to demand too much.[105] This interregnum lasted more than three weeks.[106] If it had lasted only a few days, it could have been hoped that the French would not complete their preparations quickly enough, but there could be no question of such an assumption about a period of several weeks. We remark on this precisely because the French did not complete their preparations for crossing until 24 September, and most historians have posited that everything depended on whether Suvorov could have emerged from Switzerland's high mountainous region on the 25th or at least exerted some influence on that day. Of course, it did indeed turn out like that, but if we look at it from the point of view of the cabinets and commanders four to six weeks before this decisive day, there could be absolutely no question of them reasoning on that basis, for

105. This is a critical point. Clausewitz is referring to his argument in *On War* that the political objective should determine the strategic goals and the degree of effort to be made. But this is extremely difficult to do. Furthermore, he argues, "Policy, of course, will not extend its influence to operational details. Political considerations do not determine the posting of guards or the employment of patrols. But they are more influential in the planning of war, of the campaign, and often even of the battle. . . . Nothing is more important in life than finding the right standpoint for seeing and judging events, and then adhering to it. One point and *one only* yields an integrated view of all phenomenon; and only by holding to that point of view can one avoid inconsistency." *On War*, 606. He is saying that one should figure out a clear strategic goal that matches the policy (and/or political goals) and try to maintain the connection. If things become muddled or unclear—and with a political war council made up of often competing personalities, they probably will—then there is likely to be an unhappy outcome, just as he points out. He also points out that the goal of identifying a clear political objective becomes harder if one adds allies to the mix. He is not saying that one does not need allies; rather, he is saying that if one fights with them, it is far harder to identify clear goals that everyone agrees on. See *On War*, book 8, chaps. 4–6. See also Bernard Brodie's chapter, "A Guide to the Reading of *On War*," in *On War*, 699–711.

106. This relates to his point about the role of continuous pressure and continuity in terms of beating an opponent.

who knew anything about 25 September then, and how could such tiny local and individual factors as the French preparations for crossing be the object of such particular assumptions! Also, it is our conviction that people assume this French unreadiness to be too absolute; we consider it very possible and indeed very likely that if Suvorov had attacked the St. Gotthard fourteen days earlier, Masséna also would have found the means to cross the Limmat fourteen days earlier. If this is true, then the allies' misfortunes in Switzerland are indeed to be regarded as the consequence of the interregnum, and Suvorov's route through the St. Gotthard is relevant only insofar as it prolonged this interregnum by three or four days, as we shall see in what follows. Establishing this precise relationship of Suvorov's march was thoroughly necessary, since it reveals that, in this respect, it was not accompanied by any disadvantage that was not to be regarded as balanced out by the fact that this route promised a markedly better effect than any other.

Suvorov's intention was to appear in the flank of the French line of deployment with 40,000–50,000 men and to deliver a decisive battle there. The decision was already delivered on the front before he arrived, so he came too late; there is nothing in this situation that could not have occurred from at least a hundred other much simpler situations.

Suvorov now had to fall back to his right several times; this falling back happened across the highest of mountain ranges, partly on mere footpaths, and cost the Russians perhaps 6,000–8,000 men, a mass of horses, and twenty to thirty guns. That was the effect of the route chosen, and the critic is indeed justified in condemning this route for the sake of that effect.

But the violent crisis in which Suvorov's army found itself from 24 September to 10 October, whose morale effects left the Russians and their commanders wrathful and indignant toward the Austrians, the way muscles are left nervously trembling after superhuman exertions, and the very crisis that makes Suvorov's march so magnificent and historic, obviously stems not merely from the fact that he had to beat his retreat along poor roads and lost half his force thereby, since that is a situation that occurs fairly often in the history of war without being accompanied by such morale effects; nay, the intense strength of this sixteen-day crisis lies in the fact that three times Suvorov and his corps were in the utmost danger of having to lay down their arms: in the Schächen, Muota, and Linth valleys.

Thus, given the failure of its intended aim, we see that Suvorov's march through the St. Gotthard upon Schwyz not only had to lead to the unavoidable loss of half his combat forces but also could have very easily led to the destruction of the whole force and to an extremely severe blow to the honor of Russian arms and, consequently, to an enemy victory of the highest order. We wanted to explicitly single out for consideration this downside of the measure, this great counterweight, before we judge its positive side, for it is obvious that any reflection must always set such dangers against any good results, being intrinsically equally large, receding only to the degree to which positive results are likely, and looming closer to the degree that they are unlikely.

Only now let us turn to the measure itself as a means to a positive end.

Suvorov's march through the St. Gotthard was important for two distinct reasons and may almost be considered a measure with two purposes, which necessarily increased the difficulty of the mission.

First, it is a march to join two forces separated by the enemy. Such a strategic action always has its own problems, and its crisis usually arrives at the last moment. Before that, either the enemy between the two fractions cannot reach either of them, or else the one he is already close to has fallen back or found itself an impregnable position. Once the two corps have approached close to each other and thereby also close to the enemy at a certain point, they can no longer fall back too far if they do not want to miss their opportunity to join up; now the danger is that their opponent turns on one of them and beats it through his numerical superiority before it can arrange to fight in combination with the other.[107] We find this again and again throughout the history of war, and the multitude of individual measures taken by both sides, the effort put into tactical and strategic dispositions, as well as the historians' lengthy reports of such events show this clearly enough.

The other significance of Suvorov's march was as an attack on the strategic flank of the French position.

It is obvious that such an attack is somewhat different from that which could have come about from a march through the St. Bernard into the rear of the French position. In the latter case, there could be no thought of intending to fight in combination; indeed, it was not necessary because the allies' masses were too far apart to allow their adversary to turn first against one and then against the other with his undivided force. In the case of the flank attack, *fighting in combination* with General Hotze was essential because it is in the nature

107. Much as Napoleon did repeatedly in 1796 during the Italian campaign. See Clausewitz, *Napoleon's 1796 Italian Campaign.*

of a flank attack that the enemy position should also be attacked frontally, at least on that wing.[108] Thus a strategic flank attack depends much more on an accurate calculation of the moment, on the precision of the maneuvers.

If we consider both these important aspects of Suvorov's march at the same time, their different tendencies are revealed, and thereby the difficulty of combining them.

Measures for *a strategic flank attack* normally start from a position in which one is admittedly not united but still in communication, where one can discuss everything properly and can calculate time and space accurately. Here, these measures were supposed to start from a march to link up when the enemy was between the two parts, and precise mission orders could not be given reliably.

On the other hand, during *a march to link up*, when one approaches the critical line at which the decisive battles may occur, the most compelling need arises for one of the two separated masses to try to reach the other as fast as possible, just as two drops of water quickly flow together when they have approached each other to a certain point; but that is quite contrary to the aim of a flank attack, which needs one force to move around the enemy and therefore distance itself from the other.

A proper *strategic flank attack* would have required the last joint discussions to occur no more than twenty-four hours before its execution, but they took place fourteen days earlier; *a march to link up* should have led Suvorov, from the Reuss valley at least, directly into the Linth valley as the last place where the linkup could be effected with certainty, whereas the strategic flank attack led him to Lake Lucerne.

When we also take into account the degree to which the nature of the alpine region necessarily increased all these difficulties, we can really see that for quite natural reasons, the whole mission that the Austrian general staff gave to the old commander was one of the most difficult and unsound that strategy could devise, and that if any good were to come of it, this could only be thanks

108. Clausewitz's point is that a strategic attack on an enemy flank (by which he means flank and rear) allows the enemy to turn and face the threat, unless one puts pressure on the enemy front at the same time. As such, it is not necessarily effective unless one combines these actions. Of course, if one wanted to threaten the flank of an enemy to maximize the concentration of one's own force against that enemy flank, albeit without putting pressure on the enemy front, then one risks exposing one's own flank or rear to an enemy countermove. Clausewitz discusses flanks and flank attacks repeatedly throughout *On War*.

to talented execution or indeed to blind luck, but the seeds of the most unhappy outcome could already be detected in the very mission.

We do not really need to prove that Suvorov's circular letter to the generals in Switzerland could not count as a definite plan, nor even as a comprehensive preliminary order. Muddled ideas and the struggle with a foreign tongue certainly play a large part in its vagueness and obscurity, but its faults stem mainly from the fact that Suvorov is 140 miles away from the area for which he is making his plan, that he does not know this area, and that he knows little or nothing about the positions of the subcommanders he is supposed to cooperate with and to direct.

If we highlight the main instructions in this circular letter and in what was subsequently agreed, they are the following:

1. The allied generals were to attack everywhere on 26 September to facilitate Suvorov's march through the St. Gotthard.
2. Hotze and Jellachich were to advance into the Einsiedeln area.
3. Linken was to join up with Suvorov in the Muota valley.
4. Auffenberg was to attack the Reuss valley via the Maderaner valley.
5. Rosenberg was to outflank the St. Gotthard and establish communications with Auffenberg.
6. Suvorov wanted to take the St. Gotthard and descend down the Reuss valley, and then he intended to advance on both sides of Lake Lucerne, making Lucerne his objective.
7. Hotze was to attack the right flank of the French position behind the Limmat.

Of these instructions, it is mainly the first two and the penultimate one that characterize the operation.

When one attacks an enemy line of deployment in several places at once, as was supposed to happen here, according to the first instruction, one cannot expect to be victorious everywhere, so one must take care to win at the key point, that is, at a point where one either strikes the enemy force's *Schwerpunkt* or else reaches an important objective.[109] It may hold true that Suvorov with his column, either after joining up with Auffenberg and Linken or indeed on his

109. That is, their center of gravity. For a broader discussion of this concept, see volume 1, chapter 2, note 108.

own without them, knew he was strong enough to do the job against whatever Masséna could put up against him, but we cannot see how the direction that Suvorov gives himself down both sides of Lake Lucerne, even if it were really practicable, was supposed to lead to such a decisive success that it would make up for everything that could be lost in other places. Lucerne was admittedly the seat of the new Swiss government, but it was still not a place of decisive importance. The direction toward Lucerne was certainly not in the direction of Masséna's main body, still less toward a linkup with Hotze.

If we take instructions two and six together, it is again obvious that what is envisaged is a kind of strategic approach march. Even if such an approach march really does lead to the best line of deployment in the world, at the moment of a strategic crisis, when we are seeking a decision against the enemy by attacking at every point, it is worth nothing.

Suvorov's direction upon Lucerne therefore would not have fulfilled any major purpose but would have pulled the allies' forces far apart. A victorious Hotze in Einsiedeln would have been worse off there than he was being beaten behind the Linth. How Suvorov's instruction looked when Hotze was not victorious, but was beaten before Suvorov could have an impact, has been adequately demonstrated to us by its execution.

What we miss in Suvorov's plan is therefore the combination of forces striving toward one major goal that is clearly thought out and precisely expressed, and because of that, we would have expected nothing but failure from it, even if Masséna had not preempted the allies by a day.

The last instruction, which indicates Hotze's subsequent mission and which we have taken from the archduke's account, seems to have been added by the archduke just to give the whole thing more clarity, a purpose that is not promoted thereby.

If we now cast another glance over the whole, it emerges that because of the distance in time and space at which this plan was determined, six generals—namely, Korsakov, Hotze, Jellachich, Auffenberg, Rosenberg, and Suvorov himself—who were separated from one another and at the moment of the operation were independent of one another, *thus six individual wills, were supposed to act in unison for four or five days.* That would have been more than enough for the best of plans to miscarry.[110]

110. This relates to Clausewitz's concept of friction. See *On War*, book 1, chaps. 5 and, in particular, 7.

Thus, upon closer inspection of its significance, Suvorov's march through the St. Gotthard, which probably struck the Austrian general staff as a core idea of real genius, immediately blurs into a fog of unclear aims, vague orders, and uncertain data with no core at all.

If we add to that the huge oversight that was made with respect to the lack of a road beyond Altdorf, we can well say that the idea of this march was a gigantic mistake. All the bad effects of this march result from the strategic idea itself, and even if there had not been a single error nor a single mishap in its execution, the outcome would not have been markedly better. What use would it have been if Hotze and Jellachich had advanced into the Einsiedeln area on the 26th and 27th? On the 28th, while Suvorov still had to contend with the Chinzig Chulm, they would have been attacked by Masséna and driven back across the Linth, perhaps with heavy losses. And again, what use would it have been if Linken had actually moved into the Muota valley on the 27th and joined up with Suvorov? That would not have made him strong enough to advance into the plain between the lakes without Hotze. Even if Suvorov had been in Schwyz at the same time Hotze was in Einsiedeln, the two would have been separated by a mountain ridge that in any other situation would have been counted sufficient to isolate them both.

Basically, after Suvorov had scaled the St. Gotthard, the best he could do was to move through either the Maderaner valley or the Schächen valley over the Klausen Pass and into the Linth valley, where he would have met up with Linken and drawn Jellachich back to him and could have moved to Bilten, whereby at least the small strategic advantage of his march over the St. Gotthard would have remained, having outflanked the position on the Linth between Lake Zurich and Lake Walen. But such a direction was prevented by the rendezvous at Schwyz and Einsiedeln dictated by the plan.

All the failure of this march, which is so famous for its boldness and endeavor, therefore lay in the thing itself, and it would have taken a near miracle for anything better to come of it. The fact that it did not turn out far worse, and that the complete disaster that was the downside of this operation according to our reflections above did not occur, was due not only to the Russians' own bravery but also to the major errors the French made, as we shall show shortly.

After this result of our reflections, it is probably unnecessary to add how much more sensible it would have been to march across the Splügen Pass, where Suvorov could have kept most of his artillery with him, could have stayed on a road that was difficult but nevertheless viable for wheeled vehicles throughout, could have put the difficulties of the terrain behind him at a distance from the enemy and covered by the Austrians' deployment, and consequently could have reached Hotze without his army being weakened at all.

He and his army would have been in Chur by 22 September, and the interregnum in Switzerland would have ended at that moment, whereas the route over the St. Gotthard did not bring him to Altdorf, that is, the point where operating in combination became possible, until the 26th. We cannot judge whether this alternative direction of march, this more rapid approach by Suvorov, would have decided Masséna to launch his attack on Generals Korsakov and Hotze that much sooner; but if that did not or could not happen, it is clear that the events of the 25th and 26th on the Linth would have taken a quite opposite turn, and the battle of Zurich very likely would not have taken place.

84 THE FRENCH COMMANDER

Suvorov's march over the St. Gotthard was rightly regarded as a risky operation; furthermore, Masséna's and Soult's victories over the allied generals on 25 September destroyed all the premises on which it rested, and Jellachich's and Linken's timid behavior seemed to complete Suvorov's misfortune. Nonetheless, nothing more came of Masséna's action against Suvorov than would have occurred without it; that is, Suvorov had to fall back to his right, leaving half his army behind simply from having to contend with the mountains and valleys. Such a result did not seem to correspond with the dire situation he found himself in and that initially stirred critics against the French commander. As usual, they only asked themselves how the forces should have been distributed in order to obtain a truly glorious result, that is, in this case, to properly block Suvorov in, without putting themselves exactly in the circumstances in which the French commander had to operate. Thus, they naturally found that instead of turning toward Schwyz, Masséna should have moved into the Linth valley straight away to close this last exit.

While we cannot let this type of criticism stand, we must indeed express the opinion that here Masséna showed himself to be not such a great commander and, in particular, not so decisive as a strategist as when he was a *général de division.* Nor can that come as much of a surprise to us, since Bonaparte, who certainly knew him well enough and never fell out with him, says of him in his

Memoires: "Except in battle, he was the most confused man in the world." In any case, it is certain that in the campaigns of 1796 and 1797,[111] Masséna failed to pick up the best of Bonaparte's principles from his master: *to make do with as few troops as possible at secondary points, so as to be suitably strong at the key point.*

If we imagine Masséna on the battlefield of Zurich on 26 September receiving the news that the St. Gotthard and the Devil's Bridge had been taken and that Lecourbe was in the process of retreating to Altdorf, it was really quite natural that he should hasten to Schwyz with all the forces available so as to link up with Lecourbe in one way or another or to operate in combination with him. For even if Suvorov did not have a road from Altdorf either to Schwyz or to Einsiedeln, Masséna surely could not be expected to rely completely on this fact. This was partly because he certainly did not know the details of the possible routes through these areas so accurately or with the clarity, overview, and certainty with which we know them from Weiss's atlas,[112] which did not yet exist, and the French were in the habit of regarding the points of Schwyz and Einsiedeln as the two debouches into the area between Lake Lucerne and Lake Zurich; partly because experience had taught that it was not absolutely impossible to get into the Muota valley and thus into the Schwyz area; and finally because a move directed on Schwyz was suitable for attaining not only the towns of Schwyz and Einsiedeln and, if necessary, the mouth of the Linth valley but also the city of Lucerne, which one could not entirely leave out of consideration because it was not impossible that Suvorov might turn that way south of Lake Lucerne. In a word, the direction toward Schwyz was a middle way, and that is usually preferable when events have not yet developed. It is especially important here not to ignore the fact that, as the French explicitly say, they did not know how large a force Suvorov was bringing with him; they certainly did not think it was only about 20,000 men, and if he had set off with the whole Russian army and an Austrian corps, they could have taken this force to be between 40,000 and 50,000 men. With such a force, it certainly would not have been unfeasible to descend to the plain between Lake Lucerne

111. See Clausewitz, *Napoleon's 1796 Italian Campaign.* Time and again, Napoleon concentrated strength where he needed it and completely denuded other positions to achieve success at what he had identified as the key location.

112. See *Meyer-Weiss: Atlas of Switzerland*, http://www.unibe.ch/university/services/university_library/research/special_collections/map_collections/meyer_weiss/index_eng.html.

and Lake Brienz and head for Lucerne or even for Bern. If we imagine this, we can very well understand that to Masséna on the Zurich battlefield, the mission did not seem to be one of catching a weak corps abandoned by all the rest, hiding among a maze of rocky cliffs, at the last hole from which it could still escape. *It concerned the approach of a substantial army led by the allies' top general, whose victorious sword had laid low Moreau, Macdonald, and Joubert.* What seemed to matter first and foremost was simply to contest Suvorov's emergence from the mountains onto the plain wherever he could and generally to oppose Suvorov's operations in whatever way possible.

We therefore find it quite understandable that Masséna directed his troops to Schwyz, while he personally hastened through Lucerne to confer with Lecourbe. For this, at least, we do not venture to express any explicit blame.

But we must quite definitely blame the French commander for leaving a corps of 18,000 men facing the beaten Korsakov instead of a weak division of 5,000–6,000. When one has captured 100 cannon, that is, all of the enemy's artillery, one can be pretty certain of doing the business against his troops, and there is no risk at all in leaving a mere observation corps facing such an army.[113] What is the use of a glorious victory if it does not entitle you to do that? If Masséna had done so, he could have marched off with 25,000–30,000 men, who could have been brought up to 40,000 by joining with some of the troops from Lecourbe's and Soult's divisions. This was by no means too many, for even if Suvorov had approached with just 30,000 men, he could have brought these up to 40,000 with Jellachich, Linken, and Auffenberg and then advanced on to the plain between Lake Lucerne and Lake Zurich.

In the same way, Masséna should have simply left General Petrasch under observation and had Soult return to the left bank of the Linth with the bulk of his division, so as to send Molitor's brigade to the Linth valley to support Masséna.

113. Given that he had captured so much of the enemy's artillery, it would have been reasonable to leave a small force screening Korsakov, which potentially could have freed 10,000–12,000 extra troops for a more important fight elsewhere. During wargames, students playing commanders often struggle with similar dilemmas, as they assume a great risk for a small force with no guarantee of success for the main body, despite its reinforcement. This is where the character of the commander and the role of military genius come in. A military genius would possess the strength of character and the intellect to see through the fog and friction and intuit what the opponent is up to, or to analyze his doubts while exhibiting sufficient courage to make the decision. See *On War*, book 1, chap. 3.

Masséna could not have had a proper overview of the situation until he reached Altdorf; this was on 29 September. We believe it could have reasonably been done by the 28th, but we cannot judge that too severely. On this day, Soult reasonably could have arrived at Glarus and joined up with Molitor to form a force of about 8,000 men in the Linth valley. According to our assumptions, there could have been 20,000 men at Schwyz on this day; in these circumstances, Lecourbe would not have needed to go to Brunnen but could have moved to the Klausen Pass on this day. Masséna could have attacked in the Muota valley with 20,000 men on the 30th, on which day Soult could have occupied the Bragel Pass, while Lecourbe advanced through the upper Linth valley toward Glarus. Whatever strength we assume for Masséna's corps, any portion of it that he might have sent to Einsiedeln could likewise have moved off to the Linth valley on the 30th. In this situation, Suvorov most probably would not have escaped from the Muota valley, and in any case, not from the Linth valley, to which Masséna himself naturally would have followed him through the Bragel Pass.

Thus, we see that even though Masséna initially took the noncommittal middle direction, if he had just done so by turning decisively with all his forces against Suvorov, Masséna would have had time to surround him with corps on all sides, which would have been sufficient in the narrow alpine passes to make it impossible for him to break out.

We do not by any means wish to say that the execution of the troop distribution offered here for such an encirclement of the Russian commander would have been straightforward and easy, nor that everything would have arisen naturally and of its own accord, as easily and certainly as it appears to us here on paper. Anyone who knows the quite different nature of making a decision in real life, especially in war under the pressure of great responsibility and amidst a thousand uncertainties and objections, will understand that it would not have gone off here either without *many* doubts, and that what looks so easy to us probably could not have been brought to life without the presence of a powerful will; this is why in extraordinary achievements in war, devising a plan is the easy part,[114] even though it always remains a necessary condition that the plan should be sound. But such a result as the capture of Suvorov and his army could be expected only from the kind of energy and decisiveness that

114. Again, see *On War*, book 1, chap. 3, on military genius and book 1, chap. 4, on danger in war.

Bonaparte customarily displayed, and all we wish to show by our suggested dispositions is that if Masséna had been suitably strong between the Linth and Lake Lucerne, the possibility of a success of that magnitude must follow.

Where we said in the previous paragraphs that Suvorov was in danger of losing his line of retreat three times, even as early as in the Schächen valley, we merely meant in those cases that could have arisen, in particular, if the French had arrived in force in the Linth and Muota valleys sooner and barred the exits from the Schächen valley, a case that easily could have arisen from other general combinations.

After Masséna had neglected the key element, namely, to lead and summon his troops to where another decisive battle was needed, no further major result could be expected. Indeed, what we primarily miss in the use of the available means is again, as in the battle of Zurich, the clarity and decisive power of any plan, so that we are inevitably reminded of Bonaparte's verdict on Masséna; and secondly, the energy and economy of time that were usually so characteristic of the French.

On the 27th and 28th Lecourbe lets the Russians cross the Chinzig Chulm without doing anything more than serenading their rear guard with rolling musketry. Lecourbe and Masséna waste the 29th with a canter in the Schächen valley; on the 30th the latter still does not have the forces at hand in the Muota valley for a serious attack, presumably because he does not think himself strong enough with just Mortier, and Lecourbe is still ferrying across. But on the 30th only Rosenberg's troops were at Muota; they were certainly no stronger than Mortier's division, so Masséna must have made another mistake and dispersed this pointlessly. On the 31st Masséna lets himself be completely driven from the field by Rosenberg, even though he must have outnumbered him. Now he gives up entirely on attacking in the Muota valley, even though he could have foreseen that Rosenberg was about to withdraw and there was no better way for him to pin Suvorov among the mountains than to cling to him here. He pointlessly leaves 3,000–4,000 men under Mortier in the Muota valley and moves through Einsiedeln into the Linth valley, that is, he fritters away his forces and loses two days in marching. Whether he arrived in the Linth valley after these two days, on 3 September, we do not know; at least, nothing happens, and the reserve under Klein that was to take the route from the battlefield to Richterswil seems not to have moved into the Linth valley at all, since it arrives back at Andelfingen on the 6th.

Thus, the French commander squanders his time and his troops and operates without really knowing what he wants to do. From the 30th on, he could no longer take his mission to be preventing Suvorov's advance on to the plain, for what was Suvorov supposed to do there south of the Linth anyway?

If Masséna had been as decisive as Bonaparte, he would have concentrated all his available troops at Näfels, which, with Klein's reserve, could have been about 16,000 men; with these he would have gone across Kerenzen to Lake Walenstadt on the day Suvorov moved to Elm, thrown back the troops Jellachich had pushed forward, attacked the latter general at Sargans, hurled him across the Rhine, and tried to cross the river himself so as to confront Suvorov once more in the Rhine valley and force him to fall back to the Tyrol. We do not doubt for a moment that that is how Bonaparte would have done it, but we do not feel justified in demanding it of any other commander.

We have already incorporated our observations on the actions of the Austrian generals on the Linth into the course of the narrative, so we do not wish to waste any time on them now.

But we must permit ourselves one concluding remark.

This great example shows that even if, in war, the unusual has a certain intrinsic effect because of shock and awe,[115] and thus an effect on morale, that alone is not enough; rather, such unexpectedness and awesomeness lead to the aim only when they fit in with the whole. Thus, if a bold commander resolves to do something unusual because he feels he has the power to carry it through, the first condition is always that his fine sense of judgment should find the right connection between the method and the central aim; if that is not the case, striving for the unusual easily becomes striving for wrongness, which can lead to great disaster. Here, as the French proverb says, *le sublime touche le ridicule* [things go from the sublime to the ridiculous].

115. This familiar phrase is used because it closely matches what Clausewitz is saying. Clausewitz's point is that shock and awe in and of themselves are not sufficient to achieve an objective unless they are closely tied to the broader aim. For example, if an opponent does not believe that the shock and awe are backed up by genuine will and power, or if the shock and awe are not sufficient to achieve significant military gains, they are unlikely to have the desired effect. For a more detailed discussion of the modern concept of shock and awe, see Harlan K. Ullman and James P. Wade, *Shock and Awe Achieving Rapid Dominance* (Washington, DC: National Defense University, 1996).

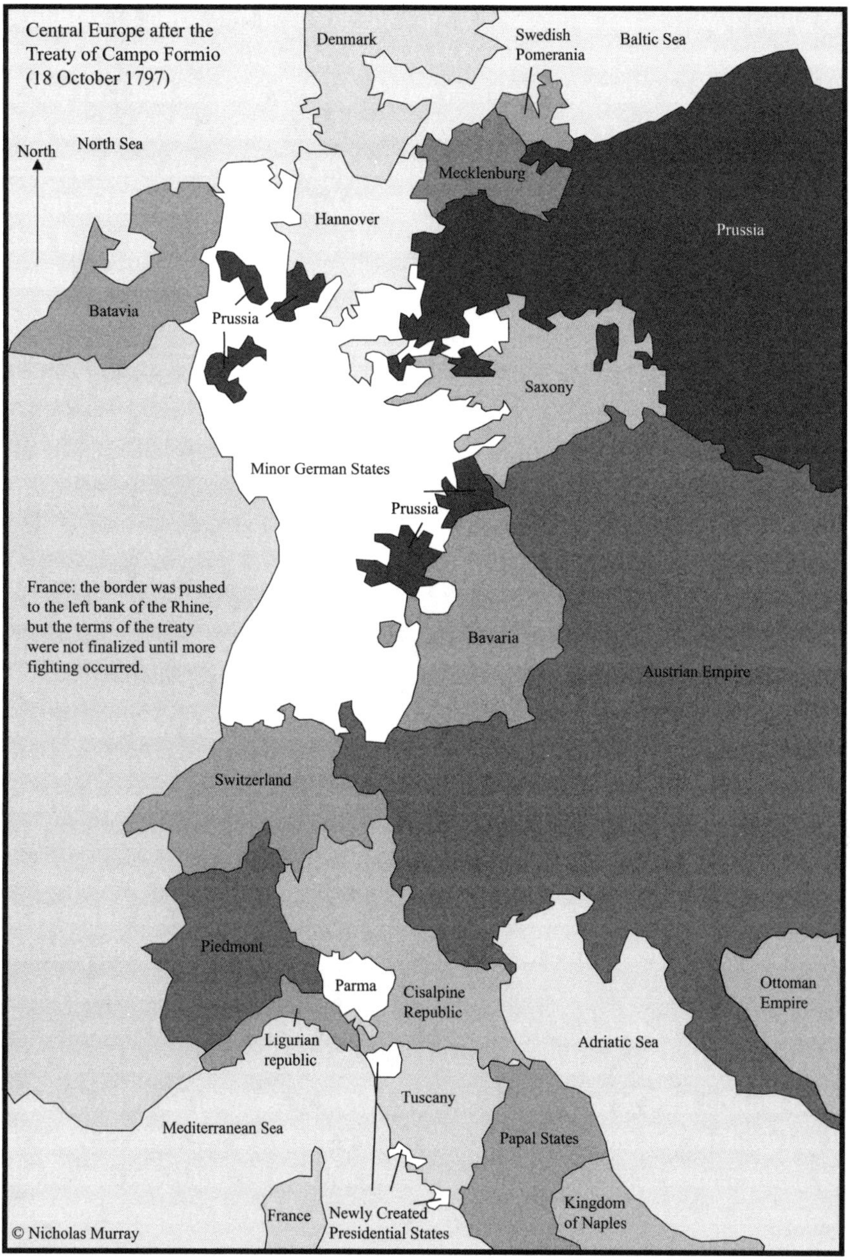

Central Europe after the
Treaty of Campo Formio
(18 October 1797)
Denmark
Swedish
Pomerania
Baltic Sea
North
North Sea
Mecklenburg
Hannover
Prussia
Batavia
Prussia
Saxony
Minor German States
Prussia
France: the border was pushed
to the left bank of the Rhine,
but the terms of the treaty
were not finalized until more
fighting occurred.
Bavaria
Austrian Empire
Switzerland
Piedmont
Parma
Cisalpine
Republic
Ottoman
Empire
Ligurian
republic
Adriatic Sea
Tuscany
Mediterranean Sea
Papal States
Kingdom
of Naples
France
Newly Created
Presidential States
© Nicholas Murray

Worms
Mannheim
Saarlouis
Neckar river
Heidelberg
Metz
Landau
Philippsburg
Anspach
Heilbronn
Karlsruhe
Hall
Rhine river
Durlach
Nancy
Stuttgart
Strasbourg
Kehl
Danube river
Offenburg
Tübingen
Ulm
Colmar
Freiburg
Rottweil
Biberach
Rhine river
Iller river
Osterach
Black Forest region
Stockach
Menningen
Schaffhausen
Lake Constance
Kempfen
Lauffenburg
Basel
Constance
Lindau
Brugg
Winterthur
Bregenz
Aare river
Aarau
Zurich
St. Gallen
Besançon
Lake Bieler
Aarburg
Lake Zurich
Rhine river
Feldkirch
Wallenstadt
Lucerne
Lake Lucerne
Glarus
Sargans
Maienfeld
Berne
Altdorf
Nauders
Lake Neuenburger
Thun
Chur
Brienz
Lake Geneva
Lausanne
St. Gotthard Pass
Splugen
Glurns
Maloja Pass
Rhone river
Nufenen Pass
San Bernardino Pass
Geneva
Bellinzona
Chiavenna
Simplon Pass
Lake Maggiore
Lake Como
Great St. Bernard Pass
Lake Garda
Dora river
Como
Sesia river
Bard
Brescia
Little St. Bernard Pass
Ticino river
Novara
Milan
Adda river
Peschiera
Oglio river
Mont Cenis Pass
Chivasso
Mincio river
Turin
Po river
Piacenza
Montgenèvre Pass
Tanaro river
Alessandria
Gap
Col Angel
Parma
Cuneo
Genoa
Maddalena Pass
© Nicholas Murray
Mediterranean Sea

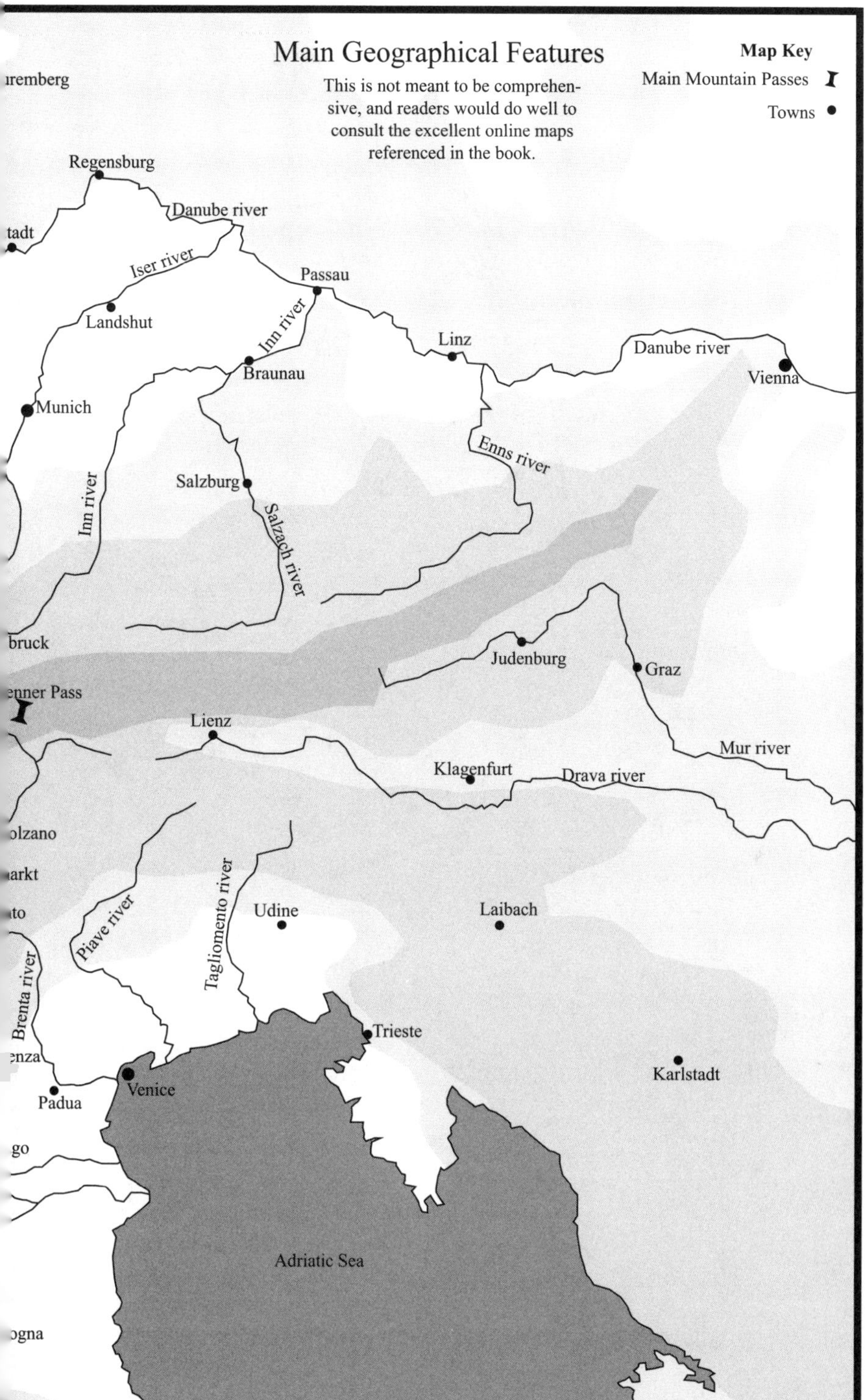
Main Geographical Features
This is not meant to be comprehensive, and readers would do well to consult the excellent online maps referenced in the book.
Map Key
Main Mountain Passes
Towns
Regensburg
Danube river
Iser river
Passau
Landshut
Inn river
Linz
Danube river
Vienna
Braunau
Munich
Enns river
Salzburg
Inn river
Salzach river
Judenburg
Graz
Lienz
Mur river
Klagenfurt
Drava river
Tagliomento river
Piave river
Udine
Laibach
Brenta river
Trieste
Karlstadt
Venice
Padua
Adriatic Sea

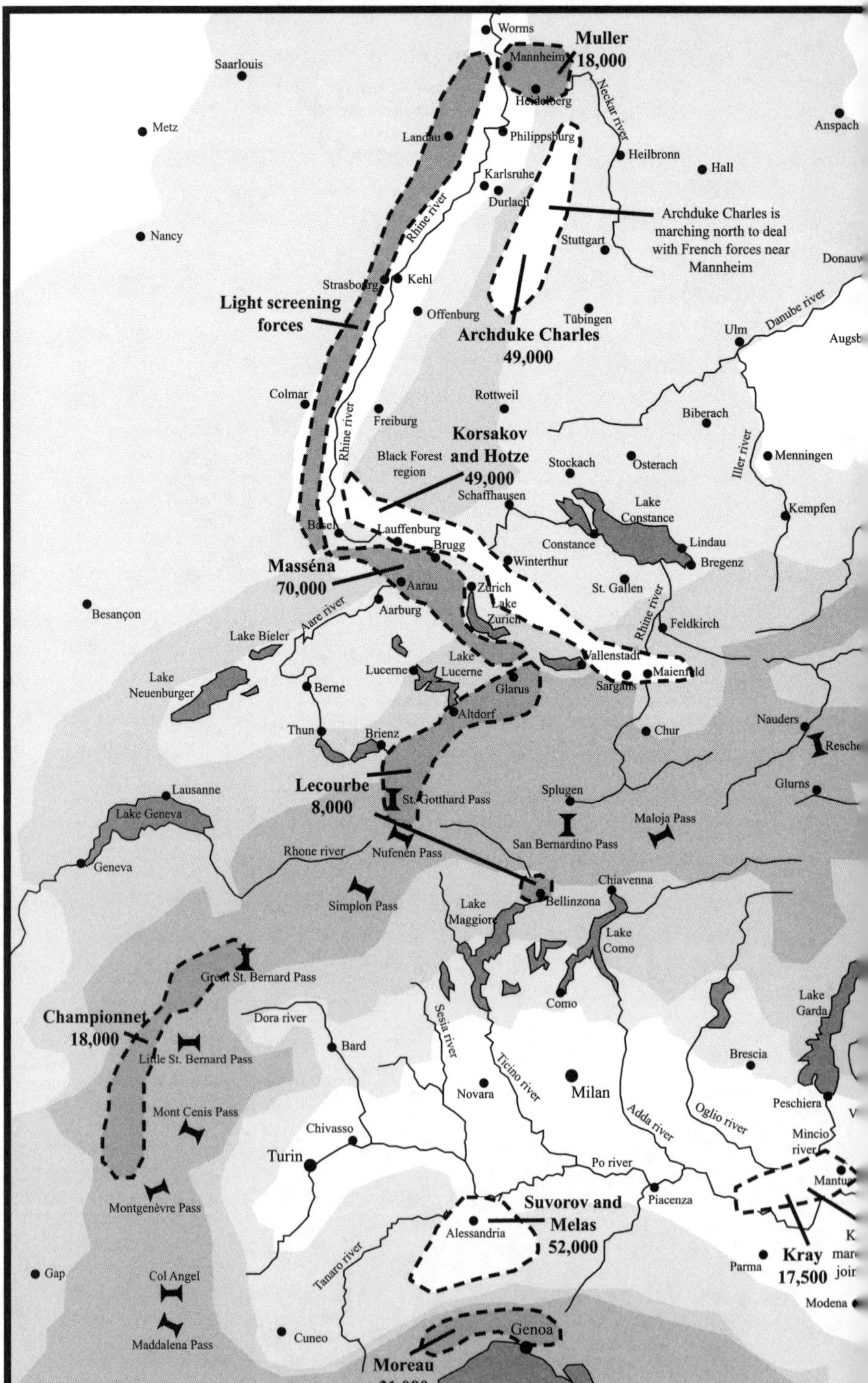

Worms
Muller
18,000
Mannheim
Heidelberg
Saarlouis
Neckar river
Metz
Landau
Philippsburg
Heilbronn
Anspach
Hall
Karlsruhe
Durlach
Archduke Charles is marching north to deal with French forces near Mannheim
Nancy
Rhine river
Stuttgart
Donauw
Strasbourg
Kehl
Light screening forces
Offenburg
Tübingen
Danube river
Archduke Charles
49,000
Ulm
Augsb
Colmar
Rottweil
Freiburg
Biberach
Korsakov and Hotze
49,000
Black Forest region
Stockach
Osterach
Iller river
Menningen
Schaffhausen
Lake Constance
Kempfen
Basel
Lauffenburg
Constance
Lindau
Brugg
Winterthur
Bregenz
Masséna
70,000
Aarau
Zurich
St. Gallen
Besançon
Aare river
Aarburg
Lake Zurich
Feldkirch
Lake Bieler
Wallenstadt
Lake Neuenburger
Lucerne
Lake Lucerne
Berne
Glarus
Sargans
Maienfeld
Altdorf
Chur
Nauders
Thun
Brienz
Resche
Lecourbe
8,000
St. Gotthard Pass
Splugen
Glurns
Lausanne
Lake Geneva
Maloja Pass
San Bernardino Pass
Rhone river
Nufenen Pass
Geneva
Chiavenna
Bellinzona
Simplon Pass
Lake Maggiore
Lake Como
Great St. Bernard Pass
Championnet
18,000
Como
Lake Garda
Dora river
Sesia river
Bard
Little St. Bernard Pass
Ticino river
Brescia
Novara
Milan
Mont Cenis Pass
Adda river
Oglio river
Peschiera
Chivasso
Mincio river
Turin
Po river
Mantu
Montgenèvre Pass
Suvorov and Melas
52,000
Piacenza
Alessandria
Tanaro river
Kray
17,500
Parma
Gap
Col Angel
Modena
Maddalena Pass
Cuneo
Genoa
Moreau
31,000
Mediterranean Sea

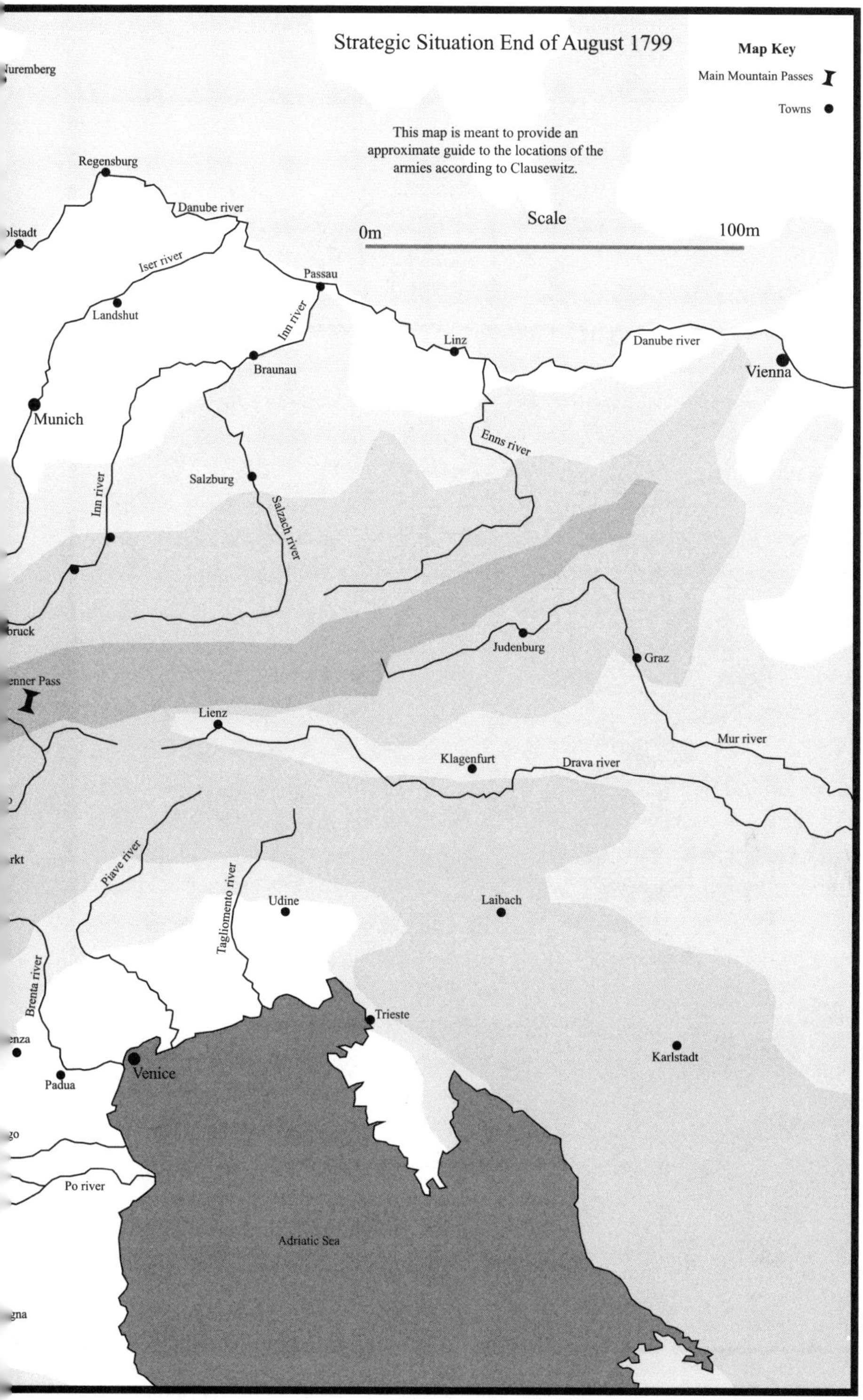

Strategic Situation End of August 1799
Map Key
Main Mountain Passes
Towns
This map is meant to provide an approximate guide to the locations of the armies according to Clausewitz.
Scale
0m
100m
Regensburg
Danube river
Iser river
Passau
Landshut
Inn river
Linz
Danube river
Vienna
Braunau
Munich
Enns river
Salzburg
Inn river
Salzach river
Judenburg
Graz
Lienz
Mur river
Klagenfurt
Drava river
Piave river
Tagliomento river
Udine
Laibach
Brenta river
Trieste
Karlstadt
Venice
Padua
Po river
Adriatic Sea

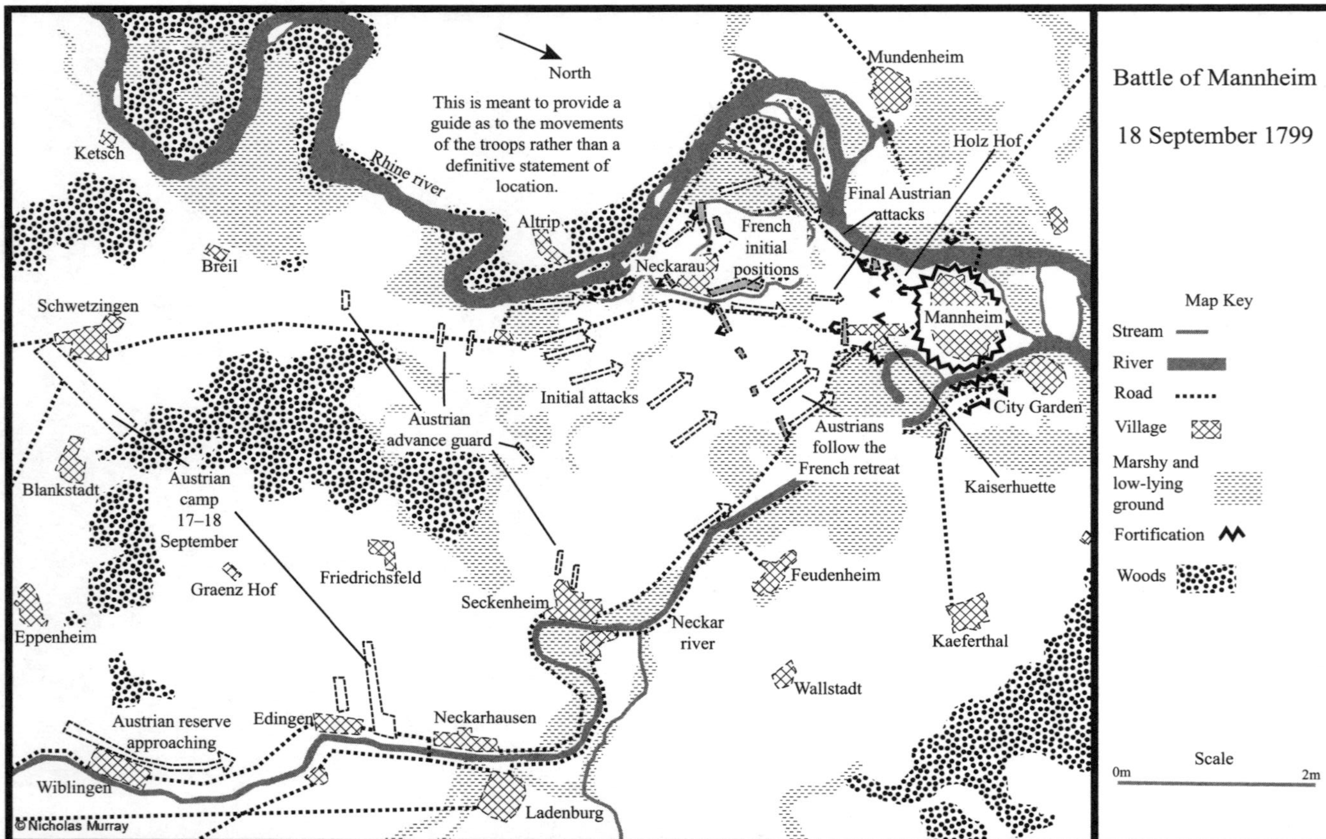
Battle of Mannheim
18 September 1799
Map Key
Stream
River
Road
Village
Marshy and low-lying ground
Fortification
Woods
Scale
0m
2m
North
This is meant to provide a guide as to the movements of the troops rather than a definitive statement of location.
Rhine river
Ketsch
Breil
Altrip
Neckarau
French initial positions
Mundenheim
Holz Hof
Final Austrian attacks
Mannheim
City Garden
Kaiserhuette
Austrians follow the French retreat
Initial attacks
Austrian advance guard
Schwetzingen
Blankstadt
Austrian camp 17–18 September
Graenz Hof
Friedrichsfeld
Seckenheim
Neckar river
Feudenheim
Wallstadt
Kaeferthal
Eppenheim
Austrian reserve approaching
Edingen
Neckarhausen
Wiblingen
Ladenburg
©Nicholas Murray

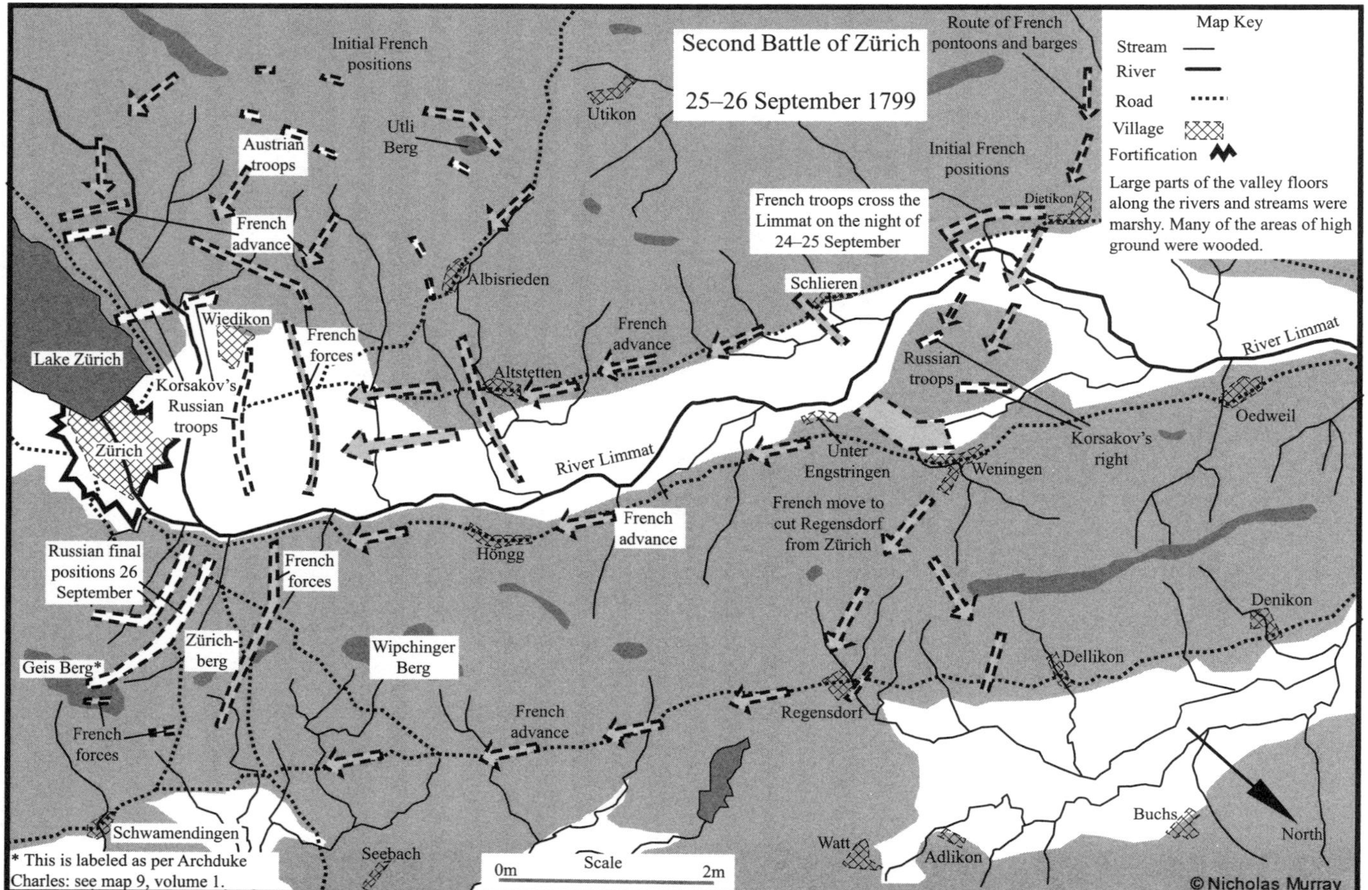

Second Battle of Zürich
25–26 September 1799
Map Key
Stream
River
Road
Village
Fortification
Large parts of the valley floors along the rivers and streams were marshy. Many of the areas of high ground were wooded.
Initial French positions
Route of French pontoons and barges
Initial French positions
Utikon
Utli Berg
Austrian troops
French advance
Albisrieden
French troops cross the Limmat on the night of 24–25 September
Dietikon
Schlieren
French advance
Altstetten
Wiedikon
French forces
Lake Zürich
Korsakov's Russian troops
Zürich
River Limmat
Russian troops
Korsakov's right
Oedweil
Unter Engstringen
Weningen
French move to cut Regensdorf from Zürich
French advance
Höngg
Russian final positions 26 September
French forces
Zürich-berg
Geis Berg*
Wipchinger Berg
French forces
French advance
Regensdorf
Dellikon
Denikon
Schwamendingen
Seebach
Watt
Adlikon
Buchs
North
0m
Scale
2m
* This is labeled as per Archduke Charles: see map 9, volume 1.
© Nicholas Murray

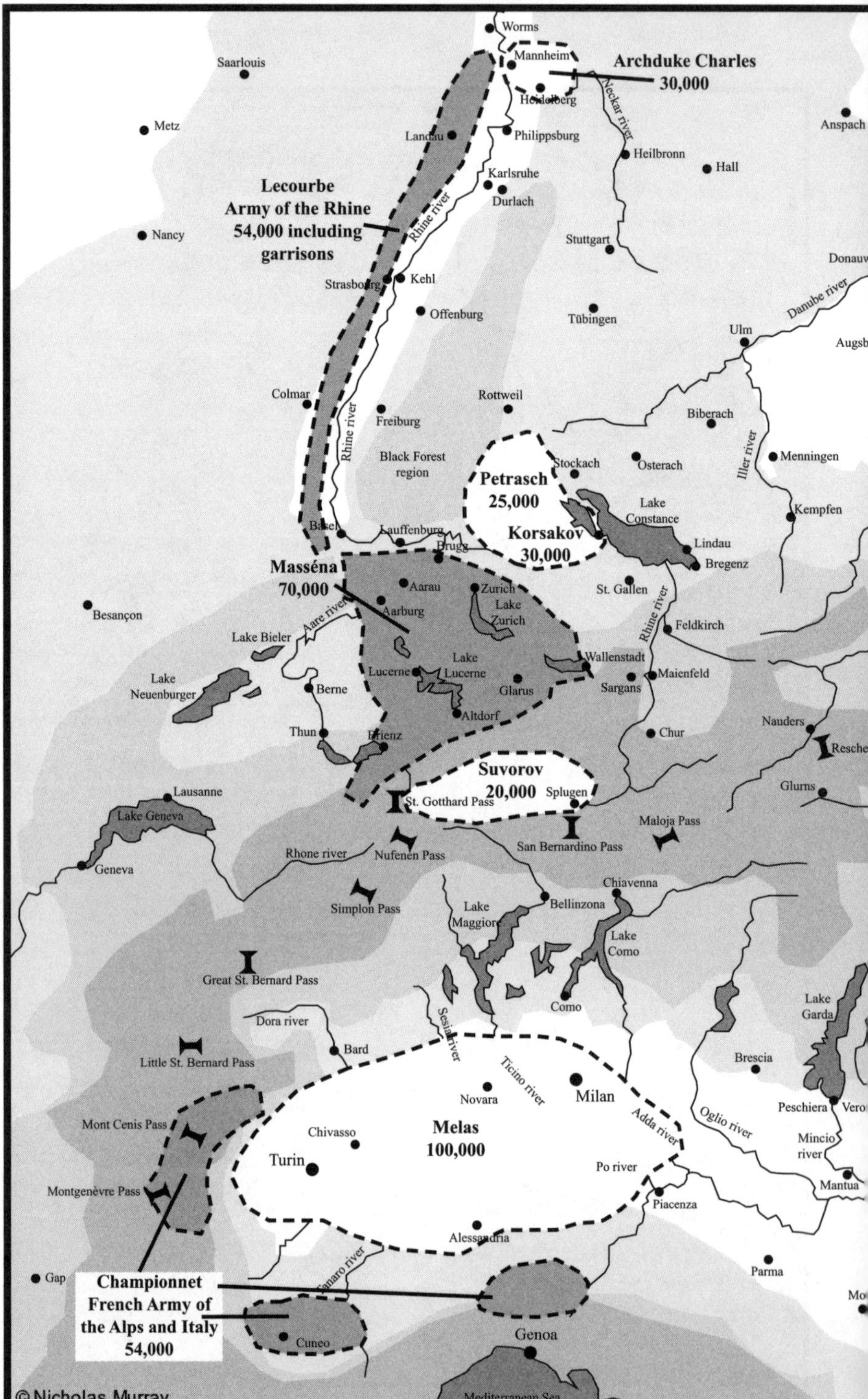
Worms
Mannheim
Heidelberg
Archduke Charles
30,000
Saarlouis
Metz
Landau
Philippsburg
Neckar river
Heilbronn
Hall
Anspach
Karlsruhe
Durlach
Lecourbe
Army of the Rhine
54,000 including
garrisons
Rhine river
Nancy
Stuttgart
Donauw
Danube river
Strasbourg
Kehl
Offenburg
Tübingen
Ulm
Augsb
Colmar
Rottweil
Freiburg
Rhine river
Biberach
Black Forest
region
Petrasch
25,000
Stockach
Osterach
Iller river
Menningen
Lake
Constance
Kempfen
Basel
Lauffenburg
Brugg
Korsakov
30,000
Lindau
Bregenz
Masséna
70,000
Aarau
Zurich
Lake
Zurich
St. Gallen
Aare river
Aarburg
Besançon
Rhine river
Feldkirch
Lake Bieler
Wallenstadt
Lake
Neuenburger
Lucerne
Lake
Lucerne
Glarus
Sargans
Maienfeld
Berne
Altdorf
Thun
Brienz
Chur
Nauders
Resche
Suvorov
20,000
St. Gotthard Pass
Splugen
Glurns
Lausanne
Lake Geneva
San Bernardino Pass
Maloja Pass
Geneva
Rhone river
Nufenen Pass
Simplon Pass
Bellinzona
Chiavenna
Lake
Maggiore
Lake
Como
Great St. Bernard Pass
Como
Sesia river
Dora river
Lake
Garda
Bard
Little St. Bernard Pass
Ticino river
Milan
Brescia
Novara
Mont Cenis Pass
Melas
100,000
Adda river
Oglio river
Peschiera
Chivasso
Turin
Po river
Mincio
river
Montgenèvre Pass
Mantua
Piacenza
Alessandria
Tanaro river
Gap
Parma
Championnet
French Army of
the Alps and Italy
54,000
Cuneo
Genoa
Mediterranean Sea
© Nicholas Murray

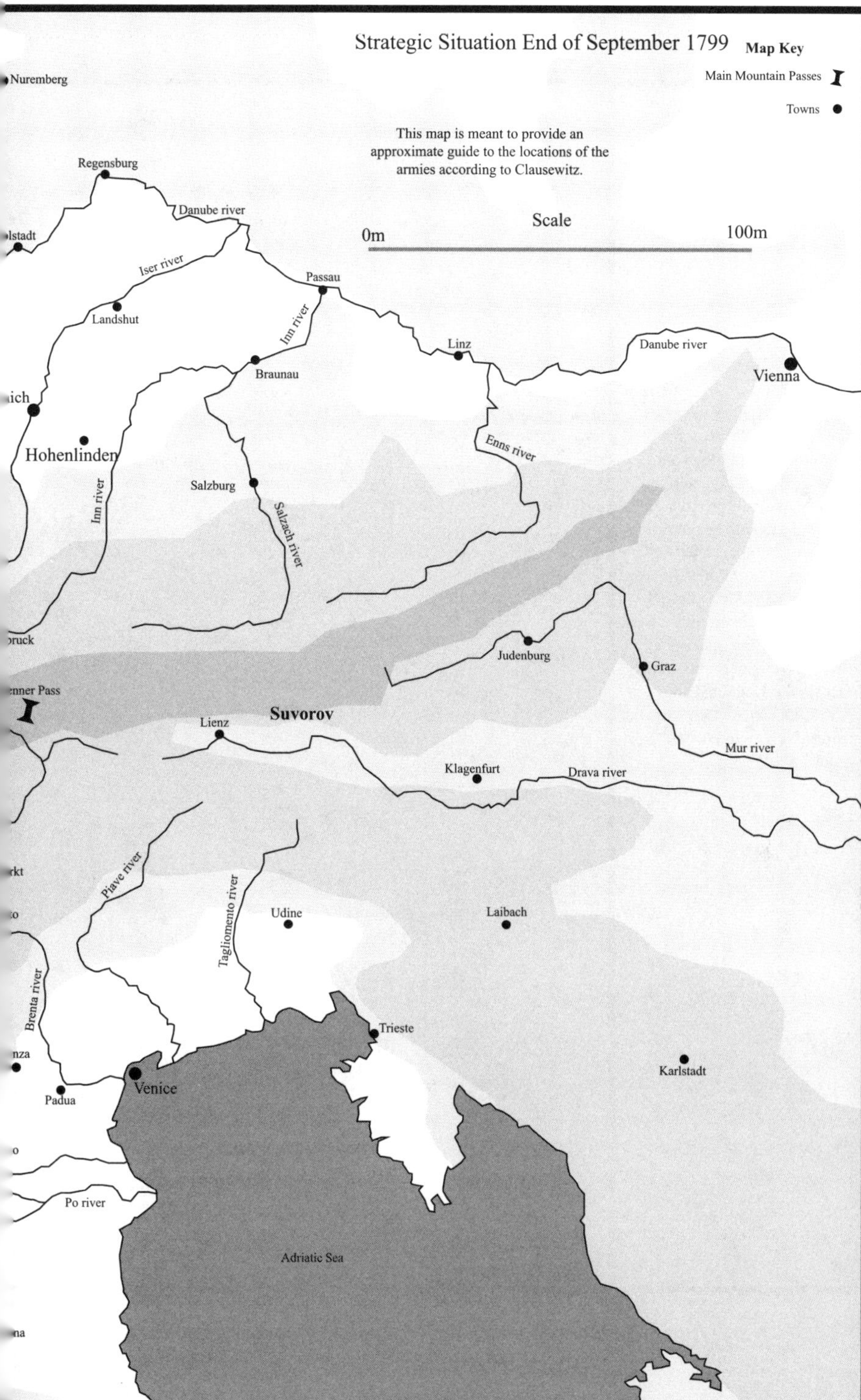

Strategic Situation End of September 1799
Map Key
Main Mountain Passes
Towns
This map is meant to provide an approximate guide to the locations of the armies according to Clausewitz.
Scale
0m
100m
Nuremberg
Regensburg
Danube river
Iser river
Passau
Landshut
Inn river
Braunau
Linz
Danube river
Vienna
Hohenlinden
Inn river
Salzburg
Salzach river
Enns river
Judenburg
Graz
Suvorov
Lienz
Klagenfurt
Drava river
Mur river
Piave river
Tagliomento river
Udine
Laibach
Brenta river
Trieste
Karlstadt
Venice
Padua
Po river
Adriatic Sea

Summary

Over the winter of 1799–1800 the strategic situation stabilized despite the Russian withdrawal from the campaigns in Italy, Switzerland, and Germany. The Austrians still held the advantage in terms of numbers and in the concentration of their forces. They besieged Masséna in Genoa at the beginning of April and French forces in Italy were widely spread across the frontier. They expected a concerted Austrian offensive would win the conflict.

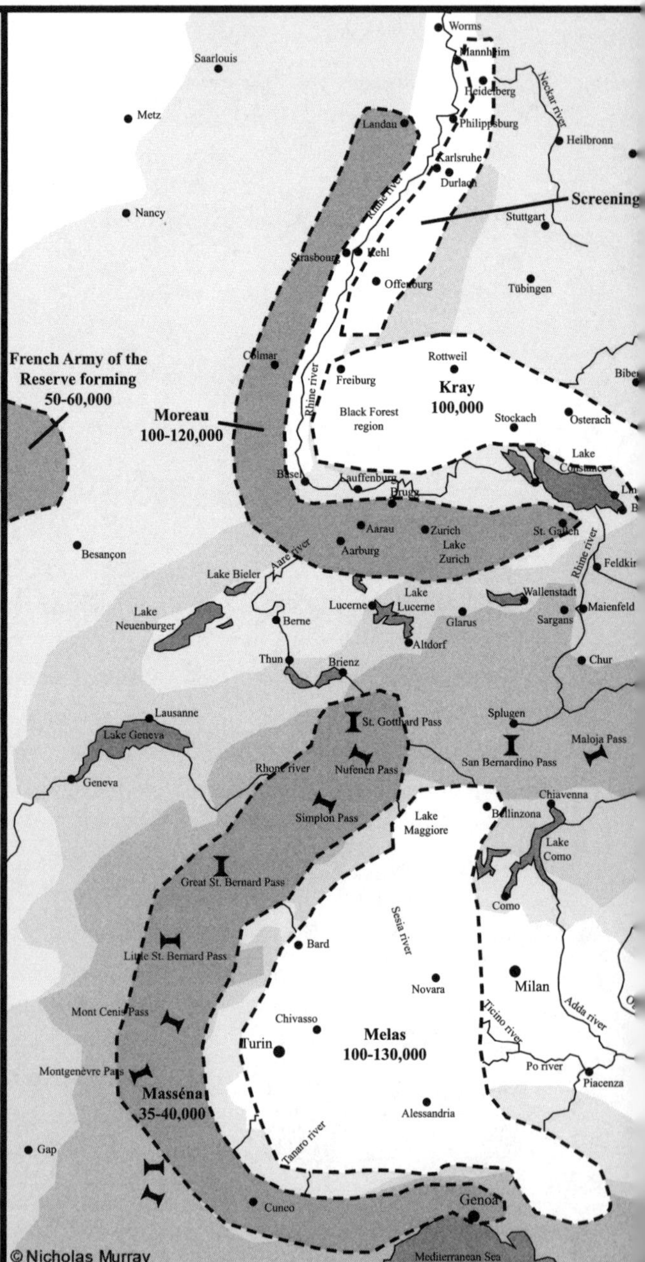

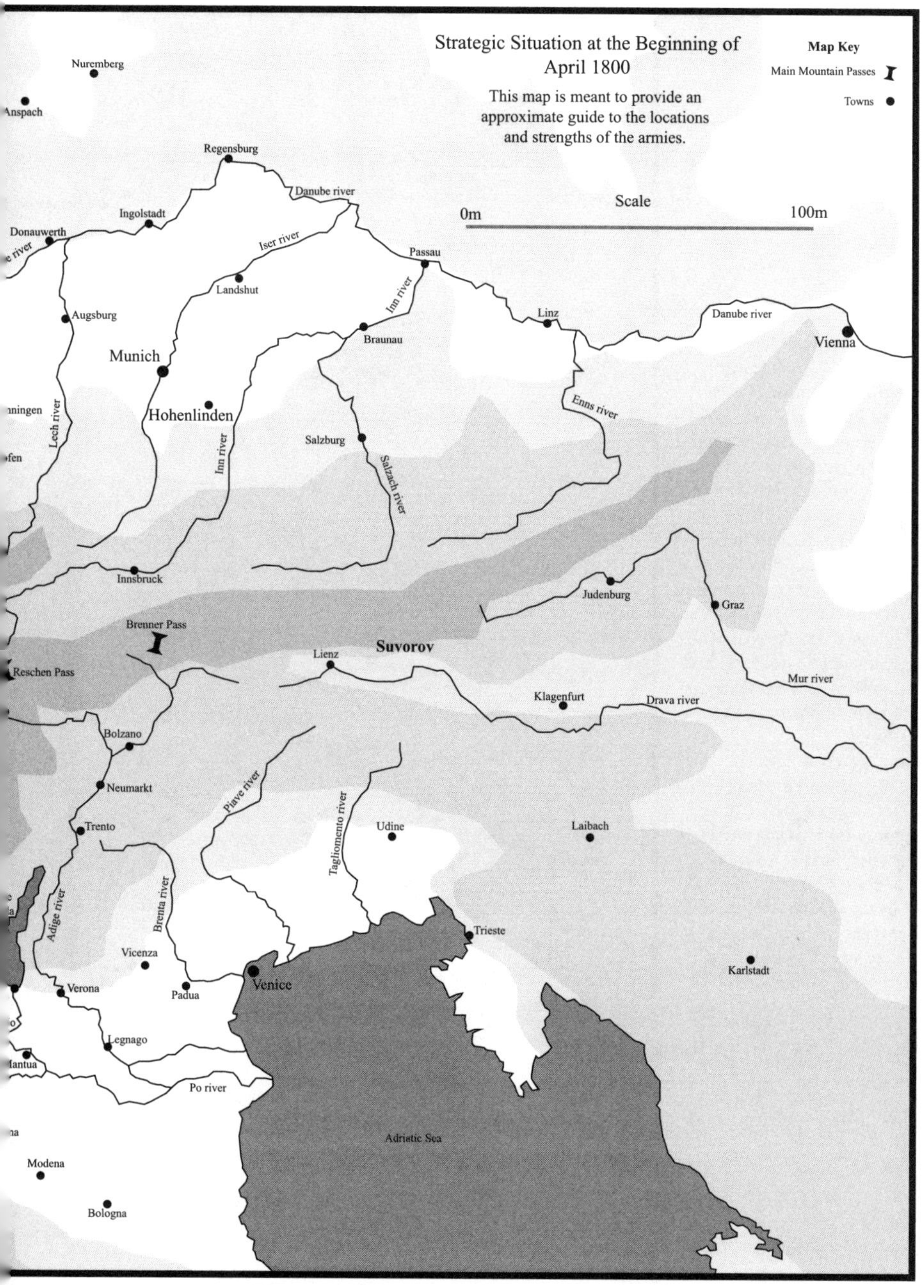
Strategic Situation at the Beginning of April 1800
This map is meant to provide an approximate guide to the locations and strengths of the armies.
Map Key
Main Mountain Passes
Towns
Scale
0m
100m
Nuremberg
Anspach
Regensburg
Danube river
Ingolstadt
Donauwerth
Iser river
Passau
Landshut
Inn river
Augsburg
Braunau
Linz
Danube river
Vienna
Munich
Hohenlinden
Lech river
Inn river
Salzburg
Salzach river
Enns river
Innsbruck
Judenburg
Graz
Brenner Pass
Suvorov
Lienz
Reschen Pass
Mur river
Klagenfurt
Drava river
Bolzano
Neumarkt
Piave river
Tagliomento river
Trento
Udine
Laibach
Adige river
Brenta river
Trieste
Vicenza
Karlstadt
Verona
Padua
Venice
Legnago
Po river
Adriatic Sea
Modena
Bologna

Summary

Following his seizure of power Napoleon Bonaparte had formed a plan to take the offensive in both theaters and personally to lead his army through the Great St. Bernard Pass with the aim of relieving Masséna in Genoa, who was cut off by the Austrians on land and the British by sea. Napoleon's advance was delayed by Piedmontese troops defending Bard, and this denied him the surprise he had wanted.

The planned Austrian offensive pushed French forces away from Genoa as they hoped, but the Austrians in Germany were forced back by the French advance under Moreau after the latter's victory at Stockach.

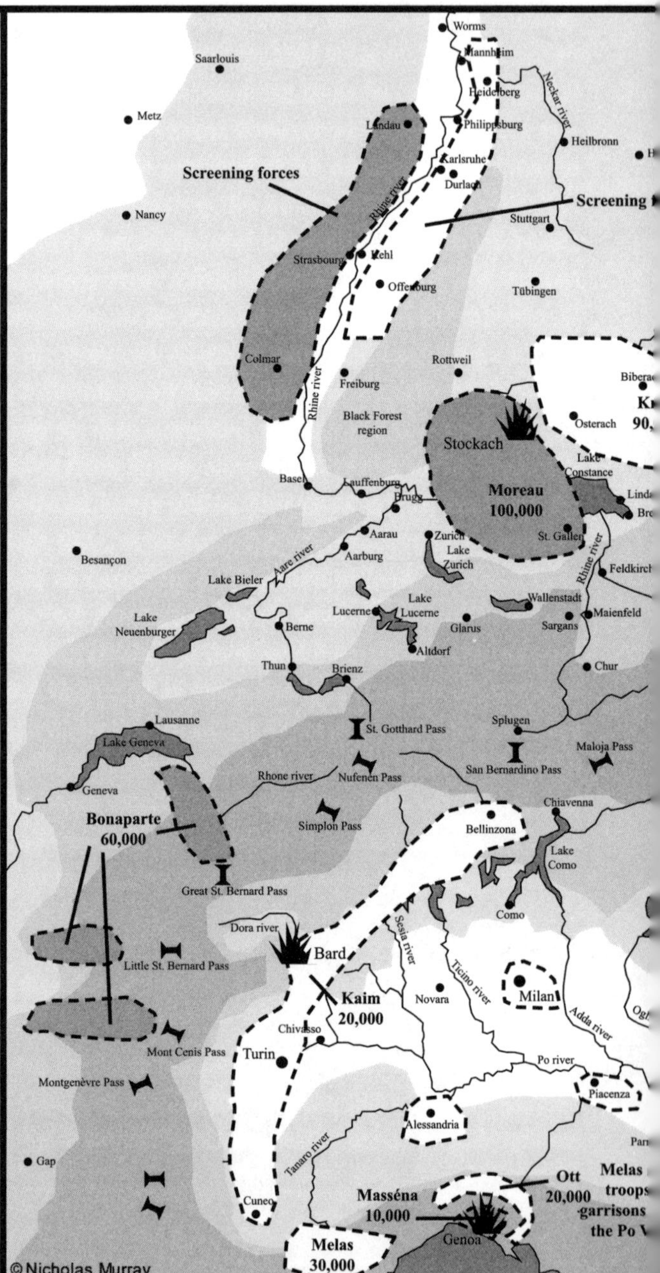

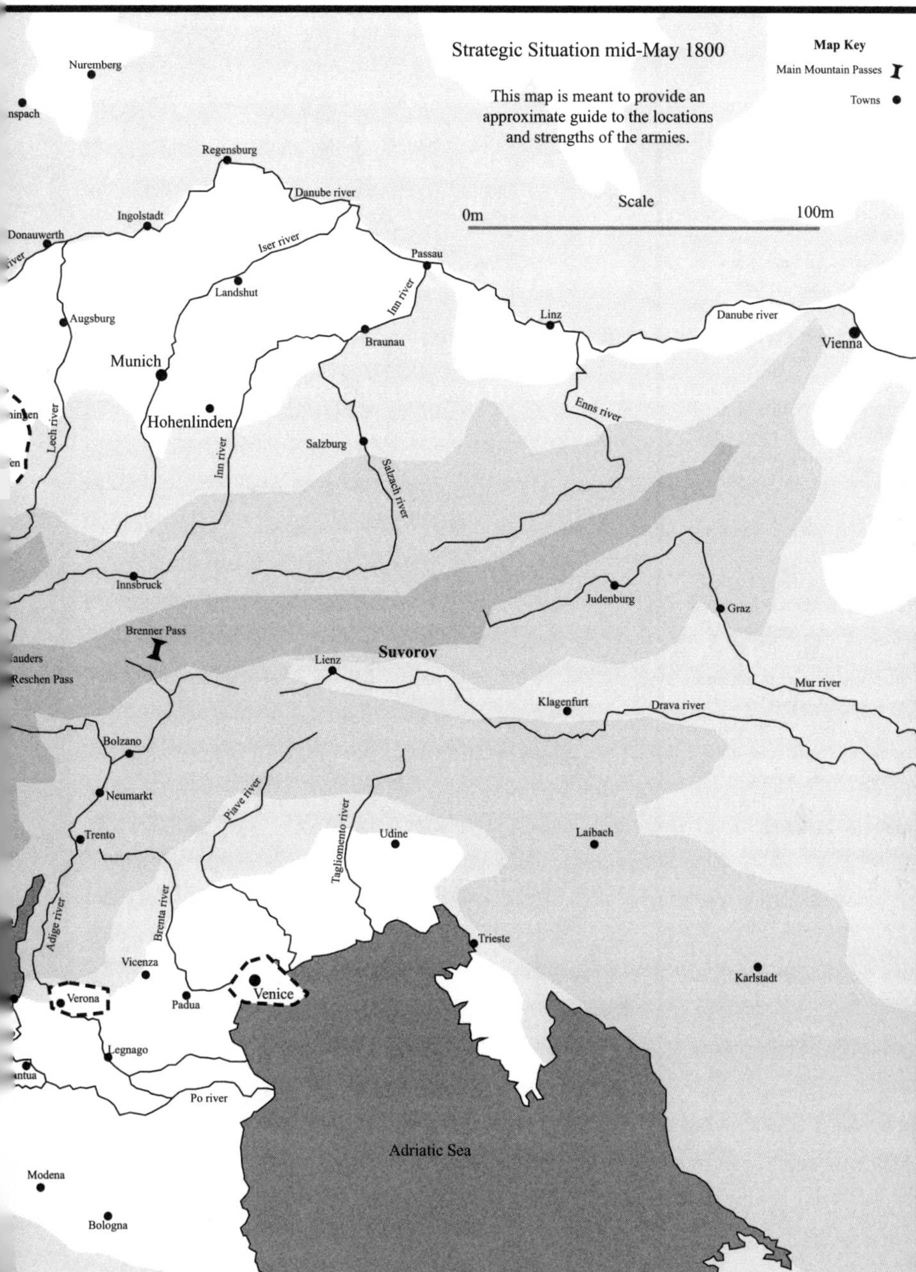

Strategic Situation mid-May 1800
This map is meant to provide an approximate guide to the locations and strengths of the armies.
Map Key
Main Mountain Passes
Towns
Scale
0m
100m
Nuremberg
nspach
Regensburg
Danube river
Ingolstadt
Donauwerth
Iser river
Landshut
Passau
Inn river
Augsburg
Braunau
Linz
Danube river
Vienna
Munich
Hohenlinden
Enns river
Lech river
Inn river
Salzburg
Salzach river
Innsbruck
Judenburg
Graz
Brenner Pass
Suvorov
Lienz
Reschen Pass
Mur river
Klagenfurt
Drava river
Bolzano
Neumarkt
Piave river
Tagliomento river
Trento
Udine
Laibach
Brenta river
Adige river
Trieste
Vicenza
Karlstadt
Verona
Padua
Venice
Legnago
Po river
Adriatic Sea
Modena
Bologna

Summary

Napoleon continued his advance to Milan to secure his lines of communication, but this decision, along with the delay he had suffered at Bard, meant he was unable to relieve Genoa in time.

The French positions in Italy cut Melas's lines of communication with Vienna.

However, Melas's capture of Genoa offered the opportunity, using British command of the Mediterranean, for the Austrians to be supplied by sea. Napoleon was forced to act and advanced against Melas at Alessandria. Although luck played a major role in the battle of Marengo (14 June), Napoleon decisively defeated Melas in the Italian theater of war. Shortly afterward, the Austrians effectively ceded control of Italy west of the Ticino River to French control, and Napoleon headed back to France to consolidate his power while continuing to prosecute the war.

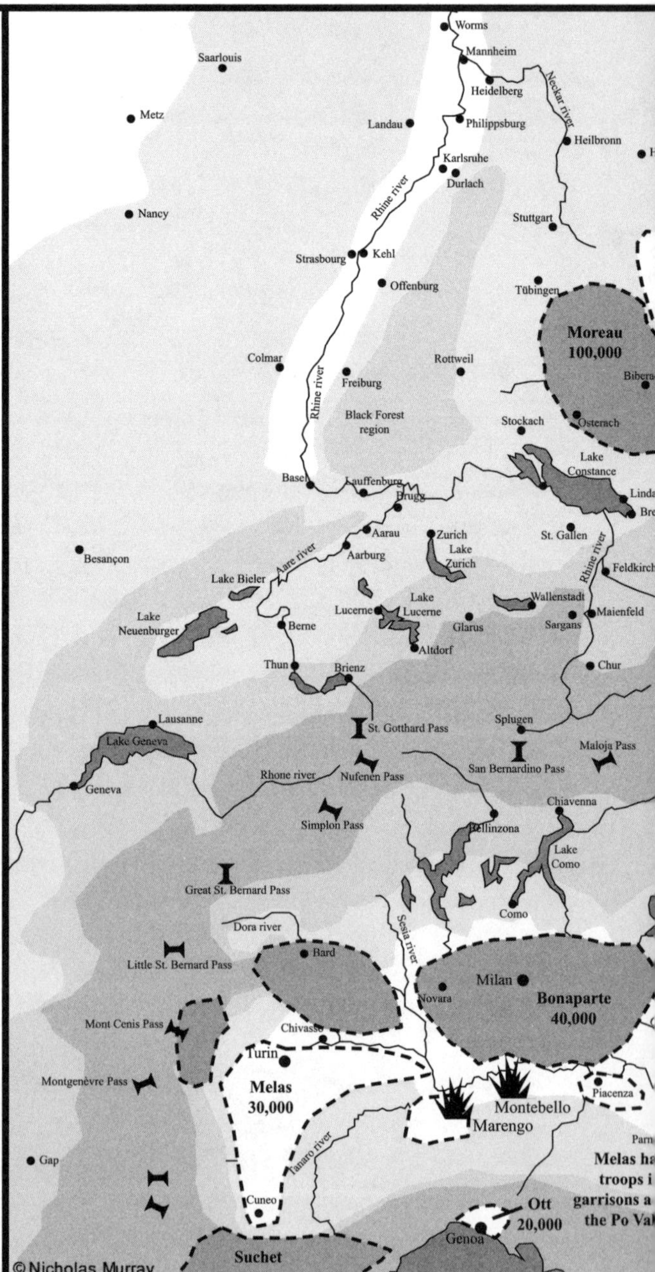

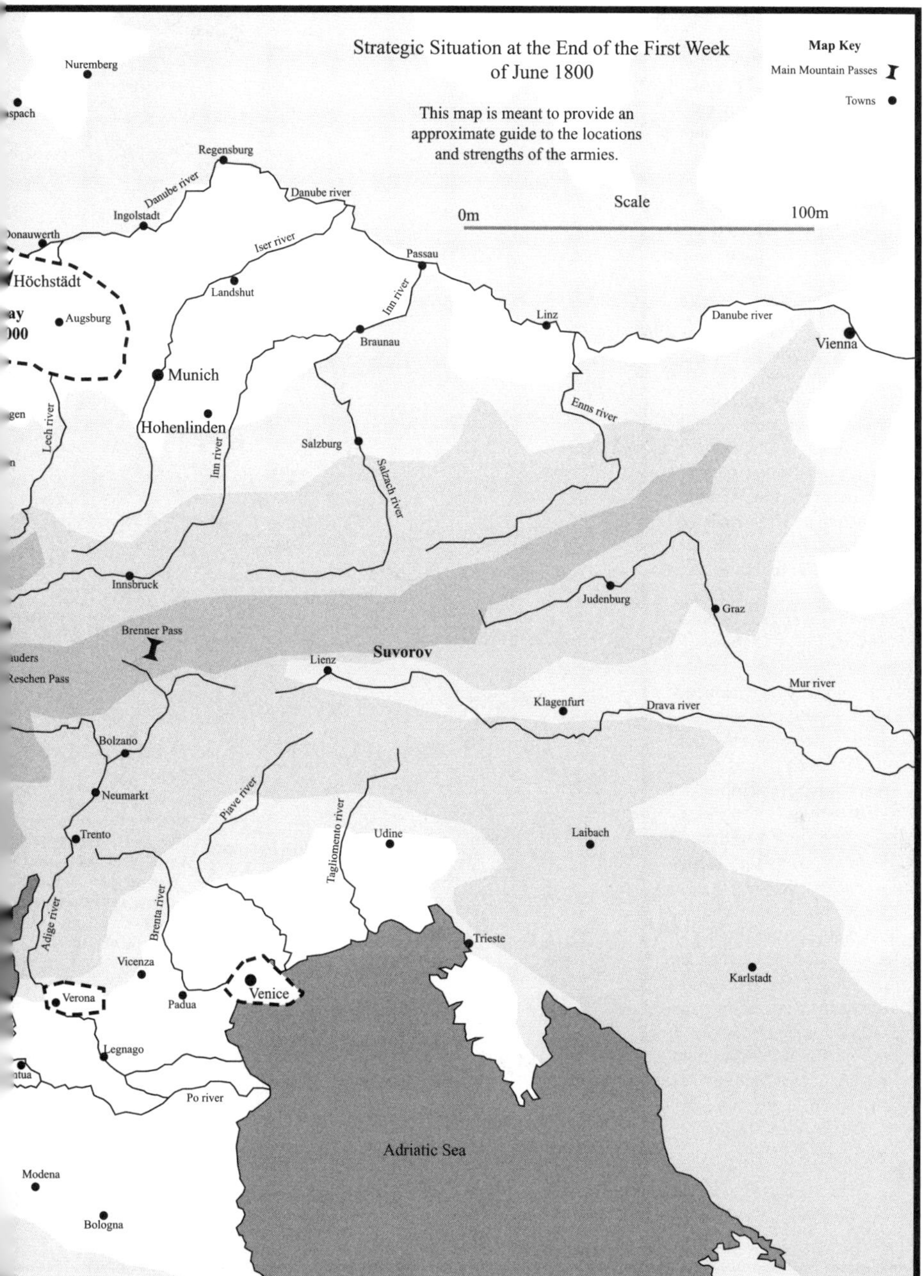

Strategic Situation at the End of the First Week of June 1800
This map is meant to provide an approximate guide to the locations and strengths of the armies.
Map Key
Main Mountain Passes
Towns
Scale
0m
100m
Nuremberg
Regensburg
Danube river
Ingolstadt
Iser river
Passau
Landshut
Höchstädt
Augsburg
Inn river
Braunau
Linz
Vienna
Munich
Hohenlinden
Enns river
Lech river
Salzburg
Salzach river
Innsbruck
Judenburg
Graz
Brenner Pass
Suvorov
Lienz
Reschen Pass
Mur river
Klagenfurt
Drava river
Bolzano
Neumarkt
Piave river
Tagliomento river
Udine
Laibach
Trento
Brenta river
Adige river
Trieste
Vicenza
Venice
Karlstadt
Verona
Padua
Legnago
Po river
Adriatic Sea
Modena
Bologna

Summary
From April until an armistice in July, Moreau's army had driven Kray from the Rhine to the river Inn. Moreau had beaten Kray at Stockach, Messkirch, and Höchstädt before the Austrians agreed to an armistice. Unlike in the Italian theater, a decisive blow had not been delivered, and both armies were still in sufficiently good shape to continue the fight. Kray's failures saw him relieved of command and Archduke John was brought in to replace him. Given John's youth, he was eighteen at the time of the campaign, he was appointed an advisor, Franz von Lauer, whom he was told to allow to run the campaign—not the most auspicious Austrian decision.

Although they had planned to launch a rapid offensive, the Austrians were too slow but still defeated a part of the French force at Ampfing, just to the north of Hohenlinden, on 1 December. Advancing to pursue an enemy they thought was falling back they ran into Moreau's main force and were thoroughly trounced. This loss led to a catastrophic Austrian retreat and French pursuit that ended with them seeking an armistice on 25 December to preempt a French march into Vienna, much as had been the case in 1797 after Napoleon marched to Vienna following his victory at Rivoli.

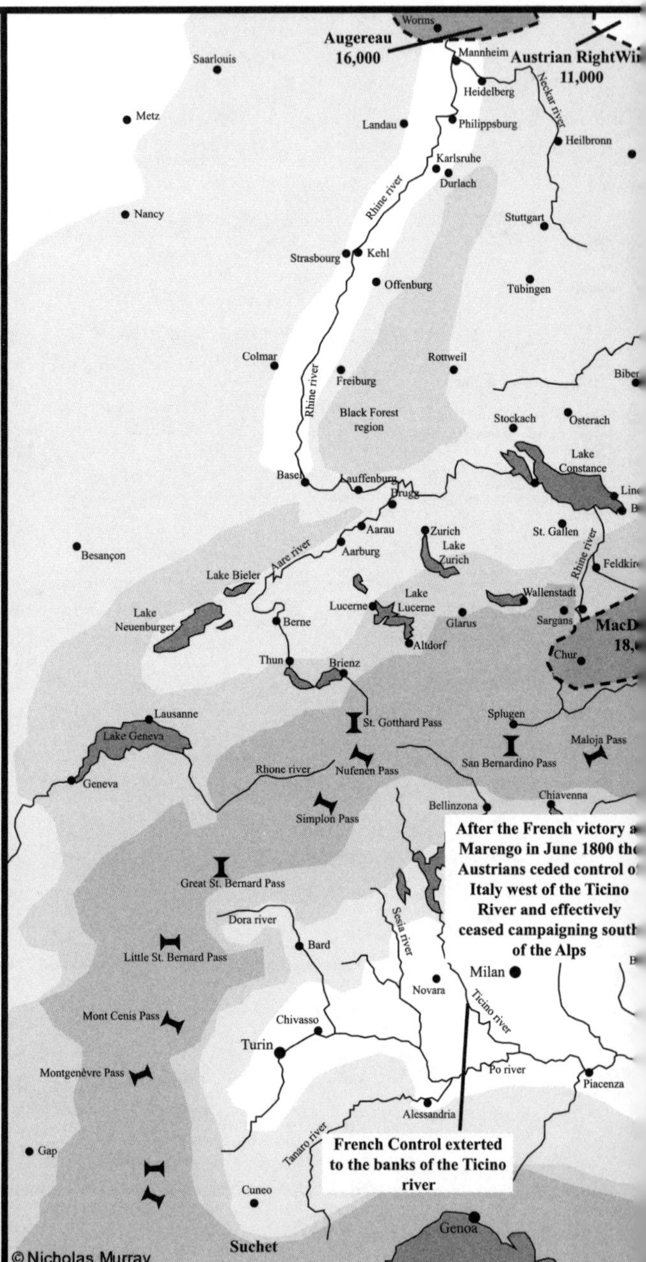

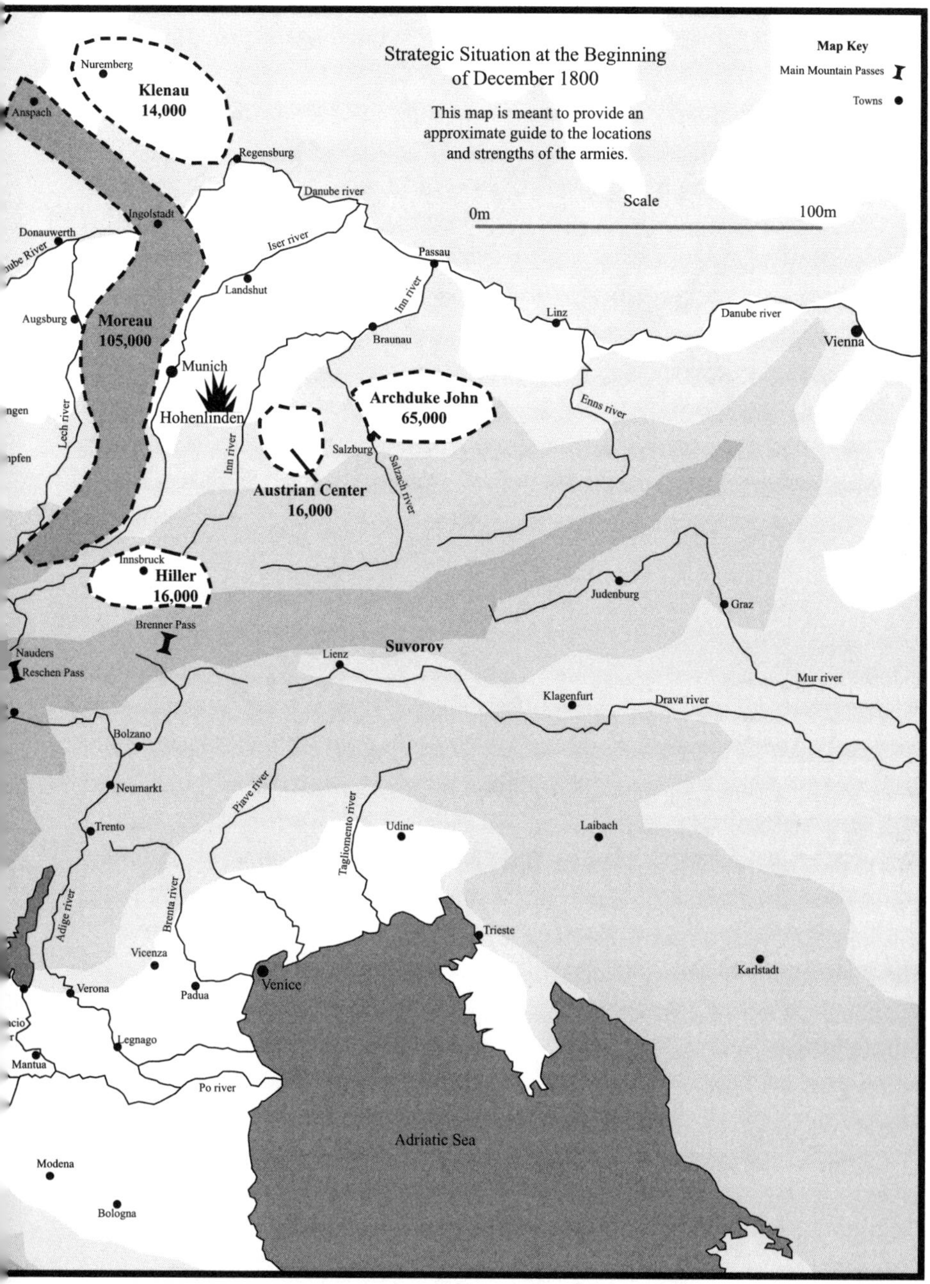
Strategic Situation at the Beginning of December 1800
This map is meant to provide an approximate guide to the locations and strengths of the armies.
Map Key
Main Mountain Passes
Towns
Scale
0m
100m
Klenau
14,000
Moreau
105,000
Archduke John
65,000
Austrian Center
16,000
Hiller
16,000
Suvorov
Nuremberg
Anspach
Regensburg
Danube river
Ingolstadt
Donauwerth
Iser river
Passau
Landshut
Inn river
Augsburg
Braunau
Linz
Danube river
Vienna
Munich
Hohenlinden
Lech river
Enns river
Salzburg
Salzach river
Innsbruck
Judenburg
Graz
Brenner Pass
Nauders
Reschen Pass
Lienz
Mur river
Klagenfurt
Drava river
Bolzano
Neumarkt
Piave river
Tagliomento river
Trento
Udine
Laibach
Adige river
Brenta river
Trieste
Vicenza
Karlstadt
Verona
Padua
Venice
Legnago
Mantua
Po river
Adriatic Sea
Modena
Bologna

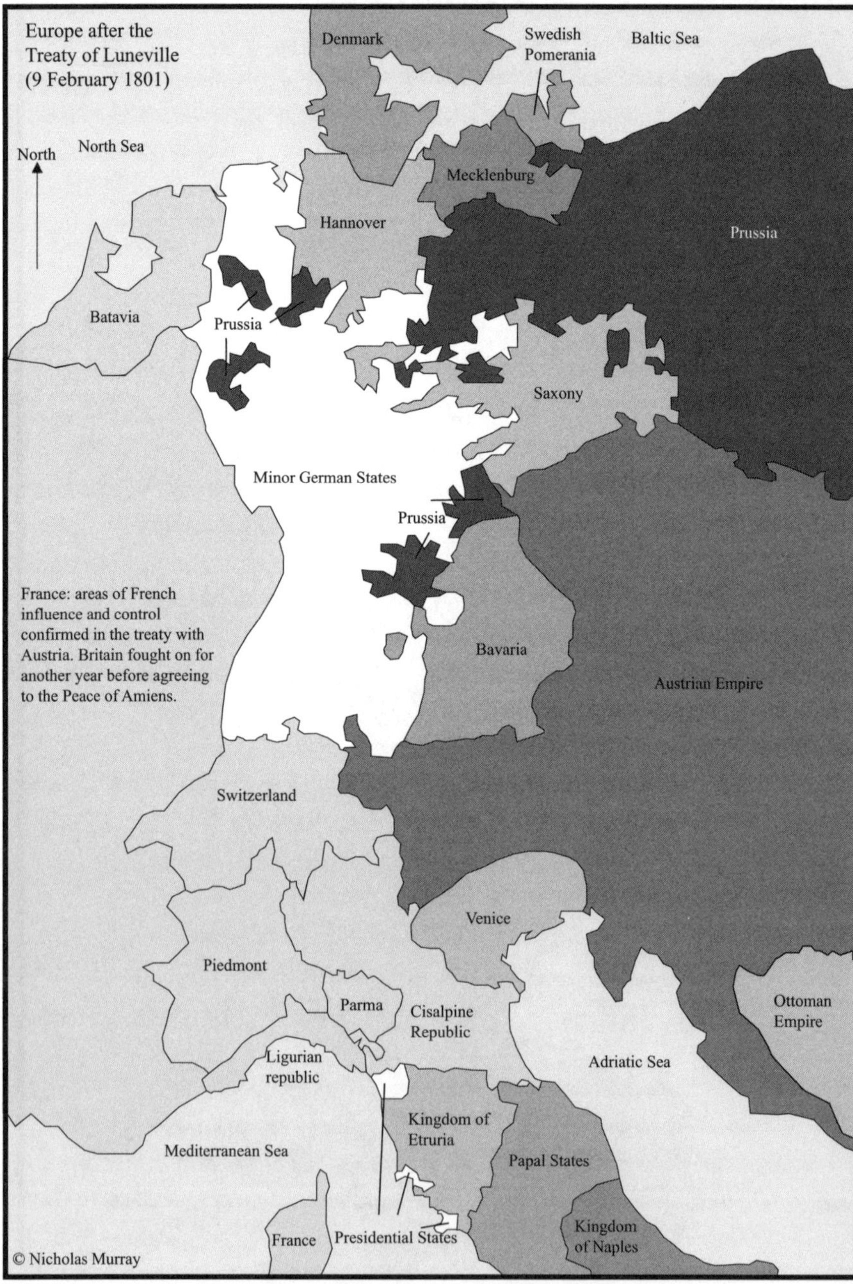
Europe after the
Treaty of Luneville
(9 February 1801)
North
North Sea
Denmark
Swedish
Pomerania
Baltic Sea
Mecklenburg
Hannover
Prussia
Batavia
Prussia
Saxony
Minor German States
Prussia
France: areas of French influence and control confirmed in the treaty with Austria. Britain fought on for another year before agreeing to the Peace of Amiens.
Bavaria
Austrian Empire
Switzerland
Venice
Piedmont
Parma
Cisalpine
Republic
Ottoman
Empire
Ligurian
republic
Adriatic Sea
Kingdom of
Etruria
Mediterranean Sea
Papal States
Kingdom
of Naples
France
Presidential States
© Nicholas Murray

8. Archduke Charles Relieves Philippsburg, Takes Mannheim, and Returns to Lake Constance

Suvorov Marches away to Swabia; End of the Campaign in Switzerland. Starray Relieves Philippsburg Twice. End of the Campaign on the Rhine.

85 THE ARCHDUKE RELIEVES PHILIPPSBURG AND TAKES MANNHEIM BY STORM

In section 68 we gave the reasons why the Austrian government decided to have Archduke Charles's army move to the Rhine. But these reasons, which related to causing a diversion for the benefit of the landing in Holland that took place at Texel at the end of August with some 40,000 men, had so little connection with the war aims that neither the Austrian cabinet nor its commander really knew what to do with this army on the Rhine.[1] To use a main army for a mere diversion is already a huge folly in itself, but besides, one can only create a diversion where there is some object of attack, and that is exactly what was lacking on the Rhine, because there could be no question of Archduke Charles carrying the war across the Rhine and the Vosges in September without holding a single fortress on that river. The fact that the French were forming a Rhine army again could admittedly be a reason to reinforce oneself there, but unless we want to deliberately introduce a false motive into the history, that cannot serve as the reason for his march away, even though it actually looks exactly like that at first glance because the French Army of the Rhine crossed

1. This brings us back to purpose and means in war (*On War*, book 1, chap. 2), where the purpose of the conflict needs to be matched by the strategic goals and actions as well as the level of effort. See also book 8, chaps. 3–6, regarding the relationship among the military objective, the degree of effort required, and the political aim of the conflict. If this is not clear, it is unlikely a commander will know how best to employ his force, short of using it for meaningless acts of violence simply to be doing something.

the river on 26 August and Archduke Charles set off for Schafhausen on the 31st. But in section 67 we have seen that he had already been under orders to do so for some time and that, by his own account, the immediate reason for his departure was basically nothing but a kind of disgust he felt at his failed crossing of the Limmat. In this, Archduke Charles seems like someone getting bored at home who reaches for his hat and stick, strolls out the door, but soon comes to a stop again because he basically does not know what to do with himself. Scarcely has he gone a few miles from Schafhausen when, before even reaching the sources of the Danube, he halts again at St. Blasien and just sends a corps off to relieve the inconsequential fortress of Philippsburg.[2]

The French were by no means lacking an objective for an offensive, since any serious advance on the Danube would have threatened the Austrian magazines and consternated the archduke. But they lacked the troops to venture so far forward. Of the 54,000 men they had on the Rhine, they could concentrate no more than 12,000 as an active army at Oggersheim and could have about 8,000 men under Baraguey d'Hilliers advance from Mainz. Little though this was, the government rightly felt that it had to be put into action in order to at least create a diversion for Masséna in Switzerland. In fact, it could have been expected that without this diversion, mere boredom or more likely shame soon would have driven the archduke back to Switzerland; he himself says: "The archduke could have wished for nothing more than enemy operations on the right bank of the Rhine that offered him the chance to fulfill the intentions of the court of Vienna, at least partly and with apparent result."[3] Rarely has a commander been seen so at a loss for an enemy.

General Müller, who was still in command of the Army of the Rhine pending Moreau's arrival, was ordered to advance as far as the sources of the Neckar and the Danube if possible. He crossed the Rhine at Mannheim on the 26th and advanced to Philippsburg on the 27th, driving off the Austrian light troops of Starray's corps that faced him.

The Austrians retreated to Durlach, Pforzheim, and Laufen, where they were reinforced by some Austrian, Swabian, and Württemberg troops.

2. Clausewitz is making the point that a commander has to have the resolve to act, not simply to do something for the sake of it because he is overwhelmed by the bigger picture. Any act needs to match the goals of the conflict. See also note 46 in chapter 7. The archduke comments negatively about his own choice too; see Karl, 2:149. He then undermines his own point later; see Karl, 2:156–157.

3. **Clausewitz** notes: "Vol. II, p 151." Karl, 2:151.

Müller now invested Philippsburg, intending to await Baraguey d'Hilliers. The latter had moved from Mainz to Frankfurt on the 28th, where he had levied a significant financial contribution. From there he had pushed his vanguard forward to Seligenstadt but did not think he could advance any further in that direction, since the minister of Mainz, Baron Albini, had mustered the *Landsturm* here covered by some detachments of Mainz, Palatinate, and Austrian troops and set 15,000 men on a war footing. General Baraguey d'Hilliers sent the larger part of his division to Müller and retreated to Mainz again with the rest. By this reinforcement, which could hardly have moved along the mountain road but rather perhaps along the left bank of the Rhine, and which arrived at Heidelberg on 31 August,[4] General Müller attained a strength of 18,000 men. On 6 September he began the bombardment of Philippsburg, which had a garrison of 2,300 *Reichstruppen* under the command of the Rheingrafen [Count] von Salm, who was the lieutenant-general of the district of Franconia. The town was soon in flames, and lacking casemates, the garrison and the townsfolk knew not where they might seek shelter. However, this problem did not last long, for the bombardment that began on 6 September soon had to cease again on the 11th.

If the archduke had carried on marching or at least had a substantial corps set off for Philippsburg straight away, it is clear that the town could reasonably have been relieved by the 7th or 8th, since it is only some 120 miles from Schafhausen. But the archduke thought there was no need to hurry; he says:

> Convinced that the possession of Philippsburg was of no great importance and that the French besieging force was not numerous, during his march out of Switzerland the archduke decided just to send off a proportionate number of troops to relieve the fortress, and to rest first at the more important point at the sources of the Danube. But because the weakness of the enemy on the upper Rhine engendered little concern for that area, and because of the exaggerated reports of constantly increasing French strength on the Middle Rhine, he was prompted to change his mind. 14,000 men remained in the chain of outposts between the Rench valley and Waldshut, 10,000 men in reserve between Waldshut and Villingen, and the archduke set the rest on the march in such a manner that 30 battalions

4. The text had September, but this does not make sense. The archduke's account has the Austrians relieving Philippsburg on 11 September. Karl, 2:157.

and 76 squadrons could be united on the Enz between Pforzheim and Vaihingen on the 12th.[5]

These thirty battalions and seventy-six squadrons constituted a force of 34,000 men, which, together with the 24,000 he left behind on the upper Rhine, makes 58,000. Since he marched out of Switzerland with only about 30,000 men, Nauendorf's corps is certainly included in that total, because Starray would have been at most 20,000 strong.

It is likely that the archduke set off from the area of St. Blasien on 5 September. Upon his approach on 11 September, General Müller raised the siege of Philippsburg and retreated to Mannheim, then back across the Rhine on the 14th and 15th, leaving Mannheim and Neckerau [Neckarau] held by Laroche's division.

A few months earlier, the French had demolished Mannheim's fortifications; now they set about urgently repairing them again.

Mind you, lying in the sharp angle of the junction of the Neckar and the Rhine and thus fairly well protected by water on three sides, Mannheim was easy to make defensible again against a coup de main; the French basically just had to rebuild three or four bastions with their associated earthworks. But they had not let themselves be content just with that. Regarding Mannheim as a bridgehead, they had constructed a fairly extensive fortification in front of the bridge across the Neckar, fortified the village of Neckarau that lay between the Rhine and the Neckar 3 miles from the city walls, and, in addition, built a large number of small advanced flèches and redoubts to connect with it. The right wing of these entrenchments rested on the sawmill by the Rhine, the left on the imperial lodge on the Neckar. The French were still working on these defenses when the archduke approached, and most of the earthworks had not yet reached their proper height. Laroche's division that was supposed to defend these entrenchments and Mannheim comprised five battalions and six squadrons, of which two battalions and two squadrons were in Neckarau, and three battalions and four squadrons were in Mannheim and its entrenchments. The fortress was very weak in artillery, since the Austrians only took twenty-three guns when they captured the place, of which some were probably Laroche's field artillery.[6]

5. **Clausewitz** notes: "Vol. II, p 156." Karl, 2:156–157.

6. See the archduke's own map. Karl, vol. 3, chart VII, https://maps.hungaricana.hu/en/HTITerkeptar/25641/view/?pg=7&bbox=-1402%2C-6929%2C10828%2C-73.

Clearly, these circumstances were of such a nature that while on the one hand the French could flatter themselves that they could remain in possession of Mannheim unmolested if their adversary had no pressing need to attack it, on the other, the Austrians could not have thought it was impossible nor even particularly difficult to take the fortress and its works by storm.

The archduke and his army had arrived on the Enz on the 12th; he followed on the heels of the French to Mannheim and, after having left five battalions on the Enz at Illingen on the road from Stuttgart to Durlach, moved on 17 September with 14,000 men to Schwetzingen, 6,000 to Edingen, and 8,000 in reserve at Leimen.

Thus the archduke and his 34,000 men had moved from St. Blasien to the area of Schwetzingen, 150 miles away, and had completely removed himself from the Swiss theater when the decisive battles there were so imminent, without having achieved anything other than the relief of the insignificant fortress of Philippsburg; if he were to retreat now, not only would the French immediately advance on Philippsburg again, but he would also be left with the powerful feeling that his operation had been utterly futile, which would be intolerable. This feeling must have been what first drew him to the idea of taking Mannheim by a coup de main. Taking a fortress by storm always has a great impact; furthermore, it never lacks for trophies; besides, Mannheim did indeed have some strategic significance as a bridgehead, and it could be hoped that if the French lost the use of this crossing, they would not threaten Swabia from the Rhine again during this campaign. Thus, by taking Mannheim with a swift coup de main, the archduke could give his maneuver the kind of purpose it was lacking—enough to satisfy public opinion for the moment, if not his future critics. Now the archduke had arrived in the Schwetzingen area with 28,000 men, and even though 9,000 of them were cavalry, there were enough infantry to make success almost certain through their superior numbers. General Müller might have reinforced the garrison at any time, but the archduke had received news that after General Müller crossed the Rhine he had sent one division to Landau and another to Holland.

On the 18th, under cover of thick fog, the Austrians moved against Neckarau and the redoubts between the village and Mannheim.

We do not wish to detain ourselves long with the details of the attack, partly because it is outside our topic, and partly because it is really not very instructive either. The corps that had camped at Schwetzingen moved along the Schwetzingen road to Neckarau; the corps from Edingen, along the Neckar to the imperial lodge; the reserve followed the latter; one battalion and seven squadrons were sent across the Neckar at Neckarshausen to threaten the bridgehead. While the infantry advanced against the entrenchments, the cavalry marched up between the two columns. The village of Neckarau was taken mainly by one battalion that had worked its way along through the meadows between the village and the Rhine and attacked the place on its right flank, while five battalions stormed it frontally. The column coming from Edingen moved from Neckarau against the sawmill [this is the Holz Hof, just to the west of the Kaiserhuette],[7] which was not able to resist for long either. When the French who had been driven out of the redoubts retreated into the fortress, inevitably great panic and confusion broke out, and the cooperation of a few of the inhabitants opening the gates from within to grant the Austrians entry was almost superfluous. The complete success of this attack was obviously more the effect of numerical superiority and of the enemy's inadequate defensive arrangements than of any especially skillful leadership, for which there was not much scope anyway, so far as we can judge from this distance in time and space. The most curious thing about this assault is that 9,000 cavalry should have participated in it without having anywhere they could go.

The day's trophies were two standards, twenty-three cannon, and 1,800 prisoners, among them two generals. The archduke does not give the Austrians' losses, but these were probably entirely negligible.

The storming of Mannheim happened at almost the same time as the battle of Bergen, which was won by Brune against the Duke of York on 19 September and decided the fate of the Anglo-Russian landing in north Holland, since from that point on, the allies were unable to make any further progress and concluded a convention for their withdrawal four weeks later.[8] Thus, even if the archduke's operation could have been expected to have some degree of effect as a diversion, it would certainly have come too late. The archduke stayed at Mannheim, busying himself with demolishing the fortifications entirely because they were not in a state to be fully repaired without great expense, and he sent away some of his cavalry to patrol toward the Lahn.

7. Karl, 2:159–162.

8. The Convention of Alkmaar of 18 October 1799 confirmed the abject end to the allied expedition to Holland. See Ross, *Quest for Victory*, 280–281. See also Intelligence Branch, *British Minor Expeditions 1746 to 1814* (London: HMSO, 1884), 40–41, https://books.google.com/.

On page 179, the archduke himself says of his operation:

> Glorious as the taking of Mannheim was, yet it benefited the English landing at Den Helder little. The distance between the two places was too great and there were too many obstacles between them for one operation to redound to the advantage of the other, nor did they both threaten the enemy to such a degree that he would be prevented from acting first against whichever caused him the most concern. For this reason the archduke's advance to the Neckar did not deter the French from sending all their available forces to the sea coast; for they rightly calculated that they need not worry about any swift and painful blow from the Rhine, and moved the rest of their troops that had returned from the right bank of the Rhine to Landau.[9]

86 THE ARCHDUKE RETURNS TO THE DANUBE

In the archduke's history he tells us nothing about his further sojourn in Mannheim, nor about the plans he had before he heard the news of the battle of Zurich; nothing about receiving this news, nor about the impression it made on him, nor about what it made him decide to do; nothing about his departure. Instead, after he has taken us from Mannheim to Zurich and the St. Gotthard and told us at length about events there, on 6 October we find him back on the Danube again between Donaueschingen and Villingen, where his army has arrived from Mannheim between 1 and 7 October, twenty-seven battalions and forty-six squadrons strong.

Since it would have taken him about eight days to march from Mannheim to Donaueschingen, we can conclude that he would have set off in late September immediately after receiving the news of the battle of Zurich. Of the thirty battalions and seventy-six squadrons he had led to the Neckar, he left two battalions and thirteen squadrons in the Mannheim area. There is therefore one infantry battalion missing, as well as seventeen squadrons of cavalry about which he tells us nothing; we can only think that they were presumably used to reinforce the cordon in the Black Forest and the Rhine valley below the Rench.

9. Karl, 2:179.

The archduke says nothing about the distribution of his forces when he arrived on the Danube, but we can roughly estimate that he had a force of 40,000 men in hand behind the Black Forest between the Rhine and the sources of the Danube and that there were about 18,000 men spread out in the cordon along the Rhine and in the Mannheim area.[10]

If the archduke and these 40,000 men had joined up with Korsakov without further ado, taking the latter under his command and returning to the left bank of the Rhine with him, there cannot be the slightest doubt that he would have either completely beaten Masséna's left wing on the Thur or else at least driven it back as far as he cared to, thus at least beyond the Limmat.[11] He could consequently have repaired the damage from the battle of Zurich to some degree, perhaps *entirely,* perhaps even *richly* repaid it, according to whether fortune favored him in doing so and the French made things worse for themselves by giving battle inopportunely. By intervening so quickly, he would have evened out the material disadvantages again, demonstrated the Austrians' goodwill, and preempted the bad impression that recent events in Switzerland were bound to make on the Russians, their commanders, and their tsar and indeed, would even have silenced their many well-founded complaints, since parking an Austrian victory right next to a Russian defeat was the best kind of rebuttal. It is incomprehensible that this chivalrous decision did not enter the archduke's mind. He was a young man, 28 years old, who had already tasted the sweetness of fame in his 25th year and could constantly use the enthusiasm his name aroused throughout Europe to fan and nourish his own ardor, even when it threatened to fade away under the pressure of real life; there was no egotism or cold calculation in his character, no narrow-minded petty politicking in his mind—we proclaim once more—it is *incomprehensible!* This way, he could have erased the total futility of his campaign up until now, which weighed on his conscience like a mountain the size of an Alp and lay in his limbs heavy as lead; this way, he could have put a stop to the utter confusion of the Austrian plans, which were like an endless

10. Readers might wish to check for themselves, but Clausewitz is right. See Karl, 2:151–180, 296–321, 360–366.

11. This brings us back to the point about concentration of effort. Had they combined, then what Clausewitz claims is quite possible. That being said, as Clausewitz observes about allies in *On War*, book 8, chap. 6a, working with allies toward a common goal is difficult unless the goal is sufficiently valuable to all parties.

bad dream, and resolved their complications, which never seemed to lead to a happy solution. But such is human nature; when strength of will fails, ideas whirl futilely through the mind, just as the compass needle on a ship spins vainly on its spindle if there is no strong arm turning the helm toward it. The cataleptic can think but cannot move![12]

We have seen how the bridges at Büsingen, Diesenhofen, and Konstanz were abandoned by the Russians on 7 October, and we know that the archduke was present and, instead of preventing the Russians from doing this, in a momentary fit of pique, he explicitly authorized Korsakov to do so. Since General Nauendorf was nearby with an Austrian corps, and also the first troops from the Neckar had already reached the Danube on 1 October, if the archduke had thought the Russians would not hold the bridgeheads, he could have used Austrian troops to do so and thus kept the Rhine crossings open. We cannot hesitate for a moment to place the whole burden of this major error squarely on him, since on page 279 he himself says:

> Abandoning the Büsingen bridgehead was an all the more premature step by the allies as they had not yet renounced the idea of a new offensive in Switzerland, which this made massively more difficult. But even if they had given up on an offensive, possession of the bridgehead could still have been very useful, because there is no more secure and enduring defense than when possession of a jumping-off point[13] constantly threatens the enemy with an attack and puts him at least partly on the defensive.[14]

He also says on page 280:

> In the situation on the Swiss border just at that time the Büsingen bridgehead could have played a glorious role, because it was late in the year

12. Clausewitz makes this point about "stolid men" in his chapter on military genius: "Stolid men are hard to throw off balance, but total lack of vigor cannot really be interpreted as strength of character. It cannot be denied, however, that the imperturbability of such men gives them a certain narrow usefulness in war. They are seldom strongly motivated, lack initiative and consequently are not particularly active; on the other hand they seldom make a serious mistake." *On War*, 106. This description suits the archduke rather well.

13. This is written as *offensiver Punkte* in the original.

14. Karl, 2:279.

> and General Masséna did not have the numerical superiority for a serious operation to force its evacuation. On the other hand this place gave the allies a free hand to harass the enemy position and to exhaust his troops through continuous small-scale operations without fatiguing their own. The bridgehead was abandoned, not because the archduke doubted the Russians' courage but because Korsakov's own repeated comments made him doubt Korsakov's determination. Nevertheless, what stopped the archduke from using Austrian troops to occupy entrenchments that only needed a garrison of 2,500 men? And even if these works were a little short of being finished, they were still defensible and could very soon have been brought to completion.[15]

From this self-criticism, we see that the loss of the Rhine crossings cannot be accepted as an excuse for the archduke standing idle on the Danube.

We see again in another place how the archduke simultaneously arraigns and excuses himself for *his inaction:*

> But right after his troops departed from Mannheim the archduke still had the means at his disposal to invade Switzerland anew, to retake Zurich, and to occupy an advantageous line for his winter quarters[16] on both banks of the Rhine between the Swiss lakes and the sources of the Neckar. Perhaps he would have carried the Russians along with him and stirred them into action, for we all like to follow someone who is decisive, and if we cannot surpass him, at least we do not want to lag behind. Nevertheless, this criticism cannot be expressed without consideration of the factors that, while not absolving it entirely, do at least enable it to be mitigated. Political considerations had taken the archduke away from Switzerland. The basis for these had not been made so clear to him that he could disregard them entirely, they had to cause him some doubt at least; and when has a doubtful commander, left hanging in uncertainty, ever acted decisively? Since the operation had to happen in two columns on either side of Lake Constance, abandoning or only weakly guarding the approaches to Vorarlberg and Graubündten for some time would have been unavoidable if each of the

15. Karl, 2:280–281.

16. The archduke discusses his actual winter quarters slightly later. See Karl, 2:322–350.

two columns was to be made self-sufficient enough not to be destroyed in detail before they could combine. Although this momentary exposure had no essential military disadvantage, it did not accord with the views of the court of Vienna, nor with prevailing opinion. On the other hand, the French Army of the Rhine was daily being reinforced and becoming better organized and more capable of threatening Germany, whose defense was solely the responsibility of the archduke.[17]

We do not wish to linger here refuting in detail the extremely weak excuses to which even the archduke himself seems to attach no great value, but instead will make three general observations.

The first is that this language sounds more like a mean, decrepit old general than a 28-year-old prince, and it amazes us to see the 28-year-old archduke not following in the footsteps of his 25-year-old self but lagging behind him. A man's life does not usually peak so soon.[18]

The second is that decisiveness is precisely the character trait that needs to be displayed when a commander is surrounded by uncertainty.[19] Uncertain though the archduke may have been regarding opinions in Vienna, he was anything but with respect to the probability of success. As far as Korsakov's goodwill was concerned, this poor sinner was in the most desperate need of a good deed, as we have seen from his advance on 7 October, so he would happily have followed the archduke, and no *perhaps* about it.

Our third and final observation is that, here again, the archduke paid too much attention to material factors and completely ignored the moral dimension. Gaining Zurich and a better line for his winter quarters was the last

17. **Clausewitz** notes: "[footnote: *p294]." This is Karl, 2:294–295.

18. In the original: "*So früh kulminirt doch das Leben eines Menschen gewöhnlich nicht.*" The choice of language is interesting, as it connects with Clausewitz's ideas about both a culmination point and military genius and youthful vigor. That the archduke already appears world-weary and cautious indicates that he is not the vigorous genius Clausewitz would like to see in charge of an army, and the fact that Clausewitz comments on his age at all in the context of culmination indicates that he thinks the archduke has already passed his peak and is beyond the point at which success is likely or even possible. See *On War*, book 1, chap. 3, on military genius, and book 7, chaps. 2–5, on the strategic attack and culmination.

19. Clausewitz has repeatedly driven this point home in these volumes as well as in *On War.*

thing he should have been worrying about; the key issue was the spirit of discord, mistrust, and hatred that had been conjured up and was bound to have been increased by the recent course of events. What counted was not the recapture of Zurich but unity and trust—not rectifying the line for winter quarters, but giving new heart—what really mattered was to summon forth new enthusiasm for the business, since the destiny of the entire campaign hung from it as if from the finest of threads. If the glow of a new victory could rekindle courage and strength once more, then not only would the collapse of the coalition be avoided, not only would Zurich and the Limmat be regained, but the whole of Switzerland would fall into the victor's lap like an overripe fruit.

But how far the archduke was from seeing things in this context is shown by the start of his following chapter, where, with truly unwitting naïveté, he says: "Masséna's efforts and even his victories in Switzerland had too little effect on the fate of the campaign in general, and did not have the glorious consequences the French government had hoped for from the success of their arms in this part of the theater of war."[20] That the French government thought this way before it knew of the split in the coalition—all well and good!—but the fact that the archduke could write that way twenty years afterward makes us exclaim as Wieland does: *he cannot see the wood for the trees!*[21]

Let us return now to the action.

87 SUVOROV MARCHES AWAY TO SWABIA

As the archduke and his army were arriving at Donaueschingen, Suvorov was crossing the mountains at Panix. The archduke was just one or two days' march from Schafhausen, so he could have crossed the Rhine as early as the 8th or 9th. But Suvorov did not reach Feldkirch until the 12th, so if the two had wanted to advance in unison, it would have cost five or six days. This delay was

20. Karl, 2:296.

21. Christoph Martin Wieland was a poet and writer of the late eighteenth-century German Enlightenment. The phrase used by Clausewitz is attributed to Wieland, and a virtually identical phrase can be found in Wieland's well-known short story *Geschichte der Abderiten* (Leipzig: Philipp Reclam, Jun., 1881), 281, https://reader.digitale-sammlungen.de/de/fs1/object/display/bsb11016459_00005.html?zoom=0.6500000000000001.

of no great importance in itself, except that at the start of October, Masséna was still engaged with Suvorov and had a large part of his forces entangled in mountain warfare; at any rate, the archduke must have assumed this was the case, so he could have hoped to find that the French on the Thur were much less capable of resistance. However, we can well understand why, if the archduke set no store by the morale value of a swift attack, that consideration did not directly decide him to act alone before Suvorov was in a position for a new advance.[22] Thus, he found it natural to wait for the latter, and the two entered into written discussions of future operations.

On 13 October the archduke received a proposal from Suvorov according

22. The archduke seems unable to decide whether he wants speed or caution. It is worth quoting several examples of this contradictory behavior. In discussing the campaign for Zurich, he says about himself: "The archduke had now fully secured his right wing through the stronger occupation of the Rhine and through the reserves positioned behind Bülach; however, he also wanted to have no worries about his left wing, as the French were still holding both shores of Lake Zürich along its entire length. This was, however, excessive caution. . . . The course of operations in an intersected area that is not well known enough and bravely defended is indeed always slow if there is no decisive superiority on one side, and the archduke had to await the approach of Hotze's corps if he wanted to create this superiority by joining up with the same. However, from this period onward, his movements were not associated with that rapidity, which was now possible and which so increases power immensely." Karl, 1:346–347. So, he wants caution to secure his base of operations, which is reasonable; he recognizes the need for rapidity but cannot manage it. In addition, when discussing the March 1799 campaign on the Lech, he writes: "The archduke's operations were better calculated. His advance from the Lech took place with great rapidity and if the French had not entirely lost the possibility of gaining the flank of the Vorarlberg before him, then the blame lay not with the Austrian general but with the political circumstances, which made his moves dependent on those of the opponent." Karl, 1:180–181. So he did move quickly but did not really gain his aim, and that was someone else's fault. Again, about the move on Zurich he writes: "In contrast, the Austrians, from the moment their opponents left Donaueschingen in order to continue their retreat to the Rhine, gained a free hand to direct their operations toward Switzerland and they hoped, through a rapid move on Zürich, to force the Swiss army [the French army in Switzerland] to vacate all forward positions before the Danube army [the French army on the Danube] would have advanced far enough through the Black Forest again to thwart this maneuver." Karl, 1:208. And, he states: "All these arrangements took place far too slowly. In the situation then pertaining, rapid action should have been taken, and the archduke did have enough forces to advance without having to wait

to which Graubündten should be abandoned, the lower toll bridge (the Rhine bridge at Maienfeld) burned, and the St. Luciensteig demolished. Suvorov then wanted all the troops in Vorarlberg to move across the Rhine at Meiningen and Höchst on the 17th, meet up at St. Gallen on the 18th, and join Korsakov at Winterthur, who was to advance in two columns from Konstanz through Bischofszell and from the area of Stein [am Rhein] through Pfyn and Frauenfeld. Until the junction with Korsakov's corps, 6,000 Austrians together with the local militia were to stay in the Feldkirch position and cover the left flank during the crossing of the Rhine.

If the archduke has presented this plan in full, what naturally strikes us first about it is that there is no mention of the archduke's army. Presumably, there was the tacit assumption that, for its part, it would cooperate at its discretion by crossing at Schafhausen with a substantial corps.

Then Korsakov's advance through Pfyn and Frauenfeld is prescribed as though there were no enemy in the area and it was merely a matter of a route march. If Korsakov were to arrive in Frauenfeld 12,000–15,000 strong, he ran the risk of being attacked in very superior force by Masséna and being utterly defeated again before even the column from Konstanz could come to his aid, let alone Suvorov from St. Gallen.

---

for Starray's arrival. He wanted to attack some point or other on the enemy line, the victory was under no doubt: a move in forced marches to Donaueschingen and the scattering of the enemy's center would have led most powerfully to the goal. However, the archduke still had doubts about Jourdan's error of judgment, which error was soon to be confirmed by the consequences." Karl, 1:233. Perhaps what shows his thoughts most clearly is a comment about Lecourbe early in the war: "Le Courbe [*sic*] gave in completely to his bold impetuous coarse character: he gave preference to the speed of the operation over its security and did not pay heed to loss of life if he hoped to purchase an advantage thereby." Karl, 1:84. Again, on the later campaign near Zurich he writes: "The execution of the plan entirely equated to the intentions of the French general and was implemented with the decisiveness that is the mother of rapidity and without which, particularly in the high mountains, no good fortune can be expected." Karl, 2:109. The entire account is littered with comments like these. Clearly, the archduke sees the need for rapidity but seems unable to manage it, and he often makes it sound as though rapidity is impetuous. Or, if he feels that he did act rapidly (and one assumes his vision of rapidity matches that of the French), he has an excuse for why the operation was not fully successful. It is as though he is justifying his lack of dynamism by pointing out that even when he was being dynamic, it still did not work. It is no wonder Clausewitz frequently takes an exasperated tone.

Nevertheless, Suvorov's plan is not entirely reprehensible; on the contrary, we are convinced that it could have been carried out successfully, because the French commander had really scattered his forces. Most of Loison's division (formerly Lecourbe's) was in the upper Rhine valley and at the St. Gotthard; thus, it could not have cooperated against St. Gallen. Mortier had the greater part of his division at Mels, Sargans, and Walenstadt; at best, he could have turned up with 3,000–6,000 men. Chabran's division (formerly Soult's), which was actually covering the Rhine in the area where Suvorov wanted to cross, had sent detachments off toward Rheineck and Konstanz simultaneously; it is therefore unlikely that it would have been capable of preventing the crossing at Meiningen and Höchst and the junction of the two columns at St. Gallen. Klein's reserve had been withdrawn to Andelfingen again. If we now consider that Suvorov still must have had about 14,000 Russians and that the Austrian corps under Petrasch, Jellachich, Linken, and Auffenberg constituted a force of roughly similar size, this means that if 6,000 of these remained at Feldkirch, Suvorov could have crossed the Rhine with 22,000 men, and it is very likely that he would have found Masséna's right wing so spread out that he could have beaten it at every point and advanced to Bischofszell without a pause to join up with the column from Konstanz. Inevitably, he thereby would have gained as much as could have been lost by Korsakov in the meantime. If we consider further that Masséna's left wing would have been pinned by an advance by the archduke, the French commander certainly would not have been in a position to stop Suvorov's advance; this must at least result in him retreating over the Töss and the Glatt and, consequently, in Suvorov and the archduke linking up unhindered. We can doubt this result all the less when we remember how poorly Masséna had understood back in May how to use his central position on the Thur to strike with superior force against an opponent advancing divided.

Of course, Archduke Charles could not have known these particular circumstances of the scattered French forces, and if he had gone along with Suvorov's plan without further ado, it could only have been to show himself ready for anything and trusting in Suvorov's personal ability, in himself, in the numerical superiority they must have had overall, and finally in luck. But the archduke did not feel the need for any great goodwill; he saw Suvorov's plan only with the eyes of a critic, found lots of risks in it, pointed these out, and proposed instead that Korsakov should meet up with him behind Lake Constance and that he [the archduke] should have a substantial Austrian column invade Switzerland. From this, it almost appeared as though the archduke himself had no intention of crossing the Rhine again with his main army. That was the last drop of water that made the bucket overflow.[23] On the 14th Suvorov replied that his troops were not suited to mountain warfare and that he had decided to detour around Lake Constance, join up with Korsakov, and then commence operations in Switzerland with him. This answer was in complete contradiction to his previous plan and was obviously nothing but an initial expression of his bitterness, an idea of the moment such as one might have during a lively debate; not that it would not have been perfectly reasonable to implement this idea, but rather because, a couple of days later, the Russian commander made a quite different decision in which indignation and bitterness actually ripened into action, while in his first reply, they only revealed themselves in an expression.

Suvorov moved to Dornbirn on the 15th and to Lindau on the 16th. Here, one of the archduke's aides-de-camp met him to invite him to a conference at which they would make their next plan. The old man took this opportunity to erupt, saying:

> Tell my lord the Archduke that I do not know how to defend, I only know how to attack; I'll advance when I feel like it, and then I won't stop in Switzerland; I'll march according to my orders, right into the Franche-Comté. Tell him that in Vienna I will kneel to him, but here I am at least his equal. He is a field marshal, and so am I; he is in the service of a great emperor, and so am I. He is young and I am old. I have gained experience by dint of victories, and I take no advice or opinions from anyone; I take them only from God and my sword.[24]

23. We have seen no evidence that Clausewitz had read Pierre-Simon Laplace's work on the surface tension of liquids (found in *Traité de mécanique celeste,* published in multiple parts from 1798 to 1829). However, given his regular use of scientific analogies, we thought it best to note this. See https://catalog.hathitrust.org/Record/100242426.

24. Clausewitz provides this in the original French: "*Dites à Monseigneur l'Archiduc, que je ne connais pas la defensive, je ne sais qu'attaquer; j'irai en avant quand bon me semblera, et alors je ne m'arreterai pas en Suisse; je marcherai selon mes orders, directement en Franche-Comté. Dites-lui qu'à Vienne je serais à ses pieds, mais ici je suis au moins son égal. Il est Feldmaréchal, je le suis aussi; il est au service d'un grand Empereur, et moi aussi. Il est jeune et moi je suis vieux. J'ai acquis de l'expérience à force de victoires, et je n'ai ni conseils ni avis à prendre de qui que ce soit; je n'en prends que de Dieu et de mon epée.*"

In front of his entourage, he exploded with bitter complaints against the archduke and the Austrians, and on the 17th he announced to the former that his troops were not fit for a new offensive and needed to rest, so he was transferring them to quarters in the rear.[25] All the archduke's representations to make him change his mind were fruitless, and it was only with difficulty that he could persuade him to let Rosenberg's division remain at Bregenz until 4 November.

At first, Suvorov wanted to transfer his troops to the left bank of the upper Danube and occupy quarters in Riedlingen, so he still would have been nearby, but his growing resentment against the archduke made him change this decision too. He indicated to the archduke that he would transfer his army behind the Lech, move his headquarters to Augsburg, and await further orders from his court. The archduke, as if he had not done enough damage already, observed to Suvorov that these encampments in the Austrian army's rear would be a hindrance, especially the headquarters in Augsburg, to which Suvorov replied with the question, "Would he prefer that I retreat to Bohemia?"[26]

While these individual tensions seem to revolve around just a tiny point of personality, they are nothing less than the symptom of the total resentment that had grown so strong in Suvorov, in Grand Duke Constantine, and in the rest of the Russian generals that they felt continuing the alliance with Austria was completely against Russia's interest—a feeling and a view that Suvorov still did not venture to express outright but that prevailed in all his reports to his tsar and that increased the latter's dissatisfaction with the Austrian cabinet to the point of total breach. We cannot know how much the archduke's last protests and his calculatedly unenthusiastic conduct contributed to this, or what could have been repaired by more temperate and considerate behavior, but in this personal interaction between the two commanders, it is important to keep in mind how men are influenced in their conduct of war by the way

25. This behavior shows war as a human endeavor and points out why Clausewitz's trinity is such an important concept. Suvorov was extremely frustrated and, as noted in chapter 7 (note 58), he had not received the mules needed for his supplies and had been forced to use many of his Cossacks' horses as pack animals. This came on top of a string of problematic issues within the alliance. However, his behavior certainly did nothing to smooth things over so that the alliance could work effectively to defeat the French.

26. "*Aime-t-on mieux que je me retire en Bohème?*"

they are treated and the role that temperament plays in this.[27] War is a human interaction and one of those where feelings play a very large part. We have no hesitation in counting this tactless treatment of Suvorov as one of the mistakes the archduke made as a commander, and not one of his smallest ones either.

88 THE THIRD INVESTMENT AND RELIEF OF PHILIPPSBURG[28]

No sooner had the archduke left Mannheim than the French advanced again from Mainz on the right bank of the Rhine. This advance was presumably not merely the consequence of his departure; most likely, upon the news of Masséna's victory at Zurich, the Directory had concluded that the archduke would soon return and had ordered the generals on the Rhine to create a diversion again, especially as Suvorov had arrived in Switzerland and Masséna could easily find himself in a difficult position. This action may be regarded as highly appropriate. While this second diversion would have come into effect too late if the archduke had shown great decisiveness and energy, that would have been due to the situation, that is, to the failure of the previous diversion; but the fact that it achieved nothing despite the archduke's indecision was due to the mistakes in its execution, as we shall show in our closing reflections.

The fact that this renewed French advance should not be considered merely a local measure by the generals commanding on the Rhine is also revealed by the changes of commander. As we have already recounted, at the end of September, General Lecourbe was named commander of the Army of the Rhine in place of the previous designate General Moreau. This was an earlier decision, probably caused by Moreau's dissatisfaction. General Müller also lost his temporary command, for unknown reasons, and General Ney arrived in his place. Since events in Holland had taken a decisive turn in favor

27. This also relates to Clausewitz's trinity and indicates that emotion, even on a personal level, should not be discounted. It is clear that the relationship between the allies was poisoned largely by small acts that were insignificant by themselves but, in their totality, undermined Suvorov's confidence in his Austrian counterparts. In turn, this helped destroy the coalition.

28. **Clausewitz** notes: "The first was carried out by Bernadotte right at the start of the campaign."

of the French,[29] the troops on their way there as reinforcements were sent to the Rhine army, which they joined bit by bit in the second half of October.

The archduke had left two battalions and thirteen squadrons of Austrians in the Mannheim area after his departure. There were six Austrian squadrons, one battalion, and three squadrons of Palatinate troops, and one battalion and one squadron of Mainz troops with the Mainz militia under Albini. These four battalions and twenty-three[30] squadrons must have come to 6,000–7,000 men, in addition to the armed locals.

The Austrians kept their main force under Prince Schwarzenberg on the Neckar, but General Szent-Kereszty[31] had been pushed forward beyond Frankfurt with some of the cavalry. On 5 October Ney sent a corps under General Lorcet across the Rhine, which drove General Szent-Kereszty back to Frankfurt and across the Main on the 7th.

On 11 October Ney and his main body crossed the Rhine at Kassel [Mainz-Kastel] and the Main below Hochheim, and a separate column crossed the Rhine at Oppenheim. The Austrians retreated on the mountain road. The Mainz militia, against which a third column had been sent under Baraguey d'Hilliers, retreated in the direction of Aschaffenburg.

The Action at Heidelberg on 16 October

The French were still receiving reinforcements every day and only followed slowly. On 16 October they advanced in three columns against Heidelberg, Ladenburg, and Mannheim. At Heidelberg, Prince Alois Liechtenstein put up vigorous resistance against General Lorcet, but the French cavalry under General Dubois-Crancé that had crossed at Ladenburg arrived on his left flank, so on the 17th the Austrians were obliged to vacate Heidelberg and Mannheim. They retreated in three divergent directions: through Sinsheim on the road from Heilbronn to the Neckar, through Bretten on the road from Stuttgart to the Enz, and in the Rhine valley to Bruchsal. The French vanguards followed as far as Wiesloch, Bruchsal, and Graben [Graben-Neudorf], but their main

29. **Clausewitz** notes: "Following the battle of Bergen on 19 September the English had reembarked."

30. The original said twenty-one, but the sum of the numbers given is twenty-three.

31. This is probably Major General Sigmund Szent-Kereszty (1745–1823).

body stayed at Mannheim and Heidelberg for another couple of days and used 3,000 men to invest Philippsburg again, whose garrison had been reinforced by one battalion.

Lecourbe had joined his army meanwhile, and on 21 October he set his left wing under Ney in motion toward Heilbronn and his right along the mountain road toward Durlach. The French gradually drove the Austrian detachments back behind the Neckar, Enz, and Murg, but this was done so slowly that they did not reach these rivers until 2 November.

The archduke and his army must have been at Donaueschingen for about eight days when he received news of the renewed French advance toward the Neckar.[32] If he had acted against Masséna right away, by the time this news arrived, he already would have been engaged in the decisive battle, and it hardly would have bothered him. Indeed, it could not do so to any great degree, since it was unlikely that the French Army of the Rhine could suddenly play a much more significant role than it had done three weeks earlier. Anyway, at this time he had begun discussions with Suvorov about a new invasion of Switzerland,[33] and the garrisons of Strasbourg and Breisach were demonstrating with sorties from the bridgeheads, so there could naturally be no question of marching off to the Neckar again; instead, the archduke contented himself with reinforcing his detachments on the Enz. However, he did believe that in this situation he had to keep his main body on the upper Danube so as to retain a central position on the roads to Schafhausen, Breisach, Strasbourg, and Stuttgart.

The archduke therefore urged the Duke of Württemberg to have some of his troops join the Austrians on the Enz to protect his country and his capital, and indeed, he caused five battalions, one squadron, and ten guns [of Württemberger troops] to be sent there and placed under the command of Prince Hohenlohe.[34] In addition, the archduke had two cavalry regiments from his army and two battalions and twelve squadrons from the outposts on the Rhine move to the Enz and Murg, giving the Prince of Lorraine command over them all.[35] Thus, by the end of October, the corps forming to face Lecourbe came to nine battalions and forty-one squadrons, or about 12,000 men, not including the two battalions and four squadrons that were with Albini.

32. Karl, 2:277.

33. The discussions with Suvorov were apparently not going well. Karl, 2:283–284.

34. Karl, 2:308.

35. Karl, 2:308.

We cannot say exactly how strong the French were, but fourteen days later, after having received a few more infantry reinforcements, they are given as twenty battalions and thirty-seven squadrons, or about 17,000–18,000 strong, so if we assume that at this time they had 15,000 men, we will probably not be far wrong. With these, Lecourbe had foolishly adopted a deployment behind the Murg, Enz, and Neckar that dissipated them across an extent of more than 45 miles.

The Action at Erligheim on 3 November

However, the Prince of Lorraine seems to have been instructed by the archduke not to undertake any offensive operations,[36] and the action at Erligheim that brought about the third relief of Philippsburg seems to have been inspired by Prince Hohenlohe alone.

On 3 November the latter general was behind Bietigheim with the Württembergers and a few squadrons of Austrian cavalry when he saw a French column advancing toward him. He decided not to wait to be attacked but crossed the Enz himself, determinedly attacked the French column at Löchgau—this was General Lorcet with Ney's advance guard—and drove it back through Erligheim and Bönnigheim. Ney himself rushed up with reinforcements but was not able to restore the situation. The French cavalry was completely driven from the field; a couple of infantry battalions in square bought just enough time for Ney's troops to quit Lauffen and other places on the Enz and were then driven back to the Heuchelberg at Gross-Gartach [Lochwald] 10 miles away.[37] This was accompanied by significant losses, Generals Ney and Lorcet themselves being wounded. The French left wing therefore retreated to Sinsheim on the 4th, as a consequence of which on the 5th, 6th, and 7th their right wing also abandoned its positions; Lecourbe concentrated his troops at Wiesloch and gave up the siege of Philippsburg again. The French left wing rested on Neckargemünd, and their right was behind the Kraich.

The Austrians had followed as far as Langenbrück and Sinsheim but could

36. Karl, 2:308–309.

37. This is a little hard to spot on a map, but if one looks just south of Leingarten, there is an area of forested hills running roughly southwest for about 6 miles toward Niederhofen.

not continue their offensive because the Württembergers were under orders not to go beyond the Württemberg border and to remain in the Lauffen area.

Colonel Wrede, with one battalion and three squadrons of Palatinate troops, linked up with the Austrian right wing at Neckarelz, and then the militia in the Odenwald moved toward Aschaffenburg.

89 THE FOURTH RELIEF OF PHILIPPSBURG BY STARRAY[38]

The two sides remained in the positions given above for nine days, during which time Lecourbe received some infantry reinforcements, as we have already mentioned. He now divided his army of twenty battalions and thirty-seven squadrons into four divisions under Laborde, Decaen, Ney, and Baraguey d'Hilliers, with a cavalry reserve under d'Hautpoul.

The Action at Alt- and Neu-Lussheim on 16 November

On 16 November Lecourbe attacked the Austrians with these four divisions in four different diverging directions.

Laborde's division was on the right wing and advanced toward Philippsburg. While the garrison units in their outposts at Alt- and Neu-Lussheim defended themselves stubbornly against the French, this time, they gave the enemy time to cut them off from their line of retreat to the fortress by a column that penetrated further left toward Waghäusel, whereby the garrison that had been 3,000 strong was reduced to 1,800,[39] so the Austrians seem to have lost 1,200 men here.

The second column, which Lecourbe himself was with, comprised De-

38. Our original copy of the archduke's history contains two pages out of place in the chapter dealing with the fighting: Karl, 2:297–298 are the same as 1:297–298 and are thus incorrect. The correct pages are found in the Swiss Digital Library's online version. Hence, for accuracy, that version was also consulted for this section. Karl von Österreich Erzherzog, *Geschichte des Feldzuges von 1799 in Deutschland und in der Schweiz*, 3 vols. (Vienna: Anton Strauss, 1819), 2:297–298, https://www.e-rara.ch/zut/doi/10.3931/e-rara-33557.

39. Karl, 2:312.

caen's division and the cavalry reserve and advanced along the mountain road to Bruchsal and the surrounding area.

The third column, formed by Ney's division, moved upon Sinsheim.

The fourth column, consisting of Baraguey d'Hilliers's division, moved to Lobenfeld in the direction of Neckarelz to observe the Neckar against the Mainz militia.

The Austrians saw or felt that they were too weak everywhere for serious resistance and withdrew behind the Enz and the Neckar yet again.[40] Lecourbe now occupied roughly the same position as before. Admittedly, it was somewhat less extended, since his right wing stood at Graben, his center at Bruchsal and Sinsheim, and his left wing at Lobenfeld. This position still extended over more than 25 miles, but General Lecourbe regarded this as unavoidable in order to cover the investment of Philippsburg on the one side and the bridge he had thrown over the Rhine at Neckarau on the other. Most likely, the line of the Neckar was also held from Mannheim to Neckargemünd, although the accounts say nothing about this. The archduke observes quite correctly that a bridge thrown across at Philippsburg would have enabled Lecourbe to adopt a position on the mountain road near Bruchsal with his force almost fully concentrated.

In this new position, another fourteen days now pass without anything happening. Meanwhile, the archduke has finished his negotiations with Suvorov,[41] the latter has departed for Swabia, and the Austrian commander has therefore been obliged to hold the Rhine in Korsakov's place. Although he could no longer contemplate operating into Switzerland, nor could any further action into Germany be expected on Masséna's part, we can well understand that he did not consider setting off for the Neckar once more, since not much more could come from that than could be achieved merely by reinforcing the troops already there. Upon the news of the renewed investment of Philippsburg, he therefore contented himself with having General Starray move to the Enz with six battalions and ten squadrons, which arrived there on 29 November. Since the Württembergers now also roused themselves again from their lethargic neutrality, this produced a combined force of fifteen battalions and fifty-one squadrons.

40. Karl, 2:312–313.

41. Duffy cites these negotiations as being extremely acrimonious by the end of October and the beginning of November. Duffy, *Eagles over the Alps*, 263.

As this force was not much weaker than Lecourbe's army, while the latter was still threatened on its right wing by the Austrian cordon in the Rhine valley and on its left by the Mainz militia, the success of an attack with concentrated force against one point of the French position could scarcely be doubted for a moment. Since the Rhine valley is cut up by innumerable small streams, ditches, and other obstacles, while the Austrians had a preponderance of cavalry, Starray preferred to strike on the high ground where he could employ this arm better; he therefore chose the area of Sinsheim for his advance.

Starray spent 1 December making his preparations. On the 2nd we find him with one column under Prince Hohenlohe on the road from Heilbronn to Sinsheim, a second under the Prince of Lorraine at Eppingen, with a third—which the official account describes as the advance guard of the second but which, in the course of the action, behaves entirely like a column in its own right—under General Görger at Gochsheim, and a reserve under General Kanisius at Bretten.

We have been unable to clarify the strengths of these individual columns. The archduke says Hohenlohe had three battalions and sixteen squadrons; the Prince of Lorraine and Görger (since he regards the latter as the advance guard of the former), five battalions and twenty-four squadrons; and Kanisius, one battalion and six squadrons, making nine battalions and forty-six squadrons altogether, or roughly the whole Austrian force.[42] No Austrian account tells where the Württembergers' five battalions and one squadron were; Jomini has them in reserve following Prince Hohenlohe.[43]

Apart from these four masses, the French were engaged in the Rhine valley and on the mountain road by the Austrians from the Rhine cordon and on their left wing at Lobenfeld by Colonel Wrede, with one battalion and one squadron of Palatinate troops that had crossed the Neckar at Neckarelz,[44] and by some of General Szent-Kereszty's Austrian cavalry that had joined him.

General Starray now intends to attack the French from his positions at the four places just described.

We are unable to present the French positions in detail. There seems to have been one division around Sinsheim that had deployed on the ridge running from Gochsheim to Sinsheim. The main position seems to have been

42. Karl, 2:317.
43. Jomini, 12:376.
44. Karl, 2:316–317.

on the Steinberg between Hilsbach and Steinsfurt, while the right wing was at Menzingen, not far from Gochsheim.

Behind the dispositions given for the attack lay the peculiar basic idea of refusing the left wing, since one of the Austrian accounts says that General Starray wanted to mount a powerful attack on the enemy's left wing (at Sinsheim) and that he found a maneuver in an *oblique line* to be the most suitable for that—hence an oblique battle order in a strategic action, since the Austrians' four deployment points were 25 miles apart and therefore could not lead to a combined action. If we strip this bizarre idea of its jargon, all it means is that General Starray lacked the courage to unite his force to attack in one place; that he feared being taken in the left flank from Bruchsal, so he left one corps in Bretten and another in Gochsheim, and even the third at Eppingen he wanted to use only cautiously and as a reserve to cooperate with the first corps' attack along the main road.

This attack was carried out on 2 December, with the following result.

Prince Hohenlohe advanced along the highway through Fürfeld on the right bank of the Elsenz against Sinsheim. The Prince of Lorraine first sent Colonel Rakichewitsch with about 1,000 men forward against the Steinberg, just to cover Prince Hohenlohe's left flank. When this detachment found the Steinberg held by a couple of thousand French, the Prince of Lorraine sent another battalion and two squadrons to support Colonel Rakichewitsch. The French held out on the Steinberg for a couple of hours but then retreated when Prince Hohenlohe made progress on the right bank of the Enz. The accounts do not tell what forces the French resisted with at Sinsheim, nor how.

Thus the French were driven off the Steinberg and out of the Sinsheim area after a couple of hours of resistance. They retreated to Horrenberg,[45] halfway from Sinsheim to Wiesloch, where they deployed again. General Starray then had General Görger advance from Gochsheim toward Odenheim, while at the same time he sent another part of the Prince of Lorraine's corps to Odenheim. General Görger found the enemy in a strong position on the heights at Menzingen between Gochsheim and Odenheim, and it seems he had no hope of driving them out of it, but the detachment sent from Eppingen to Odenheim threatened their retreat from this position and compelled the

45. The original says Herrenberg, but that must be wrong. Horrenberg is on the French line of retreat, and Herrenberg is too far south to make sense.

French to abandon it. But at Odenheim they turned and fought again, and the Austrians did not gain possession of this place until nightfall.

General Szent-Kereszty and Colonel Wrede had skirmished with the French all day at Lobenfeld, without any decisive result.

General Kanisius and his reserve moved up to join General Görger.

The French, for their part, vacated Bruchsal and the outposts in front of Philippsburg during the night, whereby Philippsburg was relieved for the fourth time.

On the 3rd the Austrians advanced again in three columns: Prince Hohenlohe along the highway, the Prince of Lorraine through the valley of the Angel [Waldangelbach] via Waldangelloch and Rauenberg, and General Görger along the mountain road through [Bad] Mingolsheim.

Prince Hohenlohe met the first resistance at Horrendorf, where the French had a strong position behind the Elsenz and made a stand until they thought they had secured the retreat of the troops withdrawing along the Bruchsal road. But they almost stayed too long because, when they arrived at Wiesloch, the Prince of Lorraine's vanguard had already pushed into the town. They therefore turned on this force and threw it back behind the Angel again. Nonetheless, the French held out at Wiesloch only as long as necessary to cover the retreat of their right wing from where it had been posted between the mountain road and the Rhine to Schwetzingen. The action at Wiesloch itself was basically a genuine fighting withdrawal, which was favored by an unusually thick fog that arose around midday. Still, it did not go off entirely without some disorder. Wiesloch was taken by the Austrians for the second time before the troops from the heights had passed through the town, so they had to make their way along the edge of the heights. The Austrians followed as far as Leimen, where night put an end to the fighting.

Until now, this two-day battle in which the two sides' mistakes offset and neutralized each other had delivered no great trophies. The Austrians counted 800 prisoners and say that they lost 500 men themselves; the French losses therefore probably would not have been more than 1,500 men. But the French commander feared its further consequences. Starray's force was all concentrated toward the town of Leimen; the French right wing was still retreating toward Schwetzingen, while the left had held its position at Lobenfeld all day on the 3rd, and Lecourbe was worried this might see it completely cut off. To preclude this consequence in the quickest way possible, on the evening of the 3rd Lecourbe requested a truce, on the pretext that he had received news that General Berthier was on his way to Vienna with peace proposals. Starray fell for it—not because he attached any great value to this news but because he did not recognize the extent of his strategic advantage. Or in other words, he did not realize how difficult his adversary's situation was—on the contrary, he was not unconcerned about what the French left wing might undertake against his own right flank. With this quite fallacious view of his own situation, which the mere request for a truce should have told him was better than that, Starray thought that if the French vacated the area of Mannheim and Neckarau without further bloodshed, this would be the surest way of fulfilling his mission of relieving Philippsburg and would carry no risk at all. He therefore agreed to the truce, subject to the archduke's approval, and since the archduke's rejection did not arrive until the 8th, the French gained four days to withdraw all their troops across the Rhine and burn the bridge at Neckarau.[46]

90 THE END OF THE CAMPAIGN IN GERMANY

Suvorov left the theater of war at the end of October.[47] The natural consequence was that the archduke could no longer contemplate any further invasion of Switzerland, even if he had still been serious about that, but he had to remain on the defensive. He reinforced the units above Lake Constance and in Graubündten up to thirty-five battalions and twenty-one squadrons, held the Rhine from Lake Constance to Basel with a strong chain of outposts, moved his main army into cantonments between Stockach and the source of the Neckar, had the Rhine below there just observed by a few cavalry and militia, and later directed General Starray into quarters between the Murg and Bruchsal as a central position for possible crossings at Kehl and Mannheim. The latter place was also garrisoned by Palatinate troops.

46. Karl, 2:320–321. There is also an irony here, in that the archduke complains about Starray's failure to maintain pressure on the French and preserve the advantages gained by the Austrians. Again, the archduke talks about the need for rapidity and continuous pressure but rarely seems able to follow through himself when the stakes are high.

47. Duffy has the Russian advance guard setting out for winter quarters on 2 November and later receiving the order to march home. Duffy, *Eagles over the Alps*, 263–265.

Masséna probably could not consider continuing his offensive into Swabia either, for if he wanted to retain the whole line of outposts in the Rhone valley and from the St. Gotthard to Lake Constance, as had been the system for the entire campaign, then out of the roughly 65,000 men he still had under his command at that time, he could have led at most some 30,000 across the Rhine. But on the far side of the Rhine he would meet the archduke with 40,000–50,000 men, and he could not be sure that Suvorov would not turn around again if he advanced into Swabia. There was therefore no prospect of a good outcome in Swabia. But even if this prospect had existed to some degree, the operation never could have become so far-reaching as to impact the Italian theater of operations and would remain nothing but a quite unsustainable vanguard pushed forward. In addition to these reasons, on 18 *Brumaire* (5 November) Bonaparte became the head of government [first consul], and it could be foreseen that the subsequent war plan would be more tailored to the overall situation.

Thus, Masséna likewise remained on the defensive and contented himself in early November with driving off the few outposts the Austrians still had on the left bank of the Rhine in the Kunkel Pass and the Tamina valley, so that communications between his own combat forces should no longer be disturbed by them.

On 31 October part of Mortier's division pushed through [Bad] Ragaz from Sargans into the Tamina valley, while smaller detachments came from the Linth valley through Elm and Flims and Loison advanced with 3,000 men of his division from Disentis through Ilanz. The Austrians were outmatched by this corps, so they abandoned the left bank of the Rhine and burned the bridges at Reichenau.

On 7 November the French even advanced through Bonaduz into the Domletschger valley (the Posterior Rhine valley), but because they did not feel they could maintain this position jutting out of their line, on 9 November they returned to the Reuss valley.

This concluded the campaign, since both sides remained on the defensive and soon recognized this mutual intention in each other. As the harshest time of year approached, they both went into winter quarters.

The Austrians did so in the positions we have presented for them above. Their left wing occupied the line of the Rhine valley in Graubündten, but we do not know in what strength nor how far up; in any case, probably as far as Reichenau, since their line of communications with Colonel Strauch's force in the Ticino valleys presumably would not have been any further back than through the Splügen Pass. No troops were left in the Tyrol, the Engadin, or the Graubündten mountains, and even if these regions could be considered threatened, they were protected by the armed locals, which provided rear security for the advanced line of Austrian outposts in the Rhine valley. The main body of the Austrian troops above Lake Constance was in Vorarlberg.

On 20 October, soon after the Russians' departure, the St. Luciensteig was completely demolished by the Austrians. Since this work faced front toward Feldkirch, it was certainly of no great value to the Austrians, least of all when, as now, the Rhine valley was occupied by only a few troops and there was no intention of seriously defending it. So long as a fortification remained there, it would always cost some battalions to garrison it, which would always be in danger of being lost as a result. Eight battalions and six squadrons remained in the Feldkirch position.

We only know of the French army's winter quarters from the archduke, and he devotes only a few words to them. One division stayed in Basel; four divisions and the reserve in the open country between the Rhine, the Limmat, and Lake Constance to cover the approaches between Coblenz (in the Aargau) and Sargans; one division in the Linth, Anterior Rhine, and Reuss valleys; and one in Wallis. From this, we can conclude that the Rhine valley was held extremely weakly.[48]

Masséna was ordered by Bonaparte to take over command in Italy in place of Championnet, and at the conclusion of the campaign, the best demi-brigades in his army likewise headed there.

91 REFLECTIONS ON THIS CHAPTER

This entire chapter consists of two diversionary operations and the reactions they provoked, since gaining possession of Philippsburg obviously mattered less to the French than drawing the Austrians' main force away from Switzerland.

The first diversion under General Müller did actually achieve its aim, but this was thanks to other factors that lay well outside the scope of its calculation

48. Karl, 2:322.

and so affected it by chance: namely, that the Austrian cabinet had promised to use the archduke's army itself for a diversion on the Middle Rhine for the benefit of the landing in Holland. Without this coincidence, General Müller's operation probably would not have lured the archduke to the Neckar any more than General Lecourbe's did.

The latter obviously did not achieve its intended aim, and we therefore cannot help thinking that if the 18,000–20,000 men used in this indirect way had been used by the French government for direct action with the main army in Switzerland, this would have been far preferable.

Diversions using fresh and intact forces, that is, without a reason related to this method, are always a mistake.

We cannot get involved in any exhaustive theory of diversionary operations here, but we can say this much: that they differ from a genuine attack in that their main object is not to gain an objective but to draw the enemy's forces away from another point; from this, we see that the forces employed for them are sacrificed for a much less *intensive effect* than if they carried out a *real attack*. One should expose oneself to this disadvantage only if the forces are not sufficient for a serious attack and cannot be transferred away from the line of operation on which they find themselves, and thus can be made useful as a diversion when they would otherwise sit idle; or alternatively, if we assume on the part of our adversary an *excessive*, we might even say a pathological, sensitivity about the point at which we direct our diversion, so that the diversion attracts an enemy reaction in disproportionate strength and thus neutralizes more combat forces than it would have done by its direct effect.[49]

After *30 Prairial*[50] the French had planned to have a new main army appear on the Rhine. This plan did not come to fruition because the landing in Holland drew their forces there, but because of it, their combat forces on the Rhine were stronger than the situation required; the fortresses needed only 20,000–30,000 men, but they had 40,000–50,000 there. This was poor

49. Clausewitz argues in *On War*, book 7, chap. 20 ("Diversions"), 562: "The main requirement is that the enemy should withdraw more men from the main scene of operations than are used for the diversion. If the numbers are even, the effectiveness of the diversion as such ceases, and the operation becomes merely a subordinate attack."

50. This is the 18 June coup that left Emmanuel Joseph Sieyès in charge and further weakened the revolutionary government, which was unpopular due to the poor conditions in France and the failures in the war up to that point.

economy of force, but that was the way it was. Since these troops could be brought into action much more quickly through a diversionary operation than if they first had to move through Alsace and the Frick valley to join Masséna, that was certainly an important reason for a diversion. The second reason that can exist for a diversion was not lacking either; the Austrian government and the archduke always cherished exaggerated concerns for their strategic rear, that is, for their magazines on the Danube, and any operation toward them would have an effect beyond its size.

We therefore find the French diversions praiseworthy only insofar as the combat forces used for them were really not with the main army and *were directed toward the Danube.*

We will examine the idea of forming a new Army of the Rhine in our concluding reflections; here we wish to pause over the objective of the diversion.

Philippsburg played a major role under Louis XIV because, at that time, the French had no bridgehead on the Rhine and because the warfare of that period revolved almost exclusively around the possession of fortresses. However, it was of almost no importance in the conditions of 1799, as indeed the 1796 campaign had already demonstrated, when the French did not care at all about this minor fortress. Besides, taking it could require three or four weeks, so it was not a diversion that promised to take effect very quickly; it still left the archduke eight to fourteen days during which he could strike a major blow in Switzerland, if he felt adequately equipped to do so. But what use was Philippsburg to the French, even if they did actually take it? They could not have found the means to provision it for the whole winter, so it would have fallen again of its own accord. The investment of Philippsburg was therefore not an effective diversion.

However, a march on the Danube would have had quite a different effect and would have had the archduke up in arms immediately. But if such a move were to fulfill its purpose, it would have to be directed at least against Ulm, in order to draw the archduke a good distance away from Switzerland; but if the French corps moved on Ulm from Mannheim, its line of retreat would be seriously threatened, and that soon would have put a stop to its effectiveness. For such a purpose, it was therefore essential that this corps be able to retreat to the Main, that is, that it had a secure crossing over the Main at Frankfurt and between Frankfurt and Mainz. The Mainz militia stood in the way of this again, and the right thing to do might well have been to cross at Mainz and Mannheim, turn first against the Mainz militia in concentric columns, disperse these completely, and then head for Ulm via Heilbronn and Stuttgart. Of course, if the archduke advanced in superior force, the maneuver would have to stop, and if the archduke sought to bring about a decisive battle, the French would have to retreat toward Frankfurt. If we take the archduke's great caution into consideration, it would not have been difficult for the French commander to retreat one step at a time and draw the archduke after him as far as the Main; indeed, the archduke might not have rested until the French were driven back across the Rhine, which would have involved him in a difficult and time-consuming crossing of the Main and obliged him to leave a significant corps there when he left.

But another difficulty stood in the way of such a diversion, in that it would have led right through the state of Württemberg, which could have caused the duke to join the Austrians with all his troops. We do not have a good enough grasp of these factors to judge what to expect in one case or the other as regards the Württemberg troops, since we have seen that these events were not without some impingement on Württemberg territory and what the consequence was; however, we must concede that if such a political consideration did determine French actions, this is not to be disapproved of in itself, and it is only to be criticized because it resulted in a half-measure.[51]

If Philippsburg really had to be the objective of this diversion throughout, then there was still one other way by which the French generals could have carried it out, apart from the one they adopted.

General Müller did not find many Austrians in this area, and presumably, those few prudently withdrew so that he could not do them any harm. His deployment during the investment of Philippsburg is not mentioned because it does not come into play. The archduke approaches with 34,000 men, Müller has only 18,000, so that makes him leave; this is quite natural. Likewise, the attempt to hold Mannheim and Neckarau is nothing unusual, since in a war where people are not fighting over any major objectives, they always attach value to small ones.[52] But he ended up with a half-measure. Why did he not

51. Clausewitz makes the point that doing something because it is militarily expedient might carry political consequences that actually make the military situation worse in the longer term.

52. Clausewitz's point is that if the overarching political objectives of the war are fairly limited in scope, one might not want to threaten something really important to

remain in the Neckarau and Mannheim position with his whole corps? Or at least with 12,000 men, if he wanted to send some back to Mainz again? There is no way the archduke would ever have attacked them.

The archduke says that when Müller crossed the Rhine, he sent some of his troops to Holland, but the French accounts say nothing about this. To try to hold Neckarau and the many small and intrinsically weak redoubts in front of the Mannheim glacis with 3,000–4,000 men was a bad and thoroughly reprehensible measure.

During the second investment, the French advance along the mountain road, the Stuttgart road, and the Heilbronn road and space themselves out in their positions behind the Murg, the Enz, and the Neckar across more than 50 miles. General Ney was facing only a weak enemy, since the archduke had left so little in this area that Ney could not achieve any great triumphs over it, but he could create a racket and have a certain amount of effect. Now, even if this broad advance had been intended to make his operation look larger than it was, which might be said to be the reason, then upon the approach of the relief corps, he should have abandoned this broad position to throw himself at the enemy's main column with concentrated force. But the broad French deployment, which Lecourbe did not alter when he arrived either, was obviously just out of force of habit because the Austrians had retreated divergently along these three roads, and it was intended to cover the Neckar crossings from Heidelberg to Mannheim. The French situation therefore would have looked quite different if they had thrown a bridge across the Rhine at Philippsburg; then they could have adopted a position near that fortress with their corps concentrated, all the more so since they were not really besieging Philippsburg and would not need much time for their departure.

But without such a bridge, by investing Philippsburg, the French certainly put themselves in an extremely stretched and strategically disadvantageous position. They had to regard Württemberg and the Odenwald as hostile territory that ran very close to their lines of retreat and communications for 70 miles. But this line of retreat was restricted on the other side by the Rhine,

one's opponents because that might cause them to increase their level of resistance, thus increasing the costs for one's own armed forces. If the costs escalate enough, they might end up being more than the original political goal was worth, thus undermining the purpose of the conflict. See *On War*, book 1, chaps. 1 and 2.

which they could not cross anywhere without a bridge. This situation was so unfavorable that it was certainly one of the most difficult of strategic problems to achieve any possibility of serious resistance against an advancing relief force. Lecourbe did not know how to solve this problem during the third or fourth investment either, since in both cases, we see him withdraw without an actual decisive battle being delivered anywhere. We believe the only way to extract the possibility of success from these disadvantageous circumstances would have been a position with the main body concentrated at Graben and light observation of Bruchsal, Eppingen, and Fürfeld. We choose the position at Graben because at least one objective would be completely achieved, namely, covering the investment of Philippsburg, and no further detachment would be necessary. If it was reported that the enemy was advancing on Bruchsal in significant force, the French general would have to seek him out there. If the enemy was divided, he could hope to beat him at Bruchsal and then, buoyed by this victory, to throw himself upon those advancing on Wiesloch and, in the worst case, at least to keep his rear free. If the enemy headed straight for Wiesloch with his main body, the French commander would likewise have to march there and immediately raise the investment of Philippsburg; then he could always hope to remain unharmed because of the success that his concentrated force should provide him at any point. However the situation turned out, if Lecourbe had just kept 15,000 of his 20,000 men with him, he most probably would have won a decisive victory at whatever point of the enemy advance he turned against; but of course, this high probability relies on the Austrians making mistakes.

Our major criticism must be that during the attack he undertook on 16 November for the fourth investment, Lecourbe was not intent on winning a significant success at any one point, even though at that time he was 20,000 strong and the Austrians on the left bank of the Neckar, including the Württembergers, had at most 10,000–12,000 men spread across a large area. But at the moment one goes onto the offensive oneself, one need not worry so much about one's strategic line of retreat. However much fortune might favor it, there was no way that an advance such as Lecourbe's of the 16th, in four divergent columns, could lead to any particular success.

Lecourbe's deployment to cover the fourth investment was no better than the previous one; even if it lay in a smaller circle, it took in just as big an arc of the circle and was more than 30 miles across from Graben to Lobenfeld.

We find it very surprising that Lecourbe turns out this way as a commander in chief, despite the French saying *tel brille au second rang qui s'éclipse au premier.*[53] He had not been just a battering ram like Augereau and Masséna in Napoleon's battles; during this campaign in the high mountains, he had conducted the most difficult of wars for six long months with his forces almost always divided. We would certainly have expected more of him in combining individual actions for a major decisive battle.

We have already given our opinion of the relief effected by the archduke during the course of our account. The third relief[54] by the Prince of Lorraine does not allow many observations, since it is an extemporized piece, a gun that goes off before the hunter has taken aim properly. But we must permit ourselves a few comments on the fourth by Starray.

In the archduke's account, he dwells on Starray's odd idea of *refusing his left wing* and makes it the basis of the whole maneuver.[55] But if we really want to take a geometrical idea as its foundation, we must distinguish two elements in Starray's advance: first the wheeling of his line of deployment, and then the echeloned advance, for if, on 1 December, he was at Bretten, Gochsheim, Eppingen, and Fürfeld, then he had already swung his front through forty-five degrees and made his line of retreat run obliquely behind his flank. A simple advance in echelon does not lead to any such rotation. Now on the 2nd, he wanted to advance in echelon from this rotated position. We are of the opinion that if it is the case that one is attacking one wing of an enemy line of deployment with one's main body, while only pinning or indeed just observing the other, it is better to divide one's force only into these two parts caused by the different tasks; it is also better to have these operate quite separately, instead of deploying a couple of intermediate corps to achieve the notion of a connected line, increasing divisions and complexity overall and dissipating forces across space unnecessarily. This idea of an echeloned battle order is taken from the tactics of older times, since this form of attack had become famous during the time of Frederick the Great,[56] being the first break with

53. "Shining so bright in the second rank, yet he disappears in the first."

54. **Clausewitz** notes: "That is, if the archduke's relief is counted as the second, because the first was achieved indirectly by the battle of Stockach."

55. Karl, 2:316.

56. Probably the best examples of this tactic were at the battles of Rossbach and, most famously, at Leuthen in 1757. For an excellent account of the latter battle and a description of oblique order, see Christopher Duffy, *Frederick the Great: A Military*

the inflexible, less subdivided orders of battle of the eighteenth century; we cannot examine here the extent to which misunderstandings occurred when people tried to revive this geometrical form, but we do not in any case believe that its mere pedigree should have assured it any particular merit in strategy. If communications are to be maintained between one advancing wing that is therefore reinforced and another that is held back and therefore much weaker, that should be done with just a few light troops, and virtually no absolute value should be attached to holding the ground between the two. Corps that are stationed between one attacking wing and another refused wing are hermaphroditic creatures that do not know which kind of action they should commit to, and that is always visible in the character of the dispositions given to them. In strategy, an echeloned deployment can only arise in defense, and even then, only up to a certain point, or else forces are wasted.

But Starray's echeloned deployment was soon altered so that the left wing formed an attack column of its own, and the only consequence of his earlier idea was that the right wing on the Finsheim road was too weak to overrun the enemy left wing and cut off the right, and in general, there were not enough forces anywhere to obtain a glorious victory and to exploit the exaggerated extent of the enemy's deployment; therefore, there were almost no trophies either.

Another question is whether Starray might not have done better to penetrate along the mountain road or in the Rhine valley to cut off the French left wing, instead of swinging his forces *left* with the aim of penetrating along the Finsheim road and cutting off the French *right*. The archduke is of this opinion,[57] calling it a refusal of the right wing by contrast with the above; but to us it seems incorrect, for if we indicate the French position by the towns of Graben, Durlach, Sinsheim, and Lobenfeld, their right wing was obviously much more exposed than the left, and that *alone decides* the matter here, since the Austrians' change of their own front could not cause them any disadvantage, and loss of time was not a consideration.

General Starray's conduct has the character of apprehensive caution, and here again, we see how rarely brave and decisive soldiers are able to maintain that demeanor when they cross *the line* and enter into the realm of command.

Life (London: Routledge, 1995), 148–154, 308–311. For Clausewitz's concept of where and how the use of oblique order might be useful, see *On War*, book 6, chap. 24 ("Operations on a Flank").

57. Karl, 2:316.

9. Melas Beats Championnet at Genola and Takes Cuneo

Fröhlich Besieges and Takes Ancona.

92 THE TWO SIDES' SITUATIONS

When we left the two sides in Italy, Moreau had abandoned his attempt to relieve Tortona on 11 September and retreated to the Riviera again, Tortona had fallen, Suvorov had marched off to Switzerland, and Melas had begun his march to the Stura, leaving General Karaczai in the Novi area.

Before we pick up the thread of our account, we must clearly picture the two sides' forces and relative positions, as well as their intentions.

We left the French army divided between Moreau and Championnet. The former was in position in the Apennines with about 30,000 men, the latter supposedly 34,000 strong in the Alps. When Championnet advanced down all the alpine valleys at the end of August and in early September, he only had 18,000 men available; the total French strength at that time therefore came to just 48,000 men. Now it might have been expected that the other 16,000 would soon enter the line as active units. But this was not the case; instead, after the battle of Novi, the Directory had made the decision to remain on the defensive in Italy and therefore to have eighteen battalions and twelve squadrons of the Army of Italy march away to Switzerland at this time to replace the troops that Masséna had to send off to the Rhine. Now, since these units would have come to roughly 10,000 men, this explains why in mid-October the two French armies were only 54,000 strong instead of 64,000.

General Jomini does not say exactly when these troops left, only that it was *shortly before Championnet assumed overall command*;[1] this was on 21 September, so we must assume their departure was between the 11th and the 21st. But we must also assume that, at the same time, just as many units in the process of formation joined the line, since otherwise, right at the time Championnet began his operations with the Army of the Alps again, namely, on 15 September, we must think of the French combat forces as being weakened by 10,000

1. Jomini, 12:322.

men, which is intrinsically unlikely and nor is it justified by any report. We will therefore probably not be far wrong if we take the two French armies to be 50,000 strong at the beginning of this chapter.

It is noteworthy that in his report submitted to the Directory on 15 September, Minister of War Dubois-Crancé[2] says: "Finally the alpine border is covered by the armies of the Alps and of Italy combined under the command of General Championnet, making 80,000 men altogether, not including 10,000–12,000 who are stationed in the rear in the fortresses and various other places along the alpine border."[3]

Jomini calls this figure an exaggeration;[4] however, since we do not find the figures for the other armies in this report to be exaggerated, this does not seem to us to settle the matter. Perhaps it was a mistake that the garrisons should not have been included; in any case, those of Genoa and Cuneo most likely must have been counted among the 80,000 men; the sick certainly are, but of course, we cannot assume there were 26,000 sick. On the other hand, we are not justified in regarding Jomini's figures as too low, since they are so precise. But for us, the most important thing is that behind the Army of the Alps there were another 10,000–12,000 men who were not regarded as available. This is most likely one of those wastes of forces that occur so frequently, in that governments think they have to preserve a kind of *strategic reserve* in this way to help in case of particular misadventure. Twelve thousand more men at Novi most likely would have delivered victory.

The main body of the French Army of Italy was on the Riviera. It had a series of outposts on the crest of the Apennines; its right wing under Miollis was behind the Stura in the eastern Riviera; its left under Victor at the sources of the Tanaro maintained communications with the Army of the Alps. The latter's right wing under Grenier was at the mouths of the valleys of the Stura, Maira, and Braita; its center under Duhesme in the Pignerolo [Pinerolo, Turin] and Susa valleys; and the left wing under Mallet in the Aosta valley.

2. Edmond Dubois-Crancé (1747–1814) had just been made minister of war on 14 September 1799, and he would serve in that position only until 10 November 1799.

3. "*Enfin la frontière des Alpes est couverte par les armées des Alpes et de l'Italie réunies sous le commandement du Général Championnet, formant ensemble 80,000 hommes, non compris dix à douze mille qui sont stationés sur les derrières dans les places et sur les divers points qui bordent la frontière des Alpes.*"

4. Jomini, 12:450n.

Moreau's headquarters was in Cornigliano near Genoa; Championnet's was at Pinerolo.

As far as the Austrians were concerned, after the battle of Novi, the allied forces in Piedmont remained about 68,000 strong, excluding Haddick's corps. Four weeks later, Suvorov marched away with some 23,000 Russians, which would have left just 45,000 men. But we find that after Suvorov's departure, the main army under General Melas was still 50,000 strong, which is partly because some of those wounded in the battle of Novi had returned to the ranks by that time, and partly because of a reinforcement of four battalions that the Austrians had brought up from the interior. After Suvorov's departure, there were no Russians left in Italy; thus, with the exception of some Russian and Turkish detachments outside Ancona, the allied army in upper Italy comprised nothing but Austrians, over whom Melas received overall command. It was divided into the following corps:

Haddick's corps: 14,500 men. Facing the St. Gotthard, Simplon, and St. Bernard Passes. It comprised the troops originally belonging to Colonels St. Julien and Strauch and Prince Rohan, and another two brigades.
General Kaim: 14,000 men. In Turin and facing the Susa and Pinerolo valleys, with its left wing under Gottesheim at Savigliano and Fossano facing Cuneo.
The main army: 31,000 men. On the move from Alessandria to Cherasco.
General Karaczai: 5,000 men. In the Novi area.
General Klenau: 5,000 men. In the eastern Riviera.
Garrisons in Italy in general: 15,500.
Total: 92,500 men.

At the start of the campaign, the Austrians had been 84,000 strong; in the course of it, they had been joined by Wukassowitsch with 4,000 men, Bellegarde (including Haddick's men and the remnants of St. Julien's) with 26,000, as well as a reinforcement of four battalions from the interior that we may reckon at 4,000, making 118,000 men. Accordingly, they must have lost some 26,000 men by mid-September, which almost seems too few, so we must conclude they were reinforced with drafts of recruits during the course of the campaign.

If we deduct 30,000 men for the garrisons and for Fröhlich's corps, as well as for Strauch and Rohan, who were facing Tharreau, that left the Austrians with 62,000 men against some 50,000.

Cuneo and Genoa were the only two fortresses the French still held east of the Alps, since Gavi and Savona, which the French still regarded as such, could not be expected to put up any serious resistance. From this, it follows that if the French wanted to remain on the defensive, their main concern had to be retaining these two fortresses, while on the other side, the natural mission for the Austrians was to complete the conquest of Italy by taking these fortresses, for which their numerical superiority was sufficient if need be.

The events we have to relate in this chapter include one battle and one siege (namely, that of Cuneo), neither of which, however, is among the higher ranks of such events; and apart from these, there was a host of small actions, which we would call insignificant if it were not that they certainly had some strategic importance, although these actions were as feeble as the faint twitchings of a cataleptic toward the will to return to life. Thus, we cannot promise that the events in this chapter are of any great interest. Furthermore, no other section of the campaign is so unspeakably badly described by both sides; the accounts fragment the events even more than the commanders' mode of warfare does; there is no coherent series of ideas anywhere, only fleeting, confused scribblings muddled in a heap and full of nonsensical contradictions, like the feeble effort of an untrained student.

Added to this is the great rupture in events caused by Suvorov's departure, which makes all the historians (ourselves included) devote a chapter to it, and which leads them to make the mistake of not picking up the thread again precisely enough, so that the two ends fail to match up, like sections of a bad map.

We shall attempt to group the numerous small actions so as to give an overview, at least, and to show their connection according to their purpose, without going into the details of every maneuver, for which both source material and interest are equally badly lacking.

On the other hand, in its larger outlines, this chapter does give rise to an important strategic question that constitutes its major interest. The French government had decided to place its two armies in Italy under one command and to give this to General Championnet. Since they had to anticipate that the Austrians would besiege Cuneo or Genoa, they devoted their attention to the idea of attacking their adversary, about which there were two different views. Moreau wanted to advance out of the Apennines; Championnet's idea was to abandon the Apennines and Genoese territory entirely, withdraw the right wing of the army behind the Roya, and advance to the attack from the northern Alps toward Novara. Since a thorough discussion of this question here would lead us too far away from the events, we will defer this to the end; for now, suffice it to say that the French government rejected General Championnet's idea and did not explicitly adopt General Moreau's. It settled for giving General Championnet the general mission of ensuring the safety of Cuneo and, if possible, relieving Tortona, which it did not know had already fallen.

From this order, it seems to follow that overall command was bestowed on General Championnet around 15 September, when his operations began; nonetheless, General Moreau did not leave the Italian army until the 21st, and it does not seem as though Championnet could give it orders before then. We must therefore consider the following operations as being carried out with divided command.

93 CHAMPIONNET TRIES TO MOVE HIS CENTER TO HIS RIGHT WING: FIRST GROUP OF ACTIONS

The actions that we have to recount from the six weeks before the battle of Genola can be grouped into four episodes, namely, mid-September, when Championnet still commanded only the Army of the Alps; late September; mid-October; and late October, which brings us to the threshold of the battle of Genola.

All these collective actions stem from the French offensive and were supposed to serve to protect the fortresses of Genoa and Cuneo, although neither of them had yet been contacted by the enemy. The historians have become so absorbed in this idea, especially Jomini, that they literally give the aim of these attacks as being the relief (*dégagement*) of Cuneo,[5] even though Cuneo was never invested by the Austrians before the battle of Genola and was even behind the French outpost line most of the time. In some respects, we can allow that we approve of a second purpose they ascribe to these actions, namely, uniting the French forces,[6] but just barely because, strictly speaking, such a junction was possible without any battle preceding it.

5. Jomini, 12:313–318.
6. Jomini, 12:318.

Championnet's first operation was designed to move his center under Duhesme from Pinerolo and Rivoli to join his right wing on the Stura. This was supposed to happen on the plain, thus close to Kaim, and he chose 15 and 16 September for its execution. We can discover nothing about the reasons for these two circumstances. It seems that he made preparations for this junction immediately after receiving the news of the fall of Tortona, because he rightly anticipated that Melas and his main army would betake themselves from the Alessandria area to that of Cuneo. If he did not attempt this sooner, perhaps it was because he wanted to wait until the advance of his left wing (covered in the previous chapter), which did not begin until 6 September, had acted as a diversion against Kaim. But we are even less able to explain why the linking up was supposed to take place entirely on the plain, that is, just a few miles from Turin, since the foothills of the Alps were certainly passable for troops in many places. In any case, a road runs from Susa to Fenestrelle through the Col de Fenestra, which General Duhesme's left wing could have taken in complete safety; then at least he could have advanced with his force united through Pinerolo toward Moretta and Savigliano, where his junction with Grenier would have been difficult to prevent.

But Championnet does not seem to have thought that the difficulty of linking up on the plain would be that great; he ordered General Grenier and his 10,000 men to advance on Fossano and Savigliano on 16 September, while General Duhesme was to have detachments advance through Rivoli and Pinerolo on the 15th to draw the enemy's attention there, but to have his main body march away quickly to the right behind those places and join Grenier.

The Action at Rivoli on 15 September[7]

This operation did not have the expected success. The column that advanced through Rivoli did reach Collegno, 5 miles from Turin, but was then defeated by reserves brought up by Kaim and obliged to retreat to the camp at Avigliana, 5 miles behind Rivoli.

7. Jomini mentions this and the following actions in 12:318–325.

The Action at Salengho [Scalenghe] on 15 September

The column advancing from Pinerolo, accompanied by Duhesme himself, got only as far as Scalenghe, 5 miles from Pinerolo, and then likewise had to give way before the superior Austrian cavalry and retreat to Pinerolo again.

The Action at Fossano and Savigliano on 16 September

Grenier's division had taken Saluzzo on the 15th and moved upon Savigliano and Fossano on the 16th. It attacked General Gottesheim and forced him to retreat to Bra, where Melas's main army arrived the same day.

The Action at Fossano and Savigliano on 17 September

Melas decided to attack General Grenier on the 17th via Savigliano and Fossano in two columns, each of 10,000 men, thus with twice Grenier's strength. The first column moved upon Savigliano, commanded by General Ott and accompanied by Melas himself. Kray commanded the other moving upon Fossano. Neither could begin its attack until toward evening, but after a short but lively resistance, both were victorious by virtue of their numerical superiority. The French were compelled to retreat from Savigliano to Saluzzo and into the Maira valley, and from Fossano to Cuneo, with the loss of two guns and a couple of thousand men killed, wounded, and taken prisoner.

Melas did not follow up his victory but took position at Savigliano.

When Melas arrived in this area with his main army, he was joined by those of Kaim's troops that were there, bringing him up to 38,000 strong, while Kaim was left with just 7,000.

On 20 September Championnet retook Rivoli, whereby no great advantage accrued to him, but Melas was all the more persuaded not to tolerate him there.

The Action at Pinerolo on 23 September

On 22 September Melas sent General Prince Lichtenstein with eighteen battalions and twelve squadrons through Saluzzo against Pinerolo; the prince sent detachments into the valleys of the Po and of Luserna, linked up with a detachment from Kaim's division, and attacked the French at Pinerolo on the 23rd, beating them and driving them back as far as Fenestrelle. Prince Lichtenstein left a few detachments in this area and then returned to the camp at Savigliano with his corps.

The Action at Susa on 25 September

General Kaim sent General Bellegarde the Younger[8] into the Susa valley with a corps of 3,000–4,000 men, which took Susa on 25 September, forced the French to retreat to the foot of Mont Cenis, and then returned to Turin, leaving a small detachment behind.

Melas felt he could now send off two brigades 6,000–7,000 strong under Kray to assist General Haddick in regaining his previous positions facing the St. Bernard and Simplon Passes, which he had lost on 6 September, as we told in section 56. Kray took over command of all these [his force and Haddick's] at Ivrea on the 29th, but the French did not feel they were strong enough to take him on. Mallet raised the siege of Castle Bard and retreated to the St. Bernard, as did Tharreau via Domodossola and the Simplon Pass to Wallis. Kray therefore returned to the main army with his two brigades. Somewhat later, Melas summoned some more of Haddick's troops to him because the late season of the year meant he no longer needed to worry about those high regions. The Aosta valley was therefore left only weakly held, and Haddick himself now took position at Ivrea, where he also served as support for Colonel Strauch, who was at the foot of the St. Gotthard.

While these efforts by the Army of the Alps were being repulsed, the Army of Italy had remained completely passive in the Apennines. Moreau had left the latter army on 21 September, so from that day, we must regard General Championnet as being in overall command of both armies.

8. **Clausewitz** notes: "At this time General Bellegarde the Elder had been called away to Vienna." Bellegarde the Elder refers to Heinrich von Bellegarde. Bellegarde the Younger refers to Friedrich Bellegarde, a brigade commander who fought at Marengo.

94 CHAMPIONNET ADVANCES AGAINST MONDOVI WITH HIS CENTER AND TO NOVI WITH HIS RIGHT WING: SECOND AND THIRD GROUPS OF ACTIONS

The French army under Championnet was organized as follows:

Right wing under St. Cyr:
- Division Miollis: 4,100 men
- Division Watrin: 7,300
- Division Dombrowsky: 4,600
- Division Laboissière: 5,000

Center:
- Division Lemoine: 7,800
- Division Victor: 8,500

Left wing under Grenier:
- Division Grenier: 8,000
- Division Duhesme: 7,500
- Cavalry reserve: 1,200

Total: 54,000 men

General Jomini gives this order of battle for 17 October,[9] so we cannot regard it as accurate three weeks earlier; it is also obvious that it is lacking those troops that were still at the Great St. Bernard Pass under General Mallet at the end of September. But we can essentially accept the organization above for the end of September as well, and we may therefore now use it as the basis of our presentation so as to give it some of the definition that is in any case so lacking from other accounts of this chapter.

Scarcely had Championnet taken over command and transferred his headquarters to Finale [Finale Ligure] than he had his center (Victor's and Lemoine's divisions and a brigade of Laboissière's under Gardanne) perform a maneuver toward Mondovi, with the intention of taking that place and then having his center link up on the plain with his left wing, which, to that end, was to advance out of the alpine valleys again. The right wing under St. Cyr, 18,000 strong, was to demonstrate in the eastern Riviera and on the Scrivia.

On 28 September the center had advanced to Villanova Mondovi on the

9. Jomini, 12:313 (plan 15).

western side of the Elero, San Michele Mondovi on the Cursaglia, and Niella Tanaro on the Tanaro and had invested Ceva. But Melas had reinforced the garrison of Mondovi and moved up a supporting corps, and also on 29 September he and the main army left its camp at Savigliano in order to push left, moving to Trinità east of Fossano on the 29th and to Magliano Alpi behind the Pesio on the 30th, whereby he approached to within 5 miles of Mondovi. His left wing under Gottesheim was at Carrù, his right under Elsnitz at Morozzo. Kray remained at Fossano with three brigades.

The Actions at Mondovi on 1, 2, and 3 October

Championnet had transferred his headquarters to Bagnasco on the Tanaro on the 30th, but he did not dare to attack Mondovi, so he let General Grenier know that he was giving up on his aim for now. After he had taken Vico on 1 October, and fairly heavy fighting had broken out on the 2nd and 3rd between General Laudon sallying forth from Mondovi and General Serras, Championnet moved the right wing of his center back from the Tanaro to the Bormida, taking position at Salicetto, while Victor remained at Villanova.

Although this advance to the Tanaro by the French center caused Melas to have General Karaczai march from Novi to Asti with 4,000 men, arriving there on the 6th, St. Cyr's operation against the Austrian left wing had no other result than that he retook Toriglia from Klenau, who had taken it on the 26th, and pushed forward to Serravalle, Novi, and Ovado on the Scrivia.

There is no word of any maneuver by the left wing.

Thus, this second attempt at unification, as these incidents were called, also failed.

We honestly admit that we understand it even less than the first, and in particular, we do not know what importance the possession of Mondovi was supposed to have in it. But the incoherent accounts from the historians would render futile any effort to gain satisfactory insight into these events. The Austrians saw these various outpost actions as merely a means for their adversary to keep them constantly harassed and engaged and thereby to hinder them from operating against Cuneo and Genoa. That is certainly admissible, and if it is not the *best* method, it would at least be an *understandable* one. But we are not justified in following the Austrian representation on this point, since the French historians explicitly state that the intention was unification of forces.

Scarcely was this series of fruitless actions over than Championnet conceived a plan for other equally unsuccessful ones. In the news that spread in early October about the events in Switzerland, the French detected a total allied defeat in that theater of war, which was probably exaggerated still more by rumors relating to Suvorov's fate. The consequence of this was that they anticipated the imminent retreat of the Austrians from Piedmont with a kind of certainty, and they were very much encouraged in this view by reports from spies. Championnet needed to take revenge on Melas for the unsuccessful actions of mid-September, so for that, he wanted to exploit the crisis of the retreat that he thought General Melas was engaged in. To make part of his right wing available for his operations against Melas in the Stura valley, St. Cyr was first to drive General Klenau away from the vicinity of Genoa, since Klenau's proximity to the city was inducing constant tension and unrest there, which could easily lead to the unexpected fall of this important fortress at any time.

The Action at Bracco on 13 October

St. Cyr remained in the area of Serravalle, Gavi, and Ovado with Laboissière's and Dombrowsky's divisions, and he ordered General Watrin and his division to eject the Austrian outposts from the southern slopes of the Apennines and march quickly to San Pietro di Vara, so as to move into General Klenau's rear from there. Miollis's division, on Klenau's front, was to stay completely quiet, while one battalion was to embark on boats and travel down the coast to land at Moneglia in his rear. But General Klenau, informed of this operation in sufficiently good time, had retreated and left only a rear guard at Chiavari on the Stura. Meanwhile, Watrin had already maneuvered very swiftly to reach San Pietro di Vara on the 12th, so on the 13th he was able to capture the three companies of *Jäger* that Klenau had left behind at Bracco to receive his rear guard; later on, the battalion constituting this rear guard likewise fell into French hands, so that they had taken 1,000 men prisoner altogether.

Klenau now took position at Sestri, while Watrin's division remained at the sources of the Vara, the Tidone, and the Trebbia.

Now the right wing under St. Cyr sat still again for ten days without attempting anything of significance.

In the center of the two armies, outpost actions occurred continually from the 8th onward, of which that at Beinette was the most significant.

Grenier had set up camp at Madonna dell'Olmo, outside Cuneo. When Melas saw the French in this area being reinforced, he decided to abandon his camp at Magliano and approach Cuneo with his main army in order to "*offer battle to the French*," as the somewhat antiquated strategic form in the Austrian account puts it. He and Kray set off on the 12th and encamped at Morozzo between the Brobio and the Stura.

The Action at Beinette on 13 and 14 October

Victor's division had strongly garrisoned the village of Beinette as a liaison post between Villanova and Cuneo. Melas had General Mitrowsky attack it on the 13th with six battalions and four squadrons; the French were ejected but returned with reinforcements in the afternoon. Now this village was fought over with great ferocity until finally, after taking it three times, the Austrians were left in possession and had taken 500–600 French prisoners.

Now in the center too, another eight days passed without any significant activity. There is no mention of the French left wing.

It is difficult to say how we should characterize this third group of actions. Klenau was pushed away so that Championnet could stop worrying about Genoa and so that he could weaken his right wing if need be, but that did not happen; Karaczai was not even attacked once. It has the appearance of an operation stopped in its tracks.

95 ST. CYR BEATS KARACZAI AT NOVI; MELAS DEFEATS THE FRENCH CENTER AT BEINETTE, LESEGNO, AND CENTALO: FOURTH GROUP OF ACTIONS

In the last ten days of October, elemental conflict reignited in a series of actions that were more important in themselves this time, but again, just as trifling in their general outcome. This new collective fight appears as though it were the resumption and continuation of that which had been left unfinished in mid-October.

We shall set down here the strategic concept that was supposed to be the reason for it, according to Jomini, although we believe that it belongs more to the historian than to the commander.

> Feeling that the snows would soon force him to leave Cuneo to its own resources, also encouraged by the news of Bonaparte's return to France, and anxious to retain an entrance into Piedmont for the next campaign, Championnet wanted to make one last effort, if not to relieve the fortress, at least to store in it all the provisions that he proposed to collect in a large foraging expedition. It was with this intention that the order was sent to Duhesme to move down through the Susa and Perugia valleys upon Rivoli and Pinerolo; to Grenier, to advance from the camp at Madonna dell'Olmo upon Savigliano and Fossano; while in the center Victor, together with Lemoine, would advance through Villanova and Beinette; and on the right, after entrusting Miollis with the defense of the Genoese coast, St. Cyr would move on Acqui with his three other divisions.[10]

Not only does this concept again lack any real objective, but the execution also immediately reveals that it does not match it, since St. Cyr did not move to Acqui but did something better instead, in that he beat Karaczai at Novi.

Since the events in the center spin themselves out for longer and carry on until the battle of Genola, let us start with those on the French right wing.

The Action at Bosco Marengo on 24 October

Karaczai, whose corps comprised just 5,000 men as we know, was between the Scrivia and the Orba in the Bosco area.[11] On 23 October St. Cyr began his march with Dombrowsky's and Watrin's divisions through Novi and with Laboissière's in the Orba valley, or 12,000 men in all. From this, we see that

10. "*Championnet sentant que les neiges allaient bientôt le forcer d'abandonner Cuneo à ses propres forces, encourage d'ailleurs par la nouvelle du retour de Bonaparte en France, et jaloux de conserver un débouché en Piémont pour la campagne prochaine, voulut tenter un dernier effort, sinon pour dégager cette place, du moins pour y faire entrer toutes les subsistances qu'il se proposait de recueillir dans un grand fourrage. C'est dans cette vue que l'ordre fut expédié à Duhesme de descendre par les vallées de Suze et de Pérouse sur Rivoli et Pignerol à Grenier, de s'avancer du camp de la Madonna del Olmo sur Savigliano et Fossano; tandis qu'au centre Victor, de concert avec Lemoine, s'avancerait par Villanova et Beinetto, et qu'à droite Saint-Cyr après avoir confié à Miollis la défense de la rivière de Gênes, se porterait avec ses trois autres divisions sur Acqui.*" Jomini, 12:330–331.

11. According to Jomini, he was in an entrenched position. Jomini, 12:334.

Watrin's division, which had occupied a position at the sources of the Trebbia after the actions against Klenau, had soon left it again. On the 24th the two sides came to blows; the action began with the Austrian outposts around Basaluzzo (on the Novi battlefield) and moved through Fresonara toward Bosco Marengo, where the main resistance took place, and it ended with the Austrian general retreating across the Bormida and the French reaping 1,000 prisoners and three guns. Yet the Austrians too had taken 500–600 Poles prisoner. Since the Bormida and the Orba were very swollen and St. Cyr had no bridging equipment, he could not cross these rivers and had to halt between the Bormida and the Scrivia.

This defeat of General Karaczai made a quite profound impression on the Austrians; it spread panic to Tortona and Alessandria and caused Melas to have General Haddick, who was no longer needed to guard the snow-covered Alps, hurry to reinforce Karaczai with five battalions and two squadrons, while he sent General Kray there with another reinforcement from the main army and transferred command of this new corps to Kray.

The left wing under Duhesme in the Susa and Pinerolo valleys was supposed to begin its maneuver at the same time as St. Cyr. However, Jomini says that it could not begin its operation before 1 November,[12] so it occurs at the time of the battle of Genola. We do not know what caused this delay; perhaps the reason was the arrival of some of the left wing's troops from the St. Bernard or of some other reinforcements.

The Action at Beinette on 20 and 21 October

In the center, Victor retook the village of Beinette on 20 October but was driven out of there again the next day by General Ott and forced to retreat through Peveragno, with the loss of 500 prisoners and two guns.

On the 21st Lemoine drove the Austrians out of Villanova and deployed his division before Mondovi, while Gardanne advanced through Ceva. Melas watched for a few days; then he began to worry about Mondovi, so he reinforced the town with a few thousand men and on 26 October sent General Auersperg with six battalions and two squadrons from the camp at Montanera to push back General Lemoine's right wing.

12. Jomini, 12:336.

The Action at Lesegno on 28 October

Auersperg marched via Carrù and Niella Tanaro, where he left two battalions, against San Michele. During the course of the 27th, he threw the French back from this place and was intending to attack Vicoforte the next day, when he learned during the night that a French detachment was at Lesegno, namely, General Gardanne's. He decided to attack this detachment in the rear that night with two battalions from San Michele, while both the battalions from Niella moved against its front. The attack was completely successful; Gardanne was surprised and had to retreat into the mountains, with the loss of three guns and 450 prisoners.

Following this defeat of his right wing, Lemoine retreated from Vicoforte along the ridge running between the Ellero and the Cursaglia to Monastero di Vasco. Mondovi was now no longer threatened, and Auersperg returned to the main army.

The Action at Centallo on 31 October

After Victor had been repulsed on the 21st and Lemoine on the 28th, and they had been more or less beaten, Grenier was next in line; he began his maneuver from his camp at Cuneo on the 28th. That day he pushed the Austrian outposts back through Centallo and Murazzo. Grenier remained in this position on the 29th, merely demonstrating against Fossano, while Victor was to move through Beinette again toward Morozzo.[13]

Melas did not let this demonstration deter him from having Ott's and Elsnitz's divisions, fifteen battalions and thirty squadrons strong, cross the Stura at Castelletto and Montanera during the night. Although they first had to throw bridges across and then had to carry out the crossing under the eyes of enemy detachments, it succeeded. Grenier's division had a hard time of it, first at Murazzo and then at Centallo, which ended up with him being beaten,

13. This was Murazzo in the original, which could have meant the village of Murasso, but it is on the wrong side of the river. We think this should be Morozzo, which is on the right side of the river and in about the right place to make sense in the circumstances. However, we cannot be certain, as both towns were on the French lines of operations.

losing four guns and 800 prisoners, and having to retreat to the Maira. The Austrian divisions returned to the main army the same day.

We cannot find a single word about why Grenier's division came into action so late.

Scarcely had the Austrian divisions retreated across the Stura again than Grenier's vanguard returned to the area where they had been fighting.

Melas received the news that Duhesme was advancing again, which decided him to send General Lattermann with six battalions and four squadrons to Turin to reinforce General Kaim. On 5 October he himself abandoned his position at Montanera and reoccupied his camp at Magliano di Sopra behind the Pesio, for no sensible reason that we can find offered, since the news that General Duhesme was advancing again[14] could not have motivated this move to the left; we must much rather think that Lemoine's division had caused him new concern.

But the Austrian commander stayed in this camp for only two days as well. On the following day he had Mondovi evacuated, and on 3 October he began his march through Fossano to Marene.

This maneuver, for which the Austrian account does not give any clear motivation either, certainly could have been caused by General Duhesme's unexpected advance and by the news of the reinforcements he had summoned to him. In particular, on 30 October, while he engaged the Austrians in the Susa valley with demonstrations, the French general had retaken Pinerolo and even occupied Saluzzo. According to the Austrian presentation, in the last days of October, General Melas was already aware of the French intention to advance in a concentric manner for a decisive attack against him now, and he wanted to betake himself to a suitable point in the Marene area from which he would be able to attack the individual columns at his convenience. But apart from the fact that the town of Marene obviously does not have the property ascribed to it, because it lies so far back that it would have been entirely up to the French if they wanted to concentrate all the troops they had between Saluzzo and Mondovi before the battle, we must still ask: what was the point of the march to Magliano on 1 November? We will not allow ourselves to make any disparaging judgment here, but we may well say that to us it appears as though Melas thought he had smacked the French good and proper at Centallo on 31 October and that, for the time being, he had nothing to fear

14. **Clausewitz** notes: "Östreichische militärische Zeitschrift."

from Grenier's and Victor's divisions. But when the news arrived that these divisions were advancing again between the Stura and the Grana on 1 and 2 November, he realized that his position at Magliano was quite unsuitable, so he moved to the one at Marene.

96 THE BATTLE OF GENOLA

On 2 November the Austrians evacuated Mondovi, and Lemoine's division advanced: Serras's brigade to Breolungi, Clausel's and Gardanne's to Carrù.[15] We write this date according to General Jomini, but we find it difficult to believe that this could have been the case while the Austrian main army was still at Magliano, and we assume that here, as in many other places as well, there is a mistake over the date.[16]

Victor's division linked up with Grenier's on 3 November by crossing the Stura. The two left General Fressinet on the right bank of the Stura with 4,000–5,000 men. Victor moved along the Stura and Grenier along the Grana until both were in the area of Genola, which they seized on the 3rd, but not until late in the evening.

On this day the Austrians abandoned Savigliano, but they held on to Fossano. How the main army's move went is not related anywhere, but we assume that it had crossed the Stura at Fossano, which is indeed quite conceivable if it happened early in the morning, since the French did not occupy the outskirts of Fossano until 7:00 in the evening.

We must therefore imagine the two sides' situation in the center during the night of 3–4 November being as follows.

The Austrian main army is 29,000 strong; since it was 38,000 strong when Melas arrived on the Stura, it is now about 9,000 men weaker. This difference would not be so surprising if we could assume a reduction of 5,000–6,000 men over these six weeks, but this is not the case; according to the tables given by the Austrians for these two points in time, at the time of the battle of Genola, the individual Austrian battalions and squadrons were each somewhat stronger than six weeks earlier, so they must have received replacements. Also,

15. Jomini, 12:240.

16. The archduke has Melas on the move on the night of 2–3 November. Karl, 2:330–331.

at the battle of Genola, the main army consisted of just forty battalions and forty-four squadrons, but when Melas arrived on the Stura, it had comprised fifty-seven battalions and fifty-two squadrons. Six of these battalions were sent toward Turin, so there are eleven battalions and eight squadrons missing, of which the majority probably went with Kray to join Karaczai, and the rest were perhaps maintaining communications between them and the main army.

On the day of the battle (4 November), these 29,000 men of the main army were organized as follows:

Division Ott: 7,600 men
Division Mitrowsky: 2,700
Division Elsnitz: 8,000
Brigade Sommariva: 2,800
Brigade Gottesheim: 4,700
Cavalry reserve (Prince Lichtenstein): 3,400
Total: 29,200 men

This force was united between the Grana and the Stura. On Melas's orders, General Lattermann was also approaching again from the Raconigi area with his 3,500 men.

The French had Victor's and Grenier's divisions, 15,000 strong, opposite the Austrian main army between the two rivers named above; Lemoine's division and General Fressinet, who together formed a force of at least 12,000 men, were on the right bank of the Stura and seemed to be heading for Cherasco. Duhesme had occupied Saluzzo but still had his main body at Rivoli, too far away to participate in any decisive battle that might occur the next day. This was still more the case with St. Cyr, who was conducting his war against General Kray between Novi and Acqui, which he had garrisoned with a detachment.

The French commander was by no means prepared for a battle; for a long time already he had been expecting the Austrians to retreat from Piedmont, and when Melas began to move, he thought[17] this expectation was finally being fulfilled. He supposedly intended to let his right wing under St. Cyr advance victoriously and then move it up to join Lemoine. By doing so, he presumably wanted to cut the Austrians off from Alessandria and Tortona, whereby they

17. **Clausewitz** notes: "Jomini p343." Jomini, 12:343.

could then be induced to vacate the right bank of the Po entirely; by clearing the right bank of the Po, he thought he could gain the prospect of clearing the whole province of Milan, and who knows what other similar lofty fantasies. This is the only way we can explain why Victor's and Grenier's divisions got stuck in so boldly against the Austrian main body, while Lemoine's division and General Fressinet did not take a *direction* to enable them to *assist the other two if necessary.* If one is only expecting to pursue, then everything is arranged for just pushing straight ahead; if one is expecting a fight, then everything is disposed in relation to the place where the fight is anticipated as most likely.

Melas saw that the French had not let their setbacks in most of the preceding actions deter them from their offensive efforts. The news of the reinforcements General Duhesme supposedly received probably led the Austrian commander to expect that he was on the eve of receiving another heavier blow. He therefore thought it best to hurl his whole force upon the two French divisions facing him without delay and made the following dispositions for the 4th accordingly.

General Ott, reinforced by Sommariva's brigade, was to take Savigliano, pursue the enemy with a small force to Lagnasco in the direction of Saluzzo, but turn his main strength against Vottignasco and Levaldigi (the road to Cuneo).

General Mitrowsky was to advance on Ott's left and act in concert with him.

General Elsnitz was to attack Genola, then march against Levaldigi and engage the enemy there until the arrival of the first and second columns.

The defeated enemy was to be pursued along the three roads through Villafalletto, Centallo, and Ronchi.

To understand these dispositions to some degree, we must not overlook the fact that in posting their right wing at Murazzo and their left at Savigliano, the French had adopted a diagonal line between the Navigliano Novo[18] and the Grana, and Melas probably thought their left wing would retreat across the Grana to Saluzzo.

18. This is probably the canal running from Ronchi via Murazzo up to Fossano. The old maps show a *Canale Nuovo* in the location Clausewitz describes; see https://mapire.eu/de/map/europe-19century-secondsurvey/?layers=here-aerial%2C158%2C164&bbox=837321.4222942061%2C5531973.615153152%2C861618.8426603564%2C5539617.317981669.

On this day the French, for their part, wanted to continue their maneuver for the putative pursuit. Victor was to take Fossano, Grenier was to move to Marene, and Duhesme came from Saluzzo at the head of 3,000 men to link up with Grenier via Savigliano.

So the two sides met on the morning of the 4th. In his maneuver toward Marene, Grenier ran into Ott and Sommariva, 10,000 strong, at Savigliano. The fighting was soon very lively and remained in the balance for several hours, so the outcome seemed to depend on whether it was Duhesme or Mitrowsky who arrived first. But since Duhesme was coming from Saluzzo, whereas Mitrowsky was quite close by at San Lorenzo, the matter could not really be in doubt. Grenier was beaten by the 14,000 Austrians under Ott and Mitrowsky and driven back onto the reserve standing at Levaldigi, so that Savigliano fell into the Austrians' hands before Duhesme arrived.

The action against Victor at Genola, where Championnet was in person, began somewhat later than that against Grenier. It lasted until midday, without success for either side; but when the action against Grenier was completely decided and Melas could use General Mitrowsky from there to support the left wing, Victor too had to quit the field and retreat to Murazzo; Melas pressed on after him, so Championnet was obliged to continue his retreat to Centallo and the surrounding area. But Murazzo was held. Not only is it said that Gottesheim's brigade could not achieve anything against Murazzo, but the Austrian official report even explicitly states that the French held the place until the next day.

While this was going on along the front, Duhesme finally appeared on the Austrian flank with about 3,000 men, took Savigliano, and advanced toward Marene. Melas sent General Sommariva against him with four battalions, to combine with the battalion that had been in Savigliano and the two squadrons that had been left in the area.

General Sommariva attacked General Duhesme. The latter, simultaneously threatened by the approach of Lattermann from Raconigi, saw himself compelled to retreat again through Savigliano toward Saluzzo. General Duhesme's heading for Marene, which appears in all the reports,[19] can only be explained by Lattermann's approach, even though there is no mention of that general in the Austrian reports.

On the 5th General Ott advanced to in front of the entrenched camp at

19. Jomini, 12:345–346. See also Karl, 2:332.

Madonna dell'Olmo, Mitrowsky remained at Centallo, while Elsnitz turned against Murazzo; Victor had already vacated this position but had left a rear guard there, which was now cut off and sought to escape across the Stura, but 400 men drowned in its waters, and the remaining 1,000 gave themselves up as prisoners of war.

On 6 November Grenier abandoned the camp at Madonna dell'Olmo and moved to Borgo San Dalmazzo, but Victor returned to the Mondovi area and took position between Monastero and Villanova.

The Austrians continued their pursuit. Lattermann moved through Bosco into the Maira valley as far as Dronero to prevent General Duhesme from linking up with Grenier; Ott and Mitrowsky moved to Conaglio [Caraglio] in the Grana valley; Lichtenstein to Vignolo on the Stura near to Borgo; Elsnitz to Madonna dell'Olmo.

On all these roads they rounded up lots of prisoners.

This battle cost the French close to 7,000 men, which is nearly half of the two divisions that were mainly engaged. The Austrians took four guns and 4,000 prisoners. Their own losses came to 2,200 men.

While Grenier's and Victor's divisions were being met by a force of almost twice their own strength, Lemoine's division stayed quietly with its right wing before Cherasco and its left between Carrù and Bene [Bene Vagienna], about 10 miles from the battlefield. It was not until the 6th that Melas sent General Gottesheim across the Stura to observe this division.

97 MELAS PUSHES THE FRENCH BACK FROM MONDOVI AND CUNEO, BUT KRAY ATTACKS ST. CYR IN VAIN

We have seen that before the battle Melas was 62,000 strong, and his losses during it came to only about 2,000 men, so he still had 60,000. The French army, on the other hand, had suffered so much in the battles, from sickness and from an increasingly damaging rate of desertion, that it went into its winter quarters with only 38,000 men; we can therefore assume that after the battle of Genola, it would not have had more than 40,000. This gave General Melas three-to-two superiority overall, which can be said to be very considerable.

Furthermore, when we consider that even if we leave out the few detachments they may have had in the Great St. Bernard Pass and north of Mont Cenis generally, the French still occupied a line about 225 miles long—from the Susa valley along the alpine range to Borgo San Dalmazzo behind Cuneo, from there along the chain of the Apennines to the Scrivia, and then again in the eastern Riviera as far as Sestri—and except for the part in the eastern Riviera, this line enveloped the Austrians concentrically, who therefore had the advantage of interior lines: that must surely convince us that after the battle of Genola, with this numerical preponderance, these positional advantages, and the moral superiority from his victory, General Melas was in a position to strike one more totally decisive blow, to smash the French army completely asunder, and to cause Genoa to fall by the moral weight of this blow.

Since we are a foe to all vague expressions and empty terminology,[20] we must describe this envisaged asunder-smashing more explicitly. By this, we envision a new attack on the enemy main body, or if his forces are so scattered that there is none such, *the core of the enemy force,* thus the division that the commander in chief is with; we envision an attack on that part with superior force and in the form of an envelopment; we imagine it being continued all the way to the sea so that this part of the enemy force is obliged to seek refuge in Genoa or to fall back to the Var, if it can still do either of these things—and we are convinced that in these conditions *the consequence of this sustained thrust with superior force at the key point*[21] would have been proportionately numerous trophies, great disorder among the enemy corps, and a major moral defeat of the adversary. After the battle of Genola, Victor and Lemoine were indisputably the main body of the enemy force; the two combined were presumably

20. Clausewitz mentions this in *On War*, book 4, chap. 8, "Mutual Agreement to Fight": "There can be no engagement unless both sides are willing. That concept, which is fundamental to the duel, is responsible for a terminology used by military historians that often results in vague and misleading notions" (245). Here he is having a dig at Jomini, but as Bassford correctly points out, there are actually a great number of similarities between the two that Clausewitz was not always willing to recognize. See Christopher Bassford, "Clausewitz and His Works," http://www.clausewitz.com/readings/Bassford/Cworks/Works.htm#_edn40. See also Antoine Baron de Jomini, *Summary of the Art of War*, trans. Major O. F. Winship and Lieutenant E. E. McLean (New York: G. P. Putnam, 1854), 9–21.

21. It is worth noting that Clausewitz uses the word *Hauptpunkte* here rather than *Schwerpunkt,* which indicates that he saw them as two separate things. See volume 1, chapter 1, note 74.

no more than 12,000 strong. If we imagine that if they were attacked by 30,000 they would be driven into the mountains, surrounded on all sides, and pushed back to the sea, then there was more than a remote possibility of cutting them off from Genoa and from the Var at the same time and thus forcing them to surrender; or if this gloriously triumphant point were not attained, at least a very disrupted and disorderly retreat accompanied by heavy losses and much straggling could be regarded as an inevitable consequence. St. Cyr was at Bosco, Rivalta, and Acqui and therefore only one day's march closer to Genoa than Victor and Lemoine were at Mondovi; whether he could have got to Genoa at all in this situation can be regarded as doubtful. If he did not go there, he would have to retreat via detours and by fighting his way out to the Var or to the Piedmontese alpine passes, and then there could hardly be any doubt that Genoa would fall; but even if he began his retreat in good time and got into Genoa, it was still possible that the victory would have increased internal unrest there to such a degree as to leave General St. Cyr (or whoever else took over command in Genoa) thinking more about free passage out than about stubborn defense. When we see General Masséna actually conducting such a defense six months later, and testing the inhabitants of Genoa to the utmost through hunger, we must not forget how very different the general situation was at that time from the time of the battle of Genola. In May and June 1800 Russia had withdrawn from the alliance; Bonaparte was at the head of the French government as first consul, forming a reserve army for the relief of Genoa;[22] Archduke Charles and Suvorov had been removed from command; Moreau had advanced into the heart of Swabia. In such circumstances, even if Masséna, besieged in Genoa, could not foresee the Austrian disaster at Marengo, he could still count on a total change of fortunes in Italy to the advantage of the French. But immediately after the battle of Genola, the coup of 18 *Brumaire* (9 November) had not yet taken place, and Suvorov's departure from the theater of operations to Swabia, which occurred on 3 October, could not have been known about, still less could all its consequences yet be assessed. Thus, at this time, everything about this campaign still looked very gloomy and hopeless for the French. Anyone[23] who attaches little value to such a difference, who does not recognize the influence of the general situation at a higher level on the actions of people engaged

22. See chapter 10 of this volume for our overview of the main campaigns following the ones analyzed here.

23. Of course, Clausewitz is again talking witheringly of Jomini.

in playing out particular episodes but regards it as a matter of chance—he has absolutely not understood the true essence of war, and we would not trust him to make any judgment at all about how the forces operating in it are generated.[24] We therefore say that after the battle of Genola, General Melas could and should have seen the French situation as a rich field for him to harvest, in which (of course, only by acting decisively and skillfully) he could have obtained the finest results in more than one way and according to more than one likely situation. A commander in wartime could never ask for more from a glimpse into the future than this, and if that is not enough to tempt his ambition, he will never achieve anything much.

But these advantages of his position, this likelihood of glorious victories, vanished entirely when, instead of acting with concentrated force against the long, thin French line, General Melas himself adopted a still longer one that enveloped their concentric deployment with another concentric one in turn and thus neutralized his opponent's mistakes, in that he committed worse ones of his own. In these conditions, he was left with no chance of doing anything major, and just as that chance disappeared, so the concentric French position facing Melas from Susa to Novi became advantageous; and *in these circumstances,* the advantage of *diverging lines of retreat,* which for a long time people in the theoretical world had foolishly regarded as an *absolute,* actually came into play.

In fact, after the battle of Genola, we see the French left wing fall back to the foot of the Alps, their center to the Col de Tende, and their right wing to Novi, while exactly because of that, the Austrian commander lapses into a kind of impotence. Even if he does not want to pursue along every radius of the enemy's retreat at the same time, which would indisputably have been the worst thing he could do, and even if he wants to follow a system whereby his main body pushes back first one French corps and then the next so far

24. The core argument here is that Jomini does not understand war because he ignores the influence of higher-level events on the troops' failure to hold out more effectively in Genoa and elsewhere at this time in 1799. Jomini's description of events blames the Directory for the failures locally, and he focuses on lack of pay, poor food, inadequate clothing, and so forth. That being said, however, these issues had consistently plagued the French army in Italy (see Clausewitz, *Napoleon's 1796 Italian Campaign*), so simply to claim that they were the cause is somewhat shallow. As such, Clausewitz is right to point this out, even if his language is harsher than may be merited. See Jomini, 12:363–366.

as is necessary for the siege of Cuneo, still he cannot neglect any of these other points entirely because his main body is not large enough to strike such *decisive blows* as to be sure of compensating for any losses that might occur elsewhere. Thus his main body, which was only about 30,000 strong anyway, becomes even more split up, and the most with which he can act offensively is 15,000–20,000 men.

So in fact, after the battle of Genola we see General Melas advancing first along the Cuneo road, then turning toward Mondovi, and finally again against the French force left behind Cuneo, so as to gain himself space for the siege of Cuneo. However, since these events occur a few days later than General Kray's attack on St. Cyr, which happens at the same time as the battle of Genola, we must consider that first.

The Encounter at Novi on 6 November

After the defeat suffered by General Karaczai on 24 October, as we have already recounted, Melas had ordered General Haddick to hasten to the Alessandria area with five battalions and two squadrons that could be dispensed with from guarding the high Alps in this late season; at the same time, he had another reinforcement move there under Kray[25] and transferred command of the whole force to the latter.

The Austrian reports do not say how strong this made General Kray's force. If we assume that after his defeat Karaczai was still 3,000 strong, that Haddick brought 3,500 men with him and Kray 5,000–6,000, Kray would have had 12,000 men, or roughly as many as we can assume for his opponent.

The latter had pushed forward as far as Rivalta [Rivalta Scrivia] and Bosco

25. **Clausewitz** notes: "The Austrian account does not say this, rather from that it seems as though General Kray just went there on his own. But since eleven battalions and eight squadrons whose assignment is not stated are missing from the Austrian main army at the battle of Genola, and since Kray would hardly have risked an attack on St. Cyr if he had only been reinforced by the five battalions and two squadrons brought by Haddick, the assumption that he took some of those ten [*sic*] battalions and eight squadrons with him is very likely. It is an incomprehensible bad habit of military historians to provide the most precise strength tables and then fail to demonstrate how these forces are used in the decisive episodes."

[Bosco Marengo], was investing Serravalle, and was about to commence its siege when Kray began his attack.

The Austrian general, who probably did not have all his troops with him until the end of October, could not cross the Bormida at first because the high water level had obliged the dismantling of the bridge. He therefore busied himself on 3 November with driving the French out of Acqui and garrisoning the town.

On the 4th Kray's bridge across the Bormida at Alessandria was back in action again, and on that day he crossed the river with his main body and moved upon Bosco and Rivalta. St. Cyr did not wait for the fighting to get serious but retreated to Novi. Since Kray was still waiting for some more troops that had been sent to him, he did not continue his attack on that day but stayed deployed on the Strada Levata[26] overnight. On the 5th he was stopped by very heavy rain and thick fog. He halted in the area of Pozzolo Formigaro.

On 6 November Kray advanced to the attack again, which initially seems to have been just an advance guard aimed at the town of Novi; but since he gained possession of the town without any great difficulty, he thought the moment favorable to go over to a general attack. St. Cyr seems to have intended to resist mainly by a defense of the heights and an attack on the enemy columns behind Novi, which he executed with decisive success. The Austrians appear to have been excessively extended again, as was their habit, since their left wing moved on Serravalle to relieve that town while the right moved on Pasturana and the Lemma, so the whole was spread over an area 10 miles across. In this situation it could not have been hard for St. Cyr to break through the center, which he did after almost all the Austrians had shaken out into skirmish lines during the attack on Novi. The result was that the wings also had to retreat now, and Kray lost the battle and with it five cannon.

The satisfaction of having momentarily relieved Serravalle in this way and learned from its commandant that he was very well, thank you, was thus paid for with a lost battle. At first, General Kray remained at Pozzolo Formigaro, but on 10 November, when Laboissière's division crossed the Orba and retook Acqui, he retreated to the Alessandria area and left just an outpost line facing St. Cyr, who stayed in his position at Novi.

It seems that this victory of St. Cyr's was neutralized by the news of the battle of Genola. However, not much could have been expected from it

26. This is probably the main road between Alessandria and Tortona via Marengo.

anyway, since Alessandria and Tortona, about 10 miles beyond, would have acted the same as they did, just as, conversely, a victory for General Kray hardly would have been consequential enough to drive General St. Cyr from the crest of the Apennines.

As for the main army, Victor turned toward Mondovi on 6 November, as we said, while Grenier quit the camp at Madonna dell'Olmo the same day to occupy the one at Borgo San Dalmazzo. Constant rain and the supposedly excessive strain on the troops meant that for three days, namely, 7, 8, and 9 November, Melas undertook nothing of importance. But during this time, the news arrived that the enemy was being strongly reinforced again on the Pesio near Mondovi, which stemmed from Victor's division marching into the area. This made General Melas have Mitrowsky's division return across the Stura to support General Gottesheim.

Furthermore, upon the news of the clash at Novi, he had General Lattermann, who was in the Maira valley with his six grenadier battalions and four squadrons, move through Alba to Nizza to forestall any consequences of St. Cyr's victory if need be.

The Action at Borgo San Dalmazzo on 10 November

After taking these measures for his left wing, on 10 November he had Generals Ott and Elsnitz attack the French in their camp at Borgo San Dalmazzo, which was occupied by the main body of Grenier's division under the command of General Richepense. The resistance was fairly stubborn, but since these two divisions may be estimated at 15,000 strong and General Richepense's troops were perhaps only a third of that, they had to vacate the position and retreat toward Vernante on the road leading to the Col de Tende.

At the same time, General Sommariva pressed forward into the Vraita and Maira valleys with a couple of thousand men, causing the French to vacate these valleys completely and retreat across Mont Viso into the Durance valley, where they went into winter quarters.

Now Melas felt he also had to bring General Lattermann back to the Vraita valley, where he had been before.

The Action at Mondovi on 13 November

Right after the battle at Borgo San Dalmazzo, Melas left with Lichtenstein's division for the Pesio to link up with Mitrowsky and Gottesheim and drive Victor's and Lemoine's two divisions out of the Mondovi area. In the strength table the Austrians give for the battle of Genola, General Lichtenstein had only the twenty-four squadrons of the cavalry reserve under his command. But it turns out that on the Pesio he had General Bellegarde and six battalions from Elsnitz's division with him, which were presumably assigned to him for this operation. The force that Melas united on the Pesio in this way would have comprised five battalions and six squadrons under Gottesheim, seven battalions under Mitrowsky, and six battalions and twenty-four squadrons under Lichtenstein, making eighteen battalions and thirty squadrons in total, or about 14,000 men. The two French divisions, of which Victor's had taken position at Monastero and Lemoine's at Mondovi, were estimated at 9,000 strong combined.

On 13 November the Austrians advanced to the attack in two columns from Beinette and Magliano Sopra [Magliano Sottano]. Lichtenstein, to whom Gottesheim was attached, led the first and attacked Victor; Mitrowsky attacked Lemoine with the other. The French resistance lasted for quite a long time, and Lemoine's on the right wing was completely successful; however, more because of his left being outflanked than because of the attack on his front, Victor was forced to retreat to Vicoforte, in the direction of the Tanaro beyond Mondovi. Now Lemoine could not hold his position any longer either, and Championnet decided to retreat. Mondovi was evacuated, Lemoine retreated in the Bormida valley to Calissano [Calizzano] at the foot of the Bernardo [Colle San Bernardo],[27] and Victor's division retreated in the Tanaro valley to Garessio.

In Mondovi, the Austrians captured five guns that were presumably not field artillery, and there is no mention of any other trophies; the Austrian losses came to about 500 men, and the French losses were probably not much greater.

Melas had just General Bellegarde and his brigade pursue in the Tanaro valley, and they took position at Bagnasco. With the rest, he turned against

27. The Calizzano valley leads southwest to the Colle San Bernardo.

Cuneo. To make the investment of this fortress even more secure, on 15 November General Ott had 3,000–4,000 men under General Auersperg drive the French detachment that was still at Vernante further back as far as the Col de Tende, which the French later vacated of their own accord because of the inhospitable season.

98 MELAS BESIEGES AND TAKES CUNEO

Melas was now at the point where he could invest and besiege Cuneo. This fortress, although enclosed between the Stura and the Gesso and approachable only on a narrow, strongly fortified front, was not without its particular weak points and could hardly be expected to put up resistance stretching out for more than four weeks, so he could hope to finish the siege before the worst of the frosts. Nevertheless, in the Austrian headquarters great doubt seems to have prevailed over the choice between besieging Cuneo or merely investing it. Although the French had vacated the exits from the mountains to the north and east almost everywhere except around Novi and had retreated beyond the mountain crests, the Austrians thought they saw preparations for the relief of the fortress of Cuneo in every valley of the Alps and the Apennines. According to their reports, several French columns were advancing, including one of 10,000 men over Mont Cenis alone. In these circumstances, a siege seemed a dubious business because that would leave fewer troops available than an investment and because raising the latter incurred no losses, whereas raising a siege would put the siege train in great danger. But on the other hand, the state of deprivation, demoralization, and rampant desertion in which the French army found itself had not remained unknown to the Austrians;[28] these reports meant it was very unlikely that the French commander would be capable of attempting a sustained and effective operation to relieve Cuneo in this late season, when every operation in the high mountains becomes doubly difficult. At the same time, taking this fortress was of quite some importance for the start of the next campaign, and besides, Melas probably felt that if he did not succeed in actually plucking this single fruit of his victory, his whole three-month campaign would appear fruitless and futile, despite his numerical

28. Described in Jomini, 12:363–365.

superiority. These reasons outweighed his concerns, so hasty preparations were made for a siege, for which the artillery could presumably have been brought from Turin, which was very close by.[29]

On 18 November Prince Lichtenstein, who had been given responsibility for the siege, moved up in front of Cuneo between the Gesso and the Stura with eleven battalions and four squadrons, while six cavalry squadrons observed the fortress from the right bank of the Gesso and as many again from the left bank of the Stura. Thus, this force comprised at most 8,000 men. Melas took position south of Borgo with the rest of his troops divided into three corps: Elsnitz was on the left bank of the Stura with ten battalions, Mitrowsky between the Gesso and the Stura with nine battalions and six squadrons, and Ott between the Gesso and the Vermagnana with eleven battalions and six squadrons. There was an entrenched central position at Borgo San Dalmazzo into which Melas intended to retreat in the event of an attack.

Although the French in the Tanaro valley had let themselves be driven out of Garessio by Bellegarde on 17 November and were now all in the Riviera, during the siege they still made a move to relieve the town from Genoese territory.

We know nothing about this attempt other than that, according to the Austrian account, on 24 November the French in the Apennines advanced again to Cairo Montenotte in the Bormida valley, to Ponzone in the Erro valley, and to Ovada in the Orba valley, and that Victor's division concentrated at Oneglia in the eastern Riviera. General Jomini does not mention any actual French maneuvers at all but merely talks about Championnet's intention to relieve Cuneo being thwarted by the unexpectedly early fall of the fortress. We cannot in any case regard this small pushing forward of their outposts on 24 November as the beginning of this offensive.

29. In essence, Melas sought to secure an object to justify the costs of his rather fruitless campaign so far. Clausewitz's arguments in *On War*, book 1, chaps. 1 and 2, point out that this is backward: first one figures out what one wants, then one devises the strategy to obtain it. Doing this in reverse order risks gaining an object that might not be what one wants, or it might not be sufficiently valuable to justify the efforts expended. Furthermore, doing this on the fly, so to speak, increases the risk of miscalculation vis-à-vis the enemy's reaction. If, however, one grabs an object with a clear goal in mind as to what the object might offer—a bargaining chip, for example—then it might be a worthwhile undertaking. Given that the Austrian Aulic Council did not seem to have a clear vision of what it wanted from the conflict from one moment to the next, such clarity of insight seems unlikely.

They also advanced again in the Tanaro valley and obliged General Bellegarde to withdraw to the position at delle Torrete.[30] These maneuvers resulted in an adjustment to the Austrians' deployment. Not only was General Lattermann brought up from Nizza to Ceva to receive Bellegarde, but Kray was also moved to the right with part of his corps through Asti to Cherasco, where he arrived on 1 December and from where he moved to the area of Mondovi a few days later. Nine battalions and twelve squadrons remained in Alessandria under the command of Prince Hohenzollern, who had been called up from central Italy to replace Karaczai. Hohenzollern was supposed to keep the French right wing constantly engaged, to maintain communications with Klenau, and to retreat to the entrenched camp at Alessandria if attacked.

Outside Cuneo, the approach saps were begun on 26 November, eight days after it was blockaded. The garrison numbered 3,000 men under General Clement. The serious demoralization of the garrison, the unhappiness of the citizenry, and the commandant's weakness meant that its surrender ensued on 3 December, eight days after the approach saps were opened. The garrison gave themselves up as prisoners of war. The Austrians found 187 guns and 14,000 *Centner* [700 tons] of powder in Cuneo, having bought possession of this fortress with the insignificant loss of 130 men.

After the capture of Cuneo, the French no longer had any positive reason for action in this campaign, and it was all the more advisable for them to stay quiet as reinforcements were on the way to them from Switzerland. Also, after nine months of continual defeats, the French army's morale had sunk so low that they could not expect any success in combat until it had been restored.[31] Faced with that, there was all the more reason to ask whether General Melas ought not to continue his offensive, drive the French out of the Riviera completely, and progress at least as far as blockading Genoa. It seemed as though such an objective was attainable without great effort and without any further crisis. The reasons against continuing the campaign are presented in the following form in the Austrian account:

30. Now the Borgo Torretta district in modern-day Ceva, it is the western part of town just north of the bridge over the Tanaro.

31. This brings us back to Clausewitz's concept of the trinity. The individual and collective emotion of an army might be sufficiently degraded that it overwhelms reason and chance, whatever the odds might be. This is one reason why Clausewitz describes danger in war as being part of friction. The emotion caused by danger must be understood if one is to understand war. See *On War*, book 1, chap. 4, 113–114.

> But arguing against it was the need to give the Imperial army some rest, to reinforce it and to reorganize it. The operation in the Riviera would have had to be continued in the Apennines from Genoa to Nizza [Nice] without interruption, and Savona and Finale would have had to be besieged, at this the harshest time of year. The Austrian army's units would have been very much weakened by this winter campaign, both in numbers and in energy, and then next spring it probably would not have been fit to continue major operations.[32]

These reasons are of such a conventional kind that they tell us nothing more than that General Melas was a very conventional man who thought that he had done enough this year and that it was time for him to have a rest. Because the question over continuing the offensive is more profound, we will take it up in our closing reflections.

99 MELAS MAKES A VAIN ATTEMPT AGAINST GENOA

Although the Austrians did not want to conduct any more major operations, there was still an attempt against Genoa in progress that had actually been intended to happen at the same time as the siege of Cuneo, so as to act as a counterblow if the enemy made preparations to relieve Cuneo. Cuneo fell so quickly that this had not been carried out, and indeed, in that sense, the operation was unnecessary. But the idea that the Genoese were extremely unhappy with the state of affairs, and exaggerated notions of their readiness to throw off the French yoke as soon as a significant Austrian corps appeared beneath their walls, very naturally produced a desire in the Austrian generals not to abandon this attempt. Klenau was presumably the one most excited about it because he was closest to Genoa and, with a few reinforcements, could easily advance to beneath its walls. But naturally the participation of the Austrian corps on the Scrivia was bound to be needed as well, because if the French were not seriously pinned there, their possession of the high ridge meant they could always attack General Klenau's right flank and rear in superior force with the greatest of ease, as the example of mid-October had

32. This was not cited. Jomini indicates that the Austrians were considering this; see Jomini, 13:41.

shown. Yet despite that lesson, the Austrians were even less careful this time, so that Klenau came off much worse.

We left General St. Cyr victorious at Novi on 6 November. None of the historians tells us how long he stayed in this position; all we find is that on 6 November Prince Hohenzollern advanced toward Novi and Gavi, driving the French outposts from the former and surrounding the latter. This thus presupposes that St. Cyr and his main body were no longer at Novi; he had probably returned to the Bochetta Pass.

After General Klenau was driven back behind the Magra in mid-October, we hear no word of him for two months. Presumably, General Miollis retreated back behind the Stura again straight away, because communications with St. Cyr would have been difficult to maintain in any position further forward, so then Klenau, for his part, could soon have advanced to the Stura again; at any rate, that is where we find him in mid-December when the attempt on Genoa is supposed to be carried out.

When some of General Fröhlich's troops became available because of the fall of Ancona in mid-November, which we will recount shortly, Melas sent an order to that general to have five of his battalions join Klenau. In addition, in connection with the intended attempt on Genoa, in December he ordered Prince Hohenzollern to reinforce General Klenau with another six battalions under General Eder, in exchange for which he would give him six others from the main army; he also sent Nobili's cavalry brigade of twelve squadrons to Reggio to reinforce Klenau. Whether the latter had concentrated all these troops by the time he began to advance against Genoa on 12 December is unfortunately not made explicit in the Austrian account; in that case, he could be assumed to have had 10,000–12,000 men, but the poor outcome of his operation leads us almost to suspect that he was not that strong. In any case, the operation lacked the essential bit: *its parts acting in harmony.*

For some unknown reason and with unknown justification, Klenau imagined that Hohenzollern would advance against the Bocchetta Pass on the 15th and send a detachment across the Scrivia, and he began his maneuver on 13 December with that assumption. On the 14th he attacked General Miollis at Sori, Monte Cormea [Monte Cornua], and Torriglia. He drove him back without much trouble and pursued him to the walls of Genoa on the 15th, while having his right wing advance to the sources of the Trebbia.[33] But Prince

33. Jomini, 12:355–356.

Hohenzollern had not been able to attack the Bocchetta that day and engage the enemy forces there, apparently because the six replacement battalions he was expecting from the main army had not yet arrived, and he felt too weak without them. Prince Hohenzollern had sent an officer to General Klenau to tell him that *after sending off his six battalions he was not in a position to operate against the Bocchetta until their replacements had arrived,* but this officer had been held up by chance delays and reached Klenau when he was already engaged in battle. This explanation casts the whole operation in a dubious light. Judging by the point emphasized above, it seems that the six battalions under General Eder had only just departed, and since they were supposed to move through Reggio and link up there with Nobili's brigade, they had certainly not yet reached Klenau; so that was a very bad arrangement.[34] In any case, it is certain that the other six battalions reached Hohenzollern too late. Finally, the accidental delay of a courier officer may well cost a few hours, but General Klenau's operation did not depend on a few hours, since it lasted three days. This is probably an attempt to gloss over something in this affair.

The Genoese on whom Klenau was relying so very much did not judge the circumstances suitable to bestir themselves, since St. Cyr was both outside and within their walls with a considerable corps. On the 15th he sent General Watrin against Klenau's right flank, in the direction of Torriglia, in roughly the same way he had done two months before. On the 16th, before daybreak, Klenau learned that his right wing had been beaten in the mountains and that his rear was threatened once again. Apparently, he set off immediately so that he himself could fall on the enemy's rear via the Val Besagno.[35] He now had two serious fights—one at Scoffera at the sources of the Trebbia, and the other at Torriglia; both of these seem to have been *actions to fight his way through,* and the result was that he and his main body did indeed successfully reach the

34. Reggio Emilia was about 70 miles east of Hohenzollern's position around Novi; then they would have had to go about 50 miles west again to join Klenau's attack on Sori, Monte Cornua, and Torriglia—dubious indeed.

35. This is the valley following the river Bisagno, which enters the Mediterranean just to the east of Genoa itself. Today, the river flows underground, and it is not clear on modern maps. But if one looks at older maps, one can trace the valley quite easily. Just east of Genoa one can see the river, and from there it can be traced north via Marassi and Staglieno before turning east near Olmo. See https://mapire.eu/de/map/europe-19century-secondsurvey/?layers=here-aerial%2C158%2C164&bbox=974856.7049330907%2C5523210.391527315%2C1023451.5456653916%2C5538497.797184349.

Stura, but he lost no fewer than 1,795 men taken prisoner. He then retreated to Sarzana behind the Magra.

Meanwhile (presumably on the 16th), Prince Hohenzollern had advanced from the Scrivia against Borgo de Fornari with part of his corps, while the other part diligently bombarded Gavi. When he learned that Klenau had been defeated, he raised the blockade of Gavi and left the mountain region.

The motivation behind the attempt on Genoa is certainly not to be deprecated, but of course, the orders for it seem to have been too pedantic and to have belonged entirely to the realm of confusion and misunderstanding.

100 FRÖHLICH BESIEGES AND TAKES ANCONA: THE END OF THE CAMPAIGN

Before we accompany General Melas's army into its winter quarters, we still have to devote a couple of words to the taking of Ancona.

As we said, after the fall of Mantua at the end of July, General Fröhlich crossed the Apennines with 7,000–8,000 men to occupy Tuscany. After achieving this main objective of his mission and well and truly scattering his corps to do so, he also sent home the locals who had been in insurrection. In September he advanced to the Tiber, and on the 20th of that month he appeared outside Rome with about 3,000 men and summoned General Garnier to surrender. But the latter had already been in negotiations for several days with the Sicilians and the English, which led to an agreement on 26 September according to which Garnier and his 4,000 men vacated the Papal State and sailed for France.

But that agreement did not extend to Ancona, where General Monnier and his 2,800 men were surrounded by 3,000–4,000 insurgents under Lahoze by land and by the Russians and the Turks by sea, although they were well supported by the inhabitants of Ancona in its defense. After the fall of Rome, General Fröhlich turned toward Ancona, but since he felt too weak for a serious blockade, he left that to the insurgents for the time being and waited for his reinforcements from Dalmatia to arrive. When these had brought him up to 8,000–9,000 men, on 14 October he moved up to the fortress that was now blockaded by him, the insurgents, and 1,200–1,500 Russians taken from the ships' crews. General Lahoze had fallen in battle shortly before, and the insurgents now came under Austrian command. Fröhlich, who had no wish to give the Russians and Turks any part in this conquest,[36] decided to conduct the actual siege with Austrian troops only and even declined a reinforcement of 2,000 Turks when it was offered to him. On 17 October Fröhlich opened the approach saps. Although the garrison was too small for the size of the fortress, which would have required at least 6,000 men, and although the fortifications were in a very neglected state, General Monnier's energy and courage enabled him not only to make up for everything he was lacking through the skillful application of extraordinary measures but also to delay the besiegers' progress through frequent and very vigorously conducted sorties. Thus he was able to hold out until 13 October [*sic*—actually November], about four weeks after the approach trenches were begun. Then, although he did not get free passage, he and his garrison did obtain from General Fröhlich their return to France on parole, not to serve again until exchanged.[37]

The main things that fell into Austrian hands were 585 guns and ten warships, of which three were ships of the line.

The Russians and Turks tried to claim the naval stores because they had blockaded the fortress from the sea, but General Fröhlich maintained that their blockade would have been so weak and irregular as to be quite ineffective, so he denied them this share of the booty.

This greed, as well as his unilateral negotiation with the commandant, was taken very poorly by the Russians and gave the coup de grace to the alliance.[38]

36. Again, we see the allies disagreeing about the object of a campaign, although this seems to have had as much to do with Fröhlich's desire for war booty. This type of disagreement undermines effective collaboration. See also note 38 below.

37. Jomini, 12:360–361.

38. Clausewitz's take on this in *On War*, book 8, chap. 9 ("The Plan of a War Designed to Lead to the Total Defeat of the Enemy") is worth noting, as there are some key ideas relating to the role of shared interest and trust: "1. The distribution of the enemy's political power. If it lies in the armed forces of a single government, there will normally be no problem. If it is shared among allied armies, one of which is simply acting as an ally without a special interest of its own, the task is hardly any greater. But if it is shared among allies bound together by a common interest, the problem turns on the cordiality of the alliance. We have dealt with this earlier. 2. The situation in the theater of war where the various armies are operating. If all enemy forces are concentrated in a single army in one theater of war they in fact constitute a unity, and the question need not be pursued. But if the enemy in a single theater consists of separate allied armies, their unity is less than absolute; yet they will still be sufficiently integrated for a resolute attack on *one* to involve the rest" (617).

The Austrians try to excuse this action by the fact that General Monnier wanted to negotiate with them alone because the Russians and Turks had not honored the terms of the earlier capitulation of the garrison of Fano.[39] General Fröhlich was obviously acting on higher instructions, and here again, we see a petty Austrian policy prevail by which they shot themselves in the foot.

The Austrian main army went into its winter quarters after the taking of Cuneo, as did Hohenzollern's and Klenau's divisions after their unsuccessful attempt on Genoa. Right after the fall of Ancona, Fröhlich had sent five battalions to Klenau and gone into quarters in Tuscany and the Marches (Le Marche) with the rest of his troops. The Austrian main army occupied quarters directly behind the line it had held in the last segment of the campaign, from the Aosta valley in the Alps, down along the river to Tortona.[40] Klenau remained behind the Magra.

The French remained in possession of all the mountain crests and had even pushed their outposts a few leagues beyond the crestline in the Apennines. Their main forces were on the far side of the Alps and the Apennines in the Riviera and on the Durance. Duhesme's and Grenier's divisions continued to constitute the left wing behind the Alps, Victor and Lemoine were the center in the Riviera as far as Savona, Watrin's and Laboissière's divisions were the right wing in Genoa, and Miollis was behind the Lavagna in the eastern Riviera.

The French army was left in the state one would expect after a strenuous and continually unsuccessful campaign combined with the effects of a thoroughly corrupt, sloppy, and ignorant administration, which is to say, it was markedly worse than how Bonaparte had found it at the start of the 1796 campaign.[41] Pay five months in arrears, a lack of clothing verging on nakedness, a lack of provisions verging on starvation, and the most arduous outpost duty along the immense line it occupied in the mountains were made even more onerous by a lack of firewood and hospitals that were poorly managed and overflowing. All this was more than sufficient to increase sickness and discon-

39. The behavior of the allied troops—particularly the Ottomans—was reportedly horrific, with widespread rape and looting and with Jews in particular being targeted. Michel-Ange-Bernard Mangourit, *Défense d'Ancone,* 2 vols. (Paris: Charles Pougens, 1802), 1:206–210.

40. Clausewitz means following the river Dora Baltea flowing down from Aosta (in the Alps) to Tortona.

41. Clausewitz, *Napoleon's 1796 Italian Campaign,* 8–15.

42. Jomini, 12:363–366.

tent[42] to such a degree that when Championnet himself fell victim to typhus in January, whole units dissolved, abandoned their posts, and returned to Genoa; others dispersed and tried to return to France; still others tried to do so in column of march *drapeaux déployés* [with flags flying]. Right in the middle of this most extreme crisis, the first beneficial effects of 18 *Brumaire* occurred: Masséna, designated commander of the Army of Italy by Bonaparte, arrived there. His energy and the authority of his reputation succeeded in bringing this desertion and mutiny under control.[43]

We cannot help making a double observation here. To wit, what a degree of courage and steadfastness it took for the French divisional commanders in this situation—particularly General St. Cyr, who took over command after Championnet's death—to persevere in positions that were under such threat. And then again, what could the Austrian commander have achieved with even the slightest blow against a mass so afflicted by dissolution, if the last spark of his energy had not gone out so soon!

101 REFLECTIONS

We said that when Suvorov departed, Melas had 68,000 men to use against some 50,000. This was a moderate superiority in numbers, to which a smaller one in morale might be added. However, if the Austrian general would not or could not continue the offensive decisively, we must put the calculation somewhat differently, in particular because we must count almost all of Tharreau's division in the canton of Wallis among the enemy combat forces against which Melas needed to have parity, so the French can then be assumed to have some 60,000 men, making the Austrian superiority quite insignificant.

As far as these forces' deployment was concerned, the Austrian line ran from Bellinzona through Aosta, Rivoli, Pinerolo, Fossigliano, Mondovi, Acqui, Alessandria, and Tortona to Chiavari in the eastern Riviera. With the exclusion of Klenau's corps, from Bellinzona to Tortona this forms a half-ellipse curving outward, so the enemy surrounded the Austrians in a *very strongly enveloping form.* When the form of a deployment deviates significantly from a straight

43. Clausewitz notes Napoleon's "energy," which is a key part of military genius, along with intellect and strength of character. Read *On War*, book 1, chap. 3, in its entirety, and one might almost mistake it for a short biography of Napoleon himself.

line, it develops certain characteristic advantages and disadvantages that may be regarded as increasing or reducing the combat forces; thus the true ratio of the combat forces cannot be determined until the form of the deployment is taken into consideration, and conversely, a judgment about the value of that form can only be made when the initial ratio of the combat forces is already known.

We cannot get involved here in an exhaustive theory of concentric deployments, enveloping versus enveloped, because that would carry us too far from our topic. We will only introduce its chief principle, whose truth will anyway be obvious to most readers without needing to be proved, namely, that *the enveloping form is the weaker but the one to which greater success belongs, and the enveloped form is the stronger but with smaller result.* Thus the first increases the scale of victories, the second their probability.[44] Accordingly, the enveloping form only suits the very superior side, and the enveloped form the weaker. Since in the present case the French were by no means superior, it seems to follow that if they wanted to let it come to a major, far-reaching, decisive battle, they would have to give up their enveloping position.

But that principle expresses the effects of the enveloping form only in the case of a major battle. For the case in which neither party seeks such a battle, where they have parity with each other and a true war of observation arises, or where one of the two parties wants to be the one to advance and attack but without putting much at stake, then, by a simple deduction from the above principle, a quite different one arises that may be surprising at first

44. This is true because the enveloper's troops will be spread out over a greater distance on the outside of the curve, so to speak. The envelopee, in contrast, is on the inside of the curve and thus has to cover less ground than the enveloper, making it stronger at any one point. The enveloper can gain greater success because of the chance that a successful envelopment will greatly compromise the envelopee's position and greatly reduce its ability to fight. Hence envelopment is risky but potentially decisive. See Clausewitz on critical analysis: "When theory has established that an enveloping attack leads to greater, if less certain, success, we have to ask whether the general who used this envelopment was primarily concerned with the magnitude of success. If so, he chose the right way to go about it. But if he used it in order to make more certain of success, basing his action not so much on individual circumstances as on the general nature of enveloping attacks, as has happened innumerable times, then he misunderstood the nature of the means he chose and committed an error." *On War,* 158; see also book 6, chaps. 2–4 and 24.

glance: namely, that *the two sides' concentric deployments then mainly have the effect of limiting the progress of the war* and thus are favorable to the defender because what primarily matters to him is to maintain the status quo, and this deployment does that for *the defender whether he has the enveloping or the enveloped form of deployment.* The proof is quite simple: whoever has the interior line constantly wins the individual small clashes that arise but cannot give his victory any consequence; whoever has the exterior line could exploit a victory but cannot achieve one. Nobody would deny that the tendency of this general principle can be outweighed by individual circumstances, but nonetheless, any brief overview of the history of war shows how very often it proves itself true in general. This is why it happens that when people see a commander on interior lines wear himself out by winning victory after victory without being able to achieve anything from it, they ascribe this to the strategic disadvantages of his position, without telling themselves that it is this very position that brought him this victory; and again, the unconstrained praise people give to interior lines stems from the inverse of this one-sidedness.[45]

In the course of the chapter we are reviewing, we find this principle broadly and well enough confirmed. Where Melas is enveloped, he obtains a series of minor victories without achieving anything, and if Cuneo had not been right under his nose in a way, in that it was actually *in front of the French line of deployment,* he scarcely would have got so far as to besiege that fortress. Likewise against the Austrian left flank, where it is the Austrians who are enveloped, St. Cyr is continually victorious without being able to achieve anything more.

Let us now pass to a more detailed examination of this case.

The French were not in any way prepared for a major, far-reaching, decisive battle, and basically, neither Championnet nor Moreau intended any such by their plan of attack. If they had actually remained on the strategic defensive,[46] that is, if they had let the Austrian commander surround Cuneo and besiege it, there is no question that their strongly enveloping deployment would have given them major advantages, despite Cuneo lying so near. With a

45. This is closely related to the analysis and explanation in *On War,* book 7, chaps. 7, 13, 15.

46. See *On War,* book 6, chap. 5, "Character of the Strategic Defense."

considerable portion of his force thus pinned in front of Cuneo, Melas would then no longer have been able to appear in superior force at whatever point of his interior line was threatened. The French then could have threatened Alessandria and Tortona from Novi, Turin from Susa, or Milan from Aosta, depending on which one or other of these places they advanced from in significant force; all these cities' only defenses were their citadels, and they were by no means of negligible value to the Austrians. Melas would never have dared to push matters to the extreme for any of these places, and there is no question that his position would therefore have become extraordinarily difficult, just as for the French it would have been a very simple matter to relieve Cuneo from their very enveloping position.

But even though the French were not equipped for a major battle, they still wanted to be the attacker and flattered themselves that they could at least drive the Austrians back beyond the Po and the Ticino. In this case, their enveloping deployment was unfavorable for them, and a straight linear one would have been preferable. But so as not to keep wrestling with fantasies, we must say that here, as is usually the case, the French enveloping deployment did not come about from their own choice nor from any predilection for this principle, but just through circumstances; and neither of the two French commanders, Championnet and Moreau, who, as we have seen, came forward with two opposite plans, could or would abandon it entirely. Moreau did not want to do so at all, but rather wanted to concentrate the main forces in the Apennines to strike an offensive blow. Championnet certainly wanted to give up the enveloping position so far as he could, namely, on his right wing, in that he withdrew this behind the Roia, but the line from Ventimiglia (the mouth of the Roia) to Bellinzona was still very enveloping, and even with the best will in the world, Championnet could not eliminate that; also, the right wing itself would have remained enveloping in a certain way because of the garrisons of Cuneo and Genoa.

We can therefore only talk about the measure of abandoning the Apennines and taking position behind the Roia. If the French had wanted to operate thoroughly offensively, this measure would indisputably have been preferable, since they had 18,000 men under St. Cyr in the mountains who could not participate in an offensive blow in the center; and if they had kept the main body close by, they would have needed only 8,000 men to garrison Genoa and thus would have become 10,000 stronger in the center, while the Austrians certainly would have used no fewer of their forces outside Genoa than they deployed against St. Cyr. We therefore certainly believe that in this respect, General Championnet was right.[47]

Nonetheless, we cannot believe that the intention behind General Championnet's plan had anything in common with that which was the basis of the famous campaign of the following year, and which it seems to border on to some degree. Given the ratio of force and many other constraining circumstances, there could be no question of an operation of such a bold and decisive kind. Also, the St. Bernard Pass was explicitly omitted from the crossing points from which the attack could be carried out, which indicates that the most original element of Bonaparte's plan, a significant corps of combined arms crossing this pass, had not yet been imagined or considered at that time.[48] It would therefore be pointless for us to enter the territory of those combinations offered by the events of the following year; suffice it to say that with the 20,000 or so men he would have had in the Alps, Championnet could never have been aiming to cut off General Melas's retreat.

The question is therefore only whether it was better to advance with the main army concentrated to attack from Mont Cenis or from Col de Tende, since the alpine crossings between them are out of the reckoning; they are not traversable by all arms and therefore could not be used as the main line of retreat except in extreme necessity.

In favor of Mont Cenis, it would have been said that one could then actually withdraw the right wing into the Roia valley, that is, behind the actual main ridge of the Alps that sweeps down to the sea at San Remo. This would not be the case if one debouched from the Col de Tende, because that ridge parallels the road through the Col de Tende to Nice at a distance of 5–10 miles

47. As one can see, the key issue facing the French was a lack of sufficient combat power.

48. **Clausewitz** notes: "However, we cannot guarantee that this omission of the St. Bernard was not deliberate on Jomini's part and designed to avoid detracting from the freshness of Napoleon's famous campaign of 1800." This is an interesting note. Given that Clausewitz was not alive when his book was published, this could have been a note to Clausewitz himself regarding the need to double-check Jomini, or it could have been another dig at Jomini for omitting the fact that Championnet considered this option in order to make Bonaparte's use of it look more original and impressive. Curiously, the French officer Niessel omits this footnote from his French translation: Carl von Clausewitz, *La Campagne de 1799 en Italie et en Suisse*, 2 vols., trans. A. Niessel (Paris: Librairie Militaire, Chapelot et Co., 1906) 2:318.

and so does not adequately protect it. An advance along the road from the Col de Tende therefore presupposes that the Apennines are still held at least as far as the line from the Col de Tende to Loano; now admittedly, this line is markedly shorter than the one in the Roia valley, but it is also less strong and is in that much more danger because it curves back less. On the other hand, in favor of advancing from the Col de Tende is the fact that in this case, Genoa and Cuneo would not need to be so strongly garrisoned; but the main reason is that most of the troops were massed here already, whereas to advance from Mont Cenis they would first have to get there with much effort and loss of time, so the Mont Cenis option virtually became impractical simply because of that. We therefore believe that on this point, preference must be given to General Moreau's plan.

But as we have seen, the French basically did none of these things: they did not vacate Genoa, nor did they move their left wing to the center. They let General St. Cyr fight his own war in the Apennines with 18,000 men, which at most could serve to protect Genoa but had no effect at all for their intended offensive. They had their center and left wing advance disunited in four columns, one upon Mondovi and the others through Cuneo, Pinerolo, and Rivoli, so that they could take part concentrically in one and the same battle. This is the most ticklish of all strategic missions because, before such columns get to strike joint blows on one and the same battlefield, they arrive on such a small circle that the enemy enjoys the advantage of interior lines to the very fullest degree; by the theoretical principle we introduced earlier, the advantage of interior lines increases as the distances decrease until the single battlefield where the culminating point is reached. Thus Championnet made it as easy as possible for General Melas to meet him in superior force everywhere.

We therefore believe that General Championnet actually should have remained on the defensive; that is, waited for Cuneo to be invested and besieged and then exploited his enveloping position to relieve the fortress. If he absolutely insisted on being the attacker, he should have furnished Genoa with the minimum garrison necessary, for which a division of 6,000–8,000 men would have been sufficient; he should have occupied Finale, the St. Bernard,[49] and the Tanaro valley with a second division of similar strength to cover the road to the Col de Tende. If we consider that the Austrians certainly would have left 10,000–12,000 men in front of Genoa, then unless they weakened

49. **Clausewitz** notes: "That is, the one in the Apennines."

their center too much, they could hardly have opposed this division with so much that the Col de Tende road would still have been seriously threatened. Championnet should have concentrated the rest of his forces between the Alps and the Apennines and advanced with them to attack along the road from Cuneo to Turin. To facilitate this attack, that part of his enveloping position that he could not abandon should have been used for a powerful diversion, in that five or six days before his attack, a corps of 10,000–12,000 men should have advanced from the Aosta valley, driven back General Haddick, and marched boldly upon Milan, which certainly would have caused General Melas to send off a considerable detachment. In the valleys leading to Mont Cenis, only a couple of thousand men should have been left to screen the concentration of the rest. With such dispositions, General Championnet's main force could have been 25,000–30,000 strong.

At first glance, it may seem that little would have been gained by vacating the larger part of the Apennines, since 12,000–15,000 men were needed for Genoa and to cover the road, while St. Cyr had only 18,000. But in his positions north and east of Genoa, General St. Cyr did not cover the Col de Tende road in any way; because he did not, Lemoine's and Victor's divisions mostly had to stay in the mountains, and that is what caused the dissipation of forces. Covering it by deploying in the St. Bernard and in the Tanaro valley naturally would not have been any absolute guarantee either, but it did not matter because the road was not an absolutely essential line of retreat for the French either, and in war, the degree to which an objective is threatened can always be measured first according to its value to us and to the enemy.

This all therefore relates to the fact that Championnet chose the wrong direction for his forces; but we may say his lack of energy and decisiveness were much greater failings, and it is these alone that explain the lack of harmony in his maneuvers and in the events.

We basically do not have much more to say about the Austrian commander.

When we consider that Suvorov took 20,000 men with him and the French were believed to still be busy forming their Army of the Alps, which was supposed to come to 34,000 men, it is quite understandable that Melas did not feel ready for a new strategic offensive and decided to remain on the defensive for the time being, waiting for the situation to determine whether or not he could invest and besiege Cuneo; we believe this decision was entirely in accordance with the habitual caution of an old man.

The concentric deployment that circumstances had bestowed on the two armies favored the defense; General Melas's position was made much stronger anyway, in that he had two bases separated by the Po, so he did not need to attach any disproportionate value to either one. Indeed, to our amazement, in the Austrian account we read little about concerns for the rear, for the magazines, for bridges, and so forth, and we see that initially the corps on the wings, namely, Karaczai and Haddick, were no match for their opponents, yet Melas did not display any particular concern about them. However, if he wanted to remain on the defensive, it was naturally necessary to oppose the enemy's enveloping position with appropriate force everywhere, which resulted in him extending his own forces almost as much.

But Melas went further still: he himself enveloped the enemy position in turn, in that he had Klenau advance in the eastern Riviera. Although this spread out his forces even more, the French were not keen to tolerate him camping outside the walls of Genoa, so they deployed a corps against Klenau, and a new concentricity of positions arose. In this, it was the Austrians who were enveloped, which proved advantageous to them as the defenders, insofar as St. Cyr could not get anywhere against Klenau, Karaczai, and Kray, for all his victories over them. Besides, since the Austrians constantly had their eye on the mood of the inhabitants of Genoa and therefore regarded it as important to stay near the fortress, General Klenau's deployment in the Riviera was all the more justified.

The general outlines of the Austrian commander's actions up until the battle of Genola can therefore hardly be disapproved of if we consider them from the standpoint of common prudence, in which standpoint Melas was certainly further confirmed by events in Switzerland. Of course, somewhat more boldness and energy in the individual episodes would have given more positive results; on the other hand, he did concentrate his forces into a larger main body than we might expect in such cases.

But after Melas won his victory at Genola with the aid of his defense, he gained such moral and physical preponderance that we can only call what he did next petty compared with what he could have done, about which we have already vented at length in the course of the account.

A second question is, then: what would the result have been if Melas had continued his strategic offensive after taking Cuneo?

When we consider the state the French army was in at this time, we really cannot doubt that continuing his offensive would have brought General Melas possession of the Riviera without further crisis[50] and would have forced the French to retreat partly to Genoa and partly behind the Var; we also must not overlook the fact that wonderfully trophy-laden victories could have occurred in individual episodes during it. The Austrians knew the state of the French army, so we should not have expected General Melas to sit back, complacent about what he had done, or to ease his conscience as a commander with the glib nonsense that "enough had been done for this campaign, and it was time to give the troops a rest so that they could begin the next campaign in good shape." We need not spend many words to convince the reader that such an assertion means nothing, since it is not a question of any pointless sacrifice of combat forces but rather one of that sacrifice obtaining certain advantages that would naturally likewise be advantageous for the following campaign, and what mattered was therefore asking whether the results were worth the new effort.

Not every continuation of an offensive leads to a situation that makes the attacker stronger; the opposite is much more in the order of things, and the question is always whether the attacker still has enough surplus of forces to maintain himself in this new situation and, if this is doubtful, whether a counterblow must be feared that will cost him part of what he has gained earlier,[51] since such a counterblow is also in the order of things. In respect of these questions, we need only consider what events were likely if Melas did continue his offensive.

Naturally, the objective of this continued offensive could only be the complete conquest of the state of Genoa, and not in any way an invasion of French territory. It goes without saying that the conquest of this state, including its capital city, would give the Austrians a situation for the following

50. This ties in with Clausewitz's concept of the role of pursuit and continued pressure. See *On War*, book 4, chap. 12, "Strategic Means of Exploiting Victory." Continuing pressure, we should remind ourselves, is important for preventing the enemy from regrouping and regaining combat power. Given the poor state of French morale, which was known to Melas, it is striking that he did not maintain contact with the French army, which was in a far worse state than his own forces. As such, he lost an opportunity, again, to inflict grave or even decisive damage on the French.

51. This ties in with Clausewitz's idea about the diminishing force of the attack and the culminating point. There is a moment, whether it is physical or mental or a combination of the two, where the advancing side runs out of sufficient combat power to achieve its aim. As such, it needs to make sure it stops before then or has sufficient strength to achieve its aim before the opponent is able to contest this effectively. See *On War*, book 7, chaps. 1–7, especially 527–528.

campaign that was not weaker but very much stronger than their present one; it is therefore only a question of which circumstances would occur before this situation was reached and whether the Austrians' forces were sufficient to survive the crisis that must occur if the French returned to the offensive with reinforcements before the fall of Genoa.

Let us imagine that the French have now been obliged to vacate Genoese territory and retreat behind the Var, but that they have furnished Genoa with a strong garrison and the hastily fortified places of Gavi, Savona, and Finale with the necessary means of defense (which is unlikely). If the Austrians now left 30,000 men in the Riviera, of which 10,000 were deployed facing the Var or remained behind the Paglione so as not to have to invest Nice, 5,000 outside Finale, 5,000 outside Savona, and 10,000 outside Genoa; and if they left 5,000 men outside Gavi besides, and as many again went off to observe Mont Cenis and the rest of the alpine passes, then, since 3,000–4,000 men had joined the main army from Fröhlich and replaced the losses suffered since the battle of Genola, out of the total strength of 68,000 men, that still would have left 28,000 for the main army, which Melas could have encamped as a reserve on the plain between Turin and Cuneo.

If the French really had held on to Gavi, Savona, and Finale, these fortresses would have resisted for a few weeks at most. Genoa could no longer be besieged in winter; we do not wish to count too much on an uprising by its inhabitants, even though that was certainly not entirely unlikely, but in any case, it could be anticipated that if this fortress remained blockaded through the winter, in the course of that and before the beginning of the following campaign, it would have to surrender for lack of provisions.

Thus, if the French really did advance to relieve the small fortresses before any of them fell, even reinforced by 10,000–12,000 men sent by Masséna to Italy from Switzerland when the campaign there ended, it still seems to us that General Melas would have been in a position to meet this crisis at an advantage. From the 38,000 men the French still had after the fall of Cuneo, if we deduct 10,000 for the garrison of Genoa, 5,000 for the other fortresses, and just 5,000 for losses suffered either from enemy action or from sickness and desertion, that would leave 18,000 men; thus, even if the reinforcements from Switzerland and the interior actually came to 20,000 men, Masséna[52] still

52. Masséna left for Paris at the end of November after the coup. If Clausewitz was thinking of this happening slightly later in the year, this should be Championnet.

would have had no more than about 40,000 men to lead to the relief of the fortresses. Now let us ask, with some 60,000 men in the position given above, would not Melas find himself in a very advantageous situation? If the 10,000 men deployed on the Var retreated when a significant enemy force approached the Col de Tende, Melas would become 38,000 strong; if the force investing Gavi was drawn on as well and only a minimum number were left there, there would be 20,000 in the Riviera. Thus Genoa would be covered, and the main army would be of such strength that it could attack the necessarily divided enemy in superior force everywhere.

Thus, we see that even in the worst case, continuing his offensive would not have got General Melas into any situation that was beyond his means.

It needs no great proof to show that if he had made himself master of Genoa in this way, the 10,000 or indeed 20,000 men by which this might have weakened his army would have been richly repaid by the advantages of his new situation in the spring, since in spring 1800 the corps investing Genoa alone came to 23,000 men.

102 CONCLUSION

In order to extract those results that emerge from the characteristics of these two campaigns as a whole, before anything else, it is necessary that we review their major outlines once more.

The campaign in Italy is basically very simple. It begins with a battle in which the French attack the Austrians on the Adige before the latter have concentrated, yet they only half win it. Then two battles (Magnano and Cossano) ensue, won by the more numerous allied attackers, which leads the two sides to the Tanaro; then another three battles (Trebbia, Novi, and Genola) occur in which the French are attacking to regain what they have lost and to rescue their besieged fortresses. Incidentally, all these events develop along one simple, direct line between Verona and Cuneo; only the situation of Macdonald's army is somewhat more complex. Victory rests throughout with the side that is generally markedly superior in numbers, so cause and effect are in their natural relationship.

With regard to Switzerland, the relationship to the Italian campaign is fairly simple, in that Italy received reinforcements from Switzerland twice before the final crisis was overcome, namely, 16,000 men under Bellegarde and 12,000 under Haddick.[53] Once the crisis had been survived, 20,000 were handed back again under Suvorov.

The campaign in Switzerland is much more complicated, by contrast, because the forces are much more divided, and fortunes alternated; it is therefore also harder to give a clear general picture. Let us attempt to simplify this with an overview.

The Austrians have 70,000 men in the Tyrol, Vorarlberg, and Graubündten and 90,000 resembling a grand echelon in quarters further back behind the Lech. The French first push their left wing forward against this rearward echelon but then halt, giving the archduke time to arrive, as it were. About a week later, the French wipe out General Auffenberg's force in Graubündten; another week later, they drive the Austrians out of the Engadin; another week later again, they annihilate General Laudon's force at Taufers. With these three blows in succession working across from the center to the right wing, within a month, they have conquered Graubündten and weakened the Austrians by some 20,000 men. All these victories are achieved by a very small force of about 20,000 men against one of 70,000 because the latter remains on local defense.[54] But after they have been achieved, the Austrian masses concentrate in the Inn and Adige valleys, that small force cannot follow up its victory any further, and things come to a standstill on the southern wing. The French now await the outcome on their left wing.

Here, the Austrians' grand echelon advances, and the issue is resolved at the battle of Stockach at exactly the same time as the last battle is fought on the southern wing, but with the opposite result. The battle of Stockach and the action at Taufers share the same birthday. But this victory at Stockach by one *Schwerpunkt* against the other,[55] which should have been decisive for the whole

53. **Clausewitz** notes: "If that is how we want to regard Haddick's departure from the St. Gotthard and out of Wallis to the foot of the Italian Alps, that took place at the end of June."

54. In wargaming this campaign multiple times at the Naval War College, students have found that the French can typically gain a temporary advantage until the Austrians get their forces organized and their plan sorted out. Obviously, this is anecdotal, but it does indicate that Clausewitz's point might be correct.

55. Delivering a solid blow to a center of gravity should be sufficient to fully beat the enemy and win a campaign. This should not be thought of as simply the battle itself but the subsequent pursuit as well. Thus, the delivery of a blow to the center of gravity needs to be sustained with continuous pressure on the same point until the

campaign, is an empty name without substance. The archduke does not follow it up, so through sheer lethargy on the part of the Austrians, events in the northern half of the theater of operations grind to a halt, just as they do in the southern half through the weakness of the French.[56]

After this first exchange of blows, rather than pursuing their victory from Stockach to the Rhine and then garnering further fruits from it in Switzerland, the Austrians content themselves with first putting things right where they have gone off track, and in the reverse order from how they pushed forward—that is, from their left wing to the center. Bellegarde conquers first the Münster valley (early April), then the Engadin (late April). Their simultaneous attempt on the St. Luciensteig fails for lack of concentration of force,[57] and the French gain time to suppress the insurrection. The Austrians now pause for another fourteen days, and Lecourbe has time to descend the Italian slope of the Alps, beat Prince Rohan, and spread alarm through the Austrian army in Italy. While he is doing this in mid-May, Hotze and Bellegarde take a third step and finally retake Graubündten, whereupon Bellegarde marches to Italy and Hotze turns toward the Rhine. The archduke has let two months lie fallow; on 21 May, after Graubündten is taken, he crosses the Rhine and drives Masséna back behind the Limmat in the battle of Zurich, thanks to his larger force. While this is happening, Lecourbe has returned through the St. Gotthard and on 28 May falls on Gavasini in the Muota valley, while Haddick, detached by Bellegarde, has driven Loison back through the St. Gotthard on the very same day. Lecourbe has then quickly turned about and half annihilated Haddick's vanguard under General St. Julien in the Reuss valley on 31 May and 1 June. Now, after the so-called victory at Zurich and this scuffle at the St. Gotthard, things stagnate for a long time, which is a consequence of the parity of

---

enemy's defeat. As such, this could be considered an operational goal with strategic consequences. See also volume 1, chapter 2, note 108, for a discussion of the term *Schwerpunkt*.

56. Again, this ties the concept of continuation to that of the center of gravity (*Schwerpunkt*). Logically, repeated heavy blows—that is, continuous pressure—against the enemy's center of gravity should be decisive, assuming one buys Clausewitz's logic about the center of gravity in the first place.

57. The point about concentration of force is important because, if one is to be successful, it is better to identify a clear strategic target, whatever that happens to be, and then focus one's blows against it. Frittering away strength against something that might not matter is simply wasted effort and distracts from the main effort.

forces. General Haddick, shunted hither and thither for three weeks by order and counterorder, finally settles down quietly at the foot of the Italian Alps at the end of June, holding the St. Gotthard and Simplon Passes. Lecourbe, for his part, retreats to the German foot of the high Alps, deploying between Lake Lucerne and Lake Zurich.

Ten weeks of complete peace go by in these opposing positions. The French are reinforced somewhat, but since they have in mind the formation of a new Army of the Rhine at the same time, and the moment of the allied landing in Holland is approaching,[58] the French reinforcements do not really become significant. On the other hand, 30,000 Russians are approaching. Finally, in mid-August, the desire to act stirs again in the French; they want to do something before the Russians' arrival but find the Austrian main army too strong in proportion to them, so Masséna contents himself with driving the Austrian left wing out of the Rhone and Reuss valleys and forcing it to retreat across the Linth. This gives the French possession of the St. Gotthard again, where they remain for six weeks until Suvorov arrives.

The Russians under Korsakov join the Austrians at the end of August; also at the end of August, embarrassed by his preponderance, Archduke Charles makes a badly planned and therefore vain attempt to cross the Aare and an even weaker one with his left wing to regain its former positions, and then moves to the Rhine to render his 30,000 men useless for five weeks with one pointless storming and two futile marches.

This leaves a great interregnum in Switzerland for these five weeks. Suvorov has lingered in Italy for another fourteen days to await the fall of Tortona, so it happens that he leaves Asti twelve days after Archduke Charles departs from Zurich; another fourteen days pass before he manages to attack the St. Gotthard, and now he, the new commander of the army in Switzerland, finds himself still on the extreme left wing of this army, separated from three-quarters of it by the enemy and an impassable alpine mountain range, and embroiled in and committed to a totally misguided endeavor in completely the wrong direction. That was more than sufficient to allow General Masséna to prepare and win the second battle of Zurich. At the same time as this major decision occurs, Suvorov takes the St. Gotthard in preparation for his own decisive battle, which is to be born among a thousand self-inflicted difficulties;

58. Clausewitz is referring to the disastrous allied campaign in Holland in 1799. See Macksey, *Statesmen at War,* for a good overview of this campaign.

even without being forestalled by the French victory, it could hardly have delivered a good result, and now it brings the Russian commander and his army into a series of dangerous situations that, combined with the losses of combat forces and military honor[59] suffered at Zurich, deliver the final blow to the alliance between Austria and Russia.

The immediate task of a conclusion such as we present here is always to explain those phenomena in which cause and effect are not in their natural relationship. There are two of those here. The allies are numerically very superior, so we must regard it as the natural outcome that they should be the victors; we must therefore examine why they were not ultimately victorious overall. The campaign is generally a decisively successful one, since the positive results entirely favor the allies, yet the alliance breaks up; we must therefore pay attention to what caused that.

Besides these two objects of our consideration, another three points in particular seem to us worth closer consideration.

The first is the strategic value of the landing in Holland.

The second, the value the French attached to having an Army of the Rhine and a separate Army of the Alps.

Finally, the third is the conclusion that can be drawn from the mountain warfare in Switzerland.

As far as the allies' failure is concerned, it is to be found in Switzerland at both the start and the end of the campaign. Naturally, we will discuss the earlier phenomenon first.

Whereas in Italy a superiority of three to two leads to the conquest of a large stretch of territory and numerous fortresses, in Germany (that is, in Switzerland, in the Tyrol, and on the Rhine) a two-to-one superiority can

59. The idea of honor relates to Clausewitz's trinity, in that the emotional aspect—in this case, honor—plays a role in decision making where pure reason might be better. For example, if the Russian commander felt that the Russian army's honor needed to be avenged for some reason, he might choose a course of action with that goal in mind rather than tying his actions to the political goals of the campaign. Also, given that it is an abstract concept, how does one regain honor in military circumstances? Does a futile blow that is a catastrophic failure but extremely brave work for this purpose? If so, what does that mean for the overarching political goals of the conflict? We leave the reader with these thoughts, as it is important to think through what Clausewitz is getting at, particularly in *On War*, book 1, chaps. 1 and 2.

achieve nothing more than reaching the banks of the Linth and the Limmat after a series of battles, some successful, others unsuccessful.

The main causes of this seem to us to be the following:

1. The different characters of the allied commanders in chief, Suvorov, and the archduke.
2. The divided command in Germany.
3. The Tyrol army's defensive mission.
4. The mountainous terrain.

We have nothing to say about the different value of the French commanders in the two theaters of operations—Schérer and Moreau in the one, and Jourdan and Masséna in the other—because the value of this difference does not seem to us to be sufficiently demonstrated.

The first of these causes cannot be an object of criticism, since one cannot make a commander be the way one wants him. There is rarely much choice, and after his campaign of 1796, the archduke must definitely be regarded as the best of the Austrian generals.[60]

But for the theoretical explanation, in this example it remains extremely important to recognize the value of the commander in chief's willpower.[61]

The other three causes lie in objective conditions that could have been either created differently or managed differently.

In our earlier reflections we have already highlighted how inappropriate it was to divide command and to shackle 50,000 men to the defense of Tyrolese soil, and we do not intend to spend many more words on this. In letting our gaze fall on it here, we only wish to show the role these things play in the whole course of the campaign, and in this way, we can trace its failure to mistakes made by the government. Had the Austrians kept their eyes solely *on striking the Schwerpunkt of the enemy's combat forces with their own* and then conquering Italy in Italy and Switzerland in Germany, they could have left the Tyrol completely unoccupied. If the Tyrol were a completely flat area, perhaps

60. In this case, Clausewitz is damning the archduke with faint praise. The archduke does well in 1796, but the Austrians lose that war, and the other Austrian generals do poorly.

61. Recall the need for military genius in *On War*, book 1, chap. 3, and for boldness and perseverance in book 3, chaps. 6 and 7, respectively.

it would indeed have been left unoccupied, since the confused notion of the value of mountains [as somehow dominant high ground] was certainly the main reason for this garrisoning of the Tyrol.[62]

As far as the fourth cause is concerned, it operated in two ways to neutralize the Austrians' numerical superiority.

First, they did not think they could advance in the flat part of Switzerland without capturing just as much of the mountainous region that separates it from Italy. This implied that before anything else, they had to retake the lost territory in Graubündten and, if possible, also gain control of the St. Gotthard.

Second, it seemed to them that the Jura mountains barred any possible entry into France, and the conquest of Switzerland was like a magnet that was too weak to attract them.

Both these notions stem from the false importance attached to mountains in general. Since we do not especially wish to go on any more about the strategic value of mountains here, as we want to do this in detail later, we will not enter into any further discussion just now. But we may take it as a given that the delaying power of the mountains was quite excessive, in that it embroiled the allies in a difficult style of warfare that did not suit them, dispersed their forces in a way unsuitable for an offensive, and crippled their progress by the mere prospect of the Jura passes ahead.

But of those four causes, next to the first, the other three are of such little importance by comparison that actually these three only exist because of it. However unlikely it was that Bellegarde could have been put under the archduke's command, however much value the Aulic Council attached to the Tyrol, and however deeply the archduke may have doffed his hat to the Alps and the Jura, if he had only been a man of great willpower,[63] he would have had the means to *drag* Bellegarde along with him not by formal authority but by example and success, the ability to use the passion of victory to tear free from the wretched paste with which a pedantic Aulic Council wanted to glue the Army of the Tyrol to that territory like a map to a drawing board, and finally, the confidence gained from a thumping victory that would have made him less worried about the Alps and the Jura.

Let us turn now to the second period of fruitless numerical superiority.

Here, besides the lack of spirit of enterprise among the Austrian

62. Clausewitz examines the role of mountains in warfare below.

63. Again, see *On War*, book 1, chap. 3, and book 3, chaps. 6 and 7.

commanders, there are two things that may be regarded as the major causes: namely, the change of roles and the direction of Suvorov's march.

The first gave the archduke an excuse not to exploit his great superiority of force in Switzerland but to depart for the Rhine. Command of the main force in Switzerland landed on a man who would not have been chosen by either government, namely, General Korsakov. This caused the colossal defeat at Zurich. This change of roles also caused Suvorov to try to direct the combat forces in Switzerland from Asti; and because he could not see directly what was going on, he remained in Piedmont fourteen days longer than was advisable and made dispositions for 26 September so that, when the Austrian combat forces were attacked by the French on the 25th, they were spread out, and half of them under Jellachich, Linken, and Auffenberg were not available to help Hotze.

As far as the second cause of the misadventures in Switzerland is concerned—the misguided direction of Suvorov's march—we have already said that we attach no great value to the idea that perchance marching via the Splügen instead would have prevented the battle of Zurich; but we maintain that even after the battle of Zurich, the allies' situation would have been much less unfavorable if Suvorov had joined the Austrians in the Rhine valley with his force intact. It is very likely that he would have used the 35,000 men under his control for a new offensive against Masséna, in which the chance of success would have been at least as much for him as against him. His march through the St. Gotthard had weakened him by approximately 8,000 men, but much worse was that for fourteen long days, his feelings of displeasure and disgust toward the Austrians grew hour by hour,[64] so far as their honesty and goodwill were concerned, as much as their capability and competence. Amidst the constantly recurring awkward situations, dangers, and exertions of the most incredible kind that he met on his way, how could his inner circle not have continually poured out the most bitter criticism of the foolish plan for his march!

Never has an army's victory been made easier by its opponent's strategic errors than it was here for the French, and if Masséna did not obtain quite such a glorious victory against Suvorov as he had against Korsakov, that is due mainly to there being less clarity in its concept.

If we look for the first seeds of the split in the alliance, these were the

64. As has been documented earlier. For example, see chapter 7, note 58, and chapter 8, notes 25 and 27.

Austrians' selfish political ambitions. Their first direct effect was that the victory in Italy did not attain its full impact; that was naturally bound to affect the conduct of the war, since victory fuels the emotions, most of all those of the commander in chief.[65] Thus the strength of the alliance weakened itself already in Italy. The second effect of the particular political aims of the Austrians and the English was the change of roles.[66] This led to the dissipation of forces on the Rhine; mistakes through ineptitude and stupidity added to this, so it was not much different from putting the cart before the horse. Of course, this has happened a thousand times, since ministers and advisers in governments never have clearly before their eyes the effect their decisions have on the theater of operations. Yet means and ends are never in such constant *interaction* as in the conduct of war; however correctly political ends may provide an initial direction, the means—*combat*—can never be regarded merely as a dead instrument; from combat itself, from its rich, vital processes, a thousand motives sprout forth that can become more important and more imperative than the original political ones ever were. War is like a ship struggling against wind and waves; one must be on it to be able to steer it, to gain advantage from the elements, and to complete the voyage however it can be done. If we consider that most well-conducted wars were conducted according to the *subjective convictions* of the commanders, and to how small an extent clear notions of the higher conduct of war were present until now, even though these are thoroughly necessary if some *state authority* apart from the commander and outside the theater of operations wants to exert a regular influence on the conduct of the war, because it can only ever consider things objectively—if we consider this, we cannot be surprised when we see the Austrian government's measures constantly verging rashly on the edge of ruin here.[67]

Two things always cause the early breakup of alliances: *secret selfish aims* and *weaknesses in the conduct of the war*. The Austrians did not lack for either of these.

65. Clausewitz is again referring to the emotional portion of his trinity and its potential effect on the conduct of operations.

66. The respective war aims were not all clearly aligned.

67. This paragraph relates closely to *On War*, book 1, chap. 1, "What Is War," and chap. 2, "Purpose and Means." The constant interaction of means and ends is of particular note, along with their relationship to the political object.

The Landing in Holland

The landing in Holland is not to be condemned but should not be seen just in the sense of a diversion. First, an operation in Holland was natural because it enabled the English to bring their combat forces into play in the most direct and effective way. Of course, this allowed it to act as a diversion as well, but the English forces alone would have been sufficient to attract enemy forces there, and the Russians could have been more usefully employed in Switzerland or Italy.[68] A second aim of this operation was indisputably to bring the forces of the Orange party in Holland into action, which naturally should have entirely ruled out a diversionary operation, since it would be despicable to rouse a party up with the intention of then leaving it in the lurch. Also, as a mere diversion, the landing in Holland would have had a perverse effect, since the Orange party naturally could not have shown its true colors and cooperated until later on, when a large part of the country had already been conquered; on the other hand, right from the beginning, a certain amount of enemy forces would have been made effective that otherwise would have been neutralized, namely, the Batavian divisions and those the French had in Belgium that could not be withdrawn from there in any case.

The operation against Holland should therefore be considered a proper attack on the French Republic at that point. If it had such a thoroughly trivial result, that was obviously due to its poor execution.

The idea that it was necessary to support this offensive by a military operation on the Middle Rhine with major forces is an empty conceit, or rather, once again, a confused notion of the act and effects of a diversion. Anyone who has spent much time on these matters will have noticed that *diversions* are the diplomat's hobbyhorse.

The Formation of the Army of the Alps and the Army of the Rhine

In forming the Army of the Rhine, the French indisputably had the intention of striking the Austrians at a very *sensitive* point, namely, on the Danube, so

68. See *On War*, book 7, chap. 20, "Diversions." The key is to draw greater enemy forces away from the main fight than one uses in the diversion; otherwise, the effort is largely useless and only serves to undermine the main effort.

as to produce a *disproportionately* large effect. An important additional consideration was that they hoped that in fertile Swabia, which had had time to recover somewhat since 1796, it would be easy to feed their troops, whereas the army in Switzerland was contending with extreme privation. Finally, by advancing into Swabia, they might perhaps be able to garrison the Rhine fortresses with 10,000 fewer men and therefore bring these into action. If they were not bothered about the involvement of the Württemberger and Franconian troops that this would provoke, we can declare ourselves in agreement with their intention in itself. But in considering such matters, people mostly proceed too superficially and do not attach appropriate importance to two things. The formation of a new army always requires a significant amount of time; since it is never put together from entirely newly formed combat forces, many *faux-frais* [incidental expenses] arise, and a mass of troops is neutralized that could have come into action sooner in the theaters of operations that were already active. The second consideration is that any division of combat forces, and especially any proliferation of formations of the first rank, is an evil to which one should subject oneself only so far as important objectives demand it. If we consider how small is the number of men to whom a government can confidently entrust command of an independent army, we cannot doubt the importance of this principle. Admittedly, we could say that we are more likely to find an outstanding talent from among *three* army commanders than *two,* but it is not proper that such a lottery should take place here. But the *much greater disadvantage of division* consists in the loss of unity of will and of operation.

It is uncertain whether these considerations should not indeed have deterred the French government from forming a new Army of the Rhine. It is not uncommon for armies to be formed to satisfy personal considerations, and we cannot know whether perhaps the main cause of this idea might not have been to remove Moreau from the main theater of operations and yet not take him out of action entirely.[69]

69. Clausewitz may be mentioning this because of the French Directory's unstable political situation and the fact that many of the commanders seem to have had their own political support within the French government. As such, it might behoove the government to give someone a command without wanting him to do anything important. It is worth comparing this with President Lincoln's use of political appointees during the US Civil War, where some pretty poor-performing commanders

On the other hand, the formation of an independent Army of the Alps emerged from a truly fundamental mistake of strategic appreciation. The reconquest of Italy and the defense of the French frontier always seemed to the French Directory to be two functions at least as different and separate as the services of church and army are for the state; therefore, in this case as in that one, two completely independent arms of the state had to be assigned to those functions. We have already experienced this stupidity in the 1796 campaign,[70] when neither Bonaparte's merit nor his success nor his presumption could entirely get rid of it. It did not occur to the famous *bureau topographique* that Italy cannot be conquered without also defending the French frontier precisely by doing so, and that if that conquest fails, there is always still time to defend the frontier. This French Army of the Alps is a worthy counterpart to the Austrians' army in the Tyrol.

Mountain Warfare

We now come to consideration of the general conclusions yielded by mountain warfare as it was conducted in Switzerland in this campaign.[71]

Before the start of the campaign, the Austrians moved into Graubündten and thereby came to occupy the Engadin and the Rhine valleys; the remaining part of the mountains, including the St. Gotthard, was held by the French as a result of their earlier occupation of the country. That is a quite natural state of affairs of a simple political nature, where no military reasons are to be asserted.

The campaign begins; the Austrians make the mistake of wanting to stay in their advanced position; the consequence is that they are driven out of it with heavy losses.

Now the French get into an enveloping and very extended position in the mountains as far as Remüs and Taufers, which will be retaken by the Austrians four weeks later, up to and including the valley of the Rhine. For now, the Austrians go only partway into the Rhine valley and leave the

---

were either given commands or allowed to stay in them longer than reasonable largely because of their political importance. George McClellan was a prime example.

70. Clausewitz covered this in *Napoleon's 1796 Italian Campaign*.

71. Clausewitz spends several chapters of *On War* discussing the role of mountains in warfare. See, in particular, book 6, chaps. 15–17, and book 7, chap. 11.

French in possession of the rest for the time being. But after another four weeks, Haddick takes the St. Gotthard from them, whereupon the French also abandon the Reuss valley and deploy between the lakes, thus out of the high mountains. They stay like that for ten weeks, then retake these areas from the Austrians as far as the Linth and Rhine valleys, including the St. Gotthard; now the Austrians stay in the Rhine valley for another six weeks until Suvorov arrives and takes the St. Gotthard for the second time.

In these various episodes, the influence the mountainous region has on the commanders' motives relates to the value:

1. That the Austrians attach to actually defending Graubündten;
2. That the French attach to high ground, in having their offensive penetrate as far as the Engadin and Münster valleys;
3. That the Austrians attach to the reconquest of Graubündten, in that they choose to begin their offensive with that;
4. That Masséna attaches to the mountains, in that, instead of summoning Lecourbe and Dessolles to join him, he has them linger there and indeed descend to the Italian side;
5. That the Austrians attach to the St. Gotthard, in that they have Haddick attack it at the end of May and then adopt an extended position in the mountains;
6. That the French attach to high ground, in that they again begin their second offensive (in August) by conquering the mountains.

While some other motives also contributed to these various episodes of mountain warfare arising—for example, in the first and third, the Austrians' political considerations concerning the inhabitants of Graubündten, and in the last, the greater likelihood of success that an attack in the mountains promised to the French—yet we must not underestimate the degree to which this direction of combat forces was mainly caused by respect for the mountains, that is, concern about getting into a disadvantageous position if they were not held.

Now if this view of the importance of the mountains in the present cases is unfounded; if it rests on an unclear picture of the conditions that disappears as soon as each individual point is examined precisely; if we can demonstrate that, under the prevailing conditions, the Alps could not exert any such dominance over the Swiss plain and that possession of the mountains was pointless for a decisive attack on the plain because victory could be obtained down there, and that, as for the defense, the archduke would have done better to stand behind Lake Walenstadt and Lecourbe between Lucerne and Rapperswil or, in another case, between Brunnen and Weesen—if all this is the case, then greatly extending a deployment so as to hold the mountains is a mistake, because any division and extension of combat forces must have a sufficient reason, and in the event this is lacking, it appears to be a dispersal of forces and therefore an error.

To imagine that on this occasion the errors were canceled out because both sides extended themselves to the same degree is to forget that one of the two must begin this erroneous direction of forces, and then the other can and should exploit this error by not committing it himself. Pointless extension therefore always remains an error, whether one begins it oneself and puts oneself in a position to be punished for it or follows one's opponent in doing so and deprives oneself of the means to punish him for it.

We do not need to adduce proof that in the 1799 campaign the Alps really could not exert any such dominance over the lower ground; as far as the Austrians were concerned, the archduke himself has admitted it,[72] and the advantage of a deployment behind the line of Lake Walenstadt is indeed too obvious to be doubted. As for the French, they managed without the mountains for ten long weeks without any disadvantage at all emerging from it. However, so as to avoid any misunderstanding, let us try to give this topic the necessary clarity and certainty by the following observations.

The dominance of mountainous terrain over lower ground can only ever show itself to be effective where the mountains run fairly close to the enemy army's line of communications for a stretch of some considerable distance.

This would be the case in Switzerland if a French army was deployed on both sides of Lake Constance and had its base in the *pays de Vaud* while the Austrians had been left in possession of the whole of the Alps, or conversely, if an Austrian army wanted to advance up to between Lake Geneva and Lake Neuchâtel with its base on Lake Constance while the French held all of the Alps. But the French main army was deployed behind the Limmat, and its base was the Jura. Even if its main line of communications was via Bern to Besançon, that was certainly not its only one. Thus, if they wanted their right wing to take position between Lucerne and Zurich for a while, they had only

72. This is covered extensively in Karl, 1:1–35.

to keep a strong brigade in Bern itself—which was there anyway to maintain internal security—so as to have nothing to worry about from the mountains.

The Austrians' position behind the Limmat would in any case have been more natural if they had kept their left wing in line with Lake Walenstadt. *Bending it forward* through the Linth and Rhine valleys as far as Disentis or, as later, into the Reuss valley as far as the St. Gotthard was not done for their own security but rather was meant to threaten the enemy's—an aim it did not achieve, since it did not cause Masséna to reinforce his right wing.[73]

To those who might say that the French were initially deployed level with Lake Constance and indeed wanted to advance even further, and that Archduke Charles had no intention of halting right on the Limmat either, we reply that a region's dominance of the strategic flank always takes some time to take effect, and if he who is thus dominated meanwhile achieves great successes to his front, there are very few circumstances in which his opponent will still be allowed to hold such a mountain region. The circumstances here were not of that kind at all. If the French had advanced triumphantly into Swabia, the Austrians truly would not have had any thought of staying in Graubündten, and it would have been just as impossible for the French to hold on to the Alps if their Swiss army was driven across the Jura and their Italian one retreated behind the Ticino. In any case, there would always be time to conquer the Alps after fighting a successful battle on the plain, and it was always a mistake to want to start with their conquest.

Yet again, one might perhaps ask, what kind of advantage arose for the two commanders if they extended themselves less? For example, for Masséna, if he were content with a position between Lucerne and Zurich and left the whole of the mountains and even the Rhine valley either to the Austrians or to its own devices, whereby he would obviously have much less territory under his control and would therefore also be poorer in terms of access to resources?

We have already described the advantages of a more restricted deployment above. For Masséna, they comprised in particular: first, being able to exploit it if the archduke lowered his guard on the Limmat or the Aare, because he could concentrate his whole force with two days' march; and second, not being in constant danger of suffering defeat by a decisive attack by the archduke and being ejected from Switzerland. If one replies to this that Masséna would not

73. Lengthening the line also served to spread out their troops over a greater area, thus reducing their combat power at any given point.

and could not exploit the first advantage because he was too weak, and the second ceased to apply because he had nothing of the kind to fear from an opponent like the archduke,[74] this question has to be answered in a different context. If the holding and retaking of mountain regions were done with that in mind, this would mean that General Masséna did not want to deprive himself of the pleasure of holding a larger area because he wanted to extract that advantage from his opponent's weakness. We would not be able to make any objection to such reasoning, but we just do not think it was actually so. First, Masséna was not yet so well acquainted with the archduke as to be sure of his business, and second, the great extent of his line at various times could not have been regarded by him and his historian as a necessary evil and an obligation that weighed heavily on him. The same reasoning applies to the Austrian commander.

We therefore believe that the advantages both commanders denied themselves and the disadvantages they both exposed themselves to, in that each mimicked the other's mistake instead of exploiting it, simply arose from an erroneous view, and we would therefore be wrong to regard the 1799 campaign as evidence that any war in Switzerland must involve mountain warfare to the *n*th degree.[75] If one wants to regard the war conducted in the Alps as simply a contest of wit and skill—that is, not dictated by an overarching objective but making use of subsidiary forces while the main forces must be passive and attempting to outdo one's opponent in courage and skill on this challenging battlefield—we have nothing against that. But of course, then we must say that only the French revealed themselves as suitably capable of that, and this easily could have been foreseen because, in mountain warfare, the enthusiasm and warlike spirit of the individual comes much more into the reckoning, from the general down to the drummer boy, and the Austrian commander could well tell himself that the circumstances and the course of the war hitherto had given the French a great superiority in that respect. It seems to us very likely indeed that this view, this sense of their superiority, contributed to the French getting so deeply involved in mountain warfare. Nonetheless, it should not be regarded as the main cause; rather, that should always be attributed to their er-

74. Who was consistently excessively cautious and often slow in his movements.

75. What Clausewitz is sniping at here is the idea that simply because a campaign is waged in Switzerland mountain warfare must predominate. This is another scientific analogy and appears to relate to Euler's work on exponentials.

roneous view of the importance of mountains. Besides, it goes without saying that such a point of view of mountain warfare is permissible only when nothing could or should have been going on with the main army, and it therefore does not excuse the extended French advance at the start of the campaign.

That is how we see the general strategic relationship between this mountain war and the campaign. It was a parasitic plant that drew strength away from the original stem.[76] Having established this, we can now investigate further the relationship between the two protagonists in this mountain war. This is now so decisively in favor of the French that, as a result of their campaign, they acquired a unique grandeur that could be understood as compensating for what they lost at the key point through overextension.[77]

At first glance, the outcome of the mountain war seems to sway this way and that in a kind of equilibrium, since the Austrians, initially driven back into the Tyrol and Vorarlberg, then advance as far as the Reuss valley and are then finally repulsed behind the Linth and the Rhine. But to evaluate the great difference between the two sides in terms of favorable results, we need only take a quick look through the individual episodes. The French successes were Masséna's annihilation of Auffenberg's corps in the Rhine valley on 6 and 7 March; Lecourbe's defeat of General Laudon, with heavy losses in prisoners, in the Engadin from 11 to 14 March; Dessolles's destruction of Laudon's corps at Taufers on 25 March; General St. Julien being half wiped out by Ménard at the St. Luciensteig on 1 May; the defeat of Prince Rohan at Monte Cenere on 13 May; Lecourbe's defeat of Colonel Gavassini in the Muota valley on 28 June; the semidestruction of St. Julien at Am-Steg and the Devil's Bridge on 31 May and 1 June, likewise by Lecourbe; the defeat of General Bey on the southern shore of Lake Lucerne; Colonel Strauch being half wiped out in Wallis; the defeat of Generals Simbschen and Jellachich by Masséna and Lecourbe on 14 and 15 August; and finally the admirable resistance Molitor

76. Remember, Clausewitz emphasizes the importance of focusing on the main goal and launching peripheral or diversionary operations only when there is a good chance of great success and said operations would draw more enemy away from the main theater than are used in launching the diversion in the first place.

77. This is where the mystical element of Clausewitz's trinity is important. He is getting at the idea that the act in and of itself has been successful and something has come out of this action that enhances French combat power: this could be viewed as something akin to psychological dominance rather than something more concrete.

and his handful of men put up against Jellachich, Linken, and Auffenberg when they tried to seize the Linth valley at the end of September. Against such a series of the most emphatic victories, albeit small in size because of the often small forces engaged, the Austrians can offer only a single one of equivalent significance, namely, the successful attack on the St. Luciensteig on 14 May; all of Bellegarde's successes in the Münster and Inn valleys were really just pushing back his opponent through weight of numbers, without taking very many trophies.[78] Prince Hohenzollern's victory of 18 May against Loison is insignificant; General Haddick's against Loison at the St. Gotthard and the Devil's Bridge on 29 May likewise offers no result that can be compared with its immediate sequel, Lecourbe's victory against St. Julien. One of the best successes on the Austrian side is the repulse of the French attack on Feldkirch on 23 March; this action quite definitely belongs to the mountain war because the Feldkirch position lies in the mountains and owes its effectiveness to them; nonetheless this event lies on the boundary of mountain warfare, since the position and the bodies of troops are larger than usual for individual outposts. In order to summarize the result of this ratio between the two sides' victories, we need only add up the two sides' trophies.

The causes of such very different results lie less in the different methods employed by the two sides than in the difference in spirit between their troops, especially the leaders. The fact that the French had their outposts up on the actual ridges more often than the Austrians did and that they echeloned more deeply in the valleys applies only to the defense,[79] and even there, it has no very decisive influence; but that marvelous force multiplication displayed by Lecourbe and Molitor can obviously be ascribed more to the effect of their ardor, their ambition, and their energy than to any particular method. In this

78. This is where the idea of psychological dominance ties in with Clausewitz's ideas about military genius, boldness, and perseverance. One has to have the intellect to collect sparse information and develop it into some kind of coherent idea; one then has to have the boldness and moral certitude to follow that idea even when things look bad. It seems that a few bad results played on the minds of the Austrian commanders and undermined their ability to assume risk or make decisions. See *On War*, book 1, chap. 3.

79. This may be so, but a difference in the two sides' defensive methods surely shows up on both sides of the coin. That is, the French offensive successes can be partly explained by the Austrians' not following the French defensive method.

respect, on the occasion of his unsuccessful attack of 1 May against the St. Luciensteig, the Austrian commander [the archduke] says the following:

> It is worth noting that in the recent wars incompetent leadership generated quite opposite effects among the Germans and the French; in the former it produced vacillation, in the latter, rashness. The French, inspired by the spirit of the Revolution to breach all boundaries and expecting every gamble to produce results, followed this impulse whenever they saw no other way out. The Germans, trained to subordinate their will, accustomed to rules and bound by responsibility, were paralyzed by indecision. Hence the French superiority whenever it concerned the simultaneous action of several men left to their own devices, while their adversaries had the advantage when they were under the direct leadership of their commanders. Hence the agility of the French in mountain warfare and the dependability of the Germans in the open field.[80]

We have already said that it is in the nature of mountain warfare to individualize the collective combat forces, in that their various component bodies are more frequently left to their own devices and thus to operate according to their own volition. This applies from formations of the first rank, that is, those under brigadiers or division commanders, right down to the individual soldier, but of course, to a decreasing degree. Down as far as the battalion commanders, though, both the likelihood and the importance of such independent action are still very high. Now if we compare the Austrian and French armies of the time with each other, the difference in their aptitude for mountain warfare emerges clearly enough from their characteristics. The French generals were young men, warlike, ambitious, some of them enthusiastic; these qualities must have made up in part for any talent or experience they may have lacked. Now if the Austrians had only confronted those men with talented veterans, then perhaps, despite their greater age and less passionate nature, these would have retained parity or even predominated. But of all the names that appear here, not a single one had made his reputation earlier or managed to do so later; we may therefore conclude that these were men with undistinguished careers who had gained advancement to these positions merely by seniority. As for the bulk of the Austrian infantry's officer corps at that time, it is well

80. Karl, 1:286–287.

known that they were not regarded very highly, while the cavalry had little or no part in the mountain warfare.[81] But there was also a very big difference between the common soldiery of the two armies. We are not talking about national characteristics, since the Austrian army was composed of so many different tribes; but it is clear that among the common soldiers, where it is more a question of strength of emotion than of mental powers, the increased morale and motivation approaching enthusiasm and fanaticism that were typical of the French army at that time must have had a profound influence whenever this motivation manifested itself of its own accord. On the other side, it should not be overlooked that, as the archduke indicated in the excerpt above, if the inert mechanism of service regulations and battle orders constrained by pure geometry is not complemented by a certain mental agility, it must necessarily cripple and stultify the inner man.

81. The cavalry was highly regarded and often considered to be among the finest in Europe.

10. Editors' Overview and Afterword

This last chapter serves as both a brief overview of the campaigns that came after those described in this and the previous volume and a brief afterword regarding how Napoleon's assumption of command influenced the outcome of the conflict. We want the reader to connect Clausewitz's ideas about military genius to a campaign that features a before and after, so to speak. We must remember that Napoleon was absent for much of 1799 before returning to France and changing the conflict from a stalemate to a resounding French triumph within a matter of months. This can largely be put down to his dynamism and brilliance. Hence this chapter provides the reader with a starting point for further examination of the campaigns that took place after Clausewitz's study ends. It does not serve as a campaign analysis or a detailed history of these events, so interested readers might want to consult other sources.[1]

As we have seen, France suffered a series of reverses on the battlefield over the spring and summer of 1799, and as domestic instability increased, there was a coup in Paris: the coup of 30 *Prairial* (18 June). This coup saw the ousting of the Jacobins and left Emmanuel Sieyès[2] as the dominant figure in the French government. Although France's military situation improved after Masséna's success at the second battle of Zurich and the threat of an allied invasion receded, there was still fear of an underlying royalist sentiment, particularly in the countryside. This played an important role in Napoleon's successful coup in November, as he had been away from France during the defeats of 1799 and was thus largely untainted by the factional politics and military failures that occurred in his absence. His successful campaigns in Italy

1. This is not an exhaustive list by any means, but it should serve as a starting point: Charles J. Esdaile, *The Wars of Napoleon* (New York: Routledge, 1995) and *The Wars of the French Revolution 1792–1801* (New York: Routledge, 2019); James R. Arnold, *Marengo and Hohenlinden: Napoleon's Rise to Power* (Barnsley, UK: Pen & Sword Books, 2005); William Doyle, *The Oxford History of the French Revolution* (Oxford: Oxford University Press, 2002); Colonel George Armand Furse, *1800: Marengo and Hohenlinden* (1903; reprint, Uckfield, UK: Naval & Military Press, 2005).

2. Emmanuel Joseph Sieyès (1748–1836) was a key revolutionary figure and one of the main instigators of the coup that ultimately brought Napoleon to power in November 1799.

in 1796–1797 and the reported success of his Egyptian expedition meant that he enjoyed great support from across the political spectrum in France. Therefore, when Napoleon returned to France in October, the main factions all hailed him as the answer to France's problems.

Napoleon seized power as soon as events facilitated the process. His own coup of 18 *Brumaire* (9 November 1799) resulted in him taking the role of first consul, with effective control over the instruments of state and military power. Although he wielded a great deal of power, his position was not fully secure; his political future largely rested on his battlefield success, and France was not safe from internal disorder nor from the threat posed by the allied coalition. As such, he needed to conclude the war successfully.

With his seizure of control, the Directory's previous incoherent plans were replaced with a much clearer vision for the coming campaigns. During the winter and spring of 1800 his armies prepared to knock Austria out of the war. Clearly, Napoleon benefited from the withdrawal of the Russian army, which began its march away from the theater of operations and back to Russia in November 1799,[3] as this reduced the threat on the continent to one enemy. In addition, the allied coalition's war aims were not coordinated. Britain still wanted to overthrow the French revolution and restore the monarchy or, at the very least, restore the 1792 frontiers and prevent the export of the revolution elsewhere. Russia had become disinterested and effectively withdrew from the war. Austria's position was more nuanced: it desired the overthrow of the French government but was not enamored with French royalists. As such, Austrian aims were a hedge, indicating support for restoration of the French monarchy but without overtly calling for it, and Austrian dreams of a broader area of influence had to be balanced against Prussian and Russian antipathy to the idea. Given the way the relationship with Russia had so quickly crumbled, it is reasonable to suppose that this was very much on the Austrians' mind when they failed to commit to any single clear policy. That the Austrian emperor was not convinced the war with France was winnable and that the government left the main decisions to the *Hofkriegsrat* [Aulic War Council] surely undermined Austrian war aims and served only to perpetuate the ongoing lack of clarity with regard to the direction of the war.[4] However,

3. Duffy, *Eagles over the Alps*, 264, 265.
4. Esdaile, *Wars of the French Revolution*, 300–302.

the Austrian foreign minister still hoped to overturn the deal struck at Campo Formio,[5] so he sought to continue the war.[6]

The Austrians acted with unusual haste and decision before the French were ready and struck at French forces in Italy, driving them west. The French army in Genoa was besieged by the Austrians, and the situation looked dire for French interests. However, Napoleon was already building up an army in lee of the Alps and was thoroughly prepared for his march into Italy to secure French control and defeat the Austrians. Napoleon's countermove was bold and ultimately decisive. He famously crossed the Great St. Bernard Pass in late May 1800,[7] surprising the Austrians with his speed and dynamism. Within a month, Napoleon's army had defeated the Austrians at the battles of Montebello and Marengo and forced their commander, General Melas, to agree to an armistice. The armistice called for Austrian forces in Italy to withdraw behind the line of the Mincio River and abandon all their previous gains. In addition, the armistice prevented the Austrians from sending troops north to fight in Germany. As such, it prevented them from shifting forces to a different campaign theater, thereby restricting their strategic flexibility. It also marked a humiliating end to a series of campaigns that had seen a number of Austrian and allied successes over the previous year.[8]

In a little over three weeks, Napoleon had regained control of northern Italy and further cemented his reputation both at home and abroad. It is thus worth reminding readers of Clausewitz's key ideas relating to genius.[9] According to Clausewitz, a genius requires physical and moral courage, decisiveness, boldness, a coup d'oeil to visualize the appropriate course of action despite any lack of clarity or certainty, an inquiring mind, and a cool head. There are other factors too, and it is clear that Clausewitz sees them as an interactive whole rather than simply as related parts.[10]

5. Clausewitz, *Napoleon's 1796 Italian Campaign*, 287n22.

6. Here it is worth recalling that Clausewitz argues that the result of a conflict is never final (*On War*, book 1, chap. 1). The Austrians were not happy with the peace settlement and repeatedly sought to overturn it. Ultimately, both sides need to agree for peace to be maintained. *On War*, 80.

7. For an overview, see Arnold, *Marengo and Hohenlinden*, 79–99.

8. Arnold, *Marengo and Hohenlinden*, 189.

9. See volume 1, chapter 1, note 36.

10. See *On War*, book 1, chap. 3. We also recommend Clifford J. Rogers, "Clausewitz, Genius, and the Rules," *Journal of Military History* 66 (October 2002): 1167–1176.

Of course, the Austrian defeat at Marengo did not end the war. In Germany, the French had already had some success in early May, defeating the Austrians at the battle of Stockach and winning a smaller victory at the battle of Höchstädt in June.[11] These had not proved decisive when the armistice in Italy paused the conflict and stopped the French advance. Both sides then took the opportunity to reorganize their armies in anticipation of renewed fighting and to see what peace negotiations between the governments would bring.

Because negotiations were not proceeding in the direction Napoleon wanted, and because he thought the Austrians were stalling for time, Napoleon decided to resume fighting and try to impose a settlement on Austria in the manner of his successes in Italy in 1797[12] and in June 1800.[13] On the Austrian side, there was no clear agreement whether to accept French terms or to renew the conflict. As Napoleon concentrated on his goal of a decisive blow against Austria, the Austrians were unclear in their political goals and their strategy. They maintained large garrisons in their fortresses and again failed to concentrate their strength effectively. The French preparations for renewed fighting, in contrast, were focused on a clear goal: beating the Austrian army and marching on Vienna, just as Napoleon had done in 1797.[14]

The French plan was clear; its main thrust saw Moreau, who remained in charge of the German theater, begin his march on Hohenlinden as soon as the armistice expired on 22 November.[15] The Austrians too sought to attack, and their plan was a good one, with their army turning Moreau's left flank; however, this called for speed of decision and march that the Austrian army simply could not muster.[16] Although Moreau was no Napoleon, he was an exceedingly able general, and the rapidity of his advance caught the Austrians by surprise.[17]

11. Arnold, *Marengo and Hohenlinden*, 214–226.

12. See Clausewitz, *Napoleon's 1796 Italian Campaign*, 257–292.

13. Arnold, *Marengo and Hohenlinden*, 206–207.

14. See Clausewitz, *Napoleon's 1796 Italian Campaign*, 257–274.

15. Esdaile, *Wars of the French Revolution*, 307.

16. See Esdaile, *Wars of the French Revolution*, 307. Again, we see the difference when dynamism is combined with boldness. Simply being bold or dynamic alone is seldom enough, as has been shown repeatedly in these campaigns as well as those of 1796–1797.

17. This again brings us back to Clausewitz's description of military genius. *On War*, book 1, chap. 3.

The subsequent French victory at the battle of Hohenlinden did not lead to the Austrians' collapse, but Moreau's pursuit of the Austrian army did.[18] In conjunction with the humiliating defeat in Italy in June, and with Vienna under direct threat from French troops, the Austrians had little choice but to request an armistice, which the French accepted. Thus, by 25 December 1800, after a campaign lasting a little less than a month, the Austrians had again been brought to their knees by the French.[19]

By contrast with the French unity of command, purpose, and action, the allied coalition collapsed. The Austrians were effectively knocked out of the war in a series of rapid campaigns, each lasting less than a month. Although formal Russian withdrawal from the coalition came only after the Royal Navy kept up its interference with Baltic shipping and Russian trade, the Russians had already quit and marched home. The Austrian government signed the Treaty of Lunéville with France on 9 February 1801. This solidified the already strict terms of the Treaty of Campo Formio[20] and further degraded Austrian power in Germany.[21] The British government was badly weakened and began negotiations with France from a much weaker strategic position. Thus Napoleon achieved victory for France against its main threat, both directly in Italy in person and indirectly by creating the conditions and overseeing the French plan overall. That he did so in two short campaigns after a year of stalemate was all the more impressive, and it prompts us to ask what would have happened if he had not left France. Obviously, that is for the reader to ponder.

Of course, the wars in Europe continued for another fourteen years, in the phase typically known as the Napoleonic Wars. The wars of the French Revolution were at an end, but their repercussions would reverberate throughout the nineteenth century both in Europe and beyond. This last point is important, and it is worth considering the world wars of the twentieth century. In the first, it could be argued that the old conservative social order

18. This returns us to Clausewitz's points about boldness, rapidity, and continuity. Here, Moreau maintained pressure on the Austrian army until it collapsed into rabble not far from Vienna.

19. Arnold, *Marengo and Hohenlinden*, 252–259.

20. See note 6 above.

21. This peace with Austria would last until 1805. But again, as Clausewitz tells us, the result of war is never final. *On War*, book 1, chap. 1.

of Europe went to war in 1914 to preserve its status and that of the countries it controlled. That the conflict overthrew the existing social and international order so completely shows us the importance of Clausewitz's point about knowing what one is fighting for and what one is willing to risk. That the protagonists then had to wrestle with the elements of his wondrous and fickle trinity[22] reminds us that even a perfect plan (if there is such a thing) can go horrifically wrong due to the play of chance and probability. That the Second World War saw revisionist powers seeking to overthrow the old order and failing, but doing so in such a destructive fashion that the international and social order was remade anyway, only reinforces the point. That is, when preparing for war, as the Austrians, Prussians, Russians, and others did so frequently during the period from 1792 to 1815, clearly thinking through what one wants to achieve, what one is willing to risk, and what one is willing to do to obtain one's goals is a much better place to start a conflict. Even doing that, however, is not enough to guarantee success. The interplay of chance and probability and human decision making militates against certainty, no matter what theorists, policy makers, and leaders want to believe. The interaction of the elements of Clausewitz's trinity also precludes precise calculation, despite the chimera that a good strategy can provide it. Thus, we hope readers will think about this last point when reading Clausewitz's many analytical examples of what leaders should do when preparing, planning, and fighting a war. After all, you might not get what you wanted, and you might end up with something not even imagined.

22. Clausewitz, *Napoleon's 1796 Italian Campaign*, 57n23

Bibliography

BOOKS AND ARTICLES

Abel, Jonathan. *Guibert: Father of Napoleon's Grande Armée.* Norman: University of Oklahoma Press, 2016.

Arnold, James R. *Marengo and Hohenlinden: Napoleon's Rise to Power.* Barnsley, UK: Pen & Sword Books, 2005.

Bassford, Christopher. "Clausewitz and His Works." http://www.clausewitz.com/readings/Bassford/Cworks/Works.htm#_edn40.

———. "Clausewitz's Categories of War and the Supersession of 'Absolute War.'" http://www.clausewitz.com/mobile/Bassford-Supersession5.pdf#zoom=100.

———. "Jomini and Clausewitz: Their Interaction." http://www.clausewitz.com/readings/Bassford/Jomini/JOMINIX.htm.

———. "Tip-Toe through the Trinity: The Strange Persistence of Trinitarian Warfare." https://www.clausewitz.com/mobile/trinity8.htm.

Bellinger, Vanya Eftimova. *Marie von Clausewitz: The Woman behind the Making of* On War. Oxford: Oxford University Press, 2016.

Berkovich, Ilya. *Motivation in War: The Experience of Common Soldiers in Old-Regime Europe.* Cambridge: Cambridge University Press, 2017.

Bertaud, Jean Paul. *The Army of the French Revolution: From Citizen-Soldiers to Instrument of Power.* Princeton, NJ: Princeton University Press, 1988.

Bonaparte, Napoléon. *Correspondance* Générale. 15 vols. Paris: Publiée par la Fondation Napoléon, Librairie Arthéme Fayard, 2004–2018.

Bowden, Mark. *Black Hawk Down: A Story of Modern War.* Berkeley, CA: Atlantic Monthly Press, 1999.

Broers, Michael. "Revolt and Repression in Napoleonic Italy 1796–1814." In *War in an Age of Revolution 1775–1815*, ed. Roger Chickering and Stig Förster. New York: Cambridge University Press, 2010.

Bulos, A. *Memoirs of Marshal Ney.* 2 vols. 2nd ed. London: Bull & Churton, 1834. https://archive.org/details/memoirsmarshalno2bulogoog/page/n9.

Bülow, Heinrich von. *Geist des Neuern Kriegssystems.* Hamburg: August Campe, 1835.

Casse, A., du. *Le Général Vandamme: et sa correspondence.* 2 vols. Paris: Librairie et Cte, 1870. https://books.google.com.

Clausewitz, Carl von. *Ausgewählte militärische Schriften.* Berlin: Militärverlag DDR, 1981.

———. *La Campagne de 1799 en Italie et en Suisse*, trans. A. Niessel. 2 vols. Paris: Librairie Militaire, Chapelot et Co., 1906.

———. *The Campaign of 1812 in Russia*, trans. Francis Egerton. London: John Murray, 1843.

https://www.clausewitz.com/readings/1812/Clausewitz-CampaignOf1812inRussia-EllesmereTranslation.pdf.

———. *Die Feldzüge von 1799 in Italien und der Schweiz.* 2 vols. Berlin: Ferdinand Dümmler, 1833.

———. *Napoleon's 1796 Italian Campaign*, trans. and ed. Nicholas Murray and Christopher Pringle. Lawrence: University Press of Kansas, 2018.

———. *On War*, ed. and trans. Michael Howard and Peter Paret. Princeton, NJ: Princeton University Press, 1989.

———. *On War*, trans. O. J. Matthijs Jolles. New York: Modern Library, 2000.

———. *Vom Kriege.* 3 vols. Berlin: Ferdinand Dümmler, 1832–1834.

Cuccia, Phillip. *Napoleon in Italy: The Sieges of Mantua 1796–1799.* Norman: University of Oklahoma Press, 2014.

Dedon, François L. *Relation du Passage de la Limmat.* Paris: Didot Jaune, 1801. https://books.google.com.

Douglas, Major-General Sir Howard. *An Essay on the Principles and Construction of Military Bridges, and the Passage of Rivers in Military Operations.* London: T. Egerton, 1816. https://books.google.com.

Doyle, William. *The Oxford History of the French Revolution.* Oxford: Oxford University Press, 2002.

Duffy, Christopher. *Eagles over the Alps: Suvorov in Italy and Switzerland, 1799.* Chicago: Emperor's Press, 1999.

———. *Frederick the Great: A Military Life.* London: Routledge, 1995.

Esdaile, Charles J. *The Wars of the French Revolution 1792–1801.* New York: Routledge, 2019.

———. *The Wars of Napoleon.* New York: Routledge, 1995.

"Franziszeische Landesaufnahme (1806–1869)." http://mapire.eu/de/map/secondsurvey.

Furse, Colonel George Armand. *1800: Marengo and Hohenlinden.* 1903. Reprint, Uckfield, UK: Naval & Military Press, 2005.

Gat, Azar. *A History of Military Thought: From the Enlightenment to the Cold War.* Oxford: Oxford University Press, 2001.

Generals Reglement. Vienna: Johann Thoman Edlen von Trattern, 1769.

Graham, J. M. *Histoire des Campagnes d'Italie, d'Allemagne et de Suisse en 1796, 97, 98 et 99.* Paris: Fournier, 1817.

Handel, Michael. *Masters of War: Classical Strategic Thought.* 3rd ed. London: Frank Cass, 2001.

Hertefeld, A. *The Game of Skat*, trans. and ed. Professor Hoffman. London: George Routledge & Sons, 1893.

Heuser, Beatrice. *Strategy before Clausewitz: Linking Warfare and Statecraft, 1400–1830.* Abingdon, UK: Routledge, 2018.

Honig, Jan Willem. "Clausewitz and the Politics of Early Modern Warfare." In *Clausewitz the State and War*, ed. Andreas Herberg-Rothe, Jan Willem Honig, and Daniel Moran, 29–48. Stuttgart: Franz Steiner Verlag, 2011.

Intelligence Branch. *British Minor Expeditions 1746 to 1814*. London: HMSO, 1884. https://books.google.com.

Jomini, Antoine Baron de. *Summary of the Art of War*, trans. Major O. F. Winship and Lieutenant E. E. McLean. New York: G. P. Putnam, 1854.

———. *Tableau Analytique des Principales Combinaisons de la Guerre, et de leurs apports avec la politique des états pour servir d'introduction au Traité des grandes opérations militaires*. 3rd ed. Paris: Chez Anselin, 1830.

Jomini, Lieutenant-Général [Antoine]. *Histoire Critique et Militaire des Guerres de la Révolution*. 15 vols. Paris: Chez Anselin et Pochard, 1819–1824.

Jourdan, Général. *Précis des opérations de l'armée du Danube sous les ordres du Général Jourdan. Extrait des mémoires manuscrits de ce general*. Paris: Charles, [1799]. https://archive.org/details/precisdesoperatioojour.

Kant, Immanuel. *Critique of Pure Reason*, trans. and ed. Paul Guyer and Allen W. Wood. Cambridge: Cambridge University Press, 2000.

Karl Erzherzog von Österreich. *Geschichte des Feldzuges von 1799 in Deutschland und in der Schweiz*. 3 vols. Vienna: Anton Strauss, 1819. https://www.e-rara.ch/zut/doi/10.3931/e-rara-33557.

———. *Grundsätze der Strategie erläutert durch die Darstellung des Feldzugs von 1796 in Deutschland*. 4 vols. Vienna: Anton Strauss, 1814.

———. *Der Strategie Erläuert durch die Darstellung des Feldzugs von 1796 in Deutschland und in der Schweiz*. 4 vols. Vienna: Anton Strauss, 1814.

Lefebvre, Georges. *The French Revolution from 1793 to 1799*, trans. John Hall Stewart and James Friguglietti. New York: Columbia University Press, 1964.

Lloyd, Henry. *Geschichte des siebenjährigen Krieges in Deutschland zwischen dem Könige von Preussen und der Kaiserin Königin mit ihren Alliirten vom General Lloyd*, trans. Georg Tempelhof. 6 vols. Berlin: Gedrukt und verlegt von Johann Friedrich Unger, 1783–1801.

———. *The History of the Late War in Germany*. 2 vols. London, 1781.

Longworth, Philip. *The Art of Victory*. New York: Holt, Rinehart & Winston, 1965.

Macksey, Piers. *Statesmen at War: The Strategy of Overthrow 1798–1799*. London: Longman Group, 1974.

Mangourit, Michel-Ange-Bernard. *Défense d'Ancone*. 2 vols. Paris: Charles Pougens, 1802. https://books.google.com.

Meyer-Weiss: Atlas of Switzerland. http://www.unibe.ch/university/services/university_library/research/special_collections/map_collections/meyer_weiss/index_eng.html.

Milyutin, D. A. *Geschichte des Krieges Russlands mit Frankreich unter der Regierung Kaiser Pauls I. im Jahre 1799*. 5 vols. Munich: Commission der Jos. Lindauer'schen Buchhandlung, 1856–1858.

Mitchell, A. Wess. *The Grand Strategy of the Habsburg Empire*. Princeton, NJ: Princeton University Press, 2018.

Montalembert, Marquis de. *Correspondance de Monsieur le Marquis de Montalembert, étant employé par le Roi de France à l'Armée Suédoise, avec Mr. le Marquis d'Havrincour . . . pendant les campagnes de 1757, 58, 59, 60 et 61: pour servir à l'histoire de la dernièr guerre.* 3 vols. London, 1777.

Montholon, Général, ed. *Mémoires pour servir à l'Histoire de France sous Napoléon.* 8 vols. Paris: F. Didot, Père et Fils; Bossange, Frères, 1823–1825.

Moran, Daniel, and Arthur Waldron. *The People in Arms: Military Myth and National Mobilization since the French Revolution.* Cambridge: Cambridge University Press, 2003.

Murray, Nicholas. *The Rocky Road to the Great War: The Evolution of Trench Warfare to 1914.* Washington, DC: Potomac Books, 2013.

Napoléon I. *Correspondance de Napoléon Ier.* 32 vols. Paris: Henri Plon & J. Dumaine, 1858.

Nobili, Johann. *Hungary 1848: The Winter Campaign*, trans. and ed. Christopher Pringle. Solihull, UK: Helion, forthcoming.

Officer of the Staff. *The Life and Campaigns of Victor Moreau: Comprehending His Trial, Justification and Other Events, till the Period of His Embarkation for the United States*, trans. John Davis. New York: I. Riley, 1806. https://books.google.com.

Ospinov, K. *Alexander Suvorov*, trans. Edith Bone. London: Hutchinson, 1944.

Page, Anthony. *Britain and the Seventy Years War, 1744–1815: Enlightenment, Revolution and Empire.* London: Palgrave Macmillan, 2015.

Palmgren, Anders. "Visions of Strategy: Following Clausewitz's Train of Thought." Doctoral diss., National Defence University, Helsinki, 2014.

Paret, Peter. *Clausewitz and the State.* New York: Oxford University Press, 1976.

———, ed. *Makers of Modern Strategy: From Machiavelli to the Nuclear Age.* Princeton, NJ: Princeton University Press, 1986.

Parlett, David. *A History of Card Games.* Oxford: Oxford University Press, 1991.

Pringle, Christopher. *Hungary 1848: The Winter Campaign.* Warwick, UK: Helion, forthcoming.

"Projekt zur Erschliessung historisch wertvoller Altkartenbestände." http://ikar.sbb.spk-berlin.de/werkzeugkasten/sonderregeln/4_3.htm.

Rapin, Ami Jacques. "Jomini at the Time of the Helvetian Republic (1798–1801)." Université de Lausanne. https://applicationspub.unil.ch/interpub/noauth/php/Un/UnPers.php?PerNum=851054&LanCode=37&menu=pub.

Rodger, A. B. *The War of the Second Coalition 1798–1801.* Oxford: Clarendon Press, 1964.

Rogers, Clifford J. "Clausewitz, Genius, and the Rules." *Journal of Military History* 66 (October 2002): 1167–1176.

Roider, Karl A., Jr. *Baron Thugut and Austria's Response to the French Revolution.* Princeton, NJ: Princeton University Press, 1987.

Ross, Steven T. *Quest for Victory: French Military Strategy 1792–1799.* London: Thomas Yoseloff, 1978.

Rothenberg, Gunther. *Napoleon's Great Adversaries: The Archduke Charles and the Austrian Army, 1792–1814.* Tiptree, UK: Anchor Press, 1982.

Ruch, Christian. "Waldstädte." *Historisches Lexikon Der Schweiz.* http://www.hls-dhs-dss.ch/textes/d/D7350.php.

Saxe, Maurice Count de. *Reveries, or, Memoirs Concerning the Art of War*, trans. unknown. Edinburgh: Sands, Donaldson, Murray & Cochran, 1759.

Schneid, Frederick C., ed. *European Armies of the French Revolution: 1789–1802.* Norman: University of Oklahoma Press, 2015.

Showalter, Dennis E. *The Wars of Frederick the Great.* New York: Longman, 1996.

Six, Georges. *Dictionnaire Biographique des Généraux & Amiraux de la Révolution et de L'Empire (1792–1814).* 2 vols. Paris: Libraire Historique et Nobiliaire, 1934.

Smith, Digby. *The Greenhill Napoleonic Wars Data Book.* London: Greenhill Books, 1998.

Strachan, Hew. "A Clausewitz for Every Season." *American Interest* 2, 6 (1 July 2007). https://www.the-american-interest.com/2007/07/01/a-clausewitz-for-every-season/.

———. *Clausewitz's* On War: *A Biography.* New York: Atlantic Monthly Press, 2007.

Strachan, Hew, and Andreas Herberg-Rothe, eds. *Clausewitz in the Twenty-First Century.* Oxford: Oxford University Press, 2007.

Von Seida und Landensberg, Franz Eugen Joseph Anton. *Politisch-militärische Geschichte des merkwürdigen Feldzugs von 1799.* Stettin, 1801. https://books.google.com.

Wieland, Christoph Martin. *Geschichte der Abderiten.* Leipzig: Philipp Reclam, Jun., 1881. https://reader.digitale-sammlungen.de/de/fs1/object/display/bsb11016459_00005.html?zoom=0.6500000000000001.

Wurzbach, Dr. Constant von. *Biographisches Lexikon des Kaiserthums Oesterreich.* 60 vols. Vienna: Universitäts Buchruderei von L. E. Zamarski, 1856–1891.

Wylie, J. C. *Military Strategy: A General Theory of Power Control.* Annapolis, MD: Naval Institute Press, 2014.

Zimmerman, F. G. *Military Vocabulary German-English and English German.* London: Hugh Rees, 1915.

Zwirner, E. J. *Die Kriegerischen Ereignisse in Vorarlberg zu Beginn des Zweiten Koalitionskriegs 1799.* Feldkirch: Druck von L. Sausgruber, 1912.

ONLINE RESOURCES

http://gallica.bnf.fr
https://www.bsb-muenchen.de/
https://www.clausewitz.com/index.htm
https://www.deutsche-biographie.de
https://www.e-rara.ch/
www.literature.at

Index